A TEST OF POWERS

THE ITALIAN LIST

A TEST OF POWERS

Writings on Criticism and Literary Institutions

FRANCO FORTINI

TRANSLATED BY ALBERTO TOSCANO

LONDON NEW YORK CALCUTTA

SERIES EDITOR: ALBERTO TOSCANO

Seagull Books, 2016

Originally published in Italian as *Verifica dei poteri*

ISBN 978 0 8574 2 335 1

British Library Cataloguing-in-Publication Data
A catalogue record for this book is available from the British Library.

Typeset by Seagull Books, Calcutta, India
Printed and bound by Maple Press, York, Pennsylvania, USA

The commissioners of the Nobility . . . voiced the fear that the test of powers in common implied deliberation in common.

Alessandro Manzoni
La Rivoluzione francese del 1789, III

CONTENTS

PART III

Of Some Critics

PART IV

For Some Books

TRANSLATOR'S INTRODUCTION

The Labour of Division

Write, I say to myself, hate those
who gently lead into nothingness
the men and women who are your companions
and think they no longer know. Among the enemies' names
write your own too.[1]

I have come not to bring peace, but a sword.[2]

Standing in a corner and saying 'I' . . . is the first precaution you must take if you wish, when the time comes, to be able to say 'we', to speak also in the name of others.[3]

The Past Is a Foreign Language

In 1993, a year before his death, in the preface to his last book—a retrospect, montage and memoir of his antagonistic friendship with Pier Paolo Pasolini—Franco Fortini reflected on what younger generations might make of texts so marked, even disfigured, by the violence and hopes of their time. The likes of Fortini and Pasolini were still invested in a history which, in the words of the latter, brought tears to their eyes at a screening of Roberto Rossellini's 1945 neorealist drama of the resistance, *Roma, Open City*. But what could move a young person today? 'And to one or two of those youths I would also like to say: just as you might learn a foreign language, try to understand our own, only apparently similar to the one that each and every day you employ in conversation or thought.

If you judge that it's not worth the effort, shut our books in haste along with the age that produced them; and good luck'.[4]

It would seem that a further two decades, along with the literal foreignness of Fortini's language and many of his reference points, could only exacerbate this predicament. To say that the themes and polemics that criss-cross these pages, made taut with political and poetic urgency, are prehistoric would perhaps be over-optimistic in its intimation of continuity. And where poetry or literary prose might gain in aura from their loss of context, it is difficult to argue likewise for criticism, especially criticism such as Fortini's, so intent to intervene in its own moment, calibrating its instruments of syntax and semantics for closely fought battles or protracted campaigns whose horizon could not extend further than, say, a decade. This criticism as cultural and political service[5] (which is the precise opposite of servitude, especially when the latter takes the guise of the false mastery of traditional intellectuals) thus appears at first as eminently expendable. Accordingly, we might think that what made *A Test of Powers* such a decisive book in 1960s Italy—the way it crystallized and articulated so many of the intellectual and political crises and contests that had fermented ever since liberation from fascism—would also be what today dooms it, at best, to the melancholy attentions of erudite specialists and antiquarians.

This translation, following that of Fortini's agonistic memoir of the Arab–Israeli War, *The Dogs of the Sinai*,[6] is a wager against the historicist council of forgetting. It is based on the belated personal discovery of a critic and essayist—as well as a poet—of the highest calibre whose range, force and insight demonstrate a singular fidelity to a tradition of Marxist literary criticism that continues to nourish those who think there is a bond between the painstaking attention to literary artistic forms and the critique of social and political orders. The demands, divergent and solidary, that had been articulated by the likes of Adorno, Brecht, Benjamin, Bloch and Lukács, animate many of these pages. The fact that they remain largely unmet is also why Fortini's writing continues to speak to our present. The fact that it can do so is something that I have tried to put to the test over the past few years, with more success than I could have hoped. It was my glad surprise at the resonance among friends and comrades of these calls to action from an extinguished galaxy of militancy and experience that bolstered the labour of translation and interpretation. But what drove this project was, above all, the conviction that the ethical intensity with which Fortini approached the relation between politics and poetics, between the forms of our cultural production and our forms of life, along with the unsparing self-reflection and self-criticism that accompanied his efforts, could prove an indispensable resource for those who would still echo the declaration from his 1958 poem 'Communism': 'I always wanted this world ended'.

I would go further and suggest that the endurance of these pages resides in their consuming orientation towards a moment of collective cultural life that Fortini approached without ever sparing himself (and others). As though living without the anticipation of posterity, assuming the full negativity of one's present, is precisely what makes these pages of criticism—an activity with the negative at its nerve centre—so strangely alive today. That is true not just of the epigrams or virtual aphorisms—more shrapnel than gems—peppered throughout these essays. It also describes a style of thought that strives to bring the formal attentiveness of poetics into the domain of political reflection and the urgency of political choices into the writing of poetry and prose, without ever deluding itself of a harmony between these registers, or losing sight of the permeation of our writing and thought by the 'economic unconscious', that is to say, by the classed structures of cultural production and capital's own formal, shaping force.

Poetics, Politics, Polemics

Yet it remains true that to appreciate the incision and necessity of Fortini's writing, and its endurance well beyond its time and context, we also need to know something of the cultural and existential force field that marked the Italy of the 1950s and 60s, in particular the world(s) of left-wing culture to which Fortini's work was almost exclusively oriented. As he once remarked: 'I don't speak to everyone. I speak to those who have a certain idea of the world and of life and a certain work in that world and a certain struggle in that world and in themselves'.[7] To reconstruct that world, and Fortini's place within it, is far more than this introduction intends. We might be warned against an academic practice that sometimes recalls the bad faith of 3D-printing replacements for demolished ancient glories. Rather, I want to provide some political and intellectual coordinates that might allow a reader with little familiarity with the Italian scene to register the force and interest of Fortini's critical work in light of the historical sequence in which these writings are located.[8]

Poetics and politics in Fortini, as I intimated in my afterword to *The Dogs of the Sinai*, are often linked by the utopian valences of form.[9] But they are also bound by *polemics*. The style and the targets, or the poetics and the politics, of Fortini's clashes evince his practice of criticism. They allow us to situate him, as they allowed him to situate himself (almost obsessively, it could be argued) among and against his peers, in a stratified and conflictive world of cultural production, between publishing houses, militant journals and mass media, between long-term capitalist strategies and the experiments in resistance of embattled minorities. They also serve to punctuate the unfolding of Fortini's work, providing a sense of the decade of efforts and contradictions that spawned *A Test of Powers*.

Polemics with his socialist and communist comrades also animated Fortini's previous collection of essays, *Dieci Inverni*, which built a complex intervention and retrospect from critical and political writings across the 'ten winters' that had followed the defeat of the Left (the Italian Communist and Socialist parties) in the 1948 elections. These texts also diagnosed the climate of Cold War constriction and repression that had stifled the expansive, emancipatory vision of socialist culture promoted by Fortini and others against the grain of the political leadership of the Left. For Fortini, as for so many of his generation, the period from 1943 to 1948 was a truly exceptional time of tragic choices and revolutionary experiments, chaos and hope. After a life lived in the shadow of fascist mystification and manipulation, it was a time that could truly be experienced as *historical*. The decade that followed was instead one of partial retreat and work at the margins, or in the harsh interstices left by a dominant anti-communist culture and an official left under the sway of Stalinism. The hostility with which his own comrades met Fortini's book led to his resignation from the Socialist Party, but even before that a key watershed had been passed, the one crystallized in the 'fateful year' of 1956.

Though some texts in *A Test of Powers* precede that date, it is evident from Fortini's own recounting that it represented a break at several levels, ushering the period in which his work would enjoy its greatest impact and influence, and for which *A Test of Powers* acts as a kind of summa, namely, the years between 1956 and 1968. Unlike for many of his contemporaries, 1956 did not represent for Fortini an ideological break, a conversion or revelation. On the contrary, it was the moment when the combination of anti-Stalinism and revolutionary questioning of cultural production that he had been advocating for the previous decade finally appeared to have found a historical opening, when projects for recomposition of the cultural left drafted in the face of more or less uniform opposition confronted that messianic 'narrow door' that Fortini often alluded to, echoing Walter Benjamin. Fortini's polemics were always principally addressed to those closest to him, rather than right-wing ideologues or left-wing party hierarchies largely unmoved by his contempt. Although such contestations were deeply personal, they were invariably about shared projects in which the capacity to embody a cultural project in particular literary and political forms was of paramount importance. The polemics with Pier Paolo Pasolini, like the ones with Italo Calvino and Alberto Asor Rosa to which I'll refer below (not to mention the clashes with numerous others comrade–antagonists over the years), did not just take place on the pages of journals but also frequently had the journal-form as their object.[10]

Cultural Work

Fortini's postwar years had been marked by the formative experience with Elio Vittorini's *Il Politecnico*,[11] overlapping with his socialist militancy and work at Olivetti.[12] While publishing copious articles on a diverse range of topics, Fortini had also tried, and by his own lights failed, to push *Il Politecnico* towards a more capacious conception of culture, one impelled by the critique of the division of intellectual and manual labour and the servile, irresponsible privileges of the intellectual caste. This already opened up Fortini's reflection to the practical rather than spiritual autonomy of cultural producers which would orient much of his work over the next two decades. Together with Fortini's marginalization in the Socialist Party (notwithstanding his continued collaboration with the party's newspaper *Avanti*!), the collapse of *Il Politecnico*—partly catalysed by a famous break between Vittorini and the leader of the Italian Communist Party, Palmiro Togliatti—left him largely bereft of an organized context in which to 'test' his proposals for cultural work in and against bourgeois society. Inimical to the cultural politics of the PCI, which he perceived as largely split between a repressive regimentation of its cadre and a cynical co-optation of non-Marxist fellow travellers (see 'Clarifications', 'Radek's Hands' and 'The Writers' Mandate', in this volume), and to the PSI's weak and ambiguous relation to its political cousin, Fortini would begin in the early 1950s to participate in small group initiatives in the young journals of a critical Marxist left. These were groups in which he would never be fully integrated for reasons of age, poetics, politics, or temperament, but which would be vital proving grounds for that idea of socialist culture that preoccupied Fortini ever since discovering the writings of Marx and Lenin, Victor Serge and André

Malraux, and joining the PSI, as a refugee in wartime Zurich.[13] To echo the title of Part II of this volume, we could say that Fortini's condition was always that of the guest, recalling that the Latin *hospes* (from which we can trace the term 'hospitality') was derived from *hostis*, enemy or stranger. The critic, and in a different manner the poet, inhabits this condition of hospitality and hostility, never settling into the ease of belonging.[14]

The first of these small political–intellectual groupings was *Discussioni*, initially little more than a samizdat circulating among young philosophers and social scientists trying to develop a Marxist culture otherwise stifled by the 'national-popular' strategies of the dominant parties. Seeking comrades from younger generations outside a 'literary society' from which Fortini had felt excluded ever since his formative years was to prove a constant, from the failure of the lefts in 1948 to the outbreak of the 1968 movement. These experiments with collective work, which merged sustained reflection on the political forms of cultural organization with intense personal relations, were always accompanied by vibrant programmatic discussions on what the collective form of the journal entailed—from Fortini's unpublished programmatic editorial for *Il Politecnico*, 'A New Culture',[15] to his collaboration with an initially marginal journal that would become key for the movement in 1968, *Quaderni piacentini*.[16] In *Discussioni*, we find an example of this in the 1951 article 'On the Possibility of a Journal' [Eventualità di una rivista]. Not for nothing did his long-time friend, the Lukácsian and Germanist scholar and critic Cesare Cases refer to Fortini in a recent autobiography not just as an 'Old Testament soul' but also as a 'theoretician of the organization of intellectuals'.[17]

In 1955, the group that had animated *Discussioni* initiated *Ragionamenti*, a small albeit crucial contribution to (and anticipation of) the flourishing of the New Left sensibilities that would erupt with the repression of the revolts in Hungary and Poland in 1956. With *Ragionamenti*, we see at the level of the organization of culture the operation of an abiding trait of Fortini's practice, to which we'll have reason to return, namely, his desire to deprovincialize the world of Italian politics and letters, opening it up to a European and indeed global dimension. Fortini, who had already worked to establish links with Sartre's *Les temps modernes* in the postwar period,[18] now collaborated with his comrades in *Ragionamenti* to promote a French counterpart of the journal, *Arguments*, edited by Edgar Morin, Roland Barthes, Jean Duvignaud and Colette Audry. The project would also be accompanied by overtures to the journal *Nowa Kultura* in Poland and *New Reasoner* (the precursor of the *New Left Review*) in the United Kingdom—the latter being the only venue to publish Fortini's critical work in English, until *Screen* translated 'The Writers' Mandate' in the 1970s.[19]

Fortini, who inherited French culture from his mother, had produced important translations of Gustave Flaubert, Marcel Proust, André Gide, Simone Weil and Paul Éluard,[20] made contact with Barthes after a critical but sympathetic review of the French edition of *Writing Degree Zero* (1953), which would be followed by a considerably more positive appraisal of *Mythologies* (1957),[21] excerpts from which he would translate in the socialist newspaper *Avanti*! The epistolary exchange with Barthes, with whom he shared a bond of friendship for some time, shows Fortini's keen sense of the need to renew the instruments of cultural theory and analysis, constrained in Italy by the weight of academic conservatism as well as by the limits of a literary and cultural historicism that amalgamated Francesco De Sanctis, Benedetto Croce and Antonio Gramsci.[22] The antagonism with which Fortini would later respond to a somewhat-belated turn by Italian intellectuals to the resources of a more 'scientific' approach to culture—in so-called neo-empiricism, neo-positivism and the neo-avant-garde, all phenomena in deep solidarity with neo-capitalism, according to him—should be put into the context of this earlier encounter. Unlike *Arguments*, which would continue until 1962, *Ragionamenti* actively consumed itself with the first true crisis of historical communism between September–October 1955 and October 1957.

Polemics in Verse

The first of the polemics that would unite and separate Fortini and Pasolini until a more or less definitive break in 1968—sealed by Fortini's unsparing response to Pasolini's notorious condemnation in verse of petty-bourgeois student protesters and apologia of the proletarian police[23]—takes place in the fateful year of 1956. It is a exemplary of the enormous (some might say, extravagant) political valence that could be accorded to cultural forms, from the composition of editorial boards to the choices of poetic metre. As the selected correspondence incorporated into *Attraverso Pasolini* records, the two writers had engaged in acute exchanges on different levels of their work, exchanging poems, discussing Fortini's possible collaboration in the new literary journal *Officina*, his review of *Ragazzi di vita* and Pasolini's forthcoming trial for the supposedly 'obscene' character of that book. The dense and detailed letters also addressed Pasolini's selection in his monumental anthology of popular songs and poems, the *Canzoniere Italiano* [Italian Songbook]. With the 'extraordinary and terrible year' of 1956,[24] there is a real acceleration and intensification in Pasolini and Fortini's relationship but also in their differences and divisions.[25]

Pasolini was not one of those intellectuals who would fall prey to the 'prodigious temptation of 1956' which, having begun with the 'triumph of Consciousness' in the 20th Congress of the Communist Party of the Soviet Union would end with the humiliation of that consciousness (and conscience) in November. Khrushchev's speech provided an alibi, a 'perverse pleasure' for those Communist intellectuals who declared their life over but comfortably rejoined national elites. Pasolini was not one of those who 'were secretly ashamed of the archaic, provincial and not very "scientific" ways in which they hoped, suffered, loved, in brief, lived as men and politicians'.[26] On the contrary, according to Fortini, not only would Pasolini give voice to the joy of the summer months of 1956 in his poem 'Il pianto della scavatrice' [The Cry of the Excavator],[27] and communicate his support for the statement on the Hungarian invasion in *Ragionamenti*, he would also publicly live his despair at the hypocrisies of official Communism through poetry. But it was precisely on the way of living the crisis of 1956, in verse, in person, in politics, that Fortini would challenge his friend.

In the seventh issue of *Officina*, published in November, Pasolini included his poem 'Polemica in versi' [Polemics in Verse], dated September–October 1956, i.e. prior to the events of Budapest.[28] Set in a dusty, sweltering Roman summer, the poem—in which Fortini recognized 'splendid passages'—despairs over what Italian communism has become, through a pitiless depiction of a Communist *Festa dell'Unità* [Unity Festival] and in notes that signal Pasolini's opposition to the ideological line taken by the Communist journal *Il Contemporaneo*. Notwithstanding what would seem a transient closeness with the left critique of the PCI, the poem also targets the call for the 'mystical rigour of an action' that Pasolini discerned in the likes of the editorial board of *Ragionamenti*. Fortini would reply with the poem 'Al di là della speranza' [Beyond Hope], also published in *Officina*. Incorporating verses written in response to Pasolini's earlier 'Le ceneri di Gramsci' [Gramsci's Ashes], 'Al di là della speranza' combines a complex and knowing imitation of Pasolini's metre with a rather ruthless dissection of his politics, psychology and persona. The confrontation between Pasolini's (and *Officina*'s) literary opposition and *Ragionamenti*'s cultural project was compounded, or over-determined, by the confrontation between two ways of living the relation between poetry and politics.

For Fortini, his more hurtful verses were written 'in hatred at the complaisance in defeat that vanquished [in Pasolini] the will to endure and in hatred at those who applauded the vitalism of corruption, between honey and slime . . . Bodies as the object of sadomasochistic delirium and the play of closeness-distance of consciousness: humiliation and victory'.[29] It is this attitude, Pasolini's posture in the most critical of political and cultural moments, that Fortini could not accept. It is encapsulated in the dual truth spoken of in the famous lines from 'Le ceneri di Gramsci' addressed to the deceased Communist leader and theorist: 'The scandal of self-contradiction—of being / with you and against you; with you in my heart / in the light, against you in the dark of my gut [*viscere*]'.[30] For Fortini, the combination of Pasolini's populist paeans to the Roman sub-proletariat and the performance of his visceral, bodily despair were the guilty mark of a privilege. Their enemies may have been the same for a time—the apparatchiks of a Togliattian cultural project that traduced Gramscian 'hegemony' into bureaucratic control and political cynicism—but for Fortini it was wrong to repeat that ancient gesture in which 'freedom and consciousness for the poet are unfreedom and ignorance for his people'.[31]

In a remarkable text on 'The Silence of Italy', written in Switzerland in 1944 and crystallizing the ethical impetus behind the cultural politics of much of his later work, Fortini had already written of 'one of the gravest penalties that can strike an individual or a society: the illusion of poetry, false poetry. In other words, one's most hidden errors and vices shouted from the rooftops, fruitlessly'. In the same piece, along with a very early invocation of the necessity for the writer of a *verifica dei poteri*, a test of powers, we find that knot of ethics, poetics and politics that would mark out Fortini to the end, and which also animates the polemics with his friend Pasolini, notwithstanding his abiding admiration for the latter's poetic brilliance: 'A bad book, a mistaken or falsified poem, an imprecise or opaque pamphlet are bad actions, simony or barratry. . . . It is necessary that the Italian intellectual *decide*: the cut that alone can make his plant bring fruit. Or else he may wish to remain in the so-called *world of culture*, with his scribe's pride, the contemptuous servility of the luxury object'.[32]

Whereas in 1956, they both struggled against the world of culture that the PCI had made, in Fortini's eyes Pasolini could not abandon the image of the poet and thus the fantasy of his privileged license or 'mandate'; he could not incorporate a criticism of capitalist culture that would necessarily take the form of a *self*-criticism, an effort not to allow oneself to be caught in the easily consumable figure of the poet–martyr (in 1964, Fortini writes in a letter: 'It is not enough, dear Pierpaolo, to despise adulation; one must not deserve it'[33]). As ever with Fortini's polemics, the criticism of one's 'best fiends' is an indispensable means to further define oneself in, and through, negation. The 'grave difference' between their political and poetic stances is clarified by Fortini in his 1990s retrospect, in a revealing passage worth quoting for the light it sheds on so many of the arguments of *A Test of Powers*:

> For me, the deaf words of political economy, 'productive forces', 'relations of production', were (are) the decisive data: the rhythmic structure of the verse, the sense of the poem and economic and social events are inextricable from one another. Unlike Pasolini, I saw worker activists in the Zeran factories, in Poland, speak into microphones and pronounce the end of an epoch just as the workers of Putilov mill had done in a city that was then called Petrograd. The fighters in Budapest too, I said to Pier Paolo, labour within themselves for your (our) poetry.[34]

The attention to the 'economic unconscious' of the poem, an abiding theme throughout *A Test of Powers* (especially 'Cunning as Doves'), is here bound closely to the question of how to relate to the poet (and the intellectual's) other. It contrasts what Fortini regards as Pasolini's instrumentally romantic and reifying relation to the sub-proletariat of Rome with a utopian attention to and solidarity with those whose lives strain towards the same ending and transformation of the world as one's own. This is an image present, in reverse direction, in Fortini's 1955 poem 'Complicity':

> For every one of us who forgets
> there's a factory worker in the Ruhr who slowly
> erases himself and the numbers
> that they carved into his arm
> his masters and ours.

For every one of us who gives up
a miner in Asturias will be obliged to believe
in silks of violet and silver
and a woman in Algiers will dream
of cowardice and contentment.

For every one of us who consents
there is a sad youth who still does not know
how much he will hate living.[35]

The pitiless judgement, of self and other, in such lines, runs through 'Beyond Hope' as well, the verses addressed to Pasolini seeming to condemn the very form of his life:

You dream among bodies and believe in their blood
good to drink, in the heat
vile and sweet. You walk judging
not judging, drenched
in others, to humiliate yourself and, at base, to win.[36]

Fortini sent the poem to Pasolini, remarkably, in view of a possible 'alliance' between *Officina* and *Ragionamenti*. Pasolini, while noting Fortini's 'moralistic and mystical abstraction', and returning implicit claims of privilege, nevertheless welcomed the contradictory claims of 'hope' emerging towards the end of the poem, and affirmed a closeness—soon rescinded—to the politics of *Ragionamenti*. Only later, in 1959, would Pasolini virulently object to what he perceived as an 'idiotic' indictment of his sexual life, to Fortini's 'tacit, unconscious, and insupressable prejudice presiding over all your critical operations on me'. He would contrast his lived attention to the sub-proletariat of Rome to Fortini's alleged idealistic enclosure: 'you, deaf, blind, locked in your house, with a wholly ideological idea of the workers and of the world in general, appoint yourself the judge of those who spend themselves, and in spending themselves, err, o how they err'.[37] Fortini's response testifies to how impossible it was to disentangle in this polemic in particular, the personal and the political, the ethical and the poetic: 'you are making a big mistake, like the Jew who always thinks of himself identified as a Jew by the non-Jew. I do not read between the lines of your biography; I read the printed ones, from the *Ashes* to *Officina*. You have very clearly expressed in them the poetics and ethics of non-choice and availability [*disponibilità*]'.

For Fortini, Pasolini's sexual life was not at stake; what he targeted for criticism was its literary presentation and form, and the (political, ethical) image of the 'Poet' that it performed. In a tone that would mark his harshest polemics, when they hit what he himself recognized as a biographical, psychological nerve—the painful experience of exclusion and illegitimacy that shaped him from his youth under Fascist racial laws[38] to his marginalization in the political movements and institutions of the left—Fortini retorts: 'From you I don't take lessons in political commitment. Use another tone with one who has paid the price. I hate, by experience, the activist political dilettantism of writers. I didn't lock myself in my house: they did. The communist and socialist functionaries who spat on my work and asked me to recognise their wisdom. They know all too well that I have always worked for communism to have the need to pamper me.'[39]

Officina *and the Limits of Literary Ideology*

But before their falling out in 1959, anticipating the ultimate break in 1968, Pasolini and Fortini's polemic in verses would be the prelude to an alliance of sorts, in the form of Fortini's collaboration with *Officina* and his contrasted and short-lived participation in its editorial board. For Fortini, division—over choices of political tactics or poetic metre, ethical stance or organizational programme—was always the way in which a communist hypothesis could actually be lived. Hence, in 1993, his reflection on what that polemic in verse meant:

> I felt—and it does not matter too much now whether I was right or wrong—that the mental conflict between [Pasolini

> and me] took place within the same side in a larger confrontation, the one that with the 20th Congress had become aware of an extraordinary possibility of opening and intellectual, moral and political regeneration, of rethinking of the past and even of recovery of an impetus that had been the one of the Resistance and that 1948 and the 'Cold War' had suffocated. And that we could exchange accusations with such frankness and harshness appeared, at least to me, as an anticipation of communist fraternity.[40]

Fortini entered into *Officina* after the collapse of *Ragionamenti*, sundered by personal conflicts and, perhaps, by the inability to translate the journal's ideological anticipation of the crisis of communism into an ampler cultural–political project, after the rapid closure of the hopes that the 'fateful year' had brought forth. His abiding suspicion that beneath Pasolini's tenuous combination of despairingly vitalist *passion* and communist *ideology* lay a 'real detachment from ideological passion, from a political and even moral thematic, and the employment of their appearance for pure expressive-stylistic ends',[41] would not go away. It was compounded by Fortini's suspicions of the limitations of a *literary* review with cultural–political aspirations, such as *Officina*, marred by the theoretical eclecticism of its contributing editorial board, its pretensions to ideological intervention and its attachment to a *role* and a *mandate* for the writer that were being rendered rapidly obsolete by capitalist transformations. Behind the guiding tendency of Pasolini and *Officina*, Fortini would diagnose a nexus of literary aristocratism and rhetorical populism, an incapacity to live class struggles in the first person and a frustration at not having any practical-political impact, accompanied by a projection of the poet's own contradictions onto the relatively amorphous mass of the plebeian, the sub-proletarian, the 'people'. Suspicious of the desire to create a new 'literary society', and an anachronistic return to the spiritualized privileges of intellectual labour; Fortini was also armed with the experience of his own 'exclusion' from literary high society (very much unlike Pasolini), and his life as a waged cultural worker—as a copywriter for Olivetti and a consultant for the publisher Einaudi, not to mention his decade of rather thankless work in trying to establish the conditions for socialist cultural work.

For the year of his active participation in the project of *Officina*, Fortini insisted on the dire need to avoid repeating—perhaps in a minor farce following the major tragedy—the errors of Communist cultural policy that he had anatomized in his *Dieci Inverni*, not least that of peddling a vague Marxism.[42] It was indeed the very sceptical reception of Fortini's major theoretical contribution to *Officina*, the text 'Lukács in Italy', included in this volume—which sought to verify the work of critical Marxism within literary and intellectual life in the Italian 1940s and 50s, contrasting Lukács with Adorno and gauging their reception in the peninsula—which triggered his resignation from the board. As he would put it in a caustic letter, 'if you are going to publish a journal of ideas, you should have some'; while *Officina* remained in his estimation 'slave to the dilettantish fashion for ideologization, and degrades itself to the traditional level of the unseriousness of "men of letters", in the worst sense of the term. "Positions" are the most fatuous excuses of intellectuals'.[43]

Officina's indefensible fault was to not fully comprehend that 'politics is something serious, like literature'[44] (recall the young Fortini's allusions to simony and barratry . . .), not to traverse the anachronistic fantasy of the man of letters as spiritual guide or romantic witness, and to continuously strive to play the game of ideology with little training or tactics, and with little reflection on the social and material conditions of one's poetic and literary activity. *Officina* for Fortini turned out to represent a kind of interim or rearguard action, fighting a two-front struggle against a one-dimensional image of 'committed' art (see 'Clarifications', in this collection) on the one hand, and an equally parochial view of twentieth-century literature on the other; while allowing itself to be circumvented by the neo-avant-gardes and their far more 'up to date' relationship to the mutated conditions of a neo-capitalist cultural industry. (It should be noted that the neo-avant-garde poet

Edoardo Sanguineti, who also responded with a poem to Pasolini's polemic, is among the targets of Fortini's critical acumen in the essay 'The Two Avant-gardes'.)

The image of literature borne by Pasolini and *Officina* was for Fortini still too wedded to the 'world of culture' and its subjective privileges, unable really to put itself materially and morally into question; in other words, it failed to connect (the criticism of) poetry with (the critique of) political economy. Reflecting on this brief and contrasted collaboration in the mid-1970s, Fortini writes that the

> [E]xperience of *Officina* served to definitely dissuade me from . . . publications that do not *explicitly* assume their own ideological-political figure . . . I feel unable to believe in *literary* ideologies and in group poetics, I can only manage to raise—spectres of contradiction and limits—the examples of verbal formality, that is to say, of poetry, in the face of those who control the political, sociological or pragmatic field, and is content with that.[45]

We will return to this question of the irreducibility of the poetic to the political, and to the political valence of this irreducibility, but it is crucial to first explore another of Fortini's polemical interventions, the one crystallized in arguably the most complex and powerful essay in *A Test of Powers*, 'Cunning as Doves' in which Fortini addresses the question of the relationship between literature and industry—which is to say, literature and the capitalism that was mutating Italy's physiognomy so fatefully during the period the essays were written. Italy's so-called economic miracle is sometimes periodized between 1958 and 1963,[46] and besides the neo-avant-garde Gruppo 63 (which included the likes of Nanni Balestrini, Edoardo Sanguineti, Giorgio Manganelli, Luigi Malerba, Umberto Eco and Elio Pagliarani), its most significant literary seismograph and venue was arguably the journal *Il menabò*, edited by Elio Vittorini and Italo Calvino.

Industry and Literature Revisited

In 1961, *Il menabò* (the title refers to the technical term for a designer's dummy, indicating the editors' vision of the journal as a kind of testing ground) devoted an issue of critical essays, stories and poems to the question 'industry and literature'. For the next three years or so, the debate engaged many of the finest critical minds of the Italian left, resonating with multiple efforts to forge languages adequate to the galloping and contradictory modernization that marked Italy's so-called economic miracle in a context shaped by the powerful presence of the Italian Communist Party, a renascence of class struggles and the gestation of the New Left. The destabilization of the nostrums of socialist realism Italian-style, but also of the official 'Gramscian' image of the organic intellectual, along with the unique participation of writers and critics in the lives of industry (especially under the wing of the enlightened industrialist Adriano Olivetti, who enlisted the writers Paolo Volponi, Geno Pampaloni, Ottiero Ottieri, as well as Fortini, in important positions within his company), created a unique climate of discussion that mingled emergent revolutionary aspirations with what might now appear, in retrospect, as the last waltz of true reformism in Italy.

Bracketing the genealogy and nuances of this debate, I want to touch here on some of the theses and positions it spawned, to present in more detail one of the contexts of formal and political debate in which Fortini operated—in the conviction that it can shed light, more broadly, on the stakes of *A Test of Powers* as a whole. Such an inquiry may also make us historically sensitive to what questions could be asked about art and artists then which cannot be posed in the same way now, primarily because of the particular moment of capitalist accumulation in which that debate emerged—upward impetus, organized class antagonism, a residual persistence of the peasantry and the lived experience of geographical and temporal unevenness.

The fourth issue of *Il menabò* opens, following an intense poem by Vittorio Sereni on a 'factory visit' ('Una visita in fabbrica', dated

1952–58) which dramatizes the poet's separation from the worker's own separation, with a polemical essay by Vittorini on 'Industry and Literature', inaugurating the programmatic coordinates of the debate. Vittorini's piece is in many ways an indictment of the formal backwardness of Italian letters, whose 'visits to the factory' (a genre often promoted by industrialists, and quite prevalent in the Italian postwar period) did not generate a novelty in representation and language to match the novelty of the 'new things' of industry. Like the nineteenth-century naturalists they unwittingly resemble, for Vittorini the vast majority of Italian writers, irrespective of their political militancy, approach industry through the model of their experience and narration of pre-industrial, or natural objects. New industrial objects, or even processes, may be added to the inventory of legitimate aesthetic objects, the factory may be entered to find a new 'slice of life', an 'iconography' of the factory and of factory work may be generated, but 'industry' is never truly confronted as a new level of human reality: its objects are 'sub-objects', most often bathed in a humanist recrimination that regards them as a threat to the writer's habitus of perception; the relation to the new things of industry is ideologically or, rather, moralistically mediated. Industry is not experienced as such but already through the symbols into which it has been transcribed by ideology (be it romantic, technocratic or Marxist).

As Vittorini writes, the 'writer speaks in a language of symbols for everything that concerns the new things and a language of things (even if now old and illegitimate; in other words, pseudo-concrete) for everything that concerns the old things of the pre-industrial world which we all continue to see with the eyes of our fathers and grandfathers—as though industry, permeating them with its rhythms, had not modified them'.[47] In a formalist inversion that could perhaps be transposed into our own present, for Vittorini there was more fidelity to the novelty of industry (of industrial communication and perception, of the machine and the relations it articulates) in the language of the *nouveau roman*, than in the seemingly more up-to-date literature of the factory which remained 'old' in its rhetoric, its way of seeing, observing or being. What discriminates between a literature capable of enduring the challenge of industry, in its linguistic forms more than its thematic contents, is its systematicity. What we are dealing with, as Vittorini's collaborators Leonetti and Calvino noted, is a 'new technical epoch' or 'a global historical experience put into motion by industry'. And, what matters is not the writer's relation to the industrial 'thing' itself but to the mutation which this thing, industry, effects in all kinds of other things; or, as a recent essay on Vittorini argues, echoing Fredric Jameson, in the way that 'the factory and industry are redrawing the cognitive maps and threaten to reduce not just literature to the irrelevance of an outdated language'.[48]

Vittorini understood totalization in terms of a system of effects: 'The meanings of a reality depend on the infinite effects that are produced in it by a certain cause. . . . And industrial reality can draw its meanings from the world of the effects put into motion by means of factories'.[49] Thus while it is formally (and politically) imperative for literature to critically adapt itself to this new industrial world, it is ultimately indifferent whether or not it visits the factory. Underlying Vittorini's emphasis on the 'new things' of industry is a vague but emphatic demand for a thoroughgoing emendation of literary language which must allow itself to be transformed, to adapt to the linguistic mutations effected by industry, to the changes in communication and media that fan out from the factory into the crevices of everyday life, the interstices of the individual psyche. In the interpretation of his collaborator Gianni Scalia (who was a member of the editorial board at *Officina* with Fortini only a couple of years before), industry is a totalized notion, 'a constitutively structural and ideological, economic and existential [signifying] complex'.[50] This means that literature must discard its iconography and ideology; that it should allow itself to register (but not necessarily represent) the anthropological mutation operated by industry (this was also the period that elicited Pasolini's threnodies on 'anthropological genocide').

This involves literature immersing itself in alienation against alienation, giving voice, as Scalia puts it, to the 'aphasia of incommunicability', to the dissociation, absence of finality and project, and apparent meaninglessness of this process without a subject that is industry—not through sublimation but by generating a 'dramatic and positive knowledge' of the new things which here requires a real comprehension of the new languages and objects of industry. This immersion into the potentially nihilistic totality of industry is a first step in a programmatic and proto-political vision of literature (present but more implicit in Vittorini), stated in rather world-historical terms by Scalia: 'The material "conditions" of industry, as objective and necessary conditions of the *development from nature to industry*, have been transformed into conditions of projectability and programmability *of nature into industry*, of identification of nature and industry'.[51]

To speak anachronistically, Scalia is proposing a reform of literature that transmutes it into the instrument of a political anthropology for the Anthropocene, for a phase beyond the opposition between nature and industry—an opposition or unevenness he notes is a precondition of classical revolutionary thought. As he puts it in his essay's final lines, the task of the writer is the common task of 'constructing a trans-industrial anthropology that will know, comprehend and transform industrial industry into human industry'.[52] What is remarkable in Vittorini and Scalia's positions, as in those of other contributors to the debate, is that in this discussion of the representability and effects of industry the problem of politics, of power, is posed in a sense as external to industry (itself referred to by one of the participants in the debate as 'the power of powers'). Political power appears as a problem of control or direction vis-à-vis an epochal process that is itself politically underdetermined, as the socialization of a superhuman process (the orientation of all participants in the debate being generically 'progressive'). In other words, we see a repetition of a bourgeois conception of the state as separate from civil society, albeit with a technocratic twist.[53] The editorial line of *Il menabò*, to the extent that there is one, moves beyond the problem of the representability of the factory and labour—the one that had preoccupied writers like Ottiero Ottieri whose 'Industrial Notebook', published in the same issue, revolves around this problem (those outside the factory don't know, those inside don't speak)[54]—to that of its systemic effects on language and representability, to industry not as an object but as an epoch and a condition. It is at the systemic level, via a notion of system charged by a dialectical negativity alien to *Il menabò*'s vision of history, that Vittorini and his collaborators meet their strongest challenge in Fortini's article 'Cunning as Doves'.

Fortini questioned the aesthetic coherence and political relevance of the then (and once again now) widespread demand for representations of capitalism; in many ways recasting Brecht's oft-quoted observation, borrowed from Fritz Sternberg, that 'a photograph of the Krupp factory or of AEG says almost nothing about these institutions'. Conversely, as he would write in 1973 about his second trip to China, 'socialism is never something that you see. You see electric plants and peasants at work, school plays and folk ballets, industrial expos and parades, not relations between men'.[55] He argued for a 'prophetic' rather than a cognitive–informative role for the artwork, which in this differed from the organizational, cognitive and negative tasks of criticism (see 'A Test of Powers').[56] To those who called for a literature of neo-capitalism, he retorted that art and literature's 'cognitive power' [*potere di conoscenza*] was to be located not in its occasion or pretext (again, unlike criticism) but in its form: 'It is the work of art's final word, and not its first, to *also* be history, psychology, philosophy and politics. We must negate with all our energies the false progressivism according to which industrial reality, in its moment of production or consumption, needs to be given literary expression because it is "important".' Accordingly, 'industry is not *a* theme, it is the manifestation of *the* theme called capitalism'. Therefore, as he writes in 'Cunning as Doves':

> [I]t is increasingly difficult today to speak of an industrial truth as distinct from the general truth of society. If anything, 'sociological consciousness' should lead us to

> conclude that we are speaking of industry when we speak about anything else, and that the difficulty in speaking about it is no different than the difficulty we encounter when we really wish to speak about something true. The mystery of political economy, which Marx had already discussed, is today (through the complete triumph of industry in society and its imminent or already consummated coincidence with the state) the very mystery of our lives, the 'essence' lying beneath the 'phenomena' (p. 133).

Against the modernizing aim to enact a kind of *aggiornamento*, and incorporate industrial production into the domain of culture and art, Fortini suggests that this supposed thematization of industry serves to disavow capitalism as a 'social unconscious'. In this regard, he indicates the insufficient totalization that the very name of 'industry' as opposed to 'capital' entails. A superficial kinship with Vittorini's arguments against 'factory literature' and for a totalizing conception of the 'new things' hides a very different conception of the relation between social form and literary form, and accordingly of the 'tasks' of literature and art. With his characteristic scorn for the mealy-mouthed illusions of gradualism, he identifies the enemy in this debate as the 'vulgarity of Generalized and Reformist Progressivism'. Capital's subsumption of culture and politics means that turning to the dynamics of production, discipline, struggle or the division of labour in the factory can easily divert critical attention from the totalizing presence of the capital-relation in what, following the Marxist theorist Mario Tronti, Fortini calls the social factory:[57]

> How can we speak of industry and literature without at least agreeing on this (but it's almost everything): that the forms, modes and times of industrial production and its relations are the very form of social life, the historical container of all our content, not simply an aspect of reality? That economic structures—in our case capitalist and therefore industrial ones—are no more and no less than the

> social unconscious, that is the true unconscious, the mystery of mysteries?

Fortini would draw from these reflections some important consequences for his poetics, and for the possibility of forging literary forms capable not of mediating or representing capital but of prefiguring, without the illusions of an affirmation, the transformations of our formative capacities under communism. He thereby signalled his distance from Lukácsian critical realism, notwithstanding his attachment to the Hungarian Marxist's conception of standpoint and his complex sympathy with many of Lukács's critiques of the avant-gardes.[58] While wilfully missing this crucial dimension of Fortini's work, Calvino's intervention into the debate, 'The Challenge of the Labyrinth'—which castigated Fortini for a kind of purist, nihilistic asceticism—is worth noting at least for its proposal of a diagonal path to the alternative posed in the arguments of Vittorini and Scalia, namely, the alternative between representing the new world of industry and engaging in a formal-conceptual mimesis of industrial reality and language (this second path being largely attributed to the 1960s neo-avant-gardes, with their anti-moral acceptance of the ambiguity of the 'new things'). Calvino, whose partisanship for 'multiplicity' would be the object of a bracing correspondence with Fortini, here tried to defend the cognitive powers of literature in terms of a different, non-Hegelian conception of totalization, one that he saw dramatized in the writings of Borges or Carlo Emilio Gadda. Calvino did not deny partisanship but recoiled from treating either industry or capital as a whole, in a far more tentative vision of the 'new things' than either Vittorini and Scalia's demand for a linguistic and anthropological updating, or Fortini's critical Marxian observance.[59]

Purity or Metamorphosis?

The debate in *Il menabò* is just one significant moment in three decades of exchanges and polemics between Fortini and Calvino. It was marked by the division of labour in the domain of cultural production: Calvino played a leading role in the Einaudi publishing house while Fortini, straining at waged subordination, worked for Einaudi as a translator, consultant and series editor.[60] The contrast between the two authors could be drawn with schematic ease, for example, by noting the antithesis between some of literary values encapsulated in Calvino's *Six Memos for the Next Millennium* (1988) and Fortini's ethical and poetic principles. 'Lightness' and 'multi-plicity' are certainly not Fortinian virtues. Such a schematic opposition could find much corroboration in their correspondence—Calvino (like Pasolini in another context) bemoaning Fortini's fanaticism, Fortini repeatedly castigating the frivolousness and complaisance of Calvino's writing.

As in the polemic with Pasolini, it is the question of morality, of its place in the discourse on literature and politics, which is often in the foreground. We could find the sources for the divergence already in their earliest writings, Calvino's 'atheist atheism' at inexorable odds with Fortini's existentialist Protestantism. But these differences of worldview, character and style can also be seen as resources when thought in contact with their epoch. The question might then be: What did such deep temperamental differences make possible in terms of a response to their age, in the forms of literature and politics? In this respect, Calvino's response to Fortini's essay 'Consigli a pochi' [Advice to the Few] a text from 1959, later collected in the first 1965 edition of *A Test of Powers* (but not included here) is very instructive. In that text, Fortini had forcefully argued, in a manner which resonates throughout the rest of *A Test of Powers*, that there exists no problem of poetry and literature that is not a problem of society; to refuse heteronomy is to lie. Echoing his comments on Pasolini and the forgetting of political economy, Fortini would argue that as all modern literature is conditioned by the relations between producers and consumers of culture, any communication that does not include those conditions—which does not reflect upon, control or test them—is false. The denial of these conditions was not just the product of the bourgeois fetish of the privileged autonomy of the literary sphere, it is also what condemned the cultural politics of left parties and of official anti-fascism. The anti-fascist left was unable to propose terms of useful collaboration to cultural producers, and thus shaded into a reformism that could only fantasize its 'hegemony' by playing on an enemy field, accepting its forms and forgetting Brecht's resounding call—at the heart of 'The Writers' Mandate'—'don't forget property relations'. In 'Consigli a pochi', Fortini would speak of the need to refuse both 'exhortatory moralism' and 'false professional humility'. He argued for:

> [A] continuously active criticism of the human-social condition which we are subjected to here and now (which should be, it should go without saying, wholly different from the 'corrosive' criticism of the existentialist-stoic kind, which is now a refuge for all sorts of laziness) and on the very narrow margins that such a criticism allows or, rather, in close relation to it—which is to say, also invested by it—a limited and professional, technically effective creative work.[61]

Calvino's response begins with characteristic irony, prefacing a full agreement with the pessimistic diagnosis of Fortini's essay, with gratitude for the way it has 'rekindled my inexhaustible passion for discussions of morality; only by having a clear idea of what virtue is can I practice evil with a light heart'.[62] Though Calvino had left the PCI in 1957, by his own avowal his approach was still marked by the particular orientation to both politics and form provided by that experience. As he remarks:

> Communism's anti-moralistic message—which I believe I have assimilated with perhaps too much alacrity—makes me believe that one should never have taboos about the tools we use, that as long as the thought or images or style one wants to put forward do not become deformed by the

> medium, one must on the contrary try to make use of the most powerful and most efficient of those tools.[63]

This anti-moralism could be combined, at least for a time, with a strong determination on Calvino's part to think about what a 'Communist morality' might be defined as. A letter to Pasolini, in 1959, about the novel *A Violent Life* is eloquent in this respect:

> In the end one can only take upon oneself and rationalize all the violence of history and nature in order to live through it with one aim in view: the Communist moral is reached only by living through what is awful with one's eyes open, constantly, because every bit of progress is always accompanied by continual defeats and deteriorations. The person who lives through this, whether a philosopher or an illiterate member of the sub-proletariat, has learnt something. All the rest is nothing, it's all just an edifying attempt worthy of a parish priest or 'Communist slush,' which is the opposite of true Communist morality. Every once in a while you seem to be on the point of unmasking the 'Communist sweetly-sick,' and to reach the moral truth of Communism, but instead you just stay there. . . . In short: virtue must *never* be represented, not under any circumstances.[64]

Fortini, shaped as he was by the lesson of the Frankfurt School, and by reflection on the specifically Italian modalities of the 'culture industry' in the midst of the 'economic miracle'—a reflection marked by his dialogue with the workerist theorist Raniero Panzieri, as several essays in this volume testify—would be far less casual than Calvino on the risks of 'deformation'. Calvino combined a broadly rationalist progressive political orientation (not shorn of notes of pessimism) with a critical embrace of the historical and formal mutations thrown up by the present. This is evident in some of his essays of the late 1950s and early 60s, 'The Sea of Objectivity' and 'The Worker's Antithesis',[65] as well as 'The Challenge of the Labyrinth'. As for Fortini, the focus would always revolve around the connection between an ethically charged poetics and a partisan, antagonistic analysis of capitalism, a connection made possible by the joint criticism of literary and social forms. Contrariwise, Calvino rebukes Fortini in the following terms: 'Criticism which remains criticism and no more, retains an enormous moral authority, but is not yet dialectical negation'; what is required is utopian fabulation beyond negativity: 'Instead of being consumed by a descriptive-analytical passion for things as they are, one must not accept reality and instead put up against it a reality that maybe does not exist but that solely because you are proposing it acquires a strength and influence of its own.'[66]

It was not just a different moral and poetic temperament but also a different practice of politics that divided them. Calvino's decade of militancy in the PCI never eventuated into the repudiation of a kind of 'Enlightenment Marxism' through which he had interpreted his militancy, so alien to the 'Kierkegaardian' foundations of Fortini's heretical communism. The essay 'The Worker's Antithesis', published in *Il menabò* in 1964, with its assertion of a non-catastrophist Marxism in which the working class guides historical mutations in an alliance of sorts with the progressive forces of capital, delineates (on the same terrain as *A Test of Powers*) the difference between him and Fortini. It is a difference very nicely encapsulated in Calvino's 1959 letter:

> In fact bourgeois cultural structures nearly always distort; for that reason our conclusions end up more or less coinciding; but what does not coincide is the love of purity that you maintain and the love of contamination, of metamorphosis, of regeneration that I uphold. (Going down this road, of course, there are ninety-nine, well let's say ninety-five, chances out of a hundred that one loses one's soul; but that's the beauty of it!)[67]

Years later, Calvino would write one of his longest and most intensely argued letters to Fortini as a response to the latter's essay on Pasolini in *Quaderni piacentini*. He salutes the essay as 'a polemic that goes beyond the subject which occasioned it (I prefer not even mentioning it here), and become the basis for a general judgement'. While Calvino goes on to develop a fascinating reflection on the difference between Fortini's anthropology and his own, with its attention to humanity's place in a non-human cosmos (returning, albeit in a different vein, to the seminal insights of his essay 'The Sea of Objectivity' and to his work on Charles Fourier[68]) at the core of his agreement is, strikingly, the formula with which Fortini parried Pasolini (and Calvino's) abiding accusation of *moralism*. Calvino—whose own polemical differences with Pasolini have been the object of considerable debate in Italy, even recently[69]—finds himself persuaded, as someone who makes 'a principle of out of the rejection or punishment of moralism', by Fortini's distinction between *moralism* and *morality*. In Fortini's article titled—in anger, but in keeping with his long-held objections to the figure of 'the Poet' and the illusions of poetry—'Pasolini is Not Poetry', he had claimed against those activists who wanted merely to dismiss this poet as an enemy of the people, after his asseverations against the 1968 movement, that:

> [T]here is no interlocutor or locutor (as pure or corrupt as they may be) who cannot be the bearer of a precious truth. Against our own moralism, we must never forget it. Moralism is not that thing which Pasolini believes it is and of which he speaks all the time. He confuses moralism and morality. Morality is an urge for coherence between values and behaviour; it is consciousness of discord. It becomes politics, it is the private name of politics. Moralism is the error of those who deny that there must be or can be values or behaviours other than those which morality has present to itself at a given moment; it believes that the contradiction is arrested, even for a moment, in the formal unity of the individual.[70]

The Weapons of Criticism

With the publication of *A Test of Powers*, Fortini confronted this 'moral question' yet again, in the guise of a polemic with Alberto Asor Rosa. In 1965, Asor Rosa brought out his own *Scrittori e popolo*—published in English in tandem with this book as *The Writer and the People*, in Matteo Mandarini's translation. *A Test of Powers* and *The Writer and the People* are arguably the two crucial interventions into literary criticism on the left of the Communist Party in the period between the caesura of 1956 and the 'red decade' that would begin with the strikes of Autumn 1967 (or in Fortini's own periodization, the 'Great Storm' between 1968 and 1973). A patient comparison between them—not to mention situating them in a broader range of crucial collections from this period, from Pasolini's *Passione e ideologia* (1960) to Umberto Eco's *Apocalittici e integrati* (1964)—is a task for another occasion. But it is worth pausing briefly on their points of friction, if only to delineate the singularity of Fortini's proposal.

Asor Rosa had participated, like Fortini, in the minoritarian but immensely consequential experience of the journal *Quaderni rossi* before the fallout that saw him join Mario Tronti and Antonio Negri in *Classe operaia*, leaving behind Fortini's friend and reference point at the moment of *operaismo*, Raniero Panzieri. *Scrittori e popolo*, with its extended critical analyses of the literature of the Resistance (including Calvino) and its long oppositional dissection of Pasolini's work, singularly tried to apply the method of workerism to a critique of *populism* (which it viewed as the chief literary ideology of the Italian left). Founding his discourse on the radical antagonism of a working class shorn of humanism or romanticism, Asor Rosa argued that populism contaminated almost the entire cultural policy and literary life of the left during the postwar period, retarding a proper grasp of the deep negativity of capitalist culture—something for which high bourgeois literature was infinitely better adapted than the consolations of the 'national-popular', with its inability to truly negate the regressive features of Italian literary culture. Much of Asor Rosa's negative programme was of course sympathetic to Fortini, not just for its opposition to the Togliattian synthesis of Gramsci and Croce, with its elision of class struggle but also for its evisceration of the illusions of the 'popular', its entreaties to leave behind literary ideology and recognize the present predicament of class conflict.[71] And yet, especially in Asor Rosa's attack on Fortini's book, their abyssal differences can be clearly discerned—differences concerning their conception of the fraught link between criticism, poetics and politics.

In the essay 'L'uomo, il poeta' (1965), originally published in the young Massimo Cacciari's journal *Angelus Novus*, Asor Rosa juxtaposes his externality to the domain of culture, already articulated in *The Writer and the People*'s claim to put forward a political (and not a cultural) criticism of literature, to the ambiguity of a poet-intellectual struggling—symbolically, metaphorically—with the disjunction between individual work and collective fate, seeking poetic forms that might anticipate political ones. At the crux of Asor Rosa's attack was the repudiation of the broad premise of Fortini's work from the Liberation onward, and of the centrality of the question of the organization of cultural production to much of the reflection in *A Test of Powers*, especially as it transpires from its key programmatic essays, 'Cunning as Doves', 'The Writers' Mandate and the End of Anti-Fascism' or 'Radek's Hands'. For Asor Rosa, the only proletarian plan that Fortini should envisage is not that of a practical collaboration in an anti-capitalist direction of proletarianized intellectuals with intellectual proletarians but, rather, the one that would 'systematically plan his extinction as the representative of a specific social body'.[72] Thus, he turns Fortini's own weapons against him, seeing him as a progressive intellectual desperately tied to an obsolete mandate, 'the last of the bourgeois intellectuals rather than the first of the Marxist researchers'.[73] Having dismissed Fortini's continued attachment to the dialectics of the intellectual, Asor Rosa also attacked the utopian moment in his communist poetics, the position voiced in 'The Writers' Mandate' that 'the literary use of language is homologous to the formal use of life which is the aim and end [*il fine e la fine*] of communism'. Asor Rosa had his harshest words against Fortini's insistence as poet and critic on the link between the poetic and the political (however negatively or despairingly this was articulated). It is worth quoting at length to give us a sense of the differences that separated these two contemporaneous conceptions of literature and communist politics.

> To make poetry today, when the terms of the class conflict have reached their extreme and essential nakedness, is nothing more than submitting to the suggestive invitation of a tradition or, rather, of a crystallized convention. I do not know how one who deals with words in a literary form, doesn't feel his tongue freeze in his mouth every time he becomes able to understand the condition in which the world finds itself. Never has necessity reached such an extreme level, never have words seemed so inadequate to their aim. Faced with the reign of necessity one must have the courage to give up on everything that is not necessary: beauty, consolation, hope, pain, pleasure, must be erased from our horizon.[74]

Asor Rosa employed against Fortini the latter's criticism of the intellectual and poet's fatuous positions and misguided civic lyricism, as evidenced in the polemic with Pasolini. Fortini's riposte bitterly and cleverly turned the table on Asor Rosa and his comrades as he discerned in their performance of revolutionary asceticism the histrionic iteration of the petty-bourgeois intellectual's self-hatred, further compounded by a drastically mistaken diagnosis about the state of the class struggle and a misunderstanding of the place of ideology (see the 'Preface to the Second Edition' in this volume; it can also be read as a retort to critics like Asor Rosa).

In one of the epigrams in *L'ospite ingrato*, published in 1966, Fortini would chide Asor Rosa for merely repeating the fallacy thrown in Fortini's face by the left Socialist leader Rodolfo Morandi in 1951, namely, the notion that affirming, as Fortini did, the 'non-substitutability of the ideological moment—that is, of intellectual experience and of its orientation or finality—was tantamount to once again proposing the caste of intellectuals as elective guides of the workers movement'. The retort to Asor Rosa was also an occasion to reassert something that marks Fortini's thinking of the relation between literary work and political emancipation, namely, that ethical imperative which is spoken here under the aegis of 'value'. He writes that Asor Rosa:

> seems to want to argue that 'values' are so much Sunday fanfare, 'supreme ideals'; and that the simple (though it's anything but simple!) experience of exploitation and alienation does not imply criteria of value. On the contrary, there is no qualitative difference between the immediate end or ends (for example: the expropriation of the boss) and the mediate ones (for example: the image of the organization of a communist society). Both are founded on the choice, which is not abstractly free, of course, but neither is it abstractly determined (it would then be a non-choice), between what is desirable and what is not, for the individual, for the class and for its institutions: choices that are organised in a system or a hierarchy and which I cannot define except as values.[75]

For Fortini the intimate, if conflicted, bond between ethics and poetics, between these two moments of 'value', is evident in his conviction that among Asor Rosa's deep failings as a critic was his inability to grasp the 'literary dimension of everything that is not poetry in verses or narrative in prose'; in other words, not to grasp—to allude to the crucial role of Lukács and Adorno's insights on this matter—*the essay as form*, the aesthetic dimensions of critical writing.[76]

This moral, but not moralistic, retort prolongs what had already been Fortini's internal criticism of the workerist position, as voiced in his letter in *Quaderni rossi*, 'Il socialismo non è inevitabile' [Socialism Is Not Inevitable], where he chided his comrades for combining (in a manner not unfamiliar from the history of communist movements) a deterministic conviction in the material exacerbation of contradictions, which had yet to be properly 'tested', with 'voluntarism, because you are asking for action in the name of a moral choice, and so much the worse for reality'.[77] Whereas it imagined itself as shorn of the pathetic contortions of the (petty-)bourgeois intellectual, this unstable amalgam of voluntarism and determinism was in Fortini's eyes a deep disavowal of its own condition which repeated, in spite of itself, the hackneyed heroisms of bygone literati. Writing in criticism of the journal which Asor Rosa founded with Tronti and Cacciari, Fortini notes that:

> From the nexus of voluntarism and objectivism and therefore of exaltation of the political-directive moment and, together, of the grim-ferocious necessity and fatality of the class-machine, the men of *Classe operaia* have drawn their natural inclination to tragic-decadent heroism. . . . They all [Mario Tronti, Alberto Asor Rosa, Massimo Cacciari] sought and found a historical idol that would act as metaphor and symbol of the Stalinist ossification of the party–mass relationship, as well as of the subjective need for virile sado-masochism or tragic decadentism.[78]

That such an unconscious return to decadentism, after the repudiation of Gramscianism and humanism, was not inevitable is perhaps most incisively voiced by Fortini in a poem in which the collective activity that Asor Rosa presented as courageously stripped of beauty and refractory to value appears instead as animated by a poetic and utopian charge. The poem, 'On the First Issue of *Quaderni rossi*', was written two decades after the experience of the journal, and published in the collection *Paesaggio con serpente* [Landscape with a Snake]:

Many hours then of the few hours
that the order of killers and the disorder
had not yet broken

he read of company structures, collective
contracts, time monitoring. And what immense thoughts
in the air of his days,
imprecise, smiling! Sharpened,
the cirrus clouds that the milling cutter
spatters and the darkened oils channel

in his sleep were the figure
of dead seed and future grass.[79]

Beyond Italy

But something more than ethical or aesthetic 'value' and the political valence of poetic form dissociated Fortini from Asor Rosa's image of criticism and politics. It was a very different idea of what the other—or, rather, the *others*—to capital might be. This was testified by poems such as 'Complicity', and by the place of China, its people and its revolution in Fortini's political and poetic imagination, as evinced in the closing essay on Lu Xun ('The Chinese Spectre') but, especially, the 1956 account of his travels through communist China, *Asia Maggiore* [Asia Major][80] and the later reflections on what he called 'allegorical countries'.[81] Ever since the wrenching 'discovery of the world'[82] as a wartime refugee in Switzerland, Fortini would stand out for his hostility to the Eurocentrism pervasive in Italian politics and letters, of which Asor Rosa's strain of workerism was an extreme or, rather, an extremist exemplar.

In 1965, a few months after *A Test of Powers*, an anthology edited by Fortini was published; it was tellingly titled *Profezie e realtà del nostro secolo* [Prophecies and Realities of Our Century]. In his capacity as a non-specialist in the world of the social sciences,[83] Fortini sought to gather texts vital for the orientation of 'an average European and Italian man who grew up in average neo-capitalist civilization', to offset what had been rendered opaque by the hidden persuaders of the culture industry, namely, 'the most important things': 'his relationship to others, public life in the whole world (there is no other), his possibility of intervention in the conditions of everyone's life; in other words, economy and politics (two names for fate). And, the possibility of being different [*diversi*]'.[84] This link between a kind of planetary publicity and a 'prophecy' of difference, of transformation, runs through much of Fortini's thought in this period, allowing him to anticipate in these pages the impending political turmoil. Such anticipation was not least made possible by his attention to authors and figures who would have been alien or inimical to a left intelligentsia either tied to an anachronistic world of Italian or European culture or confident, like Asor Rosa, in the cutting edge of its own industrial negativity. Thus, in the index of Fortini's anthology we find Frantz Fanon and Michel Foucault, James Baldwin and Joan Robinson, Kwame Nkrumah and the voices of Chinese peasants, Betty Friedan and Nelson Mandela and so on.[85]

Such a diverse range was called for in 1965, a conjuncture demanding both secular prophecy and a patient work of anticipation, a moment in which Fortini both hopefully stated that 'the greatest event of the last decade and the general tendency seem to be that of the rediscovery of the communist hypothesis on a global scale' and claimed that 'social reality now seems charged with signs that are only partly decipherable'.[86] To begin to decipher that reality, *A Test of Powers*, while wrestling with the rising fortunes of structuralism or of stylistic criticism, as well as with the products of the avant-garde, maintained a creative fidelity not just to Marxism but also to the visions and instruments that had been forged, brilliantly and tragically, by Georg Lukács and the Frankfurt School in the interwar period, and which Fortini only truly discovered in the late 1940s and early 50s. The essay 'Lukács in Italy', originally published in *Officina*, registers the impact of this encounter, while 'The

Writers' Mandate' (along with the shorter pieces on the *Threepenny Novel*, *The Calendar Tales* and the poem 'O Falada . . .') reveals the enormous significance of Brecht—whose translation occupied Fortini during this period.[87] This was, in fact, Fortini's effort to wend a way through the antinomies and blind allies of communist culture, as they presented themselves in an Italian context marked by the unmet aspirations of the Resistance, a local and *sui generis* Cold War, and the 'economic miracle'. One of his most striking reflections on the uses and meaning of Marxist literary criticism appeared exactly a decade after *A Test of Powers*, in his preface to the Italian edition of Fredric Jameson's *Marxism and Form*. Notwithstanding the incommensurability of biographies and cultural context, the divergences of method and temperament, there is also a remarkable affinity in Fortini and Jameson's respective ways of traversing and recombining the crucial positions within the force field of dialectical criticism—Benjamin and Bloch, Brecht and Lukács, Adorno and Marcuse, or indeed the outlier Sartre. In his preface, Fortini, showing great sympathy for the inclusion of Sartre (who for him, as for Jameson, preceded engagement with the Frankfurt School), and even more so for Jameson's resistance to the widespread condescension directed at Marcuse, nicely remarks on the advantages of a geographical distance (which also implies a temporal one):

> What might have seemed obvious is renewed. No one in Italy, for example, would have dealt with Lukács and Sartre in the same book and in terms of the same problems; we are compulsively accustomed to consider this as an error resulting from the minimal amplitude of the acute angle that finds its vertex in California and whose sides point towards Paris and Budapest; when instead it is precisely those remote centres (or are we remote?) that allow one to grasp positions that seem absolutely disjoined or divergent as contiguous. What's more, that distance makes it possible to assess the extent to which the theses, groups and men

> who wish somehow to escape those capitalist laws of specialization that incubate technocratic elites are instead prisoners to the times, wishes, and interests of publishing houses, even the ones that claim to be scholarly.[88]

And he concludes with a reflection that could very much serve to preface not just *Marxism and Form* but also *A Test of Powers*, illuminating its effort to link the renovation of Marxist criticism with an abiding attention, charged with utopia, to the irreducibility of the work, of poetics to politics (and vice versa), which must never be fetishized and reified into a 'temptation of the work' for that would mean abandoning the politics of criticism:

> [W]e are confronted by a *necessary* and *organic* limit of that which is here called dialectical criticism. Of course, the Marxist literary critic will not be able to refuse the 'scientific' aspects of historical, sociological, psychoanalytic, linguistic and semiological inquiry; but the uninterrupted process of totalization, the need to include in one's discourses ever-more seemingly foreign fractions of reality and knowledge, will end up subtracting not only from the critic's pages and his book the harmony and completeness which is one of the signs of so-called great traditional criticism but, by implying a continuous opening to the future, they will also *entrust the meaning of the inquiry to the mutations of history* or, rather, to a particular kind of mutation whose agents will not be generic but *specific* social forces. In this sense the lack of concreteness of Marxist criticism is its inevitable constituent; and its real critical results will of necessity have to be referred back to this or that methodological component, to criteria of inquiry that call upon other perspectives and world-views, rather than to its own Marxist ones; as though the dialectical and revolutionary criticism which Jameson discusses had as its inextricable fate to be always *before* or *after* the concrete

> operations of criticism; to be, that is, what orients, not what is oriented. This condition is perhaps also true for every other critical Marxist activity, political activity included. And what is it that is eminently unable to accept such an intolerable tension, such a pitiless negation of its essence? *It is the work*, any work, in its anti-dialectical illusion, in its standing aside, in its necessary refusal of history. When, like today, history seems to slow down and the air darkens, the temptation of the work and its apparent immobility becomes as irresistible as evening, even for one who knows that resisting it is the only way for a work to be carried out.[89]

Resistance, 1945–65

Speaking of the 'mutations of history' to which the work of criticism must be entrusted, 1965 was also the 20th anniversary of liberation from fascism,[90] and the neglected or traduced legacy of that moment—which shaped Fortini to the core—haunts the pages of 'The Writers' Mandate' and other texts collected herein, driving its animus against the integration of the Italian 'civil war' into the cultural manoeuvres of party and state apparatuses.[91] Resistance, Fortini suggested, always had to be thought together with the non-resistance (to fascism) that preceded it as a social and psychic norm. It could teach younger generations the impediments facing those who did not have the political capacities or direction to translate their subjective mutation and 'Davidic' endurance, their crucial 'use of clandestinity' into a project of power that could be put to the test, 'demonstrating how, according to Saint Just, "Those who make revolution half way only dig their own graves", but they can, who knows, teach how to make them whole'.[92] Fortini noted, to resist 'is something that implies a prior event, a retreat, a flight, and then a decision to stop'.[93] Resistance, which in retrospect could stand as the critique of official anti-fascism,[94] was not just the emblem of a choice stripped of all reference to authority, the lived locus and test of that Protestant existentialism that shaped the young Fortini; it was also the emergence of a horizon of social and human reconstruction, the anticipation of an emancipated future. Speaking to students, Fortini would characterize the partisan war against fascism and Nazism as:

> [A] moral war, an accelerated course in civic life. This was even more the case, as everywhere around us, everything seemed to descend into fury, bestiality, blindness, crime. Italians discovered that there are no absolutely immaculate causes, no groups of the 'pure', that collective actions demand giving up integrity and that remorse is inseparable from action. . . . When the violence of contradictions is raised to the level of horror, wills become implacable, neglected zones of consciousness and society come to the fore, and we discover with fright and joy that the hierarchy of men was in fact apparent and false.[95]

Two decades before, in his early text 'The Silence of Italy'—a youthful manifesto written while a refugee in Switzerland—Fortini had written of 'language as the instrument to look for one's comrades'.[96] And this it remained, though the search was inextricable from the violence of polemic, of the epigram, the epithet, the seemingly irreversible epistle, and from the whole psychic weight of Fortini's abiding experience of exclusion, of what he called 'illegitimacy'. The work of criticism like the work of politics, but also like the practice of poetic writing, of metric composition, remained for him a labour of division;[97] the latter was not the path to a complacent solitude, a separate privilege, but the arduous medium for continuing that search for comrades—the ones without whom, as his translation of the *Internationale* declaims, 'death really is the end'. Two years after the publication of *A Test of Powers*, and in the same year as the Arab–Israeli War, the occasion for his memoir of division, *The Dogs of the Sinai*, Fortini addressed a rally against the

Vietnam War. In this speech-poem, which also castigates those comrades (Asor Rosa is clearly interpellated) 'blinded by a workerism as bookish as it is allied with a decadent demonism'[98] for continuing to think that the Vietnamese struggle is regressive, merely 'a courageous grandchild that needs to grow', Fortini gives voice and vent to that emancipatory demand for division that lends its sometimes desperate generosity to his polemics, criticism, and poetry; in short, his labour:

> History and experience have taught me
> that today we must try not to unite but to divide.
> To divide ever more violently the world,
> to promote the only deep, the only true, the only fecund
>   division,
> which has become ever more clear, ever more painful
>   and necessary,
> within the unity created by the international market,
> within the unity determined by power and by oppression
> This means above all destroying the false divisions of the
>   past
> it means seeing identifying interpreting
> the confused and corrupt unity that today exists.[99]

Appendix

The following is the unsigned text that Fortini wrote for the back cover of the first edition of A Test of Powers.

How can literature exist? What could the duties of criticism be? Some of these pages raise old questions that have never been so pervasive. But right away the author shows his hand. To attempt to respond is tantamount to asking other questions: How can there exist, in history, a conscious movement towards a goal? What could the 'duties of man' be?[100] A first part is devoted to problems of Italian mores and opinion: literary criticism and the industry of consciousness, the false problem of the relations between industry and literature, the re-examination of the commonplaces about post-war literature. A set of writings on some of the major critics and theorists of the literature of our time—Spitzer, Auerbach, Goldmann, Lukács—are followed by essays and notes on Russian, French and German writers and poets, approached and read as though they were parables of the entire argument. But the book's centre is to be found in the part that with its title, 'The Condition of the Guest', alludes to a status that belongs to the writer because it is generally human. The contradictory relations between poetry and revolution, the theme of the 'end of history', the development of anti-fascist positions and the end of the Mayakovskian 'social mandate' are openly summoned, intervening, so to speak, in the first person. Only apparently fragmented by the occasions that gave rise to its various pieces, the book is intended as unified because (as its table of contents shows) it develops some constant themes and advances them at successive and different levels, with a tight and twofold movement of references, now to literature, now to the social history of our time. That is why it opens with an ironic remembrance of the fears manifested in the Versailles of 1789 by the 'commissioners of the nobility', that 'the test of powers in common implied deliberation in common', and closes with the appeal to an effective assistance against the threat that looms over us, pronounced—in Brecht's words—by an equine Orpheus that men tear to pieces so that they will not hear his prophecy.

Notes

1 Franco Fortini, *Poems* (Michael Hamburger trans.) (Todmorden: Arc Publications, 1978), p. 13.

2 Matthew 10:34.

3 Franco Fortini, 'Lettere da Lontano. A Carlo Ginzburg' [Letters from Afar: To Carlo Ginzburg], *L'Espresso* (30 March 1986).

4 Franco Fortini, *Attraverso Pasolini* (Turin: Einaudi, 1993), p. *x*.

5 See Franco Fortini, 'Per una critica come servizio' [For Criticism as Service] (1951), in *Dieci inverni, 1947–1957. Contributi ad un discorso socialista* [Ten Winters, 1947–1957. Contributions to a Socialist Discourse], 2nd EDN (Bari: De Donato, 1973), pp. 79–91. This is an important statement of Fortini's position regarding the need to refocus from a Gramscian image of national-popular cultural hegemony to the 'organization of culture' understood as the ensemble of relations between cultural production and the political-economic structures of society. What the socialist movement needed, according to the Fortini of the early 1950s, was 'a nucleus of writers-critics, capable of mediating literary works all the way to the most remote parts of the cultural body of the nation and to retransmit those impulses that are the creative response of publics' (p. 91).

6 Franco Fortini, *The Dogs of the Sinai* (Alberto Toscano trans.) (London: Seagull Books, 2013).

7 'Scrivere chiaro' [Writing Clearly], in *Questioni di frontiera. Scritti di politica e di letteratura, 1965–1977* [Border Questions: Political and Literary Writings, 1965–1977] (Turin: Einaudi, 1977), p. 125.

8 For a rough sketch of Fortini's biography in English, see my 'Communism Without Guarantees: On Franco Fortini', *Salvage* 1 (2015). Available at: http://salvage.zone/in-print/communism-without-guarantees-on-franco-fortini (last accessed on 11 June 2016). I am wholly indebted to Luca Lenzini's extremely rich 'Chronology' in Franco Fortini, *Saggi ed epigrammi* [Essays and Epigrams] (Milan: Mondadori, 2003), pp. *lxxiii–cxxix*. Though Fortini never wrote anything easily contained in that genre, an autobiography of sorts can be recomposed from the pages of *The Dogs of the Sinai*, the posthumous 'public diary' *Un giorno o l'altro* [One Day or Another] (Marianna Marrucci and Valentina Tinacci eds) (Macerata: Quodlibet, 2006), and the longer interview book with Paolo Jachia, *Leggere e scrivere* [Reading and Writing] (Florence: Marco Nardi, 1993), which traces the arc of Fortini's life through the books he read.

9 Alberto Toscano, 'The Non-State Intellectual: Franco Fortini and Communist Criticism' in *The Dogs of the Sinai*, pp. 89–129.

10 For a complementary approach to situating Fortini through Calvino and Pasolini, see Daniele Balicco's excellent essay, 'Franco Fortini e

il comunismo come auto-educazione politica' [Franco Fortini and Communism as Political Self-Education], in *Altronovecento,* VOL. 2 [An Other Twentieth Century, VOL. 2] (Milan: Jacabook, 2011), pp. 613–28, which builds on his pioneering monograph, *Non parlo a tutti. Franco Fortini intellettuale politico* [I Don't Speak to Everyone: Franco Fortini, Political Intellectual] (Roma: manifestolibri, 2007). I owe to this text many of the coordinates for my own initial encounter with Fortini's writing.

11 Fortini, 'Che cosa è stato il "Politecnico"' [What was *Il Politecnico*?] (1953) in *Dieci inverni*, pp. 59–79.

12 Fortini joined the Olivetti company in September 1947, one of several writers and intellectuals who Adriano Olivetti (1911–60)—a singular figure of progressive industrialist in the Italian landscape—brought to the company town of Ivrea (Olivetti and Fortini had met first in 1938 and then in Zurich in 1944). Fortini worked on intra-firm cultural initiatives and publications but was also centrally involved in publicity and branding. The names of the typewriters *Lexikon* and *Lettera 22* were among his creations. He also wrote in Olivetti's journal *Comunità* and translated texts for the company's eponymous publishing house (such as Kierkegaard's *Fear and Trembling*). After the attempted assassination of PCI leader Palmiro Togliatti, Fortini supported a revolt of Olivetti workers, leading to his move away from the headquarters of the firm, to work in the publicity department in Milan. The collaboration with the Olivetti firm would end in 1963.

13 Fortini was given his party card in 1944 in Zurich by Ignazio Silone (1900–78), author of the novel *Fontamara*, later a contributor to the collective anti-communist testimonial, *The God that Failed*. Silone at the time told Fortini that party membership 'will give you much more pain than joy'.

14 With reference to the condition of the guest, see also Fortini's cover text to the 1965 edition of this book, in Appendix to this introduction.

15 Franco Fortini, 'Un mancato editoriale del "Politecnico"' [An Unpublished Editorial from *Il Politecnico*] (1945/1977) in *Questioni di frontiera*, pp. 237–44. In 1945, in a text entitled 'A New Culture', Fortini advanced a notion of culture not as a sphere of bookish

knowledge or artistic excellence but (in terms that resonate with Raymond Williams) as 'the way in which men produce what is necessary for their existence, the particular manner, changing along with the changing in the means of production, in which they enter into relation with other men and with things. . . . There is no possibility for a handle on reality by the intellectuals of so-called culture if not in the *relation*, in the flow and ebb, in the exchange between the mores and forms of intellectual production (Culture with a capital C) and the modes and forms of technical (agricultural, industrial) production' (pp. 240, 242).

16 See his 'Lettera ad amici di Piacenza. 1961' [Letter to Friends in Piacenza, 1961] in 'L'ospite ingrato primo' in *Saggi ed epigrammi*, pp. 944–53, addressed to the young intellectuals who would go on to found *Quaderni piacentini*. This is a veritable programme–manifesto for the revolutionary potentials of the small, self-critical, communist cultural collective.

17 Cesare Cases, *Confessioni di un ottuagenario* [Confessions of an Octogenarian] (Rome: Donzelli, 2000), pp. 73, 59.

18 See the 1947 special double issue of *Les temps modernes* (23–24) on Italy, which included an article by the 30-year-old Fortini, 'Biographie d'un jeune bourgeois intellectuel' [Biography of a Young Bourgeois Intellectual].

19 Franco Fortini, 'Letter to a Communist', *New Reasoner* 3 (Winter 1957–58): 113–18; 'The Writer's Mandate and the End of Anti-Fascism', *Screen* 15(1) (1974): 33–72.

20 Gustave Flaubert, *Un cuore semplice* [A Simple Heart] (Roma: Lettere d'oggi, 1942); Marcel Proust, *Albertine scomparsa* [Albertine Gone] (Turin: Einaudi, 1951); Marcel Proust, *Jean Santeuil* (Turin: Einaudi, 1953); André Gide, *Viaggio al Congo e ritorno al Ciad* [Voyage to the Congo and Return from Chad] (Turin: Einaudi, 1950); Paul Éluard, *Poesia ininterrotta* [Uninterrupted Poetry] (Turin: Einaudi, 1947); Simone Weil, *L'ombra e la grazia* [Gravity and Grace] (Milan: Comunità, 1951); Simone Weil, *La condizione operaia* [The Condition of Workers] (Milan: Comunità, 1952); Simone Weil, *La prima radice* [The Need for Roots] (Milan: Comunità, 1954).

21 These texts are now included in 'Roland Barthes–Franco Fortini: Lettere scelte, 1956–1961 e quattro allegati' [Roland Barthes–Franco

Fortini: Selected Letters, 1956–1961 and Four Appendices], *L'ospite ingrato* 2 (1999): 241–72

22 Fortini and Barthes's friendship ended with a letter from Fortini in which he castigated Barthes and his comrades for keeping silent on the massacre of Algerian demonstrators that took place in Paris in 17 October 1961, while continuing with their normal cultural activities, such as a conference on Alain Resnais's film *Last Year at Marienbad*. Barthes's response was furious. Fortini's recollection and commentary on this incident can be found in two articles originally published in the independent communist daily *Il manifesto*. The first, 'Siamo ancora con la testa fuori dall'acqua e capaci di pensare' [Our Head is Still Above Water and We Can Still Think], *Disobbedienze I. Gli anni dei movimenti* (*1972–1985*) (Roma: manifestolibri, 1997), pp. 151–2, connects his 1961 polemic with Barthes to the debate raging in 1977 over the open letter signed by French intellectuals (including Barthes himself) protesting political repression in Italy. The second, 'La corsa del topo' [The Rat Race], *Disobbedienze II. Gli anni della sconfitta (1985–1994)*, (Roma: manifestolibri, 1996), pp. 214–18, includes the striking passage: 'I cannot, today, judge him; but neither can I judge myself. I only know that we are judged by our written pages, which are more pertinacious and inflexible than any inquisitor. Just as an ancient wall shows its saltpeter, those pages will end up showing not only the places of our strength and our weakness, but those of the savage injustices we had to tolerate. Language is the place where truly nothing is lost, especially error' (p. 218).

23 Fortini, 'Contro gli studenti' [Against the Students] (1968) in *Questioni di frontiera*, pp. 254–7.

24 Fortini, *Attraverso Pasolini*, p. 62.

25 As Fortini writes in 'L'ospite ingrato primo', 'between 1956 and 1959 everything suddenly seemed to take on incredible speed: between the sputniks, the Great Leap Forward and an Africa that was all on the move'. *Saggi ed epigrammi*, p. 957.

26 Fortini, 'L'ospite ingrato primo' in *Saggi ed epigrammi*, p. 915.

27 In *The Selected Poetry of Pier Paolo Pasolini* (Stephen Sartarelli ed.) (Chicago: University of Chicago Press, 2015), pp. 188–217.

28 For two important scholarly treatments of this polemic in verse, see Éanna Ó Ceallacháin, 'Polemical Performances: Pasolini, Fortini, Sanguineti, and the Literary-Ideological Debates of the 1950s', *Modern Language Review* 108(2) (2013): 475–503; and Mariamargherita Scotti, '"Una polemica in versi": Fortini, Pasolini e la crisi del '56' ['A Polemic in Verse': Fortini, Pasolini and the Crisis of '56], *Studi Storici* 45(4) (2004): 991–1021. See also Thomas E. Peterson, *The Ethical Muse of Franco Fortini* (Gainesville: University Press of Florida, 1997), pp. 44–6.

29 Fortini, *Attraverso Pasolini*, p. 66.

30 *The Selected Poetry of Pier Paolo Pasolini*, p. 175.

31 Fortini, *Attraverso Pasolini*, p. 67.

32 Fortini, 'Il silenzio d'Italia' in *Saggi ed epigrammi*, pp. 1222–3.

33 Fortini, *Attraverso Pasolini*, p. 126.

34 Ibid., p. 68.

35 'Per ognuno di noi che dimentica / c'è un operaio della Ruhr che cancella / lentamente se stesso e le cifre / che gli incisero sul braccio i suoi signori e nostri. / Per ognuno di noi che rinuncia / un minatore delle Asturie dovrà credere / a una seta di viola e d'argento / e una donna d'Algeri sognerà / d'essere vile e felice. / Per ognuno di noi che acconsente / vive un ragazzo triste che ancora non sa / quanto odierà di esistere.'—Franco Fortini, 'Complicità' in *Tutte le poesie* (Luca Lenzini ed.) (Milan: Mondadori, 2014), p. 167. My translation, first published in *Salvage* 1 (2015): 230. A similar line is taken by Fortini in a text sent to Pasolini in 1958, where he remarks on the way in which 'our lives' bear the responsibility for the waste and disarray of the *ragazzi di vita*, 'of those who from objects of ethnography and literature, of linguistic mimesis and "unflinching love" [*amore imperterrito*] we should have wanted and been able to change into subjects, into addressees, into interlocutors speaking our own language, and thus into equals' (Fortini, *Attraverso Pasolini*, p. 95). The critic Gianfranco Contini had characterized Pasolini's novel *Ragazzi di vita* (1956) as an 'unflinching declaration of love' [*imperterrita dichiarazione d'amore*].

36 'Sogni fra i corpi e credi al loro sangue / buono a bere, al calore / vile e dolce. Cammini giudicando / non giudicando, intriso / d'altri,

per umiliarti e, in fondo, vincere' (Fortini, 'Al di là della speranza' in *Tutte le poesie*, p. 179).

37 Fortini, *Attraverso Pasolini*, p. 115.

38 Later, in a dialogue with the poet Franco Loi, Fortini speaks of his condition as one of feeling 'unrecognized, not fully integrated', a condition of 'impropriety, illegitimacy, marginality'. Franco Fortini and Franco Loi, *Franchi dialoghi* (Lecce: Piero Manni, 1998), pp. 26, 40.

39 Fortini, *Attraverso Pasolini*, p. 117.

40 Ibid., p. 80.

41 Ibid., p. 77.

42 Ibid., p. 97.

43 Ibid., p. 104.

44 Ibid., p. 108.

45 Ibid., pp. 138–9.

46 See Paul Ginsborg, 'The "Economic Miracle", Rural Exodus and Social Transformation, 1958–1963', in *A History of Contemporary Italy: Society and Politics, 1943–1988* (Basingstoke: Palgrave, 2003). Ginsborg notes that 1963 is a political watershed of sorts, as the Italian Socialist Party enters government with the Christian Democrats, giving rise to the *Centro-Sinistra* (Centre-Left). For a comprehensive treatment of the political, cultural and economic mutations that shook Italy between the 1950s and early 60s, see Guido Crainz, *Storia del miracolo italiano. Culture, identità, trasformazioni fra anni cinquanta e sessanta* [History of the Italian Miracle: Culture, Identity, Transformations Between the 1950s and 1960s] (Roma: Donzelli, 2005).

47 Elio Vittorini, 'Industria e letteratura' [Industry and Literature], *Il menabò* 4 (1961): 17.

48 Stefano Giovannuzzi, '"Industria e letteratura". Vittorini, *Il menabò* e oltre: Metamorfosi di un dibattito' ['Industry and Literature': Vittorini, *Il menabò* and Beyond: The Metamorphosis of a Debate], *Levia Gravia* 14 (2012): 7.

49 Vittorini, 'Industria e letteratura': 20.

50 Gianni Scalia, 'Dalla natura all'industria' [From Nature to Industry], *Il menabò* 4: 96.

51 'Dalla natura all'industria', p. 109. This could also be seen as a reprise of Lukácsian 'second nature', though now shorn of its dialectical impetus.

52 Ibid., p. 113. Fortini scathingly alludes to this notion of the 'trans-industrial' as a mystification of capitalism in 'Cunning as Doves'.

53 I owe this observation to Matteo Mandarini.

54 Ottiero Ottieri, 'Taccuino Industriale' [Industrial Notebook], *Il menabò* 4: 21–94. Fortini refers to Ottieri's contention in 'Cunning as Doves'.

55 Franco Fortini, 'Ancora in Cina' [Once Again in China] in *Questioni di frontiera*, p. 192.

56 Elsewhere, Fortini defined his notion of criticism as presupposing 'specialist and technical knowledge, necessitating a certain degree of identification, pronouncing judgements of value; but [criticism] does not aim either at the scientific knowledge of literature nor at "the adventure of a soul among masterpieces": its purpose consists in the implication of various orders of knowledge *on the occasion and with regard to* the knowledge of a literary object'; see 'Critica' [Criticism] in *Ventiquattro voci per un dizionario di lettere. Breve guida a un buon uso dell'alfabeto* [24 Entries for a Literary Dictionary: Brief Guide to a Good Use of the Alphabet] (Milan: Mondadori, 1968), p. 163. For insightful comments on Fortini's conception of criticism, see Pier Vincenzo Mengaldo, 'Appunti su Fortini critico' [Notes on Fortini the Critic] in *La tradizione del Novecento. Nuova serie* [The Tradition of the Twentieth Century: New Series] (Florence: Vallecchi, 1987), pp. 407–14.

57 For the rich theoretical and militant dialogue between Fortini and *operaismo*, see Balicco, *Non parlo a tutti*, which pivots around the encounter with Panzieri and Tronti.

58 As Mengaldo notes, the historical and aesthetic significance of artworks lay for Lukács in 'their capacity realistically to represent, typifying them, the tendencies of society on the basis of those who can be predicted or hoped to be victorious within it; for Fortini, instead, it is in the intensity with which the conflicts and contradictions of the bourgeois world are lived in the work, in the capacity of the work to embody not so much the voice of "progress" as that of opposition and utopia which perhaps emerges especially by way of negation, as

a kind of photographic negative, a spectral double [*controfigura*]'; see 'Appunti su Fortini critico', p. 411.

59 Umberto Eco mirrors Calvino in his critique of Hegelian–Marxist poetics entitled 'Del modo di formare come impegno sulla realtà' [On the Manner of Forming as a Commitment to Reality], *Il menabò* 5: 198–237. Calvino enthusiastically welcomed Eco's piece in a letter dated 5 May 1962; see Italo Calvino, *Letters, 1941–1985* (London: Penguin, 2014), pp. 227–8, for the beguiling references to a common project of 'cosmic' literature. Fortini later acerbically identifies Eco and Calvino as cultural figures who, notwithstanding their qualities, fit the contemporary complexion of the culture industry all too well. See 'E subito spariscono, II' [Right Away they Disappear, II] in 'L'ospite ingrato secondo' in *Saggi ed epigrammi*, pp. 1099–1100; 'Calvino 1', 'Calvino 2' and 'Eco' in 'Breve secondo novecento' in *Saggi ed epigrammi*, pp. 1137–40, 1142–3.

60 Fortini—who had reviewed Calvino's *The Path to the Spiders' Nest* for the Socialist paper *Avanti*! in 1947—was invited by Calvino to publish reading notes in the *Notiziario Einaudi*, and to serve as an editorial consultant in 1952. The testiness of these editorial relations is evident in a letter to the publisher Giulio Einaudi (November 1959): 'Fortini too must be kept on a leash, and should be contacted frequently because only in this way can his overwhelming excesses be toned down' (Calvino, *Letters*, p. 192).

61 Franco Fortini, *Verifica dei poteri* (Turin: Einaudi, 1965), pp. 32–3.

62 Calvino, *Letters*, p. 174. Calvino clearly enjoyed questioning Fortini's *gravitas*. In a letter from 28 May 1957, in part responding to Fortini's complaints about the absence of reception for his travelogue from China and the USSR, *Asia Maggiore*, published by Einaudi in 1956, wrote: 'I sense a hint of bitterness in this letter of yours and in a previous one. Excellent: we are living in a dark period, there is absolutely nothing going right, and the only consolation we have is to think about the brevity of life. I have to say that in this situation I am absolutely fine, and I am giving myself up finally to total misanthropy, which I now discover corresponds fully to my true nature. But you seem to be still anxious about something or other. Ha, ha! Don't worry, it will just get worse and worse' (p. 132). For the relationship between Calvino and Fortini, see Giuseppe Nava, 'Le ragioni dell' altro: il carteggio Calvino-Fortini' [The Reasons of the Other: The

Calvino-Fortini Correspondence], and Mario Barenghi, 'La purezza e la metamorfosi. Calvino *vs* Fortini' [Purity and Metamorphosis: Calvino vs Fortini], *L'ospite ingrato* 1 (1998): 119–34, 135–40.

63 Calvino, *Letters*, p. 175.

64 Ibid., p. 178. This moral concern was very much present in Calvino's early aesthetic reflection on the negativity, 'irrationality' and amorality of much contemporary literature, which official Communism was so prone to simply condemn. In an important public lecture in 1955, Calvino declared: 'In every real poem there exists a lion's marrow, nourishment for a rigorous morality, for a mastery of history. . . . We are in an age of alarm. Let us not confuse the terribleness of real things for the terribleness of written things, let us not forget that it is against a fearsome reality that we must fight, taking advantage of the weapons that a fearsome poetry can provide us'. 'Il midollo del leone' [The Lion's Marrow] in 'Una pietra sopra' [A Stone on Top] in *Saggi* (Milan: Mondadori, 2007), pp. 25, 27. For Calvino's communist militancy and resignation from the party, see Paolo Spriano, 'Un Calvino rivoluzionario' [A Revolutionary Calvino] in *Le passioni di un decennio* [The Passions of a Decade] (Milan: Garzanti, 1986), pp. 11–32.

65 See 'Il mare dell'oggettività', 'La sfida al labirinto' and 'L'antitesi operaia' in 'Una pietra sopra', pp. 52–60, 105–23, 127–42. Unfortunately, the key essays from this period of Calvino's literary and political production are yet to be translated into English.

66 Calvino, *Letters*, p. 175.

67 Ibid., p. 175. This sentiment was even more strongly and colourfully present in a letter on Christmas Eve of 1959 from the USA, in which Calvino, having jocularly lamented Americans' lack of Hegel, and alluded to all the money one could make setting up a 'Hegelian college', speaks of his horror of American monotheism, and the fact that 'I am more than ever polytheistic in everything and I think truth only exists in the multiplicity of Gods and in this sense I loved America'.—Italo Calvino and Franco Fortini, 'Lettere Scelte 1951–1977' [Selected Letters, 1951–1977], *L'ospite ingrato*, p. 106.

68 See Italo Calvino, *The Literature Machine: Essays* (New York: Vintage, 1997).

69 There was a fierce debate in the late 1990s in the Italian broadsheets, set off by the publication of Carla Benedetti, *Pasolini contro Calvino. Per una letteratura impura* [Pasolini Against Calvino. For an Impure Literature] (Turin: Bollati Boringhieri, 1998).

70 Fortini, *Attraverso Pasolini*, pp. 45–6.

71 See Fortini, 'Nazional-popolare. 1959' in 'L'ospite ingrato primo' in *Saggi ed epigrammi*, pp. 924–5.

72 Alberto Asor Rosa, 'L'uomo, il poeta' in *Le armi della critica. Scritti e saggi degli anni ruggenti (1960–1970)* [The Weapons of Criticism: Writings and Essays from the Roaring Years (1960–1970)] (Turin: Einaudi, 2011), p. 115. For a much more conciliatory, recent presentation of *Verifica dei poteri* and *Scrittori e popolo*, in the context of a didactic reconstruction of their literary and historical context (including the debates on Pasolini and in *Il menabò*), see Asor Rosa's own *Breve storia della letteratura italiana. II. L'Italia della nazione* [Brief History of Italian Literature, II: The Italy of the Nation] (Turin: Einaudi, 2013), pp. 313–15.

73 Asor Rosa, *Le armi della critica*, p. 126.

74 Ibid., p. 132.

75 Fortini, 'Per Asor Rosa. 1965' in 'L'ospite ingrato primo' in *Saggi ed epigrammi*, pp. 987–8.

76 Fortini, 'Asor Rosa, gusto' [Asor Rosa, Taste] (1965) in *Un giorno o l'altro*, p. 342.

77 Fortini, 'Il socialismo non è inevitabile' [Socialism Is Not Inevitable] in *Saggi ed epigrammi*, p. 1383.

78 Fortini, 'Classe operaia' [Working Class] (1966) in *Un giorno o l'altro*, p. 362.

79 'Molte ore così delle poche ore / che l'ordine degli uccisori e il disordine / non avevano ancora spezzate / lesse di strutture aziendali, contratti / collettivi, controlli dei tempi. E che pensieri immensi / nell'aria dei suoi giorni, / imprecisi ridenti! Acuminati / quei cirri che le frese / schizzano e gli incupiti olii convogliano / a lui nei sonni erano figura / di seme morto e di erba future' (Fortini, *Tutte le poesie*, p. 397).

80 Franco Fortini, *Asia Maggiore. Viaggio nella Cina e altri scritti* [Asia Major: Journey to China and Other Writings] (Donatello Santarone

ed.) (Roma: manifestolibri, 2007). Originally published by Einaudi in 1956.

81 *Paesi allegorici* is the title of the fourth section of the 1977 essay collection *Questioni di frontiera*, and comprises essays on Solzhenitsyn and Lu Xun, as well as reflections on Fortini's second trip to China in 1971, and the further mutations of that revolution.

82 I am alluding to the title of the memoir of her wartime communist conversion by Luciana Castellina, *Discovery of the World: A Political Awakening in the Shadow of Mussolini* (Patrick Camiller trans.) (London: Verso, 2014).

83 Fortini also briefly edited the Piccola Biblioteca series for the publisher Einaudi. For Fortini's tenure at Einaudi one can consult Luisa Mangoni's compendious and fascinating chronicle *Pensare i libri. La casa editrice Einaudi dagli anni trenta agli anni sessanta* [Thinking Books: The Einaudi Publishing House Between the 1930s and 1960s] (Turin: Bollati Boringhieri, 1999). For reproductions and detailed analyses of Fortini's reader's reports commissioned by Einaudi and Mondadori, see Valentina Tinacci and Marianna Marrucci, *"Meglio peccare fortiter". Poeti e versificatori, ritardatari e aggiornatissimi nei pareri di lettura di Franco Fortini* ['Better to Sin *fortiter*: Poets and Versifiers, Backsliders and the Up-to-Date in Franco Fortini's Reader's Reports] (Pisa: Pacini, 2013).

84 Franco Fortini (ed.), *Profezie e realtà del nostro secolo* (Bari: Laterza, 1965), p. *vii*.

85 Fanon would remain a recurring point of reference for Fortini, see his 1992 article 'Bring Back Fanon', *Salvage* 1 (2015). Available at: http://salvage.zone/in-print/bring-back-fanon (last accessed on 11 June 2016). Fortini's friend and comrade Raniero Panzieri had played an important role while working together on the project to publish Fanon's work in Italian at Einaudi. See the letter from Giovanni Pirelli to Panzieri in Frantz Fanon, *Écrits sur l'aliénation et la liberté* (Jean Khalfa and Robert Young eds) (Paris: La Découverte, 2015), p. 576.

86 Fortini, *Profezie e realtà del nostro secolo*, pp. *xv*, *xxiii*.

87 See especially the anthology of poetry and songs co-translated with Fortini's wife, Ruth Leiser, which features an important introduction to Brecht's poetics: 'Bertolt Brecht' in *Poesie e canzoni* [Poems and

Songs] (Ruth Leiser and Franco Fortini trans) (Turin: Einaudi, 1961). Leiser and Fortini also published translations of *Mother Courage, St Joan of the Stockyards* and *The Threepenny Novel.* Fortini translated *The Calendar Tales* with Paolo Corazza. Brecht also played an important role in Fortini's dialogue and friendship with Roland Barthes. See Judith Lindenberg, '"La langue travaillée par le pouvoir": Franco Fortini et Roland Barthes face à Brecht' ['Language Worked by Power': Franco Fortini and Roland Barthes Confront Brecht], *Revue de littérature comparée* 328(4) (2008): 429–42.

88 Franco Fortini, 'Introduzione' in Fredric Jameson, *Marxismo e forma* (Naples: Liguori, 1975), p. *vii.*

89 Ibid., pp. *xvii–xviii.*

90 See Philip Cooke, *The Legacy of the Italian Resistance* (New York: Palgrave, 2011), pp. 83–112.

91 For the Resistance conceived in the frame of 'civil war', see Claudio Pavone's remarkable historical and moral study, *A Civil War: A History of the Italian Resistance* (Peter Levy trans.) (London: Verso, 2013). It is interesting to note that Pavone was one of the young editors with whom Fortini collaborated in the early 1950s in *Discussioni.* In 1994, Fortini referred to Pavone's book as 'the most serious and beautiful "moral" history of the Resistance' in *Un giorno o l'altro*, p. 343.

92 Fortini, 'Ancora sulla resistenza' [Once Again on Resistance] (1965) in ibid., p. 347.

93 Fortini, 'Le resistenze' [Resistances] (1965) in ibid., p. 349.

94 Fortini, 'Un' "altra" storia' [An "Other" History] (1965) in ibid., p. 353.

95 Fortini, 'Ventesimo della Resistenza, in una scuola' [Twentieth Anniversary of the Resistance, in a School] (1965) in ibid., p. 355.

96 Fortini, 'Il silenzio d'Italia' in *Saggi ed epigrammi*, p. 1218.

97 His 1962 'Poetica in Nuce' [Poetics in a Nutshell] includes the directive 'Against the amplitude of register. For division within the spectrum' ('L'ospite ingrato primo' in *Saggi ed epigrammi*, p. 962). In a review of Fortini's poetry collection *I destini generali*, Pasolini had linked Fortini's 'moralistic hypersensibility' to a resistance to the poetic but, more specifically, to Fortini's 'obsessive modification' of his language against the lures of inspiration; see Pier Paolo Pasolini,

'I destini generali' (1958) in *Passione e ideologia* (Milan: Garzanti, 2009), pp. 510–13. More pointedly in the 1969 text on 'Fortini's Obsession' (that word again . . .) Pasolini had rebuked Fortini for the martial references throughout his work, writing acidly that 'Fortini, to my mind, needs to feel at war, because only in that case does he exist and finds a necessity in his own existing'; see 'L'ossessione di Fortini' in *Scritti sulla politica e sulla società* (Milan: Mondadori, 1999), p. 1192. On the 'divisive' character of Fortini, see also Pier Vittorio Mengaldo's extremely insightful essay, 'Per la poesia di Fortini' in *La tradizione del novecento. Prima serie* (Turin: Bollati Boringhieri, 1996[1975]), pp. 411–29.

98 See this 'Pro-memoria' or memo from 1965: 'To those who continue to preach a Eurocentric workerism, to treat the Chinese as "underprivileged" and to exclude the under-developed from the leadership of the world revolution we should counter with the universal proletarianization created by the capitalist international. To those who dream of struggles of the "poor" against the "rich", "coloured" against white, underdeveloped against developed, we should instead oppose the international of the exploited and the discourse of the Marxist–Leninist tradition' (Fortini, *Un giorno o l'altro*, p. 349).

99 'Storia ed esperienza mi hanno insegnato / che si deve oggi tendere non ad unire ma a dividere. / A dividere sempre più violentemente il mondo, / a promuovere l'approfondita, la sola vera, la sola feconda divisione, / divenuta sempre più Chiara, dolorosa e necessaria, / per entro l'unità creata dal mercato internazionale, / per entro l'unità determinata dal potere e dall'oppressione. / Vuol dire anzitutto distruggere le false divisioni del passato, / vuol dire vedere identificare interpretare / l'unità confuse e corrotta che oggi esiste' (Fortini, 'Intervento alla manifestazione per la libertà del Vietnam' in *Saggi ed epigrammi*, p. 1402).

100 An allusion to Giuseppe Mazzini's *Doveri dell'uomo* (1860). Throughout *A Test of Powers*, I have chosen not to conceal the gendered character of Fortini's universalism, opting in most instances to leave *l'uomo* as 'man', rather than rendering it with 'humanity' or 'human being'.

Translator's Acknowledgements

Luca Lenzini, director of the Centro Studi Franco Fortini and its archive, provided indispensable help and support throughout the translation and editing of this book. His unmatched knowledge of Fortini's work and fidelity to its ethical and political drive have allowed me to 'test' the translation as the project advanced. Gabriele Pedullà's comradeship and critical erudition were vital as I made my way through Fortini into the field of Italian literary criticism and poetics, which he masters like few others. Many of the editorial notes with which I've tried to orient readers unfamiliar with Italian literature and political history owe much to these two immensely generous readers. My gratitude also goes to friends and colleagues who provided help and encouragement at various stages of the project: Daniele Balicco, Matteo Mandarini, Luisa Lorenza Corna, Elisabetta Nencini, Tyrus Miller, Fredric Jameson, China Miéville, Gail Day, Steve Edwards, Benjamin Noys, Jason Smith, Evan Calder Williams. And to Brenna, who accompanied this hopeful task from the beginning, and across the islands. This book would not have been possible without the immoderate trust that Naveen Kishore has put in this List, and the work of everyone else at Seagull Books. To paraphrase Fortini, translation too can be an instrument to look for one's comrades.

Preface to the First Edition

(1965)

Nearly all of this book's pages were written after 1955. For a few years afterward, I had continued to work under the illusion that my back was covered by a political side and by a solidarity of opinions. We believed that debate and the 'battle of ideas' on the so-called Left press could still set themselves apart from the ambient editorializing. Intellectuals played an obvious part in the East European cases of 1956 and 1957, and among us too spirits were moved. Not long afterwards, French authors came forward, like characters in a Racine play, to make themselves heard *pour la dernière fois*. Like some kind of paroxysm of life, the great historic claim of the intellectual and moral guides of the Left gave—along with the Left itself—its last gasps.

In this volume you will find, for example, the title essay, which is from 1960. In it, I reprised a figure of the critic that belongs to another tradition: the critic as other than the specialist, as the one who discourses on the real relationships between men, society and their history with reference to, and on the occasion of, the metaphor of those relationships—which is what literary works are. Of course, I believe that the image I proposed of the critic's activity continues to be correct; but the past few years have made it almost unbelievable. It presupposes *a* society, a modicum of agreement with one's environment, even if this only amounts to a circle of friends or to a conspiracy of the kind of which Belinsky once spoke.[1] What surrounds us instead is Society, the passive result of the disintegration of every particularity. A 'civil society', which is to say, a 'de facto' society.[2] The industrial and political classes continue to keep personnel posts open in newspapers, journals, publishing houses and university chairs even for literary criticism—and serious scholars, intelligent essayists or sharp journalists often come to occupy those roles. But they are now condemned to a fiction: beyond that civic society for everyone and no one there can be no other. This is why the survival of a critic of the kind I've just mentioned—a critic-essayist—places him in a zone which is traditionally considered conservative, if not reactionary.

In the 1960 essay, I voiced another doubt that pulled pathetically at the page. This doubt concerned 'an error in the reading of social reality'. And if I'd been mistaken? For modesty's sake, I speak in the singular. What if class determinations, my 'petty bourgeois' autobiography, my Jacobin taste and gestures, etc., had cloaked reality behind a screen of phrases? Had my old friends been right—these old friends, now indistinguishable from my new foes, who had gathered in the democratic and 'scientific' opposition or in the 'scientific' and democratic majority? Now I am sure I may have erred. But I also know that they were not and will never be right. A possible objectivity does not coincide with the fable of coexistence, nor does the reality of the world coincide with the world of generalized and scientific exploitation.

Isn't this meant to be an introductory note for a collection of literary writings? Why the digression? Why—let's be frank—does the activity of literary critics seem ever-more *superfluous*? Perhaps because criticism is in fact less and less a matter of evaluation and more and more a programmatic-methodological discourse or a subjective variation, that is, something unverifiable, untestable? The evaluative tradition of criticism has really come into conflict with the more recent forms of interpretive criticism. Modern (though a half-century old) exegetical methods—stylistic, semantic, neo-formalist, structuralist criticisms, with their many subspecies and varieties—call on a host of particular disciplines to situate their results (even if they don't always state this intention) in the ambit of the so-called science of literature, considered as one of the 'human sciences'.

Those methods were widely experimented on in contemporary literature as well; as everybody knows, this is what took place from the Russian formalists to Auerbach, from Contini[3] to the most recent French critics. But when they weren't looking in them for pretexts for regional inquiries (by the linguist, the sociologist, the scholar of metre, etc.), the practitioners of those methods, as they intervened into contemporary literature, were bound to equate them with criticism as such: this is because the distinction between non-contemporary and contemporary literature is not an empirical and chronological distinction (nor can it be idealistically dissolved in the name of the contemporaneousness of history for the historiographer) but corresponds to the distinction between a historical-evaluative judgement (or a perspectivalism from the past to the present) and a judgement of tendency or taste (or a perspectivalism from the present to the past). If the practitioners of those methods wished to escape the loathed 'world views' and the choices of tendency, which is to say, of perspective, they were compelled to stamp out historical-evaluative judgement, to treat the distant in the same way as the near. Descriptivism is rich, combative, irreplaceable—but who will voice the discourse that comes *after*? The opposite of the specialist, the much-maligned critic-essayist? Behold the swarms of exegetes, brimming over with dossiers whose ostentation cannot but aim to intimidate, unload their critical neologisms on the latest author; as though we too were born yesterday and did not know that the worst evaluations are unconfessed, and the worst use of methodologies that refuse standards of value is an ideological one, namely, the smuggling in of a standard of value. For many writers and people of letters, burnt by real or factitious political disappointments and careful to swim with the current, those critical methodologies appear piously to interpose themselves between literature—which is always and necessarily deemed lacking and suspect—and the feared basis of the 'sciences', held in high regard by the powerful. And so, in a manner dictated by a long Italian tradition, from those linguistic, semantic or other instruments of severe philology, they squeezed out some other aesthetic or even all manner of criteria of interpretation.

We can understand then why the past few years have again posed questions that from the Romantic Age to today had found no shortage of formulations and responses. How is literature possible? And, how is literary criticism possible?

Until 15 or 20 years ago, though the paradoxes and antinomies of literary writing (and to a lesser extent of critical writing) were so well known that an entire Italian literary current—'hermeticism'—had based itself on them, questions of this kind could not have been phrased in such a blunt tone. In our country, literature still had its place, simultaneously privileged and isolated; and the 'illegality' and 'impossibility' of poetic discourse, the aphasia that constantly threatens it (as also happens, albeit in a different way, to criticism and the essay), were like a reflection in the consciousness of the authors of the silence that surrounded them, of their separation from society. Is this not, as many have recognized, one of the main themes in the poetry of Montale?[4] After all, the organization of culture had not changed much since the times of Leopardi and the publisher Stella.[5] People of my generation had the chance to get acquainted with it: literary Florence, Crocean Naples, liberal-socialist Turin . . . Today, on the other hand, that organization, where it survives, has lost any selective or critical function. Today, the challenge to the legitimacy, to the 'place' of literary or critical discourse, comes directly from outside, besieging the author. It is not the ill-defined 'world' but the specific 'world of the book', of 'culture', of 'literature', which strips him of the last shreds of social decorum, casting doubt on his pastoral vocation, all the more so as his audience and public expands. Because the writer does not write for *the* public, but for *a* public—or for no present public, which amounts to the same.

Up to this point, however, while the argument remains generic, it can only be of very modest interest; things change when the challenge that contemporary society poses to literature is considered in an entirely different way or, better, when it's reversed. It will then be a question of that criticism which the 'real movement'—the movement that in fact struggles against the present class society—levies against the condition or status that revolutionary organizations and their ideologues sought to attribute, over the last half-century, to poetry.

That is the theme of many of the following pages. The theme is the relationship between communism and anti-fascism, between anti-fascism and committed literature; and if we pronounce here the word 'end' with regard to anti-fascism, it is with a precise aim which is not just polemical but also concerns the history of culture, in the certainty that a reinterpretation of our recent history and of our contemporary literature is long overdue, though work on it has begun. Just a few years ago, all the themes that recur in these writings would have appeared bizarre or pretentious: the urgency of freeing oneself of the notion of 'organic intellectual' for the sake of each and every one's direct insertion in the national and international political class struggle; the need to seize all the instruments of interpretation and intelligence that capitalist culture puts at our disposal to employ them against the visible or invisible nexuses that tie that culture to the system of stabilized inhumanity; the necessary inclusion, which now conditions any thinking, including critical and poetic discourse, of the perspective of the so-called underdeveloped countries.

Today this is even starting to seem obvious. Division, the interruption of false solidarities, of false unity (which I have hoped for ever since I perceived how many precious goods were being wasted and tarnished by some, by us, beneath the semblance of those values) becomes a reality. This is not my doing, or someone else's, but the objective pressure of things in the minds of men. In the 'envoy' that can be read in the final pages of 'Cunning as Doves', some benevolent friends discerned a fit of eloquence. No doubt it is difficult to avoid the bad taste of the beautiful phrase when you are speaking, or think you are speaking, alone. But I hope that today those friends understand that I was serious. I hope they'll forgive me.

Contrary to the appearances and even to the letter of many of these pieces, I think that today one can 'move to prosecute'. I would like the younger readers to grasp this, even if this book can seem entirely negative. It is not a matter of short-term 'hopes': when you've spent 20 years of your life trying to leave behind the moral parameters of the previous 20 years, you may still have some time for naivety but not for illusions. Is there a risk of mistaking personal difficulties for indisputably universal situations, to turn biography into mythology? Of course. But if I reread what I wrote in 1957, in the conclusion of *Ten Winters*,[6] I say to myself that it really is true: when you no longer have any hopes for yourself, you begin to see more clearly. We can move to prosecute: in the register of practical, that is, political, action, and in the one, more paradoxical than ever, of the literary word. The latter *can* traverse the body of its addressees, one day, only if it accepts to be voiced without a hope of echo or return. After all, how can we convey that our hope is not in a chronological future but (as a friendly phrase goes) 'my future is nothing but the present of an other'?[7]

I wouldn't want anyone to be scandalized by the fact that in these pages you can encounter expressions and forms of language that belong to religion and metaphysics. I don't employ them by accident. They help me to make explicit a continuity of aims which I think exists between the intentions that those languages interpreted and our own. In ages of retreat and defeat—as ours is, at least here in Italy—it is inevitable that language betrays an incaution not granted to action. Reason and knowledge then appear to be entirely on the side of those who believe they are fully at one with effective reality. But the only thing that matters is that those to whom these writings are directed bring forward the conditions that will render useless every allusive, oblique, double discourse—like this one is, still. They will have to advance infinitely farther than I have been able to in the 'verification of credentials', the 'test of powers' in which, very rightly, the 'commissioners of the Nobility' discerned the premises of 'deliberation in common'.[8]

If writing is a work of delation and double-crossing and there is no language save that of slaves (and masters), then to write, to want poetry or literature, is also to allude (never more than allude) to a different possibility of codification of the real and of language.

So, to the question 'how is literature possible?' I can only respond as follows: to one who by dint of his class origins or election lives at the border between certainty and precarity, between participation in existence and its denial, and who has thus trained himself to detect the hidden air pockets where social reality seems most solid and compact, to hear unpredicted hollows underfoot—to such a person, the Other, the Different, though it may at first have appeared with the bewitching and repulsive mask of the Sacred, can end up revealing itself for what it really is, namely, composed of men. Not of everyone or anyone, but of a part. Not transfigured by historical or geographical or social distances but, rather, made similarly—even if they originate in those distances—to the everyday faces we meet, to our own visages: in their complex, articulated, occasionally contradictory action towards an end that is sometimes subjectively conscious, sometimes objectively determined by a non-individual consciousness.

Those men—and we are to be counted among them—near or far, do not cease being able to turn again into the Other or the Different; through the office of poetry, their swarming can again become ungraspable, their (our) countenances blurred into a darkness that other centuries would have called 'the night of the soul.' But in fact they continue to move in the direction of our most obstinate reasons, with the will of one's first years, almost confused with the revelations of childhood. They come to light. That motion of theirs has an internal law, it organizes its own risk through a kind of metre, it has its own way of pressing forward through clauses and cadences; it seems and perhaps is the same motion as that of works of poetry, written or to be written. *This is how, as though from another shore, literature is possible.*

In the first part of this book, I've brought together writings on the condition of the writer and critic and on some false problems, like that of eroticism in literature or the relations between industry and letters. The last essay in this part instead reconnects to a rather passé theme, a matter of discussion about a decade ago: What can the writer *do*?

I cannot, as one should, thank those who have helped me to compose this book, because there is none among my acquaintances who, through listening or discussion, has not collaborated in it. I certainly would not have written anything without the words of objectors or adversaries, but especially without the apprehensible eloquence and silences of true enemies. The past few years have furnished the latter with potent and miserable instruments of persuasion and fright, vocabularies of resignation, chemical verbs that alter everything while leaving everything apparently intact. I have sought to understand them. Among the first few who resolved to run the risk of deciphering the new language, which is mortal, Raniero Panzieri is no longer alive to stop me from writing his name.

Notes

1 Vissarion Grigoryevich Belinsky (1811–48), Russian literary critic and friend of Alexander Herzen and Mikhail Bakunin. [Trans.]

2 A play on *di fatto*, meaning both 'in fact' and 'common-law' (as in *coppia di fatto*, common-law couple). [Trans.]

3 Gianfranco Contini (1912–90), literary critic, historian of literature and philologist, author of studies on Dante, Petrarch, Gadda and Montale among many others. In Italy, he was a pioneer in stylistic

criticism (of the kind associated with Leo Spitzer, and discussed in this volume) and the philological analysis of authorial variants, placing key emphasis on the genesis of the text, and largely avoiding aesthetic or psychological speculation. Like Fortini, he participated in the short-lived partisan Repubblica d'Ossola during the Resistance. Fortini writes about Contini's critical edition of Dante's poetry in 'A proposito delle *Rime* di Dante', *Il Politecnico* 31–2 (July–August 1946): 54–8; now in *Saggi ed epigrammi*, pp. 1247–59. [Trans.]

4 Eugenio Montale (1896–1981), arguably the foremost Italian lyric poet of the twentieth century, was awarded the Nobel Prize for Literature in 1975. He also produced important literary criticism and numerous translations of both prose and poetry (Shakespeare, Gerald Manley Hopkins, James Joyce, T. S. Eliot, Jorgé Guillen, Dorothy Parker, etc.). For Fortini's appraisal, see 'La pietra e la coscienza' (Stone and Consciousness—a reference to Jean-Paul Sartre's *Being and Nothingness*], in *Saggi Italiani;* now in *Saggi ed epigrammi*, pp. 614–17. Fortini discerns in Montale 'the construction of defences against a historical reading of social truths, a will not to know, proper to one who insists on identifying the cause of poetry with that of the privileged', carried out with 'images that are the only *nekyia* [ancient Greek term for necromancy] of the Italian bourgeois intellectual class, its only authentic descent into the netherworld of its own inauthenticity' (ibid., p. 615n2). But he also acknowledges their profound impact on him: 'Stiffened and indestructible, Montale's poems have represented for me the very paragon of poetry understood as vigil [*veglia d'armi*—a reference to the investiture in scouting] and royal art [a reference to Plato's *Statesman*]' (ibid., p. 617). Fortini and Montale had also exchanged letters in the early 1950s, when Fortini, while praising the older poet's work as the most important poetry being written in Italian, took the occasion of Montale's dismissive obituary for the French communist poet Paul Éluard to contest his rightward drift. See Franco Fortini, 'A Montale 1952' in *Un giorno o l'altro* (Marianna Marrucci and Valentina Tinacci eds) (Macerata: Quodlibet, 2006), pp. 116–25; Eugenio Montale and Franco Fortini, 'Le lettere antagonistiche (1952–53)' [Antagonistic Letters] (Romano Luperini ed.), *Belfagor* 34(6) (1982): 685–99. On Fortini's assessment of Montale's poetry translations, see 'Montale traduttore di Guillén' in *Nuovi saggi italiani* (Milan:

Garzanti, 1987), pp. 142–9. For Montale's poetry in English, see *The Collected Poems of Eugenio Montale, 1925–1977* (Rosanna Warren ed., William Arrowsmith trans.) (New York: W. W. Norton, 2012).

5 Antonio Fortunato Stella (1757–1833), pioneering publisher and supporter of his friend Giacomo Leopardi (1798–1837) whose *Operette Morali* he published in 1827. [Trans.]

6 Franco Fortini, *Dieci inverni, 1947–1957: Contributi ad un discorso socialista* (Milan: Feltrinelli, 1957); 2nd EDN with a new preface (Bari: De Donato, 1972). [Trans.]

7 The phrase is from the poet and essayist Giacomo Noventa, pen name of Giacomo Ca' Zorzi (1898–1960) whom Fortini met in Florence in the 1930s and who exercised a major influence on his initial intellectual formation. Noventa's poetry, written in Veneto dialect, is discussed at length in 'Noventa e la poesia' (1956) in *Saggi italiani;* now in *Saggi ed epigrammi*, pp. 528–44. His critical and political writings are appraised in 'Noventa Politico' (1970), from the same collection (ibid., pp. 764–70). See also Franco Fortini, *Note su Giacomo Noventa* (Venezia: Marsilio, 1986); Elena Urgnani, 'Fortini Lettore di Noventa', *Allegoria* 21–2 (1996): 80–91. [Trans.]

8 *Verifica dei poteri*, the expression from which both this book and an essay collected herein take their title, refers to the certification or verification of credentials which in constitutional law defines the procedure to ascertain that a member of parliament has been properly elected, that his nomination and appointment are in keeping with legal perquisites; in international law, and in the operation of various assemblies and collegial bodies, it refers to that procedure whereby one certifies the legitimacy of delegates and representatives. While keeping this technical meaning in mind, as reflected in the book's epigram by Manzoni, given the ampler meaning accorded to the noun *verifica* and verb *verificare* in Fortini—who employs both insistently across his writings—I have opted for a somewhat elliptical translation, 'test of powers', which retains the agonistic and antagonistic sense of Fortini's concern with the 'verification' or 'testing' of critical and political positions. [Trans.]

Preface to the Second Edition
(1969)

'Regressive' Poetry and the Refusal of Literature

I need to take into consideration the most serious criticisms that have been directed at this book. As for the truly crucial ones, since they reached me indirectly—having been written in code in the social reality that I live in—they cannot receive an adequate response on this occasion. For example, not a few young people sensitive to political problems reacted to the thesis ('The Writers' Mandate and the End of Anti-fascism') that concludes by pointing towards the existence of 'regressive' elements in art and poetry. Some glimpsed here a kind of defection of so-called commitment or, worse, an opportunistic retreat under the mask of a rhetorical-heroic posture. I don't know how useful it is to recall that the term 'regressive' was not intended to have a purely negative meaning. It can be wholly negative only for those who believe that everything must be subordinated to the primacy of immediate political struggle.

It would be necessary to take up the argument from the beginning and explain again through which mediations poetry, thanks in part to its 'regressive' features, *can* be a decisive moment of that totality 'man' (needless to say, in its specification in terms of society, class, etc.) which is the object of the political moment. Yet, many have noted that the youngest and those most resolutely set on desiring new forms of associated life say they have little or no interest in literature or poetry. It is easy to prophesy that we will all pay quite dearly for the refusal to seek the true reasons for that disinterest, because it is easy to feel that a unanimous appeal to the most serious motivations of writing and poetry rises up from the most anti-literary documents of the new struggle against the present society. (One of the deep reasons, for example, behind the power of certain Chinese texts is not their literary quality but, rather, their open or implied formal reference to a type of communication which is 'literary' because it is eccentric to Western forms of communicative writing of a scientific type, or because it wishes to grasp together the everyday-ness and the totality of the addressee.)

I am obviously not speaking of the examples of dire literature occasionally present in the writings of the youth, especially in the Spring of 1968 and in Paris; I am speaking of some fundamental exigencies of the new political and most often anti-political forces, which will no doubt continue not to recognize themselves in literature properly and vulgarly so called, but which in fact affirm models of behaviour and projects of freedom that have as their equivalent not *what* poets and men of letters say but the way of using language that is specific to poetry and literature. This distinction may appear all too subtle and sophistical, which is why I will return to this argument in a moment. Yet not too much time will need to pass for what I am saying—what I am repeating from reflections both richer and more coherent than my own—to begin to be better understood. Those who claim to be poets and men of letters should hold dear today's contempt and indifference towards poetry and literature, evident proof of love and passion for truth, and for the modes of being that poetry and literature should also embody. They rightly meet with such contempt or indifference to the degree that they are not sufficiently poets or men of letters, not because they are so too much; in other words, to the degree that they are not sufficiently convinced and committed first to know and then to resolve into that single dimension the other dimensions of experience and duty.

Use of Language and Forms of Life

One of the criticisms levied against me concerns an assertion made in the essay on the 'Writers' Mandate', to wit, that the literary use of language is homologous to the formal use of life which is the end, in both senses of the term, of communism. I have been told that a formal use of life, the idea of a form capable of ordering existential chaos, is typical of the bourgeois rationalism preached by the stratum of intellectuals who take themselves—or, rather, took themselves, in the Romantic Age—to be the lawgivers of humanity.

When I speak of a formal use of life, I mean the possibility of giving not so much an order but an intention to one's existence; it is that intention which reorders past and present. In the history of the Greco-Christian West and then in Protestant-bourgeois history, this proposal has taken the lineaments of an ought, which for at least two centuries has been an idealist one. But all the formulas that refused the ethics of conscience, Christian salvation or Kantian universalism, even proposing the transmutation of all values, nonetheless ended up with a *savoir vivre*, with a project of life. The communist one—when it speaks of the free development of one and all—is no exception.

What should perhaps be pointed out instead is that when one speaks of finality (the *terminus ad quem* of the novel according to Georg Lukács), it is difficult not to employ references to bourgeois rationalism, but it is not difficult to see how it cannot exhaust the issue. First, because the communist transformation of social relations implies the modification of the relationships between rational and irrational as well as between the conscious and the unconscious; and then because when we speak of a use of life, we mean a use of life in its entirety. The contradiction that my critics have asserted—between the radical opposition art/life (which belongs to classical German thought as it does to every classical thought) and the formal or pedagogical character which that thought accords to artistic expressions—does not exist. Friedrich Schiller's name should suffice. That conservative or Romantic reactionaries increasingly forgot the opposition (though one should say the distinction) between art and life for the sake of a vitalism in art and a vitalist aestheticism only proves that bourgeois culture has a history. Besides, in order to parry the accusation of an aestheticizing perspective (as if the suggested homology implied a life treated as an artwork, or something to that effect), it will be enough to say, or to repeat, what we mean by 'literary use of language'.

At least for those who do not equate reality and language, using language to literary ends means structuring a complex communicative organism on the basis of multiple intentions, varying in their degree of conscious clarity, aimed both within and without the communication that unifies them. Artistic-literary making has itself and its consequences as its object; it is both transitive and intransitive. Now, this ambiguity or ambivalence can be registered in every partial achievement of existing or acting, in the order of will, intellect and praxis, in every exercise of freedom. It therefore also accompanies the whole prospect of a formal use of life—which is an end in itself and is its own contents; it is individual and collective. But here the analogy must stop. The word is not the thing, and literature is not life.

It is true that the use of literary language proposes frameworks for the ordering of existence; but that order is consumed as figure and phantasm. To put it in psychoanalytic terms: it does not become 'need' nor does it ask, like the 'question', for an answer. It remains 'desire'; and in that sense it contains a regressive, youthful or puerile element. This is why only in art (understood in the widest sense) and for it, in the literary use of form, that achievement assumes *the form* precisely *of an object* that functions symbolically, in which proposal and proponent coincide.

But why do I continue to think this is an important confrontation? Why, among the criticisms that have generally been directed against my 'formalism'—and I will try below to say in what sense they can be accepted—do I now privilege this aspect which seems somewhat irrelevant? Because *if we denied the reality of that symmetry between the literary use of language and the 'formal' use of life*—at least in those that are already its 'liberated territories'—*we would no longer understand why or for what reason there exist a set of relations between the overall historical movement of a given society at a given time, its particular and partial movements, its individual biographies and 'forms', in particular, its artistic and poetic 'forms'; and the claims of any historiography or sociology would turn out to be absurd.* Now, I can easily accept that the correspondence between a given stylistic structure and the structure of a historical-social body has not been demonstrated, and may be indemonstrable; but I cannot say that the correspondence between a historical–social body and the structure, say, of behaviours, is equally indemonstrable. I don't think I am saying anything scandalous, or even new, by putting in parallel—without the ridiculous pretence of unearthing determinisms dear to the positivism of a hundred years ago—the articulations and the deep or superficial styles of inter-human relations (with everything that this term implies in Marxist thought), and the ones, be they superficial or deep, that compose artistic-poetic 'forms'.

In this book, I have also spoken of 'imitation of history in perspective' and I think it is now possible to better understand what I meant. The imitation or mimesis of 'nature' is the pivot of very ancient and modern 'realisms'. I continue to maintain that it is a substantially valid standard of judgement. Now, to say that the 'mimesis of nature' is really the 'mimesis of history' is an obvious notion, at least from classical German thought to Lukács. Except that, in the conception of modern realism, that mimesis of history has been seen and interpreted especially at the level of some elements of the work—'situations' and 'characters', for example—and not others, and in terms of one 'genre' in particular (the novel), rejecting as so much degraded formalism the search for that same 'imitation' where it operates in less visible if equally profound ways. In terms of the formula I advanced, when I say 'language' I obviously mean the major as well as the minor 'signs', from 'literary genre' to the phoneme. Even the 'formal use of life' implies, and will increasingly imply, both lofty vocations and imperceptible choices.

From the above, we can draw some suggestions for useful developments and clarify, among other things, the reasons and limits of this book's basic arguments. But I would like to insist some more on the criticisms directed at me for having employed the notion of 'form'. On the one hand, these 'materialist' criticisms—which recall, to shame me, the Romantic-bourgeois origins of that notion (forgetting that formalization is only a secondary or meta-language, inseparable from the existence of any human language whatsoever)—accuse me of wanting to propose to the 'proletariat' a rational-bourgeois consciousness managed, for the *n*th time, by 'intellectuals'. On the other, it is these very criticisms which extol and mythologize a 'materiality' that serves as bare 'formless' plutonium, according to a phallic conception of 'revolutionary forces', which is itself not alien from the typical bad conscience of the 'intellectuals' of yore, who in Italy are sadly still active and preaching. Perhaps we could ask ourselves—and the discussion would then shift to the contemporary quarrel on the relationships between political avant-gardes and 'masses'—to which class relations do we owe the most typical models of those situations. But also whether the place that literature and poetry (and their 'authorized personnel') have had and can have within conscious sociopolitical movements, after more than half a century of conflicts (amply recalled in the pages of this book), is not so tragically precarious precisely because the figure of necessity and play that poetry proposes is the least distant from the one, inscribed into the future, of the most clear-sighted revolutionary will. This is a proposal that ignores the opportunities of place and time and wants everything *now*, because it feigns it is a being while it is nothing more—although this is not little—than an image.

We are then told that subaltern classes, at least in our country, live in a culture that can be defined as a (not necessarily contradictory) combination of elements inherited from past historical phases, of ones currently received-imposed by the dominant class, and, last, of creative modifications carried out on both of these. What's more, the history of the revolutionary avant-gardes involves the desire to clarify for the subaltern classes the ideological composition of their culture, to push them to reject and destroy it, either wholly or in part, so as to take on other ideological criteria, other standards of judgement and behaviour.

It could be said that when revolutionary minorities or avant-gardes tend (vis-à-vis the fractions of the subaltern classes that are the immediate objects of their action) to replace the ideological-cultural elements received-imposed *onto the present* by the dominant class with the results (the values, the methods) achieved by the avant-gardes in the course of their ideological conflict with the dominant class, there results that deviation and that error which political jargon terms dogmatic-sectarian deviation and the error of subjectivism.

When the self-same minorities or avant-gardes tend instead to privilege the cultural elements of the subaltern classes, inasmuch as they constitute their *past*, and to make of their rediscovery or integration the substitute for the values imposed onto the present by the dominant class, there results that deviation and that error which are termed the populist deviation and the error of nationalism.

In the first case, one proposes to the subaltern classes the last and highest cultural form of the dominant class, namely, its maximum degree of self-consciousness. This perspective is implicit in all the theories and practices of 'creative minorities'; it is also present in Leninism which, not by accident, has its origins in the refutation of Russian populism. Among such minorities, the hatred for the cultural elements imposed onto the subaltern classes is at least equal to the scorn for the ideological inheritance of the oppressed classes. So it often happens (we see examples of this every day) that, since this twofold negation gives rise to the imagination of a void, the latter is filled by postulating as ever-present in the subaltern classes a high potential for ideological nihilism—which is instead nothing but the projection of the unconscious self-destructive will of intellectual minorities deracinated from the values of both the dominant and the subaltern cultures. I am not saying this is the rule. But it is certainly the danger.

In the second case, it seems instead that the revolutionary minorities or avant-gardes want to repeat, along with the entire fraction of the subaltern classes that they can influence and organize, the latter's exit from the ensemble of ideological-cultural values of the dominant classes. But the ideological foundation which in the first hypothesis the avant-gardes assumed by instating themselves as guides may reveal itself insufficient to organize subaltern culture. The more elements received from the past have been worked up by the life experience and conflicts of the subaltern classes, the more they become allies or competitors (and sometimes adversaries) of the 'advanced' culture of the minorities. The latter will then want to unite themselves or, rather, merge (at least partially) into the subaltern classes or the 'ideologically oppressed'. In effect, by affirming past or present values more than values that still demand to be embodied, the populist attitude represents a secession, organized as a defence against the attack of new 'values' which the most advanced sectors of the dominant class adapt or dissimulate in order to have them accepted by (or to impose them upon) the subalterns. Populist resistance may have an objectively revolutionary meaning and impact—for example, in the defence of national cultural elements against imperialist disintegration—but it will enter into crisis when it finds itself obliged once again to face up to contact with the other; this will always be an agoraphobic crisis, the price paid for the ideological-cultural (and thus also ethical and aesthetic) welding of revolutionary minorities and the subaltern class.

The ideological task is therefore not that of giving form to a formlessness (the solution typical of bourgeois rationalism), to revere a formlessness (the solution of vitalist and avant-garde extremism) or to defend a catalogue of forms (the populist solution), but to criticize the mystified image—that is, the illusory form—that the oppressed class has of itself. Not through the traditional process of awareness-raising and becoming-conscious but with a proposal of activities and praxes which will be formalizing or, if you will, emancipatory. I am speaking of *behaviours able to expand the available domain of existence, to transform into choices the largest possible quotient of fate, to create authenticity with fragments of inauthenticity.*

We thus return to—no longer as a generic affirmation but as a specific itinerary of political action—the theme of the formal use of life. Referring to the experiences of the past few years, it should be recalled that in and through the various current political and social regimes or, rather, almost independently from them, groups and strata have achieved or been granted the possibility to decide for themselves, to formalize a wider sector of their existence than was previously available to them—by privilege or the fight against the privilege of others, by affluence or revolt. These groups or strata ultimately ended up refusing, for the love of the concrete, every final ought, due to its remote and imperative nature; putting forward again, in the intervals or even the niches of the present, anticipations of non-individualistic concreteness or 'happiness'. It's not worth repeating here the theoretical refutation of those attitudes; they contain a precious, irreplaceable element of futurity. What 20 years ago was objectively regressive, today can take on an entirely different value. They effectively lay claim to aspects of existence that manifest a solidity or permanence that are far greater than those of sociohistorical features. No 'eternal man', rather, aspects of history that have taken on the apparent constancy of 'nature', like the succession of ages and generations, mortality, the sphere of biological needs or that of the unconscious; I would also add some kinds of workmanship, and, at least for some of its aspects, language.

It is useless to hide it; to lay claim to those aspects also implies putting forward again and re-evaluating models of behaviour and of language-thought whose structure is mythical or symbolic. We may warn of the dangers of this path, but we can't avoid the practical and immediately political question of how to not separate the register of rational-scientific *certainties* from the potent and present demand for *truth*; not only of *knowledge*[1] then but also of *wisdom*.[2]

One Should Not Give Up on Anything

> To write poetry today, when the parameters of class conflict have reached their extreme and essential nakedness, is really to give in to the suggestive invitation of a tradition or, rather, of a crystallized custom. I do not know how those who treat words in a literary form avoid having their tongues freeze in their mouths every time they manage to grasp the condition in which the world finds itself. Never has necessity reached such an extreme level, never have words been as inadequate to their task.[3]

These words (by Asor Rosa), though written as polemic against both my poetry and my arguments, in this book, about literature, had initially found me in extraordinary agreement. It was precisely what I had repeatedly said at various points in this book. The inadequacy of the word, the aphasia induced by the spectacle of the real, the consciousness that contemporary poetic illusion is sustained only thanks to a 'crystallized custom'—these situations are far from foreign to the moderns. I myself have often hyperbolized them because I wanted to strike at two (symmetrical and ultimately dispelled) optimisms: the optimism of 'participation', of the 'commitment' which in forms old and new wished to 'serve' the revolutionary Cause, and the (apparently opposite) optimism of neo-positivist, technologizing, avant-garde anti-ideologism. With this book and the numerous metaphors that comprise it, I had precisely sought to articulate that 'freezing', only retaining at the very most an ironic and sinister hypothesis about poetry, resounding in the void. In other words, I was persuaded that, faced with what appeared as successive episodes in the cultural and political degradation of the socialist revolution in Europe, the sole possible unbending defence was the one which, precisely by talking about something else, inflexibly indicated the First and Only Necessary Absence.

The criticism directed at me was also an accusation of insufficient coherence: He who preaches silence, I was told, should start by shutting up. I was told that the situation was extreme; that 'we must give up on man,' that 'beauty, consolation, hope, pain, pleasure must be erased from our horizon;' that 'the class struggle does not pass through ideas, values, culture.'

At this point, I started to understand where my mistake lay. Of course, to say 'at this point' and 'I started' is a metaphor. The criticism of that error had not begun as a disgust with aestheticizing and pseudo-religious formulas, such as the ones I've just quoted. No, it had started in the facts, surrounding me, of these past years.

Today, I think that my mistake did not lie in the survival of an obstinate literary vocation or presumption, with its vices and ornaments, in discourses that claimed to concern ideology or politics. (We are creatures of our own past, after all, which is the source of the worst but also the best. I too could repeat that I am not so interested in what is done to man but in what he does with what is done to him.[4]) Nor was my mistake to be chalked up to what even my most benevolent friends chided me for, namely, coquetting with the allegories of religious language.

No, *my mistake was*, truth be told, *not having sufficiently defended the irreplaceability of poetic and literary discourse*. It was the mistake of having excessively praised the aphasia, the tragicness, the impossibility of the literary word, to have given in not only to the proud temptation of a denial of one's vocation but also to have incited others to do so; whereas one can turn to a new vocation only with the aim of attaining within it a degree of authenticity and value higher than the one that preceded the change or conversion.

If one believes in the inter-human circulation of works, that degree is what counts, not the point of application of one's energy vis-à-vis truth. In brief, if there's a mistake in this book—and there's more than one—it is not unrelated to what I have glimpsed in the phrases quoted above. There is truly an aestheticism in every *declared* desperation; there is pseudo-religiosity in everyone who continues to call *only* political revolution what he should recognize, for example, as *the projection into history of an act of faith in the non-demonstrable bond and presence of the living, the passed and the coming.* Without wanting it, and perhaps expressly denying it, in these writings of mine there was something that made me partake in an avant-garde of virtuous 'demons' and its dogmatic-sectarian risks.

One cannot repeat too often that we should not forget how the movement of the real does not coincide with the movement of our heads. Those who accuse me of theorizing my private affairs are right. But do I need to repeat, yet again, that *today only the proclaimed and manifest acceptance of a subjective point of view appears capable of diminishing the risk of an involuntary ideological mystification of our neighbour*? At the same time—why not admit it?—such personal affairs simply reflect, in our society and then in our heads, a change that has taken place far from here, where the political fate of the world is decided.

Let me recall that in the years when most of the pages of this book were written (1959–64), for the majority of the politically aware Italians, the formula of anti-fascist unity still stood—in its most authoritative interpretation, that of Togliatti's communism.[5] The *new* Left opposition was the prerogative of very few young and not-so-young people—ignored, mocked and boycotted by *all* the cultural and political forces of the 'historical' Left (union, parties, publishing, press). Little or nothing was known about the existence of a new opposition in the USA (the first events in Berkeley date from Autumn 1964). The Sino-Soviet conflict and the movements of the Third World were still, in 1962, talked down in the communist press. To announce or wish for—as one reads in the 1965 preface—'the interruption of false solidarities, of false unity' in our country could not have been done at the time without an extra effort, meaning an extra gesture. The interruption or rupture, whether intellectual or political, with people of my age was almost the opposite of its selfless intent; it was the proud proof of a coherence that could not reach its true addressees immediately because that rupture separated me and those close to me from the instruments of communication managed by the bloc of the governing and of the official—and accepted—opposition. It placed itself—in a proper communication system—under the heading 'poetry'. There's nothing strange in the fact that it can still be read as such.

The true break with the past only came when we were no longer a lonely few. Now the worst temptation, for one like me, would be that of the flight forward. The mocking or impatient smile with which the politicized youth or the young politician may meet these words neither cheers nor disturbs me. My service does not pass through him any more than 20 years ago it passed through the intimidation of Stalinist apparatchiks. Yet service it is. Who said that the writer must stand before the 'people' like the water buffalo before the kid who pulls it along and plays with it? As young as they may be, it is difficult to see the newest politicians having the grace and gaiety of the boy from the rice fields.[6]

This brief comment on criticisms received has mutated into a criticism of my work. 'As though from another shore, literature is possible,' I wrote in these pages, in 1964. Well, when one declares so eloquently that he wishes to be on the side of the dying and not the unborn, it means that he still isn't or, better, that he has yet to understand that the other shore does not exist and that the dead and the unborn exist with us on *this* shore. I was, we were, too fascinated, in those youthful years of massacres and unreal cities, by the void and the nearness of annihilation for our verses and prose not to carry nostalgia for it. We were almost never able to pluck 'the living flower'.[7] Now I am starting to understand that the great literature and great politics of our century is the one that wields

Negation with the joy of an Affirmation, and that for it the world is dense with reality, as full with the dead and the living as a page of Marcel Proust or a Cultural Revolution. There's truly reason to be scared of one's own weakness, of the paucity of the tools—of virtue and knowledge—that we've retained; of the irretrievable delay with which we've taken up a more difficult path.

What does all of this still have to do with Marxism? With what right do we still use the word 'revolution', with its irresistible trail of metaphors? This is how the title of the book sounds, even for its author.

I believe that signing off on the proofs of a reprint, an author, at this point, should not say anything at all. He can't make promises. Like an amputee, he can feel a pain where his books used to be, his verses and his prose; the age of confidence is gone and it is impossible to rewrite them. The rest is matter for another book. Or, more likely, for another man.

Notes

1 *sapere*. [Trans.]

2 *sapienza*. [Trans.]

3 Alberto Asor Rosa, 'L'uomo, il poeta' [Man and Poet] in *Intellettuali e classe operaia. Saggi sulle forme di uno storico conflitto e di una possibile alleanza* [Intellectuals and Working Class: Essays on the Forms of a Historical Conflict and a Possible Alliance] (Florence: La Nuova Italia, 1973), p. 265. [Trans.]

4 Paraphrase of a famous dictum by Jean-Paul Sartre. [Trans.]

5 Palmiro Togliatti (1893–1964), co-founder of the Italian Communist Party, and its general secretary from 1927 to his death. For Fortini's marked personal and political antipathy for Togliatti, see *inter alia*, '*Il Politecnico*, un discorso aperto' in *Un dialogo ininterrotto. Interviste 1952–1994* (Turin: Bollati Boringhieri, 2003), pp. 167–9. [Trans.]

6 Likely an allusion to a photograph from Vietnam. Fortini was active in the movement against the Vietnam War; see his speech at a

demonstration in Florence on 23 April 1967, reprinted in *Che fare* 8/9 (May 1971). [Trans.]

7 Fortini often alludes to the famous passage in the young Marx's Introduction to his *A Contibution to the Critique of Hegel's Philosophy of Right*, which reads: 'Criticism has plucked the imaginary flowers on the chain not in order that man shall continue to bear that chain without fantasy or consolation, but so that he shall throw off the chain and pluck the living flower'; see the interview 'Le catene che danno le ali' [Chains that Give us Wings] (1981) in *Un dialogo ininterrotto*, pp. 298–310. [Trans.]

PART I

The Literary Institution

I

Eroticism and Literature

Is it possible for erotic representation 'not be judged differently from any other representation?' No more impossible (according to an *incipit* that is often evoked, both for its share of truth and, even more, for the portion of error that may be glimpsed in it) than a critical reading of the *Divine Comedy* undertaken as though it was just another poetic work. The trouble is that one thereby runs the risk that the reader will miss one of the specific traits of Dante's *oeuvre*, namely, its ability to stand aside and let us go on our way, 'only gazing'.[1] When eroticism is represented like any other thing, what vanishes is eroticism itself.

In a society of generalized repression, the specific repression of eroticism is the most glaring and thus presumably the least important. Eroticism is the commonest and most recognized of taboos. It is indirectly charged with all the severity of so many other prohibitions, becoming their screen. Every relatively rigid society probably tends to establish a scale of visibility for prohibitions. Only if it has projected its entire capacity for hypocrisy onto the sexual-erotic, can a society feign to fear for its institutions on account of license or debauch. That is what appears to be happening in Italy today. This is the first proof of the naivety of the apostles of sexual revolution: true conservatives don't ask for anything better than to be attacked on the terrain of mores—as long as this is an end rather than a starting point.

That Medea should not murder on the stage is a valid precept for poetics, not erotics. To be more precise: erotics and poetics make different usages of figures or metaphors. What I mean is that pornography or the *film cochon*[2] or striptease or any other form of erotic excitation have their excellent reasons to exist but on condition that they are able to exercise all their power, to urge eyes and hands, to loosen collective sexual behaviours. Otherwise they may be classified (as is the case) among those semi-pathological forms of eroticism that rehearse repression without ever reaching the final act (not even that of Wagner's *Tristan*), that is to say, the reversal of repression, as certain tribal ceremonies are able to do. The obstacle to something and its delay are two different things; and different again are the obstacle and the delay that forget their object even when it is so close. Partial sublimations are the worst kind. If we compare bad faith to bad faith, specifically artistic and poetic bad faith has the advantage of being correctly fulfilled; of being, on its own terms, completely consumable. It is an effigy. Artistic and poetic representation does not trigger any kind of lacrimation, or any set of behaviours, except for very slowly mediated ones. As we know, every art always says something other than what it seems to be saying, and its object is by no means 'the reality of life' (this stubborn and perhaps necessary naturalist illusion of which the questionnaire[3] speaks) but the *truth* of life. Which is something else entirely. And why should the obstacle—which Freud perhaps did not identify as such but glimpsed as a necessary component of the libido (and there's those who argue that there's no erotics without a violation of taboos)—not also be transferred, albeit clandestinely, unto the most liberating of representations? It is possible in fact to think that the taboos linked to erotic representation may largely fade or disappear altogether. Employing contemporary techniques of conditioning, it would surely be possible to control the reactions of the masses and lead them to accept not only the literary or theatrical representations but also the journalistic, televisual and filmic representation of all the particulars of what the law codes term carnal congress. In a few years, in the Sunday supplements . . . We need only remind ourselves of the rapid shift, under our very eyes, of the frontiers of the permissible. One must really be exceedingly candid to think that our need for darkness can be exorcized at such little cost.

I wouldn't say that in contemporary literature eroticism is really perceived as something 'healthy, necessary, natural and religious' (a series of equivalences that is, moreover, contradictory). Wherever I turn I'm increasingly less likely to read the praises of health or nature, which basically means of immediacy—that great decadent myth, broadcast by right and left, by progressive Jesuits as much as by optimistic post-Marxists and radical-liberals of all stripes. Nor could it be otherwise when the two most dauntless anthropologies of our age, the Marxist and the Freudian, are founded on the notion of false consciousness.

It is difficult not to get the impression that the greater sexual freedom of the present, which is the object of the discussion, is in fact nothing more than a greater facilitation of sexual exchanges, a more widespread tolerance and a resolute choice for banality. For there to be a 'reasonableness' of Eros which is not tantamount to cynicism, erotic morality would need to appear in the light of day and be (or begin to be) integrated into the world of non-eroticism, which is to say, of production and work. Instead, the opposite takes place: productive 'reasonableness' determines (and increasingly deforms) its erotic counterpart. We should not be fooled by cinema or advertising, nor mistake some limited sectors (like haut-bourgeois or artistic milieus) for the reality of a productive society. In offices and factories, at least here in Italy, the public repression of the erotic and its repressive containment in the private sphere lead to the permanence of truly archaic forms of sexual-erotic tension (from the intensely erotic atmosphere of the offices that a French sociologist has rightly brought to our attention to the notoriously lewd language of some groups of workers, especially women, in the workplace). This is anything but freedom or reasonableness. And this is but a case—the most obvious one—of the retardation of the culture of feelings or passions in comparison to the culture of information and intelligence; a retardation that the current developmental phase of capitalist society seems intent on maintaining.

This is confirmed by the extreme contradiction between the type of culture hinted at by the dress of the average Milanese female office worker and the one indicated, as soon as she opens her mouth, by her lexical and ideological choices. Outside the workplace, in leisure, an erotics and a sexual ethics, which is also an ethics of production and profit, flourishes all the more: with the patterns of weekly and seasonal migrations, the means of transport and communication and so forth. I am not sure, for example, if others have registered the precept of corporate exogamy under a neo-capitalist regime, whereby sexual exchanges between employees of the same company or firm are perceived as something that is better avoided or is openly disapproved by the executives' gaze. So, come evening, the young males of Bank *X* or Plant *Y* escape incest and cross the urban forest towards the gates of other plants or other banks.

The direction of the change therefore seems to go from archaic forms—characterized by strong pressures and a proportionally high erotic tension—to forms of mystified freedom which rehearse the script of eroticism but in fact hint at something else: ambition, envy, power, vanity. Just as in the world of production and profit, feudal or mercantile ethics has been replaced by bourgeois reasonableness, and today by the advice of *good will*[4] campaigns, so is erotics, within reach of every conscience, as democratic and flavourless as artificially fed chickens and weeklies. As weakened as it may be, the Christian tradition's idea of sin seems, in comparison, to uphold a less mystified freedom.

The relationship between socioeconomic repression in the world of profit (that is, the regime of class domination and absence of democracy in the choices on which production and consumption depend, and on whose major decisions our collective fates ultimately rest) and the apparent non-repression and license in the world of erotics (apparent but in fact debased) is thus extremely clear. All official or clerical *pruderie*, with its censorship and buffoonery, is a basic (even crude) ploy, a rearguard skirmish that the men of 'progress' have let themselves get mixed up in—thus revealing their complicity.

That is why those who go around today preaching sexual freedom are in my eyes little different from reactionaries. Were I coherent, I shouldn't move a finger nor add a signature to prolong the ridiculous tug of war between clerics and anti-fascists, an alibi for conflicts that no one wants fully to recognize and confront.[5] Do we need to recall that a century ago the epithet 'bourgeois' meant severity, moralism, philistinism, good sense and moral order, while today the 'neo-bourgeois' (in industrially-advanced societies and in that part of Italy that counts as such) advertises his liberalism in matters of sex, reads the most 'risqué' books, laughs at censorship, tolerates his daughter's use of not-very-Catholic expressions, only likes avant-garde art and so on? Such a tolerance in matters of sex is now rendered possible by certainty in what concerns the efficacy of true taboos, the socioeconomic ones. In the last and bloodiest days of the Algerian War of Independence, a French acquaintance of mine, a long-time Left militant and supporter of the Algerian cause, accused me of 'Stalinism' for having interpreted in political terms a film like Alain Resnais's *Last Year at Marienbad*. 'Don't you understand,' he told me, 'that you can make love and, ten minutes later, be on the street and *se battre avec les flics*,[6] and the two things are separate? It is an abuse of language and of intelligence to mix them up or try and reduce them to a unity.' I understood very well. And the examples had been chosen with remarkable precision. All you needed to do was open a newspaper and the practice of dissociation was there, narrated and propagandized day after day. The society of which I speak is founded on institutionalized dissociation, everybody knows it; and if that dissociation is fought against, it is not in order to rebuild the fictive unity of the bourgeois person but because today capitalist ideology no longer aims at that unity—instead it stabilizes and fixes *only* separate functions, the functional separations that defend it.

We must give their strongest and most literal meaning to some phrases of Marx: not only to the one that says that 'The immediate, natural, necessary relation of human being to human being is the *relationship* of *man* to *woman*,' but to the following one, also from the same *Manuscripts*: 'private property does not know how to transform crude need into *human* need. Its idealism is *fantasy*, *caprice* and *infatuation*.'[7] This is the best definition of debased eroticism, of what Marx himself calls 'putrefied nature'[8]: fantasy, caprice and infatuation, demeaned and reduced, reminding one of those manuals, purchasable for a few cents, where in austere scientific language desperate American spouses are taught the manipulations that should remedy their frigidity.

It is not possible to understand the presence of eroticism in contemporary literature unless one sees it as the attempt to juxtapose a 'truth' (that of the dissociation between eroticism and the 'other' life, or that which denies any 'other' life outside of eroticism) to the 'falseness' of the ideological industry that wishes to mediate sex, eroticism and love, and to affirm a hypocritical unity of human existence. The more that film, TV, advertising and fashion offer erotic proposals in the only form that is practicable and unfortunately necessary today, namely, as splitting and flight from one's identity, the more they effectively line up in defence of the last unitary notion, that of 'love'. That is why literature, as long as it continues to believe that its main mission is to *oppose* mass myths rather than to *educate* that very mass (in other words, to the degree that it is snobbery at the service of privilege and the perpetual reconstitution of an ideology for leaders), has found itself forced, for half a century, to repeat two attitudes: the first sees eroticism as waste, squandering, vexation, vanity, contempt, cruelty, compulsion to repeat, regression or cynicism; the second turns it into a privileged form of consciousness and revelation, be it 'black' or 'white'. Everyone can decide for themselves which authors to class under the two attitudes. Obviously, these have as much to do with truth as eighteenth-century sadisms or romantic sentimentalities. And we can soon expect, as 'black' eroticism pierces through cinema, that writers will rediscover the 'pink' kind.

In conclusion, we should refuse any rationalist and libertarian optimism towards erotics as well as towards any enterprise of dis-alienation that does not intend to pass through the eternal narrow gate of the mystery of mysteries, that of *political economy* and of its *practical criticism*. We should also refuse any operation at the summits, that is any undertaking led by sexual avant-gardes as well as any reformist descent of erotic mores from enlightened strata down to those who are presumed as retrograde. We should accept instead, without resorting to easy remedies, the miseries and the chains, the miserable chains of contemporary eroticism as one of the conditions of consciousness necessary to pursue—in the organized, inflexible and, in this sense, 'scientific' transformation of the man–nature relationship—that lessening of the traces of original sin which alone—according to Baudelaire's profound insight,[9] paradoxical in its formulation, and thus the object of immoderate praise or hasty mockery by sexual-Catholics or rational-libertines—can constitute progress: personal and present progress as well as collective and future progress.

1961

Notes

Original publication: 'Otto domande sull'erotismo in letteratura' [Eight Questions on Eroticism in Literature], *Nuovi Argomenti* 7(51–2) (July–October 1961). *Nuovi Argomenti* was founded in 1953 by the writer and journalist Alberto Carocci (1904–72) and the novelist Alberto Moravia (1907–90). It is worth noting in this respect that Moravia's novels were considered at the time to contain pornographic elements, even contributing, as the opening of the Swedish archives has recently shown, to his exclusion from the Nobel Prize in Literature. Later, after Pasolini became an editor, Fortini would turn down an offer to participate in *Nuovi Argomenti* for literary and ideological reasons. See 'Caro Pasolini' (1965) in *Un giorno o l'altro*, p. 344. [Trans.]

1 '*solo sguardando*' (Dante, *Purgatorio*, Canto 6). [Trans.]

2 Smut film (in French). [Trans.]

3 This essay is a response to a questionnaire prepared by the journal *Nuovi Argomenti*. [For the original version of Fortini's text, including the questions, see 'L'erotismo in letteratura' in *Un dialogo ininterrotto. Interviste 1952–1994*, pp. 38–45.]

4 In English in the original. [Trans.]

5 This is an instance of the systematic concealment of authentic class antagonisms beneath apparent contrasts—which Italy has experienced for over a decade but which in France, under the Third Republic, has lasted much longer.

6 Fighting with the cops (French). [Trans.]

7 Karl Marx, 'Economic and Philosophical Manuscripts of 1844' in *Early Writings* (Rodney Livingstone and Gregor Benton trans) (London: Penguin, 1975), pp. 347, 359. [Trans.]

8 Ibid., p. 359. [Trans.]

9 'Théorie de la vraie civilisation. Elle n'est pas dans le gaz, ni dans la vapeur, ni dans les tables tournantes. Elle est dans la diminution des traces du péché originel' (*Mon cœur mis à nu*, LIX) ['Theory of the true civilization. It has nothing to do with gas or steam or table-turning. It consists in the diminution of the traces of original sin'] [Charles Baudelaire, *Intimate Journals* (Christopher Isherwood trans.) (Westport: Hyperion Press, 1930), p. 85.] I am not surprised to find this same quote from Baudelaire in Marcuse's *Eros and Civilization*. What sets Marcuse apart from the countless preachers against the repression of the instincts is the clear consciousness that every individual (which is to say, not 'political') 'anticipation' searches for 'a non-repressive reality principle' in the past, à la Jung, or in some pipe dream of the future, bereft of a historical guide.

II

A Test of Powers

1. Over the past several years, the sites of opinion and literary taste have been shaken by the surge and spread of what are to us new forms of the culture industry, which have transformed the appearance and function of the traditional mediating organs between authors and public—publishing houses, bookshops, journals, political and cultural groups. Literary society has put up even less resistance to motorization than our historic town centres. Unlike their foreign colleagues with their maturer modernity, writers have been unable to adapt, that is to react to their environment. The most backward elements of Italian society also play their part in softening the brutality of the shift, which thereby loses any of its pedagogical value. Contrary to what happened in the Paris of a hundred or a hundred and fifty years ago, or more recently in the United States (and, albeit with radically different motivations, in the Stalinist USSR), the explicit subordination of the intellectual and the artist, and therefore of the critic, to the interests of the dominant class in the phase of the mass-culture industry has not gone through a tragic phase here in Italy. Each and every day, the 'naked, shameless, direct, brutal exploitation' that transforms 'the poet, the man of science' into 'paid wage labourers', according to Marx and Engels' old *Manifesto*, finds those who would clothe it and hide its shame.

Just as there was no anti-fascist emigration among Italian writers that could be compared to the German or Spanish one, so too the culture industry of the past decade has found a thousand ways to maintain the illusion of critical independence. Even the different political blocs have made their contribution. Engrossed in immobile conflicts among currents, some intellectuals and critics managed to believe, for flashes of time, that they could take on the same role that in France was played, and not for long, by a Sartre, Camus or Mauriac—in France, where, notwithstanding the general decadence of the literary and cultural elites, the organization and stratification of cultural instruments has remained unchanged for so long that authors and critics regard it as a truth of nature, like the course of the Loire. Here in Italy instead, at least until yesterday, many militant critics thought they were still running around wearing the uniform of Marxism and Catholic spiritualism, ignoring that on their backs was already printed the name of a company producing cultural tyres or literary toothpaste.

> We will exclude from our investigation the conscious or unconscious hucksters of criticism. . . . However, with the critics as with the writers, the mass of mediocre and corrupt scribblers furnish an environment that cannot be eliminated from our considerations. For this environment must affect the professional critic when he judges contemporary literature and the writer when he evaluates contemporary criticism; it establishes the atmosphere which helps to determine—whether or not they are aware of it—their evaluation of each other.[1]

The essay containing these words dates from 1939. It has lost none of its actuality. In Italy, the last few years alone suffice to show, with blinding clarity, that the 'constant vacillation between examining the content in literature from an abstract social or political point of view and examining form from a subjectivist point of view represents no real progress or constructive evolution' and that 'the sociological investigation of literature offers no escape from narrow aestheticizing subjectivism. On the contrary, it draws criticism deeper into the morass.'[2] That is because today we are really witnessing within the language of criticism both *the formalization of sociological investigation* (classifications derived from sociology, which are precious tools in the philological-linguistic moment, tend to forget their own origins and to establish themselves as critical categories, such as those of linguistic 'levels', of semantic 'choices', of 'areas' and so on), and, inversely, *the sociologization and pedantic pseudo-scientific classification of an untestable vitalism*, or of the recurring intuitionism which, ashamed of its own cultural nakedness, today wears (just as it did half a century ago) clothes borrowed from positivism, from the terminology of the *sciences humaines*. Needless to say, there's more than one sociology, more than one formalism; Barthes's sociologism is something other than the one learnt by old men desiring rejuvenation or young men desiring to age. Above all, there are different degrees of preparation, sensibility and intelligence. We are not interested here in the exception but in the rule, the average. And the average reproduces—duly updated and reciprocally integrated—those dead antitheses that Lukács spoke about more than 20 years ago and which among us were delayed by the Crocean dictatorship (an example of how a 'delay' can sometimes be more positive than a belated 'progress' . . .) and by the years of a dominant if uncertain Gramscianism; antitheses that only the unfolding of the current condition has made visible to the naked eye. The field of literary criticism, for example, is one in which—I am still speaking of the 'average'—the rigorous research of men like Giulio Preti[3] risks vulgarization, or even vulgarity. If Pietro Citati[4] heralds the agony and useful death of our literary society such as it has been configured until now, he is really just asking for that recognition of the modern world which has already been carried out where—having bid farewell to the hypocritical illusions of rebelliousness and independence—there is no literary society in the Italian or French or Spanish sense of the word; where, as in the USA or England, the producers of literature or criticism accept the rules of the commercial and social game, or if they do not, it is not as artists or critics but as private citizens and on the basis of their own opinions and interests, not of a particular intellectual profession. Perhaps Citati's proposals only intended to reconstruct literary society at a higher level; to increase membership in the Jockey Club of international high literature. Nausea at false aristocracies may be a noble feeling, but I know no aristocracy more dubious than the one that affirms the existence of values invisible to the worldly gaze while at the same time granting itself, or someone else, the capacity to discern them, which implies partaking in those supreme values. There is a foolproof clue to identify the equivocal aristocracy of intuition, isolation, the gift, or grace: it links values to persons more than to works. To persons and corporations of persons ('great' writers, for example) and not to their works, which are always collaborations, both in their genesis and their consumption.

2. Is a kind of criticism that does not profess its agnosticism or indifference towards 'world-views', or negate itself in the so-called science of literature, possible? Of course it is. But repelled by neo-positivist presumptuousness as much as by the poverty of pseudo-Marxist scientism, the scholar of contemporary literature[5] finds everything ready to welcome his discourse about the present, based on a well-tested all-purpose practice, a mix of cynicism, moralism and intuitionism. The culture industry, as we've said, needs this kind of eclecticism; at least as much as it needs to manufacture the new avant-gardes. The more it instrumentalizes and demeans to the rank of mere profit factor the hyper-discredited intellectual—who, thanks to the noted privilege of self-consciousness, humbles and extols himself, eclipses himself and then makes himself shine again—the more it needs to invent seemingly irreducible or aristocratic minorities. One of the most pressing interests of economic and political ruling groups lies in maintaining the illusion of spontaneity and independence, the moral foundation of the system.

That illusion is projected in advertising balance sheets and the budgets of the industrialists of culture; in each case, they evaluate with quantitative precision the demand for freshness and authenticity originating from those strata who every day deprive themselves and others of them.

Meanwhile, the more glaring differences between academic criticism, rapid-response criticism and militant pamphleteering have diminished considerably. The sensibilistic and intuitionist language of post-Idealist or hermeticist-oriented criticism has been replaced by those of the neo-philologists (in the universities) and—vacillating between stylistic criticism, semanticism and sociologism—of contemporary criticism.

The differences of yore have not been lessened by a movement towards a greater homogeneity of critical language and method, which would borrow its authority and philological probity from academic criticism and the fluency or force of its intervention into public opinion from the other forms of criticism. If that movement had begun in the immediate postwar period in left-wing publications, it was soon exhausted: those were the fleeting years of op-ed professors and aesthetes, contrite and conflicted by the awfulness of the events of the war. The abandonment of the idea of a unitary criticism, the refusal of every unitary idea of criticism, has led, in the academic context, to a neo-philological revival and, in the context of militant criticism, to aping the approaches and results of Anglo-Saxon criticism. This was due to the admittedly legitimate reaction against the verbalism of late idealist criticism and the inconsistency of ideologism of a Marxist type, though, lo and behold, it also coincided with a mutation in the political balance of forces. As far as contemporary criticism is concerned, the new subjectivisms, which have sprouted up again on the 'right wing' of criticism, and the new objectivisms, which lay claim to a science of literature that would envelop and liquidate Marxist demands, are two facets of the same retreat.

The first group accepts the world as it is and assigns the writer and critic a base and grandiose task, full of sin and repentance: the servitude and greatness of traditional clerisy. Nuances of taste, preparation and intelligence matter little: it does not make a great difference that one lives off pathetic nostalgia, the other off vibrant scepticism and a third off scornful snobbery. What is essential is that being dead to the world, as trumpeted by such writings, always means being dead to *a* world, and accepting another real, concrete (and temporally powerful) one. They are better informed than the generation that preceded them; they have studied and read more. But their position within Italian society is proportionally the same, and will remain the same, as that of a Serra, a Cecchi, a Pancrazi or a De Robertis—that of a lame humanism.[6]

The second group, those belonging to a Left to suit all tastes, also accept the world as it is, as proven by the fact that they transfer the task of changing it unto specialisms and techniques. They too believe in Providence. But while for the ones (the Pampalonis,[7] Citatis, etc.) Providence is of the Christian or Manichean sort—'God above' or 'the prince of this world'[8]—for our paladins of neo-Enlightenment, a combinatorial optimism is at work—everyone should dig their own garden, someone else will take care of the synthesis.

The very few divergent examples truly seem to belong to a species on the verge of extinction—or of rebirth. The critic who understands his task more or less as I do—that is along the lines of the great Romantic and post-Romantic criticism, up to Lukács—finds himself denied his political purpose and ultimately pushed to the two extremes (I am thinking of a Cesare Cases, but also of the best moments of a Bàrberi Squarotti or a Luigi Baldacci[9]): academic essays on the one hand, information on the other, perhaps deluding himself that this is not the case. Cases, for example, is careful to hide his desperation beneath the appearance of the solid optimism of 'conventions'. More or less consciously, he places his 'values' in the safe-deposit boxes of conservation, detesting all avant-gardes, forgetting that Lukács spoke of Goethe from a country on the socialist path, between two five-year plans, and that two people (especially two critics) who say the same thing do not say the same thing.

3. Today, an essential part of critical activity is invisible. The fundamental choices are made in the editorial boards of publishing houses, on which there converge those judgements from whose balance or imbalance stems that act of cultural or commercial policy (as well as of critical orientation) which is the *publication* of one or more literary works. By this, I do not mean to say that *true* criticism is the one exercised by the readers of publishing houses or by the critics and literary scholars they employ, and that critical *truth* is the one deposited in the archives of publishers. I do not mean to say it, for the ritualistic and conventional character of the article or essay retains its critical *raison d'être* because of the formal deference demanded by its publicity, which cannot exist in the so-called frankness of private judgement. But there is no doubt that today—if not always, at least often—the critic performs an indispensable technical function vis-à-vis an industrial and commercial apparatus, and, what is more, in the act of performing it, becomes the vehicle of ideological and political perspectives in a way that carries infinitely more responsibility than accrues to the narrator or poet. Even if moved by the most disinterested search for value, anyone who exercises a critical function in the great organs of publishing or in other organs of mass culture, such as newspapers and weeklies, cannot ignore that the culture industry could not survive, at least in its present forms, without that mass of useless or bad books cluttering his desk.

Robert Escarpit tells us that in France between 60 and 70 per cent of book production never reaches a profitable volume of sales.[10] Supposing that the same is true for Italy, we can infer that it is precisely the 60 or 70 per cent of bookshop flops that guarantees the relative independence of the critic. If the economy of publishing did not make it so that the success of one book compensated for the failure of three, there would neither be prestige publishing production (the 'feathers in the caps' of so many publishers) nor would the critic have the luxury every once in a while, in the columns of a newspaper or weekly, of busying himself with books that only interest him and his friends. The chaos of tastes is the condition for 'good taste', idiocy is the ground for intelligence, etc. The exceptions confirm the rule. There is no critic who, besides his public scale of values, does not have a private one, or one reserved for a few intimates only. He lets it be glimpsed, every once in a while, like a sacred image, even by his common readers, namely, those who pay to know what he thinks.

We find the critic in all the phases of cultural production and circulation: from the phase of conversation, of the literary or salon circle (whether elite or semi-political), of the journal for a select few (where particular tendencies or tyrannies of taste are forged), or of editorial consultancy for the newspapers, radios, TV stations, etc. that decide and directly affect the success of this or that publishing initiative, and all the way to the final phase of placement and consumption. It is evident that *written* criticism is simply the part of this activity that lies above the surface.

In each of these phases, the critic is delegated by ideological, political and economic groups. There are critics who take part in more than one moment: the senators and undersecretaries of criticism, who, like some writers, think they are merely heeding the wishes of the Nation. They are simultaneously university lecturers, directors or consultants for book series, authors of prefaces, translations, introductory essays, regular critics for newspapers and weeklies, directors or editors of literary journals, jury members for literary prizes, public speakers, advisors to social groups or socialites. Grand Almoners of the ideologies in power or of the constitutional and complicit opposition, they sometimes tell the great and the good about the vanity of the world, as Bossuet once did.[11] Zealous advocates of the severe distinction (or confusion, it's all the same) between literature and politics, they accordingly guarantee themselves irresponsibility and impunity in both sectors. Their accents, even when they call themselves socialists, resemble those of liberal articles in the newspapers of the Confindustria.[12]

But I hear it said or I tell myself that these conditions, though menacing and miserable, do not infringe on the capacity to exercise the critical virtues for whoever may want to possess it. In truth, it has perhaps never been possible to write without believing that in the end there is justice in this world and that when all is said and done good work, work carried out conscientiously, bears fruit, assumes authority, achieves recognition.

In this sense, the critic cannot fail to share, at least in our society, that condition of living death that is perhaps necessary for the exercise of any virtue. But for the critic the dangers are worse than for the poet: he is by definition a go-between, a medium, a place of transit and encounter; he needs a conversation, a society. And since the acceptance of death is necessarily intermittent, in practice, when a real exchange is forbidden, the small group that remains will display the vices of cliques, the mysticism of minorities, the tendency to arbitrariness. In the end this amounts to an acceptance of the vulgarity of the greatest number. It's a well-known fact: whoever thinks it is enough, in order to separate oneself from it, to denounce the vulgarity of others will find himself contaminated by it, in his most aristocratic pretensions.

I cannot persuade myself that the supreme virtues of a critic are foresight and the ability to bet on highly valued stocks in the bourse of the future. Not only because of a reasonable scepticism about the wisdom of that future. But especially because it is an untestable quality. You can't refuse your own natural judges, that is to say, your contemporaries, and then expect them to listen to you. The poet can appeal to future justice, the critic cannot. The critic is bound in a vital, direct relationship with his contemporaries; a relationship that only in particular epochs is the privilege and peril of the novelist and the poet. We all know that there is a way of being wrong (for example, of Lessing on Corneille, or Lukács on Proust or Brecht) which is richer and truer than many minor truths.

Today the critic can also be judged by the degree of his consent to a condition that deforms his purpose. Not unlike the poet or narrator, all of the elements of his work—argument, type of choice and motivations, structure of the text, stylistic elements—are, at one and the same time, the expression and communication of a vision of the world, of the present and the future. The critic judges himself much more than he judges others. Or rather, this is precisely what grounds the legitimacy of the judgement of value that much criticism today is inclined to refuse. The motto from the gospels is addressed to the critic: 'Blessed is he who does not condemn himself in what he approves.'

Finally, to the question of what the function of the critic in our country is, I would have to answer as follows: to make choices, identify arguments, construct discourses, employ languages that are choices, arguments, discourses and languages that can be desired for a society in which 'the free development of each is the condition for the free development of all.' From this perspective belonging to the humanist-Marxist tradition, which envisages a 'pedagogic province'[13] and an education of every man by every other, the critic is expected—if he shares it—to place himself right away at the level of *common discourse.* This obviously does not mean any discourse whatsoever. This discourse is common precisely because it seeks a commonality of objects and arguments beyond the mystification of fake cultural democracy. But insofar as he is a critic on the basis of a specialism—a literary specialism—and thus, in a certain sense, insofar as he represents this specialism, he will also need to be at all moments a critic *of* literature, of the position that literature occupies in the ensemble of human life and culture, a critic of literary institutions, and of institutions *sans phrase*. In other words, a critic of society: a political critic.

This is the critic-philosopher and critic-writer of whom Lukács speaks to us in his essay; and the critic-historian, of which Lukács himself is an example. This idea of criticism, which stubbornly refuses to leave us, is basically the one that belonged to romantic humanism and which persists, in other humanisms, to our present day. It is based on the quest for the past, present, or possible dignity of man, on his *unity*. The literary critic has as his object a work which, to the degree that it is non-discursive, non-analytical, but rather synthetic, has, or claims to possess the very complexity of the 'world', of 'life', of 'man'. Engaging in the work of criticism and developing a critical discourse means being able to speak *about everything* with reference to a concrete and determinate occasion. The critic is therefore truly *the other* of the specialist, the philologist and scholar of the 'science of literature'; he is the voice of common sense, an ordinary reader who acts as a mediator, not between works and the public but between specialisms and particular activities (or particular 'sciences') on the one hand, and the author and his public on the other.

By contrast, Sainte-Beuve's definition of the critic as one who knows how to read and teaches others to read,[14] aside from forgetting the obvious inversion, retains the typical reactionary formula of the mediator between strata or castes or classes; whereas, to my mind, a positive mediation can only take place between moments of the ideological superstructure. Because he knows that the works of which he speaks are not only private and untestable discourses but also the effect and image of the real ways in which men are with one another, the critic at first forbids himself from knowing more about the world than his author tells him. But he subsequently accords himself the right, which belongs to every reader, to compare those experiences with his own so as to judge their meaning, coherence and implications. And, in the contradictions between that organized universe of words, expressions, images and thoughts, his own 'world-view', and the circulation of different interpretations of the real in the society in which he lives, he establishes reactions and relations, situating his own discourse. Finally, he entrusts this discourse to a form which, though it tends towards the lucidity and coherence of historiographic and scientific discursivity, also accepts the moment of expressivity as one of its necessary moments, as a margin of arbitrary choice that *can* amount to a deeper interpretation and a closer cleaving to the object, namely, to the literary work under consideration and to the reality shared by the author and the critic.

The critic of whom I speak cannot really be set apart from the essayist. I know very well that today the traditional notion of essayism is looked upon with understandable repugnance as a tradition which, at least in Italy, has been marked by arbitrary choices, fake elegance, belletrism. Still, I wonder whether it is possible for a formalization of critical discourse or a 'science' of literature not to be matched by a 'form', in the *literary* sense of the word. I have always thought that, at least in Italy, the study of the essay *as form* has been neglected.[15] Many Italian essayists have written as though, exiled from Paris or Oxford, they had found themselves obliged to explain good manners to an audience of provincials; they didn't feel they had to pose the problem of the legitimacy and function of essayistic forms; they were essayists by literary right, which is to say, by birthright. On the other hand, the so-called Left has always viewed those investigations as useless formalisms and has always taken as its model (as one can tell in Muscetta[16] or Cases) the German and Russian democratic and socialist essays of the nineteenth century, often with stylistic effects which—I hope my two friends will forgive me—remind me of the character of Ehrenfried Kumpf, the plump and jovial theologian of Thomas Mann's *Doctor Faustus*.

In my view, instead, there is no contradiction between the defence of the essay, as a form of critical discourse proper to the idea of the critic I have just outlined, and its 'scientificity', understood not just in terms of lexical-expressive rigour but also of its adaptation to its addressees.

4. Summing up the Marxist contribution to literary criticism, Lucien Goldmann[17] has written that the essential tools created by Marxist thought appear to him to be:

i. The concept of *signifying structure* (or universal dynamic structuralism), which implies those of *coherent world-view* or *possible consciousness*.
ii. The concept of *socialist realism*, which, despite the abuses of Stalinism, remains valid as the affirmation

of the relationship between the content of the work and the overall social reality (or degree of correspondence), and thus as the need to 'distinguish between works that reveal social reality and works that mask it'. It is socialist because, to the degree that today's realism breaks through 'static phenomenal appearance', it cannot fail to register some of the trend-lines of socialism, which a Marxist understands as an essential factor of progress.

iii. The notion of the unitary structure of form and content, which nonetheless retains the idea of a dependence of the former on the latter, and thus their conceptual distinction.

If the third point is a cause for obvious perplexity, the first appears to be shared by several currents in structuralism, even though—as Goldmann himself notes—these do not insist on the signifying character of human structures, and tend to reduce 'world-views' to psychological and cultural phenomena. I cite these formulas from Goldmann because I think they point to an increasingly important tendency in an area of French criticism which, without resorting to a self-interested 'liquidation' of Marxism, tries to fuse historical discourse, sociological discourse and aesthetic evaluation in some sort of interminable addition and synthesis which, though it implies contributions from all the *sciences humaines*, does not rule out the *mise en forme* of critical prose, in the twofold sense—particularly dear to this writer—of logical-scientific *form* and literary *form* (or, as one says, 'writing').

A critic with an entirely different formation, Maurice Blanchot, espouses a contrasting conception of the critical act, one that 20 years ago had a lot of resonance in Italy. It brings together, without unifying them, the irrationalist vocation to universal communication (or the mimesis of the vital-spiritual flux) and the vocation—which should properly be termed crypto- or pseudo-Marxist—to overcome the division of labour (and of specializations) in the name of human unity. The first component—which has a heretical, hyper-romantic origin, and until very recently would have been associated with surrealism—is basically a tendency to anarchy, an affirmation of the underground, of the deep anti-historicity and anti-institutionality of life, which, in the very gesture of refusing values posits itself as the supreme value. For this component, rigidity is the only negative. It will therefore envisage criticism as a kind of river Styx, flowing parallel to the rivers of life and literature. Generalized semantics leads to the same consequences, and it matters little that it replaces the obscurity of 'life' with the Brownian motion of 'signs': the universe becomes a prodigious metaphorical series without an object; it is because it is. The circularity of critical discourse is then naturally mistaken for an indistinct unity.

The respective positions of Goldmann and Blanchot do not have counterparts in our Italian context: the development of the first was hindered both by the Crocean tradition and by the insufficient grounding of studies and investigations originating from literary criticism of a Marxist type, at least until a few years ago; while the second attitude, though it was widespread in the hermetic tradition, has always carried among us an explicitly conservative or openly reactionary ideological connotation.

5. To one who sees the task of the critic along the lines that I've summarized, the current situation offers two divergent paths: the criticism of pretexts and the criticism of positioning.[18] The first will tend to move beyond judgements of value, to circumvent them; the second, to dwell on them.

The change that has intervened between the age of Lukács and our own is exactly this: back then, the Marxist critic could exercise both kinds of criticism at the same time. Ever since, though the 'whence' has stayed the same, the 'whither' has changed, moving farther towards the horizon. The dominant Lukácsian theme of these past few years, that of 'critical realism' (with its manifest traits of compromise), is the effect of the weakening or, rather, the transformation undergone by the entity that back then mediated the discourse of the critic: I mean the Party. Attacked by Zhdanovites, Lukácsian realism could always invoke or await the dialectical turns of the Party, pointing through it to the prospect of socialism. But in the struggle for peace, detente, coexistence, the 'whither' of socialism is deferred, transformed. It must be redefined, but that has yet to happen. The Marxist critic today will continue to reply that socialism is the prospect of the human species but he will be far less certain than the Marxists of previous generations about what this affirmation implies; he has turned from the great universal prospect to events in his own nation; he asks what socialism could mean *for us*. He notices that most of the information he has about the society in which he lives does not come from the part that he has chosen, but from the enemy side. His resistance to the enemy ideology seems to diminish by the day—as always in these cases—and turns into faithfulness to principles, that is, into a regime of double truth.

The critic who refuses to collaborate with those who can furnish him with some sociological insights and data concerning the objects of his discourse risks believing, for example, that a novel published today is the same *thing* as a novel published a hundred years ago, that it occupies the same literary, cultural and social space; he also risks making the mistake of those who first study a type of craft production that has been in existence for centuries while ignoring that its finished products are packaged, sold and bought as ornaments. If this same critic affirms that all this doesn't eliminate the here-and-now of the object of criticism, nor the dialogue between critic and work, nor the objectivity of the real in which author, critic and public communicate, we will need to tell him: Can't you see that, in spite of your claim to be making choices on the basis of a method and a criterion of value, by exercising your trade on a finished object that has reached your table with the label of literary work, you are limiting yourself to confirming the system that produces these works?

As far as I can see, there's no escape: either one considers the object of contemporary criticism as a pretext, an occasion, a cue for some discourse or other—in which case one's method is not exercised because of a value-laden choice but is at best involved in the choice of pretext (this is, in fact, often the case)—or we wish to place the books and authors whereof we speak in a historical, ideological, aesthetic order—and then that schema and that order need to be continually tested on the social, productive and cultural context which produces and receives those books and those authors. Today, in our country, how can one refer, when it comes to the observation of a literary work, to normal climactic and atmospheric conditions? How can we take for granted the apparent motion of the stars at the latitudes of Rome or Milan? Note that this is not a question of methodology but of simple philology. We need to inventory the instruments of criticism, to test their powers and verify their credentials, to decide at what sea level our calculations begin, within what arc of meridians and parallels we deem our discourses valid. Writers sometimes put these questions to themselves instinctually, because to them their 25 or 25 million readers are often but metaphors; but for the critic, 25 readers (I'll rule out the 25 million!) are really 25 non-metaphorical persons. And if the poet really can do miracles, the critic must not.

I will be told that there's no criticism without history or philology; this is tantamount to saying that a 'world-view' is not enough, that all around the critic there must be a whole host of investigations, projects, studies and interpretations with a certain degree of ideological homogeneity, which cannot be deduced from principles or classics. *Carmina possunt vel coelo deducere lunam*;[19] but the critic must know what the morning papers say. If what has been said above about the current situation of our country is true, that ideologically coherent cultural elaboration will need to be the critic's element, his homeland, his vital place, that space where knowledge and action are integrated. It cannot be constituted by postulates of conscience or private cults. In other words, to borrow an old formula, there is no criticism outside of an organization in which the critic participates, which he contributes to determining, and which tends towards hegemony. Today, however, the principle: *cuius regio eius et religio*,[20] the foundation of the most hypocritical coexistence, sadly appears to have become official for Italian criticism as well.

That I, as a critic, make a choice in the corpus of Italian letters, as methodologically reasoned as can be, saying, for example, Cassola[21] if, Pavese[22] maybe, Calvino well,[23] Lampedusa no etc.; or that I argue for the immeasurable greatness of the *Pasticciaccio*,[24] the *Romana*,[25] or the *Gattopardo*[26]; without my argument taking account of the structure of the Italian literary, editorial and economic society that promotes these authors as opposed to others, and of the real conditions under which these works are read, their relevance vis-à-vis other works of contemporary literature and so on; without me as a critic electing, denoting, calling on my collaborators, delimiting the area of my address (an election and delimitation that takes place especially through the choice of *a* critical language)—all this simply means giving up de facto on that idea of criticism that I have recalled and illustrated above, and entrusting one's investigation instead to the whim of historical forces. Like Vigny's *bouteille à la mer, Dieu la prendra du doigt pour la conduire au port*.[27] I can already hear the retort: this distance, maintained in a Lukácsian fashion, between great historico-ideological curves and the short or extremely short waves of the sociological-political survey is the only one that can guarantee the great breadth of the visual field and, in the long run, real efficacy: *but then one is not engaging in contemporary criticism. Or, if one deals with contemporaries, they will become pretexts, heraldic personages*, like Mann or Kafka for Lukács, and one will provide only some 'cartoons', so that the 'workshop' can deal with the details.[28]

But we neither are nor wish to be the Marshals of Great Criticism: *the pretext, then, tempts us as a kind of retreat*; *the space it allows us to introduce between our circumstances and our judgement can resemble those walls of air, more impenetrable than ivory, which despair erects between our pages and the world.*

So it is that for a few years we have partaken in the puerile, stubborn proposal and reproposal of working programmes or group plans aiming at a possible homogeneity of method, a prospected unification of critical language, a synthesis of the main literary realities of the past and present, subjecting to control all the various agencies and mediations of critical discourse. We have fantasized about the journal that would give an example of 'political' discipline, a 'democratic university', an authority independent from the big business of publishers and the limelight of fashion. At the same time, there is, in the author of these lines, an ever-greater distrust in the possibility of climbing out of the valley of false spontaneity and false organization into which we have descended, a sense of uselessness and fatigue at the failure of every attempt and the prudent laziness (or shall we say *omertà*) of our peers, the suspicion that we've misread the environing social reality—these leave us gasping for air.

The question of whether we're making a mistake in critical method, in poetics, and ultimately in life is one and the same with that (which has always haunted the best politicians of the revolutionary opposition) of whether there's a possible error of method in the aim of 'transforming the world'. Resistance to the 'world', once deemed heroic, suddenly and horrifyingly appears as an infantile refusal of the barren truth. Disappointment unleashes self-punishing passions. Scaevola glories in his error in the very act that makes him powerless to put it right . . . [29] 'So, what do you demand from us in the end?' our more generous interlocutors often ask. And we do not dare to reply as we should: 'greatness', that is, 'truth'. Others instead, perhaps more intelligent, citing Valéry's Pindar, say: 'Do not ask for an immortal life; take on works that it is granted you to finish'[30]—to them, one knows not how to reply. The aim and writing of criticism, which first moved towards the object and the public, towards 'testable' discourse, now retreats to the diary, to confession—the pretext that is, yet again. Soon enough we arrive at the memories of the manuscript, the bottle beyond the grave.[31] We drift towards what we most detested, that limbo where old enemies, mixed up with old comrades, smile with scorn or regret. All that is left is the hope, not at all groundless, that in spite of it all, some of our letters from prison, scrawled on the back of failed operational plans or projects for breached fortifications, will bear witness, *if read on both sides of the sheet*, to an objective truth that we did not know—or only glimpsed in our dreams—we possessed.

1960

Notes

Original publication: 'Otto domande sulla critica letteraria italiana' [Eight Questions on Italian Literary Criticism], *Nuovi Argomenti* 6(44–5) (May–August 1960). The other respondents to the questionnaire were Cesare Cases, Armanda Guiducci, Eugenio Montale, Alberto Moravia, Carlo Salinari, Sergio Solmi and Elémire Zolla. The range and significance of the participants testifies to the intense public attention lavished around this time upon the problems of literary criticism, at a time when national traditions were being tested by the irruption of structuralist and semiotic methods (1960, among other things, saw the translation of Roland Barthes's *Writing Degree Zero* into Italian). On *Nuovi Argomenti*, see the unnumbered note on p. 91 in this volume. [Trans.]

1 Georg Lukács, 'The Writer and the Critic' in *Writer and Critic and Other Essays* (A. Kahn ed. and trans.) (London: Merlin, 1970), p. 196.

2 Ibid., p. 198. [Translation modified.]

3 Giulio Preti (1911–72), philosopher who played an important role in the introduction of phenomenology, logical positivism and the philosophy of language into Italy, in the ambit of a lifelong critique of the idealist orientation of Italian thought. [Trans.]

4 Pietro Citati (1930–), writer and literary critic. [Trans.]

5 *il contemporaneista* [Trans.]

6 Renato Serra (1884–1915), Emilio Cecchi (1884–1966), Pietro Pancrazi (1893–1952), Giuseppe De Robertis (1888–1963), literary critics. [Trans.]

7 Geno Pampaloni (1918–2001), journalist and literary critic. [Trans.]

8 A reference to the Bible, John 12:31: 'Now is the judgement of this world: now shall the prince of this world be cast out.' [Trans.]

9 Cesare Cases (1920–2005), Germanist and Marxist literary critic, Lukács scholar and lifelong friend and interlocutor of Fortini; Giorgio Bàrberi Squarotti (1929), literary critic and poet; Luigi Baldacci (1930–2002), literary critic. [Trans.]

10 See Robert Escarpit, *Sociologie de la littérature* (Paris: PUF, 1958).

11 The Grand Almoner, or *Grand aumônier*, was the officer in charge of the religious branch of the French royal household under the *Ancien Régime*. Jacques-Bénigne Bossuet (1627–1704), French bishop and theologian, renowned for his sermons and funeral orations as well as for his defence of absolutism and the divine right of kings. [Trans.]

12 General Confederation of Italian Industry, the national chamber of commerce and employers' federation, a major force in Italian politics and the proprietor of the newspaper *Il Sole 24 Ore*. [Trans.]

13 A reference to an episode narrated in Johann Wolfgang von Goethe's *Wilhelm Meister's Travels Years, or the Renunciants* in *Goethe's Works, Volume 8* (Thomas Carlyle trans.) (London: Anthological Society, 1901), p. 207. [Trans.]

14 Charles Augustin Sainte-Beuve (1804–69), French literary critic. Close to Victor Hugo and his circle, he was the target of Marcel Proust's posthumously published *Contre Sainte-Beuve*. [Trans.]

15 A reference to Theodor W. Adorno, 'The Essay as Form' in *Notes to Literature* (Shierry Weber Nicholsen trans.) (New York: Columbia University Press, 1991), pp. 3–23. [Trans.]

16 Carlo Muscetta (1912–2004), Marxist literary critic and intellectual. [Trans.]

17 Lucien Goldmann (1913–70), French Marxist philosopher and sociologist of literature of Romanian origin. His masterpiece, *The Hidden God*, which was translated by Fortini and Luciano Amodio into Italian (*Pascal e Racine. Studio sulla visione tragica nei "Pensieri" di Pascal e nel teatro di Racine*, Milan: Lerici, 1961), is discussed later

in the essay 'Deus Absconditus', pp. 311–18 in this volume. It is likely that Fortini met Goldmann via Cesare Cases in Zurich in 1943. See Alessandro La Monica, 'Franco Fortini a Zurigo. "La guerra a Milano" e altri inediti', *L'ospite ingrato* (27 October 2008), available at: http://goo.gl/2nzd8v (last accessed on 13 August 2016) [Trans.]

18 *sistemazione* [Trans.]

19 'Charms can draw down the very moon from the sky.' Virgil, *Bucolica: Ecloga Octava*. [Trans.]

20 'Whose realm, also his religion.' The political-theological principle whereby the religion of the ruler should determine the religion of the ruled. Adopted at the Peace of Augsburg between Catholic and Protestant forces in 1555. [Trans.]

21 Carlo Cassola (1917–87), novelist, best known for *La ragazza di Bube* (1960). For Fortini's estimation of his work, see 'Di Cassola' in *Saggi italiani*, now in *Saggi ed epigrammi*, pp. 676–90. [Trans.]

22 Cesare Pavese (1908–50), novelist, poet, translator and editor at Einaudi. See Fortini, 'Di Pavese' in *Saggi italiani*, pp. 665–72. [Trans.]

23 The friendship and critical—oftentimes polemical—dialogue with Italo Calvino (1923–85) accompanies a large swathe of Fortini's writing life. Fortini reviewed several of Calvino's works, and writes about Calvino in, among others, the posthumous *Un giorno o l'altro* (Marianna Marrucci and Valentina Tinacci eds) (Macerata: Quodlibet, 2006), pp. 168, 495, 507–10, and *Breve secondo novecento*, now in *Saggi ed epigrammi*, pp. 1137–40. For their captivating correspondence, which intermingles sympathy and contrast, see *L'ospite ingrato, Annuario del Centro Studi Franco Fortini* I (1998) as well as the letters to Fortini in Italo Calvino, *Letters, 1941–1985* (London: Penguin, 2014). Calvino, in turn, reviewed Fortini's first poetry collection, *Foglio di via e altri versi* (Turin: Einaudi, 1946) and his novel *Agonia di Natale* (Turin: Einaudi, 1948; 2nd EDN *Giovanni e le mani*, Turin: Einaudi, 1972). See Italo Calvino, '*Foglio di via* di Franco Fortini', *L'Unità* (14 July 1946), now in *Saggi ed epigrammi*, pp. 1057–60. [Trans.]

24 Carlo Emilio Gadda, *Quer pasticciaccio brutto de via Merulana* [*That Awful Mess on the Via Merulana*], 1946/1957. With its linguistic pluralism and 'baroque' expressionism, which sought to register an irreducibly complex reality ('that awful mess'), Gadda's book

marked a crucial departure from neo-realism. For Fortini's own critical estimation, see 'Gadda' and 'Gadda 2' in *Breve secondo novecento*, now in *Saggi ed epigrammi*, pp. 1146–49. [Trans.]

25 Alberto Moravia, *La romana*, 1947. English translation: *The Woman of Rome* (Lydia Holland trans.) (New York: Farrar, Straus and Giroux, 1949). [Trans.]

26 Giuseppe Tomasi di Lampedusa, *Il gattopardo*, 1958. English translation: *The Leopard* (Archibald Colquhoun trans.) (London: Vintage, 2007). See Fortini, 'Contro "Il Gattopardo' [Against the Leopard] in *Saggi italiani*, pp. 720–30. [Trans.]

27 'God will take her by the finger to lead her to port.' Last line of the poem 'La bouteille à la mer' (The Bottle to the Sea) by Alfred de Vigny. [Trans.]

28 The analogy is to the preparatory drawings (called cartoons), *cartoni*, that the likes of Raphael would produce, and on the basis of which the assistants in their workshop, *gli aiuti*, would, for example make tapestries. [Trans.]

29 A reference to the Roman legend of Gaius Mucius Scaevola who, captured by Etruscans in the process of trying to assassinate their king Porsena, thrust his hand into a sacrificial fire without a grimace of pain to prove his courage and contempt for the suffering of the body. [Trans.]

30 Paul Valéry takes as the epigraph of his poem *Le Cimetière Marin* the lines from Pindar: 'Do not, my soul, seek immortal life, but exhaust the field of the possible.' [Trans.]

31 Fortini is crossing François-René de Chateaubriand's *Mémoires d'Outre-tombe* with Edgar Allan Poe's 'MS. Found in a Bottle'. [Trans.]

III

Clarifications

1. The so-called 'literary ontology of the *Novecento*'[1] was a small myth at the level and to the benefit of a restricted circle of authors and critics from the 1930s.[2] Some of us, myself included, were lucky enough to have our literary activity coincide with the criticism of that myth and of the taste of that decade. Between 1948 and 1952, when the restoration also made itself felt in literature, it seemed futile to take up that argument again, so patent were the aims of those solemn sacerdotal gesticulations. Today those same men can even strike 'progressive' attitudes; they have already fulfilled their servile duty.

The idea that the literature, especially the poetry, of our century has developed according to special criteria and characteristics that are absolutely innovative in contrast with the preceding epoch, making it possible to compile a 'canon', has long been advocated by critics like Bo, Ferrata, Anceschi and many others.[3] But who takes it seriously any more? Attacked from all sides, over the past 15 years its own partisans have substantially corrected it. In the beginning of the twentieth century, taste silently shifted from the Florentines to Gozzano, Campana took the (modest) place that belonged to him, next to Jahier one could now also read Michelstaedter, Rebora became a central figure, a Tessa or a Clemente were no longer just dull figures from the suburbs and provinces.[4] Reluctantly, the knowledge dawned that in the 30s, a poet of Noventa's stature had been active, and that Pavese had also written *Lavorare stanca*.[5] The *Novecento* schema was shattered. Too much, we could even say.

Because when certain categories appear to have been left behind, one of the self-defence tactics adopted by those who had first erected them is to negate them all, to shuffle the cards. Today, in any case, the category of the literary *Novecento*, its 'ontologism', its 'absolutism', appear to me as unusable polemical formulas, nothing but expedient straw men.

The mistake of the review *Officina*[6] and of so much *anti-Novecento* polemic—a mistake, I must say, that was *not* my own—was to ignore the extent to which our 'literary *Novecento*' was but an episode in late-symbolist and avant-garde European literary culture. To criticize the irrationalism and mysticism of that poetics, and therefore the conception of the world of the philosophy (and politics) from which it originated, meant opening up a discussion about contemporary Europe, its historical roots and prospects. This is what *Officina* could not and did not want to do. Its polemic against the twentieth-century right was 10 years too late; what made it appear new was the simultaneous polemic against commitment and social realism.[7] It was no accident that it tended to suggest a poetics that was 'civic' but 'uncommitted' to political factions. (Luckily, the Centre Left,[8] taking on and then liquidating the spectre of anti-fascism, now suddenly shows how easily satisfied some of my dear friends were back then.) An inquiry into the European origins of the Italian *Novecento* would have helped us to understand, for example, that literary and artistic currents that were marked by a deep and serious irrationalist vocation dominated and continued to dominate the field in Europe, in the name of cultures and philosophies that did not in the least lay claim to idealism. Next to them, their Italian counterparts appeared as so many residua of a neo-classicist common sense. Neither Proust nor Joyce, neither Kafka nor Musil, to mention the first and habitual names that spring to mind, came from an idealist tradition. Every defensive manoeuvre has been worthwhile, as long it allowed one not to see the class structures of modern literature and not to have to draw the consequences—which are not necessarily those of crude negation. Rather, those consequences lead both the 'committed' and the 'uncommitted' much deeper into a zone of severity with no escape and no deceit.

2. It is false to say that in the immediate postwar period (1945–48) to speak of *engagement*[9] meant to register or support the subordination of literature to politics. This argument is (and was) the self-interested invention of scholars who already aimed at political restoration and only secondarily at literary restoration. It was used by Bo, and many others, against the literature of so-called neo-realism, which saw itself as ideologically close to the political left. That invention (the fellow traveller of a kind of local intransigence) amounted to making people believe that the poetics of the authors who had come onto the literary scene just after the war was not just violently heteronomous but, rather, directly subordinated to (communist) politics. Between 1947 and 1950, the Italian restoration had an interest in confusing the term *engagement* with the most foolish Zhdanovism. In 1948, Vittorini, with the idealist and evasive motto 'art is a natural *engagement*', unintentionally falsified the meaning of the struggle waged by his journal *Politecnico* against the political control of Central Committees and, though he had no reason to fear either prison or death, stepped back in line. In the spirit of compromise, the Central Committees both spoke and didn't speak; they preached artistic-literary Zhdanovism to the less canny and permitted a kind of limited freedom to the more clever.

But the notion of *engagement*, which is broader than its French-existential meaning, was not really born with the Second World War and the Resistance. Let us imagine that it had never in fact existed; two-thirds of our century's most important poetry would become incomprehensible to us.

So *which* Italian writers accepted the function and privilege of being 'pipers' of the Party? Here too we have to dispel a fable that has been widely spread among the young by some far-from-disinterested teachers. The call for civic responsibility in culture and the criticism of the taste and poetics of the decade 1932–42—since this is really what we're dealing with—do not coincide either chronologically or conceptually with the French watchword of literary *engagement*; in any case, the latter does not coincide in the least with the subordination of literature to the propagandistic contingencies of a particular politics. It suffices to recall the extremely violent communist opposition to the *engagé* Sartre, whom the Soviet press called 'a hyena with a typewriter' and whom the Italian Communist press happily depicted as a pig. Again, aside from a few socialist and communist journalists and commentators, who among the writers supported or practised the subordination of literature to politics? Back then, it was very clear what the abstract polarizations of the Cold War were obscuring: that the social and political participation of the literary work takes place in the moments of its genesis or its function, that is, *before* or *after* its creation. And *because* of this, the demand for radical transformations of society grew stronger, and for the poet's work too. Those transformations would act as decisive components in the author–work–reader circuit, in its first and third moments. In January 1946, Pavese, just to pick an example, had already written *Di una nuova letteratura* (On a New Literature); Vittorini's letter to Togliatti was written prior to January 1947. Nor are we dealing with exceptions. All one needs to do is go back and read what was being written at the time in the publications of the Left. You will find that almost invariably what are denounced as the greatest sins of the fascist era are the subordination of culture to political expediency and the dissociation of the former from latter. No one would have imagined that 'politics' could have the restrictive, negative meaning of a propagandistic manipulation or an impassioned moralism. Politics stood for 'the life of societies', for our *own* life.

3. The idea that the literature of the *ventennio*[10] or, better, the literature of artistic prose and lyric poetry, first *novecentesca* and then hermetic, had represented the 'Italian path' to cultural anti-fascism was not born with the restoration that took place after 1948. It is instead a pivotal idea, a myth scrupulously prepared *before the fall of fascism*, grounded on the equivocations of anti-fascism, namely, on its frontism, which saw the likes of Gide and Brecht align on the same side. That idea circulated in unwritten form during the war among that skein of authors and writers who were close to liberal or liberal-socialist anti-fascism. Its most accomplished and authoritative formulation, considering the context and the moment, is to be found in an essay by Gianfranco Contini, from the Swiss journal *Lettres*,[11] introducing an anthology of Italian literature ranging from Campana to Vittorini. In that text he explicitly argued that Italian cultural 'resistance' should be located in the refusal of our best writers to put one's mouth to the social and Tyrtaeic trumpet.[12] In postwar Italy, that thesis became almost official. No political force or organized group emerged to refute it; no one openly reversed the thesis to affirm that, beyond Mussolini's fascism, there was a class and a generalized ideology, and that the literature of abstention and ascesis, of the 'inner realm' or *das innere Reich*, was the faithful voice, the pious mirror of that class that had made and unmade fascisms. This was also because not a few among those whose joint responsibility *ex silentio* should have been registered were, at least temporarily, on the communist side or fellow travellers; they were authoritative and influential, tied to all the others by bonds of friendship or intrigue, and communist cultural politics was then, as always thereafter, largely 'national' in kind. In a country where one could find no more than a dozen university professors ready to refuse the oath of allegiance to the *Fascio*, it was absurd to speak of a purge of the literati; instead, they were duly promoted to the rank of resisters. What's more serious is that this contributed to obscuring, retarding, blocking and ultimately distorting the historical–political debate on fascism. And on anti-fascism.

4. How can one pretend to ignore that the arrest of the revolutionary development of the most consistent type of anti-fascism, the Marxist one—notwithstanding its incredibly serious deficiencies—is the economic-political fact that has allowed the Italian cultural caste (in the name of conservative, liberal and catholic forces, but not without joint socialist and communist responsibility) to recuperate, almost intact, the three or four decades that go from 1920–25 to yesterday? Now that almost two decades separate us from the age of fascism, we must warn the young from the most dangerous illusion: the one that tends to make people believe today that political and cultural responsibility can be kept apart in what concerns the faulty evaluations of fascism and anti-fascism. I myself took every opportunity back then to urge going beyond appearances and framing in terms of history and philosophy what seemed, but was not, a matter resolved in terms of power.[13] Today, however, I must say that every belated trial against the literature and poetry of the 1920s and 30s that does not above all involve a critique of the politics (both cultural and non-cultural) of the subsequent period, that is, of the period that has taken us from 1945 to now, and does not contain and constitute a political proposal in its own right, is a sheer waste of time.

Historical justice cannot be done unless the future too is engaged. The responsibility of others, past for our present can exist only to the extent that we come to be responsible for the future. Choosing descendants means choosing a tradition.

That is why we can, if we so wish, forego thinking, saying or alluding towards what image of humanity, nation or man our research as men of science or poetry, and our struggle as partisan men[14] should strive; we can forego knowing if that thing which has been dubbed as Socialism (and which and how and when) was or is about to become an alternative to our global, Italian, individual history, at least from 1914 until tomorrow; we can pretend—some among us do so marvellously well—that the very problem of Socialism (production and culture, pedagogy and institutions, ethics and economics) either no longer exists or is a problem for specialists, or perhaps it is a problem for us but only as specialists or 'citizens'.

'Who moves us?' 'Where should we be moving towards?' These questions may be wrong. We can avoid posing them or answering them. How many around us, and among the best, have not already done so! But let us at least listen to the silence that surrounds us.

1962

Notes

Original publication: 'I giudici naturali ovvero contro gli stoici' [The Natural Judges, or, Against Stoics], *Rendiconti* 4–6 (November 1962). [Trans.]

1 *Novecento,* literally 'twentieth century', but here also refers to a trend in Italian letters. Fortini closely linked the term to the notion of 'the modern' and subjected it to trenchant criticism. [Trans.]

2 The expression, already frequent in the literary review *Officina,* reappears in the piece by P. Bonfiglioli ('La storiografia delle riviste e la «Schuldfrage» del Novecento' [The Historiography of Journals and the *Schuldfrage* of the Twentieth Century]) in *Rendiconti* 2–3 (June–September 1961): 51–69. These 'clarifications' are drawn from my response in *Rendiconti,* from which I have omitted what could have been perceived as polemic against Bonfiglioli.

3 Carlo Bo (1911–2001), Catholic literary critic and chancellor of the University of Urbino from 1947 to 2001, theoretician of hermeticism, on which he published an influential essay 'Letteratura come vita' [Literature as Life] in the journal *Frontespizio* in 1936; Giansiro Ferrata (1907–86), literary critic and series editor for the publisher Mondadori; Luciano Anceschi (1911–95), literary critic and phenomenology-oriented philosopher, he defended the poetic tradition of hermeticism and his journal *Il Verri* (founded in 1956) played a prominent role in the rise of the neo-avant-garde. In his *L'ospite ingrato,* Fortini had two epigrams for Carlo Bo: '18. [For Carlo Bo]: Carlo Bo does not like my verses. / My verses do not like Carlo Bo'; and '107. Carlo Bo: No.' (*Saggi ed epigrammi,* pp. 888, 1016). [Trans.]

4 Guido Gozzano (1883–1916), poet linked by some literary historians to the *crepuscolarismo* (from '*crepuscolo*', twilight) movement,

of special significance for his narrative poetry; Dino Campana (1885–1932), poet and author of *Orphic Songs* (1914); Piero Jahier (1884–1966), poet and translator, an important author during Fortini's teenage years; Carlo Michelstaedter (1887–1910), writer and philosopher, author of *La persuasione e la rettorica* [*Persuasion and Rhetoric*] (1910). As Luca Lenzini notes in his preface to Fortini's *Saggi ed epigrammi* (pp. *xxxii–xxxiii*) Michaelstaedter's sense of the tragic would strongly resonate with young Fortini, as evidenced by his early article, 'Su Michelstaedter' (1938–39) and later reflections such as 'Un biglietto di Michelstaedter' [A Note from Michelstaedter] (1974) in *Saggi ed epigrammi*, pp. 1199–1203, 465–570. Clemente Rebora (1885–1957), poet. See Fortini, '*Frammenti lirici* di Clemente Rebora' [Clemente Rebora's *Lyrical Fragments*] in *Saggi ed epigrammi*, pp. 1706–52; Delio Tessa (1886–1939), poet who wrote in Milanese dialectic; Vittorio Clemente (1895–1975), poet. [Trans.]

5 Cesare Pavese, *Hard Labor* (William Arrowsmith trans.) (New York: Ecco Press, 1979). [Trans.]

6 A journal of poetry and literature founded by Pier Paolo Pasolini, Roberto Roversi and Francesco Leonetti, published from 1955 to 1959. Fortini collaborated with *Officina*, and was briefly part of its editorial board, in the context of which he was often spurred to polemics with Pasolini that would occupy him up to his friend's murder and beyond. For a critical introduction and anthology of the review, see Gian Carlo Ferretti, *'Officina'. Cultura, letteratura e politica negli anni cinquanta* [*Officina*: Culture, Literature and Politics in the 1950s] (Turin: Einaudi, 1975). For Fortini's arguments with Pasolini, see the correspondence and commentary included in Fortini, *Attraverso Pasolini* [Through Pasolini] (Turin: Einaudi, 1993). [Trans.]

7 In October 1958, for an internal discussion in the review *Officina*, I had written the following: 'I don't think it's appropriate to focus the critical activity of an entire year of the publication on a critique of methodology. [. . .] I think that the steps that need to be taken require taking for granted the outcome of the anti-avant-garde and anti-*novecentesca* polemic; and to go beyond it, identifying the 'inheritance', which is to say, the lineage of works, not just Italian

ones, which we consider to constitute our ancestry. This problem of heredity is of very great moment because it can, in most likelihood, lead us to recognize the non-existence of a properly Italian inheritance, following the historical fractures experienced by our country; in other words, the recognition of almost symbolic ancestors belonging in fact to all the European inheritances. Moreover, this also means developing an approach to all the major contemporary literary currents. [. . .] It's a matter of exercising one's critical judgement about contemporaries through a system of references consisting of rapid allusions to literary currents and authors, both national and foreign, which we consider important. The force of a group that aims at renewal is measured by its capacity to crystallize acceptances and refusals along determinate axes. [. . .] Our essay-writing, precisely because it is essay-writing, is not a rigorously scientific discourse but, instead, a literary one; which is to say, it is formal, factual, and thus an example, a proposal, a challenge or an allegory at the level of its own language, meaning that it is contemporary, placed between the objectivity of a tendentially homogeneous and univocal critical vocabulary and the subjectivity of an individual expressive-communicative vocation. [. . .] What sets us apart from the neo-empiricism of Calvino–Vittorini and a widespread neo-positivism is not simply the affirmation of a priority of culture over literary expression; it is the will to practice this thesis of priority in the course of the exercise of criticism . . .'.

8 *Centro Sinistra*, a reference to governments led by Christian Democracy with the support, whether active or passive, of the Italian Socialist Party, PSI, among other parties. The year 1962, in which this essay was published, saw the formation of Amintore Fanfani's government with the crucial abstention of the PSI, which had previously been in opposition. The first government of the Centre Left proper, with participation of the Socialists, was led by Aldo Moro in late 1963. [Trans.]

9 In French in the original. [Trans.]

10 Refers to the two decades of Fascist rule (1922–45). [Trans.]

11 [Gianfranco Contini, 'Introduction à la littérature italienne contemporaine', later included in *Altri esercizi. 1942-1971* (Turin: Einaudi, 1972).] *Lettres* was printed in Geneva; its editorial board included

P. Courthion, Ch. Guyot, G. Haldas, M. Reymond, A. Rousseaux and J. Starobinski. Contini's essay was published in the fourth issue of 1944. [It was around this time that Starobinski and Fortini first met. They would carry on a correspondence, now held in the Archivio Fortini.]

12 A term derived from Tyrtaeus, the Spartan war poet of the seventh century BCE. [Trans.]

13 For many years, before and after the war, Giacomo Noventa rightly insisted on the need for greater study of the 'theories of fascism', namely, of the authentic and pre-eminent forms of culture and thought of the first 20 years of the century in our country (together with their sources and their foreign equivalents) that had not so much laid the groundwork for fascist ideology as interpreted a social reality that fascist solutions had allowed to prevail over other realities.

14 *uomini di parte* [Trans.]

IV

Cunning as Doves

1. Those articles in the fourth issue of *Il menabò*[1] that reflect on the mutations induced in human beings by the objects of contemporary industry forget that the object is the sensuous and the sensuous is human activity, praxis.[2]

They claim: 'Industry drowns us in production, in its new "things", provoking all sorts of nauseas, estrangements, mistaken fixations, monstrous relations with ourselves and others'. Yet I've always thought that the fascinated contemplation of a condition of the working class envisaged purely in terms of the man–machine relationship, along with that other enchanted pastime, the immersion into 'objectivity', were two typical errors (or perhaps just one) of non-dialectical materialism. In Marx's descriptions of consuming sub-humanity, the strongest stress was always put on liberatory action. (And there's no work of anticipation, bordering on science fiction, which does not insist instead on the reduction of man to thing, or on the transformation of the thing into a horrid creature; whence the importance accorded to the animal, that animated 'thing'.) Do we want to shed light on the relationship between object and user, object and producer? Why then obscure the human origin of objects? Were they receptive to citations from Marx, I could remind some friends of the third thesis on Feuerbach,[3] where the enlightenmental and paternalistic consequences of that error are foreseen, all the way to the modern crusades of architects and designers, and the sociological angst of those who make horrified condemnations of contemporary man, plunged into the quicksand of commodities, just so they can avoid remembering that all of this presupposes man's own condition as a commodity. In Chaplin's old film, *Modern Times*, what is tragicomic is not the assembly line or the Tramp's obvious and anarchic reaction but the seriousness of the other workers, their interest in the proper flow of production, their conviction that they're doing their duty, because they're not alienated from the machines but from the owners of the machines. (This is one of the many points of contact between Chaplin and Brecht.)

Do we need to recall that industry produces not just objects but also human relationships and 'ideas'? 'The same spirit that constructs railways with the hands of workers, constructs philosophical systems in the brains of philosophers'.[4] Among those ideas is also the one that things have a decisive importance for man, not as an answer to a 'human' need but 'in themselves'. ('The Fetish Character of the Commodity and its Secret' in *Capital, Volume 1,* Book 1, Chapter 4 was published in 1867; and Lukács's essay on reification and the consciousness of the proletariat was printed in 1923.)

2. The writer (like anyone else, for that matter) starts from a sensuous-phenomenal domain that is already organized in accordance with schemata that become all the more apparently objective the more they are in fact passively endured. These are the schemata of culture, ideology and world-view. They pertain, in the writer's case, to that particular type of (class) tension and contradiction that in our world accompany the components of that sector of intellectual activity, and those who characterize themselves as artists or writers. As a consequence of that tension, and to the degree that he is an authentic writer and artist (to the extent that this is his specific task), he consciously assumes, challenges and can overcome (always within the limits of self-consciousness) received ideologies, world-views and standards of judgement, as well as inherited languages.

This relationship between passivity and activity, devotion and innovation, begins to be produced along with the dawning awareness of that apparently superficial occasion which is the 'theme' or 'object' of the work. I do not wish here, even cursorily, to take up the problem of choice in what concerns literary themes again; in what the writers of *Il menabò* disparagingly refer to as 'iconography'. But, instead of recalling the rather ample contemporary consensus about the crucial importance of the explicit subject (or theme) of a literary work, we should recall how for every different and possible 'level' of reading of a work there are corresponding intentions, themes and subjects internal to that work. That way we will avoid the opposite yet kindred mistakes on the one hand, of an aestheticizing underestimation of the explicit, primary, manifest 'subject' and on the other, of an overestimation due to simple 'sociological contingencies' (the literature on the 'condition of the working class', for example, or on the 'sea of objects' . . . [5]); recognizing instead that *if there exists a privileged theme, namely, a 'theme of our age', there is no privileged 'subject' that can convey this theme.* Take a quick example: the conflict between the leftovers of the *Ancien Régime* and national-bourgeois society is certainly the privileged theme in the European reality of the Restoration, but it is no less at home in the metaphors of the historical novel than in those of the novel of character and mores; that theme is not to be found in Manzoni more than in Balzac despite the absolute difference in their subject-matter. I say this in order to argue that for the writer the world of industry, whatever its importance may be (is it necessary to say that it is decisive? that it is the 'narrow gate'?), is not (by comparison to other parts of the social body, the peasant world, say, or that of the craftsman) an elective path into the 'theme of our age' and, further, into the plenitude of artistic representation. This is true, if anything, of the very general historical theme of the 'fundamental conflict' of which the world of industry is both a manifestation and a component, albeit an essential one. Today, and in the present condition of our society, we really do not need the historical novel to know history, the psychological novel to know psychology, philosophical poetry to know philosophy or political theatre to know politics. We must apologize for these platitudes. Or, better said, we may continue to need such genres in two opposite ways: the first, regressive and conservative, mere information dressed up in literary garb; the second, insofar as it is poetic, is in some way also prophetic. The latter is related to the power of *knowledge* contained in artistic form, not to its occasion or pretext. It is the work of art's final word, and not its first, to *also* be history, psychology, philosophy and politics. We must negate with all our energies the false progressivism according to which industrial reality, in its moment of production or consumption, needs to be given literary expression because it is 'important'. It is particularly imperative for someone like me who affirms the primacy of industrial production in the determination of our social destiny, who places the *whole* of the *verifiable* duty of men in the identification and destruction of the capitalist roots of our society (and thereby of a mode of production and appropriation) to react against the current literary 'progressivism'. The latter blackmails every position and every consciousness that truly wish to negate the present society, putting forth elements that can indeed be used for the sake of knowledge-action but alongside ever-heavier doses of reformist banalities—which in practice means diversionary ones. Such 'progressivism' has always justified itself, moreover, with the vile argument of the backwardness of the masses. Backwardness compared to what? Compared to the radical-progressivism of reformist leaderships, incapable of understanding the 'progress' of the masses except as an 'ascent' to their own level . . . (The adjectives to label these assertions of mine already exist, 'sectarian' is one of them. Indeed, I believe we have been suffering for some time from a lack of 'sectarianism', that is, of the aptitude to *separation*, the only path to new unities.)

Every progress in the so-called scientific knowledge of society appears matched by a diminution in literature's informative capacities and an increase in its metaphorical latitude. And as has always been the case in the history of all literatures, a poem on little birds in the woods—in its structure, internal articulations and semantic tension—can interpret and therefore *formally* overcome a given 'world-view', the reflection of a given class relation and productive regime, and thus be the bearer of a mediated practical energy as great as that of other figurations of 'private history', without thereby exhausting the truth of a work of poetry.

So the relationship between the world of industrial production (or of consumption, to the extent that it is specifically linked to industry) and the aspect that language evokes by direct or indirect representation in literary work will interest, if at all, only the historian of society and mores. A relation that instead concerns literature as such is the one between the human relations engendered by industry and the writer as man, citizen, producer and consumer—in that biographic experience which is so strangely omitted from current considerations on this theme and which implies, among other things, a sociology of the men of letters as professionals. A debate on industry-and-literature would benefit from a reflection, perhaps a statistical one, on the changes (in my view considerable) undergone by the economic and social status of writers in Italian society over the past two decades. It is very likely that the personal relationship with industry as a source of income has become far more widespread and decisive, if not for the writer who lives from his pen then at least for his whole intellectual environment—in which he frequently socializes, from which he often receives his commissions and by which he has been named as a writer. Just compare this environment today with the literary or cultivated world of 50 years ago. Film, radio, TV, major newspapers, press offices and corporate research centres: the writer today no longer depends, whether as a teacher or civil servant, on the state as the representative of the collective that could bestow the chair, the appointment, the funds; nor from agrarian rent, with its air of aristocratic eternity; nor from the print struggles of militant political groups, but directly from the private or state culture industry. However, at least in the ambit of publishing—due to the complexity, subdivisions and articulations of its productive mechanism—this still allows for the illusion and individualism of craft. The old phrase from the *Manifesto* is realized to the letter: the writer is waged or salaried by one part of society. Socrates' ironic request has been realized.[6] But the Prytaneum today is subsidized by an industrial conglomerate, according to the well-known principle that 'what is good for General Motors is also good for Athens'. The difference with socialist societies is that the capitalist ones finance their own opposition, nullifying negation; while in socialist society, since every opposition is immediately political, it represents a possibility of real antithesis, a 'thorn in the flesh', a real contradiction.

3. It is very difficult to debate using Vittorini's terms, if 'archaic' and 'old' are for him synonyms of negative, and 'new' of positive. Is a tree archaic and a TV new? That is a kind of reasoning that doesn't cease to surprise me.

Likewise with 'ideology' and 'things'. Ideology, in his essay, never means what it usually does in historical and philosophical language, whether Marxist or otherwise; instead, it is nothing less than the operation of the intellect or 'rational consciousness'—'culture', even. Needless to say, the meaning here is still pejorative (but very different from the traditional one of 'defensive formation'); 'ideology' and 'ideological' here mean 'thought', 'science', 'reasoning' and 'mediation', but also 'abstractness', 'formalism', 'bookish', 'politicking' and 'dogmatism'. In other words, the negative. 'Things', instead, represent health and candidness. Vittorini does not just desire to privilege immediacy; he ultimately wants to conclude that, having been replaced by the categories of Old and New, history does not exist; relations of mere cause and effect do but they are necessarily incomplete, and no one should ask themselves—under pain of the soul's death penalty, namely, 'ideology'—what modern industry lives off, who animates it, who produces it, whom it benefits; to put it briefly, the subject-matter of contemporary economics and politics. The world of industry is contrasted with that of nature simply in order to inform us that the latter has been definitively replaced by the former; a conclusion that every historicism had already reached. But then industry just stands there, contemplated in its quality as a 'thing', governed by opaque 'natural' laws, like a hippogriff or a dinosaur. It is not by chance that Vittorini (precisely at the point where he grasps the difference between the informative-descriptive moment of industrial life and the interpretation of the changes effected 'in every other kind of thing', that is, in the entire social body by modern industry) is only able to speak of new 'objects' and new 'gestures'. He thereby accentuates, with this updated 'thingism',[7] his erstwhile behaviourism, instead of speaking of new relations among men, that is, of new feelings, values, thoughts; terms which to his ear ring of the psychology he despises. Vittorini does not seem ever to have gotten over the knot tying empiricism and spiritualism (the old category of 'life'). But he is a writer; in other words, he expresses himself also and in particular by hammering continuously on the same point. Instead, someone like Scalia[8]—whose formation and character are wholly different—has returned to that knot by dint of what to my mind is an excess of culturalist impatience.

According to Vittorini, on one side we would have things (nature or industry) and on the other the writer, who is all the more authentic insofar as he manages to establish a direct and vital intuitive relationship with things; linguistic facts would then be the expressive metaphor of that experience. Inasmuch as it pre-exists and informs every new experience, what language bears within itself by way of already-thought thought, that is, by way of inheritance, would be mere repetition, falsification, academicism and death; whence an absolute accessibility of language and, in the end, the ill-famed (surrealist) transmutation of abstract subjectivity into abstract objectivity.

It is true that in this piece by Vittorini, 'industry' stands for 'technics', that is, for the 'way of making things'. Who was that trade unionist who told me, some time back, of the marvellous collections of short documentary films on individual productive operations that German unions employ in their discussions with business owners? Those trade unions are what they are—mere instruments of class collaboration—to the exact degree that they accept the separation between the technical moment and the political or all-embracing one. To equate industry with technics (or with technology, to employ the common and telltale Anglicism) means conferring upon industry a rational fatedness that it does not have. It is a purely apologetic discourse. And no apologist is as effective as the one who does it in good faith.

For Scalia instead, everything is communication and sign: beneath names there is nothing. Unlike Vittorini, he does not see ideology's vice in the betrayal of authenticity but, rather, in the strange urge to revive a tension that had long been happily placated. In their writings, Vittorini and Scalia are in agreement in their stand against mediations—they want for words to be stones (Vittorini), or stones words (Scalia)—on condition that the ones and the others never be human beings, never be *history*, never be real contradiction or negation of negations. In those pages where he summarizes the current situation of the 'civilization of machines' for the man of letters, Scalia sketches out the direction of a useful and worthy experience. But that writer he invokes, who in order to write needs to have such a solid knowledge of the sociological profile of contemporary industry, would find himself unemployed, or reduced to paraphrasing science; in other words, to exercising an ornamental, if noble, subaltern function.[9] This writer would have overcome all the paradoxes of writing, along with the derisory character of the operation of literature, its ever-possible lack of justification (which is not at all the 'irrationality' that many talk about but, rather, the reflection of a missing or deficient justification, purloined but potentially recoverable, of man with regard to himself). This writer would be so useful, though free and uncommitted, as to lose any of his margin of error. In other words, he would be a non-writer.

4. Many have confined themselves to repeating Ottieri's observation according to which, when it comes to the world of industry, those who know don't speak and those who speak don't know.[10] I think the reason for this is to be sought, not especially, or not only in fearful awe but also in the fact that the absolute seriousness of productive processes and their social consequences is so great (even when, as one can legitimately hypothesize, the professional seriousness of their leadership is lacking) as to impose upon literary metaphor a very strenuous demand: industry is not *a* theme, it is the manifestation of *the* theme called capitalism. This is especially the case the greater (and growing) is the extramural importance of modern capitalist industry. The accusation of archaism that Vittorini has levied against American and Russian naturalist novelists of industry means, I think, that those writers spoke about a world of industries to a world that did not yet entirely belong to industry; while it is increasingly difficult today to speak of an industrial truth as distinct from the general truth of society. If anything, 'sociological consciousness' should lead us to conclude that we are speaking of industry when we speak about anything else, and that the difficulty in speaking about it is no different than the difficulty we encounter when we really wish to speak about something true. The mystery of political economy, which Marx had already discussed, is today (through the complete triumph of industry in society and its imminent or already consummated coincidence with the state) the very mystery of our lives, the 'essence' lying beneath the 'phenomena'.

To speak of my own affairs, I can say that the relationship with the modern factory appeared to me, right after the war, as something to tell the 'others'; and later, in some verses, as a relation between the 'inside' and the 'outside' of the factory. But the more, with the passing of our years, the neo-capitalist universe around us grew, the more it became useless to speak of the moment of the worker; it was products (plastic materials, as a typical example) that offered a key to reality. Of all the images one can propose in the world of modern production, only one has seemed to me to be able to figure—in my capacity as an author of poetic verse—something very severe, only imperfectly decipherable and rich in its ambiguity. Only one, beside the more obvious ones of the modern city or of the 'ordinary industrial countryside';[11] I mean the moment of the interruption or end of work; or rather, the moment when, with the interruption or end of the work of the factory, the historical character of the industrial landscape becomes more evident. It is the moment of the Polish October, of the great assemblies in the factories of Warsaw.[12] In the register of revolutionary decision, it reminded me of another time when—I had spoken about it in a poem—the industrial demobilizations of the postwar period had triggered violent tensions, subsequently neutralized by neo-capitalist reconstruction. I saw the 'lifeless factories' of the years 1948 to 1951 as the image and warrant of the 'slow justice accompanying us'.[13]

Let me add that today I believe one way of escaping the vulgarity of Generalized and Reformist Progressivism is the one—which I attempted in more than one of my compositions—of hinting at the recovery in a communist society of the values of pre-industrial society. Besides, they are so essential to the peoples of the Third World that no revolution can be true for them if, as Fanon tells us, it does not verify those values.

5. For some years now, and with increasing frequency, we have been the recipients of the following argument:

> Start the chronology when you wish. But, and not just in the West, consider depoliticization, indifference to

ideologies, irony about 'world-views'. Today one advances through sectoral or regional truths, eliminating metaphysical 'residues', universalistic frameworks, the snares of feeling. Anthropology and phenomenology have either absorbed or dissolved the old claims of historicism. But take note: interest in or deference towards this or that finding of the social sciences is not enough. We demand deference towards the political meaning of this new situation, that is, towards the death certificate of every revolutionary movement or, better, of the very notion of revolution. Reformism, yes—similar opportunities for everyone in the respect of liberal liberties. And an information network and opinions capable of resisting the cruder forms of the culture industry; that is, to make them less crude. The supreme good is peace; let us then promote disarmament, especially the atomic kind. But you must also recognize, with the naked eye, the consequences of this altered situation in a finally adult world, in the field of arts and letters! The revaluation of formal elements or the peace between the generation of prewar formalism and the very recent one does not really take place in the archaic formulas of 'art for art's sake'. What is required instead is a voluntary self-limitation either in contents or in addressees, or both; a genuine, systematic realization of the old dream of having done with eloquence. That literature should offer itself as a universal, which is to say, humanistic discourse—this is a dream from a pre-electronic past. Literature has come of age; it accepts without shrieks of rebellion the organizing structures imposed upon it by contemporary Western society; and considers these nigh on unchangeable. In any case, they are preferable to disorder, as your Goethe used to say. We do not want the revolt of surrealist papa's boys or the useless rehabilitation of corpses 20 years after their deportation. Having settled upon a sector of reality, literature will attack it with an analysis which is all the more rational to the extent it is arbitrary; and the operation of synthesis will be at the reader's leisure. Literature will avoid all accusations of irrationalism and intuitionism because it will be both lucid and predetermined; to the degree that it offers objects and objectivity, it will even be 'materialist'; and it has already done away with that whole sequence of post-Romantic degenerations, from expressionism to politically committed art, from surrealism to existentialism. In the rigorous sense of these terms, it will be a chapter in semantic and linguistics. Without any nostalgia for the category evoked by the adjectives, it will be more 'classical' than is generally thought; at least in what concerns its satisfaction under the assured protection of the Prince. It is ridiculous to brandish against this art (abstract, informal, objective or whatever name it may receive tomorrow) Lukács's old arguments against the avant-garde. It is true that, refusing every dialectic, this literature and this art partake in the eternal hendiadys of naturalism and symbolism; but they do so with force and irony that stem not just from modern scientific achievements but also from the certainty that by now—as Edoardo Sanguineti[14] already remarked some time ago—we have turned the avant-garde into an art for museums (and fashion houses), something as reassuring as drawing-room paintings, but which creates an order in which great and even extraordinary talents may develop. The relations with industry are by now established and clear. If they are less clear in Italy, it is because Montecatini[15] or Fiat do not yet seem directly interested in the publication of young Italian authors; but the time is near, or at least the relationship between large industry and universities or publishing is increasingly more evident. Inequalities in information rather than in development.

> The world, in any case, is compact. Men are no longer divided into classes but into strata and functions. Africa is so backward and China too distant and famished. Socialism was a fable, dreamt throughout a century. Though it has not avoided horrible sufferings, it has managed to push a part of Asia and Europe towards the technoscientific benefits evolved by the capitalist world . . .

These arguments—some, not the least significant, coming from the very milieus of Italian communist leadership—were met with important responses by C. Wright Mills, last year, in the pages of the *New Left Review*.[16] But Scalia, though he cites this prematurely deceased American sociologist, does not appear to have taken them into consideration; Vittorini neither. I do not intend to attribute to the two of them all the foregoing theses, just some of them. Each one supplements the other, in *Menabò* and beyond, so as to cover a pretty significant 'ideological' area. And so, we are back with the industry–literature relationship.

6. How is it possible to speak of industry—of large and medium, modern, neo-capitalist, Italian industry—and forget that our sources of knowledge are not down there in the bibliographies but circulate immediately inside and among us, in the form of 'views' and 'notions' (alienation, automation, costs, piecework, industrial dispute, surplus-value, proletariat, exploitation, socialism, welfare state, modern technology, etc.)? That between industry and us there stands culture, a whole culture, and that the idea or opinion that we forge about industry has no common measure with so many of our other opinions, positions and ideas about particular questions? How can we speak of industry and literature without at least agreeing on this (but it's almost everything): that the forms, modes and times of industrial production and its relations are the very form of social life, the historical container of all our content, not simply an aspect of reality? That economic structures—in our case capitalist and therefore industrial ones—are no more and no less than the social unconscious, that is, the true unconscious, the mystery of mysteries?

It would seem that this obvious Marxist premise has not, either now or ever, managed to cross the minds of the directors and editors of *Il menabò*.

In this regard, it is very important than in the unwritten premises of some authors in *Il menabò*, and then in their explicit conclusions, by 'industry' is understood *only* the complex of productive operations, with particular consideration for industrial work and for the relation between machine and worker, or the one between product and consumer. The human problems of the industrial mechanism will be kept in mind, but it is *essential* that they will deem it possible to speak of industry while bracketing the *economic* characteristics of that very industry; not least the socioeconomic laws that in a given context determine, or tend to determine, one kind of consumption rather than another (including ideological consumption, and thus *Il menabò* itself). It is *essential* that in an authoritative discussion, in a review of high literary standards, one argues about modern industry and about its relations with literary expressions speaking of alienation, reification, 'the sadness of workers', democracy at all levels and 'trans-industry', but *not* of capitalist criteria of production, the purchase of labour-power, surplus-value, capitalist planning, the relationship between investments and trade union action and so on.

This context of arguments and omissions is objectively part of the ideology that the current phase of development of neo-capitalist industry brings about in Italian society. So much so that we encounter it along a very wide front of ideologization, from certain Communist positions all the way to some Christian-Democrat ones, passing through Social Democrats and Socialists. It is worth noting that, in *Il menabò*, this ideological aroma is more redolent in the theoretical writings, while the creative ones really do not seem to have breathed it in as much.

This cannot surprise anyone who takes into consideration the successive phases through which our guiding ideologies have passed over the past 15 years. Is it or is it not in the interests of neo-capitalism or of state monopoly capitalism to avoid any objective revolutionary connection between the 'backward' demands of the Third World and the 'advanced' ones of continental proletarians? And is the price to be paid for avoiding such a connection (in keeping with a classic model that has been active in other places and times, albeit in different guises) not in fact—besides a greater proletarian share in capitalist profits—the participation of a section of the workers' leadership in entrepreneurial planning at the level of both company and state? This is among the reasons why those in France who deny the existence of common interests between the intransigent military right and the economic right in their country are not entirely wrong. It is pretty obvious, to the extent that the state in Italy is readying itself to take on functions analogous to those of large industry, that the fundamental authoritarianism stemming from those kinds of non-democratic planning will be joined by a degree of greater 'democratization' of civic life. It is easy then to anticipate the resolution of a number of obvious contradictions: for example, the well-known contradiction between trade union and political votes at Fiat will come to be resolved either in the direction of a degradation and irrelevance of the political vote or in that of the restriction of the trade union vote, so as to eliminate the need for the current 'anti-democratic' pressure. . . . I don't think I am saying anything new in stating *that the current phase of neo-capitalist development demands that a wide swathe of socialist themes come to enter the language or the tasks of industrial directorships*; in the sphere of the cultural and literary superstructure, this is evident in the liquidation of the old spiritualist and irrationalist 'right-wing' criticism, in the acceptance of sociologism as a surrogate for political discourse and in the recuperation within the reformist order of authors who until a few years ago represented not just an opposition but also an alternative. I have said elsewhere that the advent of neo-capitalism has replaced the mediation represented by political parties with the industrial-corporate mediation of publishing. But the real relation between men of letters and industry does not take place in publishing, nor indeed in the professions; it is celebrated in the intangible ideological aura generated by the corporations. And it is *superfluous* to say that the man of letters is all the less prone to admitting this, to the extent that the self-same ideology tends to proclaim that he enjoys the independence of the craftsman, and to isolate him in an 'Indian reserve' of humanity and spontaneity. Until a few years ago, there still existed those who refused collaboration or cordiality not just to the falsely repentant fascist but to their own political adversary, especially if that adversary was a public spokesperson, a responsible persuader. But those were the last icebergs of the Cold War. Today instead we witness the exact replica of the situation that obtained between 1934 and 1939 when, with the exception of the extremes represented by naive and explicitly fascist writers on the one hand, and declared anti-fascists (who in any case were silent or periphrastic) on the other, the immense majority of writers and men of culture was simultaneously fascist and anti-fascist, sometimes dining with the authorities, other times on the verge of being censured by the police or the party federation. Today Calvino spends his holidays on the shores of the sea of Objectivity and no longer notices (*masca eris et ridebis semper*!)[17] that the mask is so close-fitting as to coincide with his very face, making him resemble innumerable Italian literati and thereby assuring him equal place in our literary histories. Besides, how is one to avoid all this democratic tolerance if there's no publishing house, no literary prize, no public institution that does not impose it?

Let us then say, only somewhat in jest, that the ideological canon of many of our contemporaries appears to have become that of the basic unity and identity of the world's historical development; so much so that if specific differences are omitted or downplayed (chalking them up to historical delays or uneven development), all that remains is resemblances. Resemblances between the existing bourgeois and the bourgeois to come. The reduction of the different to the similar: that is, the reduction of socialism and communism to the liberal-capitalist tradition. 'The whole world is, or will be, one village'—thus rings another one of their principles.

Invoking the controversy over the degree to which collectivist regimes (for example, the Soviet one) impact on the condition of the working class—the degree and type of modification of the human condition induced by the collectivist structure of the socialist economy and its superstructures—the structure of Western and Italian industry will be bracketed in a discourse on 'industry and literature'. One starts from the unproven identity between the alienations, reifications, etc., in societies with capitalist and socialist structures, not in order to indicate (even if proof of this identity existed) what their central motor is and what relations it entertains with literature but simply in order to get rid of the very question. Or to substitute it with unfounded arguments, mere phrases about democratization and 'trans-industry'.

Nor is this happening only in *Il menabò*, where Vittorini has reprised his anti-historicism (though it could be said that the myth of cruel purity that was associated with his name 20 years ago is overshadowed by the other face of the same myth, that of a kind optimistic and creative corruption); and where Scalia invites literature to a historical–sociological repast of such magnitude as to send it to sleep dreaming of a democratic–scientific–literary Jacob's ladder, where everything is in everything, and vice versa. It's happening more or less everywhere, at least in Italy and France; the number keeps growing of those who tell you about Man, with an invisible capital letter, and about ever-more complex techniques to approach Him; and there rears its head, as one might expect, 'deep' Man, the human essence or condition, which turns out to be same at the assembly lines of Renault or ZiS,[18] because the cars and the productive apparatus are the same and so is the human 'nature': the union, once again, of positivist materialism and spiritualism.

(Are my criticisms facile? I know I could be mistaken. I know that the future can prove me wrong and bring to pass what Scalia and others, on the basis of some books, prophesy: the revolution without tears, the revolution without revolution, the beyond of industry thanks to the enlightened conversion of politicians to science . . .)

7. So are we no longer to inquire whether—as was indeed thought by the highest thinking of the modern age—the deepest cause of the division between men and between the parts of each individual man is still to be sought in industry, in the mode of producing and the property structure of the means of production? That is, in the most powerful cause of the tensions and paradoxes on which literature and poetry thrive? We are no longer allowed to think, it seems, that that cause is the power of man over man that is exercised today in the accumulation and reproduction of capital.

No one yet dares to treat the apparent attenuation of ideological and social conflicts in our country as a triumph of a kind for human reason. But (this, at least, is what transpires from the issue of *Il menabò*, and from the tone in which it has been generally discussed), one no longer hopes or fears to seek, in the society that surrounds us, 'the weakest link'. In the last 10 or 15 years—this is the theme of 'ageing' about which André Gorz has spoken brilliantly in a recent piece[19]—every one of us has come to be part of the amalgam, the cemented concretion, the conglomerate. Where is the fissure, the furrow, the crack? The one that, according to the Gospels, pits father against son and brother against brother; and according to Hegel, men in deadly struggle for recognition; and according to Marx, classes in conflict until their negation? And yet to 'bring the sword' into the world has been and remains one of the tasks of poetry.[20]

But here I see I have erred; the last affirmation is the first that my interlocutors deny. At most, they grant that the task of literature and poetry is to generate the sense of their own failure, their paradox; but not, as I instead continue to believe, of a failure and a paradox that are lodged like fierce precious worms in the very kernel of reality—especially of that reality that appears to be the most seamless and solid—and not in literary expression.

8. Today, like the worker who has not lost his class consciousness and the political leader who has not accepted a professional consciousness, or a consciousness merely oriented towards success, the writer knows or should know that the struggle for communism begins again now. *It begins again precisely at the lowest point in its arc, where nothing appears to support it—a point we have already reached or are about to.* Prophecy came easy to me, five or six years ago. In the West, but perhaps also in the East, beneath the themes of economic demands and those of government and parliament those of a 'qualitative leap' are being advanced. This is a leap that the three decades of Stalinism had led the world revolutionary movement to abandon. And this is happening precisely when the power with which the capitalist system invests and governs every part of society is most total. Due to a contradiction that inheres in their very existence, the most evolved forms of today's capitalism are incapable of founding a society of persons rather than roles. It is a matter of resolving in western Europe and therefore in Italy the very problems that the formation of socialist states and the emergence of the Third World have left unresolved among us, namely, the problems of a 'non-modern' progress, one 'not based on affluence'. To affirm these things means affirming that literature cannot accept the status that neo-capitalism has offered.

I am quite aware that what I'm saying here is at the limit—and perhaps beyond it—of the sensible and the reasonable. Before it judges others, this is something that casts judgement on the one who speaks. But if one lacks the courage to face that judgement, one might as well stop writing. I mean to say that the writer, if he has understood the present terms of the class struggle, must not only leave behind the phase of solitary or group revolt, together with the phase of revolutionary participation, which belonged to him in the first 35 or 40 years of the century, which is to say, in various forms, until the Second World War; he must also—and I'm talking about us, about Italy—give up the 'sociality' which is the sole miserable leftover of the commitment to historical responsibility which in 1945 was proposed to many, even in ways, as we know today, that were relatively independent from party ideologies.

Precisely because he knows what industry is, the writer I am referring to knows that speaking about industry is like speaking about his deepest ego, and therefore that only a long chain of metaphors can take on the risk of that discourse. I do not think it is in any way either useful or necessary to establish a direct relationship between the knowledge-for-action required by every action that considers itself to be revolutionary—in other words, a scientific knowledge or one that claims to be such—and the particular knowledge (of the industrial world) that can derive from literature (perhaps, as Vittorini says, as a 'representation of servitude that contains a project of freedom'). I say more, I who for 20 years have argued for seemingly opposite positions: even the now threadbare polemic in the domain of poetics against the so-called 'literary ontology of the *Novecento*'[21] and against 'irrationalism' and related ills, belong to the ideological tunics that neo-reformist and neo-industrial progressivism loves to see draped over the choristers of the literary and artistic world. Today in Italy, to advise writers to turn their attention to industrial sociology or the invention of new relationships between 'men' and 'things', with an eye on the 'things' of industry, probably means keeping alive a pseudo-progressive misunderstanding. Better instead to indulge in sheer play, mockery, arcadia. Between the ennui and the tiresome land-surveying of much cosmopolitan 'thingism', and that same 'thingism' that today or tomorrow will sprout in Italy not without historical–social condiment—I'd rather have the French kind, which is harmless. Or better still, nothing.

The cultural and interdisciplinary circulation in which, according to our social-Kennedyites,[22] the writer should partake is not only 'esperanto-like' (as Aldo Rossi has referred to it[23]) but also lacks a motor—nor can it say what forces, besides the sheer love of the true and the good, will push it towards Circular and Generalized Democracy. Faith in the revelatory and liberating function of literature—which is and has long been the dynamically positive substance of Vittorini's argument—instead seems to generate from within itself and to imply (accepting, as it does *de facto* and *e silentio*, the current sociological-political framework of literary production) the perpetual recreation of artificial avant-gardes. These lightly armoured, fleet-footed avant-gardes run in advance of those who instead sweat the no-longer-despicable wages of the culture industry and the literature of utility; but not so fleet as to forget the connections, in a perpetual exchange of slogans and personnel.

The question no longer concerns literature, but morality and politics. If one agrees that the principal ideological characteristic of the forces that are economically and politically dominant in Italy today is the absorption or neutralization of any protest or negation that presents itself as tending to universality, it should be clear that the first way to frustrate the expectations of those forces is not to furnish the literary alibis and the good progressive conscience that they require (and will increasingly require).

Today, any literary expression that represents a servitude in such a way as to make an illusion of freedom immediately possible, serves an illusory freedom. And those who agree that there are no distinct and different freedoms to aim at, that freedom is, as Lenin thought, one and only one for a given time and a given situation, indistinguishable from the path leading towards it, will understand why, at least here and now, in the current literary and political climate—what Roversi[24] calls 'this great dance beneath the cherry tree'—it is best not to invoke the name of truth in vain, and to leave the imperturbable apologists to their simony. I think that today it is up to the coherent Marxist and socialist to disdain the noble anxieties beneath which capitalist reformism hides its substantial optimism, its conviction that it has succeeded in securing progress and democracy for our country. Today one must not do anything publicly to distinguish the ideology of a functionary at ENI[25] from that of a functionary in the PCI, if some find that distinction difficult to make; nothing should be done to distinguish a speech by Togliatti from one by Giolitti,[26] if some find that lack of distinction pleasant. It's the only way for those who need to understand and distinguish to understand and distinguish. I wonder if we should not try to preserve the residual revolutionary capacities of language in a new estrangement, different from the Brechtian kind but oriented by it. Paradoxically, and amid peals of laughter, the poetics of the occult and the hermetic may be rehabilitated. Make yourselves as innocent as foxes and cunning as doves.[27] Blur your tracks and your identities. Poison the wells.

Only now—despite being as old as the October Revolution—do I seem to grasp how many meanings dwell in the final words of the *Manifesto*: that change can come to societies or individuals only at the extreme of a wretchedness-need that is seen and accepted; when that wretchedness-need no longer has any form other than that of a servitude, of a material chain. And that the world that we (that you) have to win really is a whole world. This is why I think that today (and this is advice I give myself, not a precept for anyone else; though in the hope that it's grasped by the better sort) to wish to write about industry, factories, workers, trade union and political struggles is to be a fellow-traveller of conservation. To understand the world around us is also to be concerned with industry, factories and workers, with trade union and political struggles. It is to act within them. This I believe must be done. And never to withhold one's word, where there is a true possibility of inflicting a salutary offence upon the offenders and a just injustice upon the unjust. But as a writer—at least to the extent that I have the opportunity to communicate with a public—I tell myself that I want to appear the most abstract, the least committed and useful, the most 'reactionary' of writers. I would like it if upon reading a poem of mine about roses one drew away one's hand, as if touching a reptile's slime. The managers of industrial and progressive culture have always glimpsed in my complexion something that dissuades them from the temptation to trust me. Today I would like for my pallor (ours, my friends) to be all the more unnatural, confected—and undefined. I would also like to stop making compromises with the ardent or fatigued intellectuals of my generation; with that part of myself that resembles them. I would therefore like to be able to greet them, and if needs be revere them, flatter them—with perfect mendacity. It's not easy. Like some kinds of industrial action, those who set themselves such aims in the field of literature have already been anticipated in the balance sheets of power; much sought-after, then, like prize game. It is easy instead to be confused and to confuse oneself with the worst scoundrels of protected rebellion or with eccentric latecomers. It's enough to make one seriously think that one should cease writing, or publishing.

But all we need is to remember how we welcomed, at the beginning of our lives and only yesterday, the words that taught us in what direction to look for our comrades. Then in what I write, or others will, there may be, like the thin metal file hidden in the lifer's bread, a metallic part. May only he who has asked for it, and thus deserved it, be able to take it into his possession. Smuggled in a shape that all, enemies included, can communicate; but destined only for him and those like him.

1962

Notes

Originally published in *Il menabò di letteratura* 5 (1962). *Il menabò* was founded and edited by Elio Vittorini and Italo Calvino in 1959 and wound down in 1967. [Trans.]

1 Elio Vittorini, 'Industria e letteratura', *Il menabò* 4 (1961): 13–20; see also Gianni Scalia, 'Dalla natura all'industria' [From Nature to

Industry], 95–114; and Agostino Pirella, 'Comunicazione letteraria e organizzazione industriale' [Literary Communication and Industrial Organization], 115–20. My text owes much to Mario Tronti's 'La fabbrica e la società', which I read in draft form, and was then published in the second issue of *Quaderni rossi*, 10 days or so before *Menabò* 5. [*Il menabò di letteratura* was a literary review founded by Italo Calvino and Elio Vittorini in 1959. They published 10 issues, irregularly, in collaboration with Einaudi before closing in 1967. The term *menabò* is a technical expression in the language of publishing for a draft page layout, the equivalent of 'paste up'.]

2 See Karl Marx, 'Economic and Philosophical Manuscripts (1844)' in *Early Writings*, pp. 341–58.

3 'The materialist doctrine concerning the changing of circumstances and upbringing forgets that circumstances are changed by men and that it is essential to educate the educator himself. This doctrine must, therefore, divide society into two parts, one of which is superior to society. The coincidence of the changing of circumstances and of human activity or self-changing [*Selbstveränderung*] can be conceived and rationally understood only as *revolutionary practice* [*umwälzende Praxis*].'—Karl Marx, 'Theses on Feuerbach' in *The German Ideology* (C. J. Arthur ed.) (London: Lawrence & Wishart, 1987), p. 121.

4 Karl Marx, 'Rheinische Zeitung No. 195, 14 July 1842, Supplement' in 'The Leading Article in No. 179 of the *Kölnische Zeitung*' in Karl Marx and Friedrich Engels, *Complete Works, Volume 1, Marx: 1835–1843* (London: Lawrence & Wishart, 1975), pp. 195–202; here, p. 195. [Trans.]

5 An allusion to Italo Calvino's essay 'Il mare dell'oggettività' [The Sea of Objectivity], *Il menabò* 2 (1960), now in the collection 'Una pietra sopra' (1980) in *Saggi*, pp. 52–60. [Trans.]

6 In Plato's *Apology*, Socrates proposed that as a benefactor to Athens he should be granted free meals in perpetuity at the Prytaneum, the political and spiritual centre of the polis. [Trans.]

7 *cosismo* [Trans.]

8 Gianni Scalia (1928–), literary critic and editor—along with Fortini, with whom he was often at odds—of the second series of *Officina* in 1958–59. [Trans.]

9 Vittorini has also reached this conclusion, which is consistent with his overall argument. Like Houdar de la Motte, who could not understand why on earth one should say in verse what is so much clearer in prose, Vittorini affirms that the modern sciences have made literature nearly impossible. In jest, but only partially, we could paraphrase an old joke: a little 'science of man' (sociology, anthropology, linguistics) takes us away from literature, *beaucoup nous y ramène* [a lot leads us back to it]; meaning that literature regains that 'impossibility' or paradoxicalness which is its most common mode of existence. [Antoine Houdar de la Motte (1672–1731), French dramaturge and critic.]

10 Ottiero Ottieri (1924–2004), novelist and author of *Donnarumma all'assalto* (1959). His *Taccuino industriale* was published in *Il menabò* 4. Like Fortini (as well as Paolo Volponi and Geno Pampaloni), he was employed for a period of time by Adriano Olivetti. [Trans.]

11 Fortini, 'A Cesano Maderno' in *Una volta per sempre* (Milan: Mondadori, 1963), p. 63. [See also *Tutte le poesie* (Luca Lenzini ed.) (Milan: Mondadori, 2014), pp. 276–7.]

12 Fortini, 'Al di là della speranza' in *Poesia ed errore* (Milan: Feltrinelli, 1959), p. 237. [See *Tutte le poesie*, pp. 179–81, 792–7. For Fortini's response to the 1956 Polish uprising, see *Attraverso Pasolini*, p. 68.]

13 Fortini, 'Ad una straniera' in *Poesia ed errore*, p. 154. [See also *Tutte le poesie*, p. 140.]

14 Edoardo Sanguineti (1930–2010), poet and theorist of the neo-avant-garde, translator, novelist, critic and member of parliament for the PCI. For Fortini's critical views on him, see 'Sanguineti' in 'Breve secondo Novecento' in *Saggi ed epigrammi*, p. 1175; and the essay 'Two Avant-gardes' in this volume. [Trans.]

15 An Italian chemical company founded in 1888, it was the quasi-monopolist of the chemical industry in Italy. Montecatini merged with Edison in 1966 to create the Montedison company. [Trans.]

16 C. Wright Mills, 'Letter to the New Left', *New Left Review* 5 (1960): 18–23. [Trans.]

17 'You shall be a mask and you will laugh forever', quoted from Victor Hugo's *L'homme qui rit* (The Man Who Laughs, 1869). [Trans.]

18 ZiS (Zavod imeni Stalina, literally 'Plant named for Stalin') was a Soviet car factory, active between 1931 and 1956, when it was renamed ZiL. [Trans.]

19 André Gorz, 'Le vieillissement', *Les temps modernes* 187 (December 1961): 638–55; and 188 (January 1962): 829–52. [Trans.]

20 Matthew 10:34: 'Do not think that I have come to bring peace to the earth. I have not come to bring peace, but a sword.' [Trans.]

21 See the previous essay in this collection, 'Clarifications'. [Trans.]

22 An ironic play on Communist condemnations like 'social-fascist' or 'social-imperialist', this refers to people on the Italian left supportive of a rapprochement with John F. Kennedy's policies. [Trans.]

23 Aldo Rossi (1934–99), philologist and critic; he intervened in the debate on industry and literature set off by *Il menabò*, with articles in journals like *Paragone* and *L'approdo letterario*. Rossi's term here is *esperantistica*. [Trans.]

24 Roberto Roversi (1923–2012), poet and intellectual, co-founder of *Officina*. [Trans.]

25 Ente Nazionale Idrocarburi, Italian state oil and gas company. [Trans.]

26 Giovanni Giolitti (1842–1928), Italian liberal politician and five-time prime minister. [Trans.]

27 A chiasmatic play on Matthew 10:16, 'I am sending you out like sheep among wolves. So be as cunning as serpents and as innocent as doves'. [Trans.]

V

Literary Institutions and the Progress of the Regime

Many current discourses on literary institutions and manners mix near and far horizons, descriptions of fact and declarations of duty. When the one speaking is himself an author, it can happen that, being accustomed to free creation, he refuses institutional mediations but then, precisely because the discourse is a different one, superimposes on them a variable degree of prudence and tactics.

By literary institutions I refer to the system of formal conventions that in a given society define certain forms of communication and expression as literature, as well as the ensemble of activities whose object is already existing literature, namely, criticism, publishing, the investigations of the sociology of literature and so on. In what follows I will exclusively employ this second meaning. What I will argue makes no claim to originality: it would not have been formulated without the writings and recent conversations of friends. And especially not without the arguments of eight or ten years ago. With the immense difference that those were addressed to the cadres of a party who are no longer, or which is no longer. The assertions that follow might in part seem obvious. But to whom? Best not to move further until, having tested their degree of truth, some practical consequences have been drawn from these observations.

My premise is that, over the last decade in Italy, there has been no apparent progress in the organization of literary institutions, with the exception of some areas of academic philology and criticism. The forms and customs of literary publishing and critical commentary in newspapers, periodicals and audiovisual media, journals, prizes and so on, have remained unchanged despite the high sales figures and the industrial standards applied to literary publishing. Only the scale has changed in proportion to the increase in turnover. The points of sale supported by commercial advertising base themselves on immutable premises: to promote a given product as what brings order into disorder or disorder into order, but in any case guarantees a spiritual advancement thanks to having originated in a group (the authors) whom another group (the publishers–critics) continues to invest with ancient magical powers.

'The last decade': I refer to the years following 1956 (self-liquidation of the organizations of cultural mediation of the political Left and takeover of their function by publishing companies). In parallel with certain recent governmental strategies, it seems likely, however, that economic-political power will delegate to publishing more explicit ideological-cultural tasks.

(Avant-gardists and their foes are both ready and willing to put everything in doubt and bury the carcass of belle-lettrism. Not to alter the structures of literary institutions. To engage in lengthy disputes about capitalism and the culture industry, Marxism and revolution. Not to actually alter the status of their profession. Books will stay closed or open, pianos played or burnt; but the rules of succession, editing and combination will remain unchanged.)

But the path of modern capitalist power (national and international programming, the integration of all antagonisms) has precise requirements. It has already led to a modernization of education. It has entrusted schools with the pre-selection of its labour force. It has already replaced a class pedagogy grounded on 'humanism' with the one, still anchored in class, of the disciplined consumer. Scientific research represents a further step. The process of concentration and rationalization will eventually introduce modifications into the regime of publishing and then in all those other elements that have allowed Italian literary institutions to retain their characteristic flavour.

It is also likely that the model is the United States, and now also England and Germany. France too is already embarked in this direction. Private or public bodies investing capitals in the establishment of modern universities will also impact the 'departments' of literary studies; they will fund research and publishing projects, they will reorganize the service performed by critical information and make it truly efficient. It will be in the interest of the culture industry itself (that is, of the 'factory of consciousness') for truly independent critics to exist, ones clearly distinguishable from current specialists in social relations and marketeers of literature. The last remainders of a literary milieu will disappear in favour of an extended, serious and decent variety of literary studies. Only those employed in the business of free creation will be allowed on probation, albeit under surveillance.[1] (We read in an Italian journal that our epoch, grounded on the scientific spirit, maximally restricts the communicative possibilities of the arts and letters. I think the diagnosis is correct.)

All of this is standard operating procedure in a developed capitalist country. If we're surprised, it is because we are not more advanced, because the managers of the contemporary culture industry believed, rather naively, in what they were told over the last three decades by a few outdated figures, that is to say, in the advertising value of certain literary myths. The golden age that led some writers, including some of my peers, to believe that they possessed a moral power, rapidly came to an end. They, or others in their place, will enjoy a moral power as the direct delegates of the system but not as its inspirers or critics.

At this point, it would seem that the argument should come to a close with some hypotheses. But any hypothesis for the contemporary organization of literary culture premised on the *immediate* historical struggle against the capitalist system is groundless. Like with any other form of organization of associated life, 'prefiguration' (if it doesn't stem from the most immediate and visible negation) is a pleasure that we should forbid ourselves the more we really advance. Or rather, the degree of its diminution is perhaps a measure of real progress. Starting now, the very notions of 'organization', 'culture' and 'literary institution' must know that they can be negated or overturned by the mental forces of men in the act of their revolutionary unfolding. Let us recall the negative definition of communism: 'The real movement that abolishes the present state of things'.

A friend warns me not to fall into the customary illusion of trusting in my readers' baseline consensus. But these words are not addressed to anyone. They are only for those who already agree on the importance of not compromising with society in general and with the society of literary institutions in particular or at least only so far as is strictly necessary the better to damage it. A reader of the final two pages of an article of mine in *Il menabò* on industry and literature benevolently imagined that I had been possessed by the sublime.[2] I'd like to dissuade him from that opinion. I said what I said, literally and in every sense. My addressees are those who don't let themselves be fooled by the sophism with which the various fractions of Italian (and non-Italian) literary culture have tried to make people believe that the disengagement of literary creation from its subordination to political ideologies could be extended to literary institutions. The sophism has been argued proclaimed reiterated over the past few years in the pages of innumerable journals and under many different signatures: *we have ended up believing that the forms in which journals are edited, articles are drafted, book series directed, research promoted or funded by universities or publishing houses, unpublished texts judged or published texts distributed, that either these forms don't exist or that they coincide with a mythical and unimpeachable culture industry or that they melt into the mists of industry-and-literature.* In practice, just as the industry–literature relationship hid the one between capital and waged workers, the new wine of the latest critical trends or new international experiences came to be poured into the old organizational structures, fundamental choices in literary questions continued silently to obey the criterion of profit, critics to sob over the culture industry and then pass by the till, tiny journals to proliferate in every jurisdiction, debates to plague houses of culture, etc.

This means that the recruitment and selection for literary studies are carried out so as to guarantee certain outcomes. 'I'm a coward, yes, but listen' [*Son vigliaco, sì, ma 'scólta*].[3] As a matter of fact, they all say they agree with you; in practice, though, one doesn't want to ruin his relationship with his publisher, the other needs to publish a book and has placed his hopes in Y's review, a third hopes to be in the shortlist, a fourth already is, a fifth can't say what he thinks about Z because he took his wife away from him, a sixth is about to leave for a semester at Salt Lake City University, a seventh thinks there's much to expect from the next writers' congress in Kiev, an eighth is suffering from a nervous breakdown, a ninth is dead and a tenth must still be born.

This argument, it is worth repeating, is concerned with literary institutions and their organizations. Just as we have witnessed with scientific research (especially in advanced capitalist countries) and, moreover, with the literary institutions of Soviet countries themselves, the problems of organization, as they become the very problems of autonomy and the choice of priorities, also modify the creative substance of literary activity, or at least impact upon it. In practice, most of those concerned will merely behave as they have until now: either ascend the university hierarchy or seek patronage, individually or as a group, from publishers, parties, monopolies, regions or states; basically, offer themselves as technical personnel for the rationalizing transformations that capital's plan foresees or implies. A minority, comprising authors or scholars shaped by the mores of yesterday or the day before, will continue to perform the threadbare and picturesque comedy of 'freedom' and 'moral authority'. Now to propose, as is rather obvious, the aim of self-management in literary institutions amounts to recommending a set of behaviours that in part remains within the bounds of the system, and in part transcends those bounds. Self-management, the kind that scientific researchers envisage, signifies the whole complex of guarantees and assurances that should take the exercise of literary institutions (from criticism to editorial choices, from teaching to research) away from the criteria of profit or privilege. The word alone suffices to shed light on so many contradictions; it shows that to pose the problem is to see it immediately overtaken by an incomparably broader political context. I repeat: the very word self-management interrogates us (as has never been seriously done) about the real functioning of the two main systems that we know of for the organization of literary institutions: that of universities and foundations in the advanced capitalist countries, and that of literary civil service in socialist societies.

More simply and immediately, it is also necessary to propose and enact, with modesty, the construction of *models* for investigations, studies, critical or essayistic writings, for the management of literary institutions; *not in competition with the existing ones* but as one among the innumerable forms of participation in the 'real movement that abolishes the present state of things', that is in the general political action for *communism*.

Must I recall how much patience, modesty, capacity for contempt, 'pathos of distance', deliberate resignations and laborious ironies are implied by these suggestions? But no one ever ordered us to be writers, nor told us that it would be easy to concern ourselves with literature in this way. We can always do it (and indeed we know how) in that other way, without the moralism, asceticism and other ugly things that the foregoing reflections seem to entail.

But the real way to avoid these is by not being alone in sharing them; I mean not being alone even in a group, exposed to the obvious temptations of the church awaiting the advent. Beyond individual or group solitude stand those in whose name we take on the right to administer the discourses of poetry and of literature. Do they exist? We should cast doubt on a proof as feeble as the increase in vital senses and aptitude for survival that we feel in ourselves when we think of them—hope makes a dreadful advisor. Yet the hypothesis should be declared. It is what authorizes the painful and necessary virtues which this text has once again tried to recall.

Of course, this presupposes an order of common refusals. Among these is the refusal to answer a considerable number of people who may ask in the name of what values we are speaking. 'General Gallifet observed the group of prisoners . . . and sought out his victims. Now he chose old men, declaring that "they had already seen a revolution, so they were guiltier than the others".'[4] Though they have not seen a revolution, those who are as old as I have seen enough to be considered 'guiltier than the others'. No explanation is owed them. Let them figure it out for themselves. For those who only know the world of the last decade, they should not look in our arguments for those 'values'. We can only hope that from the imperceptible but unmistakable aberration of the most brilliant trajectories they will infer—as it seems astronomers have sometimes done—the existence of a temporarily invisible celestial body; and that they may then manage to identify it. That such a body may correspond to my friends or to something quite different has an importance that is inversely proportional to its capacity to change the system.

1964

Notes

Originally published in *Quaderni piacentini* 3(14) (January–February 1964). [Trans.]

1 *in libertà vigilata*, literally 'in freedom under surveillance'. [Trans.]

2 See 'Cunning as Doves', pp. 125–50 in this volume.

3 A line from Giacomo Noventa's poem 'El povaro me dise', in which a poor man and a rich man both tell the author, in identical verses,

that they are cowards because they have old parents, a young wife and children to feed; to which the poet's voice replies to kill them all, whereupon they'll be freed of regrets and cowardice. [Trans.]

4 Edgar Monteil, *Souvenirs de la Commune, 1871* (Paris: Charavay Frères Éditeurs, 1883), p. 132, quoted in P. M. Kergentsev [Platon Mikhailovich Kerzhentsev], *La Comune di Parigi* [*Istoriia Parizhskoi Kommuny, 1871*] (Rome: Edizioni Rinascita, 1951[1940]), p. 559. The original French is quite different: 'coming across a group of prisoners General de Galliffet [misspelled in Fortini's quotation] . . . made a selection among the men, pointing them out with his finger and asking them: "Are you an old soldier?" "Yes, my General." "I know my way around, as you can see. Stand there." . . . "Send them to the firing squad".'

VI

Two Avant-gardes

1. Taking up again a theme from Lukács, we could argue that the so-called historical avant-garde is founded on the rejection of the category of mediation. As we know, the avant-garde attitude is born with Romanticism, out of a very strong sensitivity to contradiction and conflict. This contradiction and conflict became extremely acute for some European intellectuals when the Rousseauian and Jacobin revolution revealed itself as the mother of the philistine bourgeoisie. The knots of the historical avant-garde come to the surface at every twist in the development of industrialized societies, at least from the Napoleonic era onward.

That contradiction knows nothing of the dialectic; it is a juxtaposition or polar oscillation between absolute subjectivity and absolute objectivity, between abstract irrationality—namely, the refusal of the discursive, dialogical, communicative moment for the sake of association, involuntary memory and dream—and abstract rationality, that is, knowability by way of discourse, in the particular naturalistic and positivistic acceptation of the idea of 'reason'. The avant-garde seeks shelter in one or other of these extremes, or experiences them simultaneously, in a manner well known to the whole of the mystical tradition. The pages of the first *Surrealist Manifesto* are exemplary in this regard.[1]

In a polemical tract by Roland Barthes (*Critique et vérité*, 1966), I happen to find defined as 'stupid', 'all these aesthetic-cum-moral oppositions between a man who is organic, impulsive, automatic, unformed, unrefined, obscure, etc., and a literature which is self-controlled, lucid, noble, glorious by virtue of its restraint of language . . . given that psychoanalytic man is not geometrically divisible', etc.[2] Even without calling on psychoanalysis, we can recall that such a 'stupid' opposition can only be overcome dialectically; otherwise I simply don't understand what is meant by the shifting *avers* [recto] and *revers* [verso] of man (a notion that Barthes borrows from Lacan[3]) 'whose roles language continuously transmutes'.[4] We all know that the rational–irrational antithesis is magnified by bourgeois culture but is only resolved by the avant-garde in the simultaneity of opposites. We therefore continue to employ it precisely because it alludes to a very precise historical legacy; it is one of the points where the avant-garde has in no way overcome the culture it thought it was fighting against.

2. The avant-garde's movement of escape regarded itself as antagonistic to a society and a culture which in most of their social, economic and political expressions still wished to think that all mediations were still possible, especially in the name of history and progress, and accepted the tearing asunder only as a kind of 'spiritual aroma', in the register of sentiment and thought. The hegemonic culture wanted to believe that real mediations were possible; in other words, it denied class division. This is the sense in which the first and major avant-garde, the one of the solitary nineteenth-century heralds of the storm, could appear to prophesy the conflicts, revolutions and massacres of our own century. Yet the split of the bourgeois-positivist type, between scientific rationalism and decadent yearning, between democratic 'prose' and aristocratic-symbolist 'dream', still enjoyed a wide margin of survival between the end of the nineteenth century and the beginning of the twentieth.[5] In this sense (but only in this sense) the historical avant-garde of the first decade of the century really is full of scorn and rupture, it attacks the terms of that dispute, it mocks them, unmasking the reality of a deep consensus . . . and, in more than a few cases, readies itself to replace it. Let us not forget that the idea of (reformist) progress or transformation (including the revolutionary kind) was bound to be repugnant to the historical avant-gardes, or at least to a large part of them. And, when it was not (as in the case of the Russian Cubo-Futurists) it was because of a vital misunderstanding that the subsequent events were quick to clarify, sometimes bloodily; this misunderstanding was due to the apparent parallelism between the destructive moment of political revolution and that of the artists and writers of the avant-garde.

3. It so happens that one of the elementary characteristics of the societies of 'new capitalism' (as they have manifested themselves together with their technological and economic development over the last 15 years but which, as in the USA, were observable by the sociocultural gaze well ahead in time, namely, on the eve of and during the Second World War) *is the tendency to attenuate or expunge from many of their ideological expressions the possibility of employing the category of mediation*, together with the register and sense of historical movement. (Not by chance it seems that much of Catholic thought, in order to survive, has become the heir and defender of what remains of humanism.) The techno-scientific universe, cybernetic codes, the rationalization of production, forecasting techniques, everything that takes inspiration from a mathematical kind of logic, is perfectly consonant with the ethics of consumption and its lack of foresight, with the liberation of instincts, with permanent absurdity and so on. Anarchist negation is once again predictably blossoming on the same trunk as productive power and the neo-capitalist order (the military aspects included). We are not dealing with a new development; it is the apotheosis of a process that has continued throughout our century. The now compulsory silence about everything of which 'one cannot speak'—the incommunicable and ineffable side of life—rekindles, even in mockery and sarcasm, that 'sense of mystery' that the old Neapolitan humanist,[6] at the beginning of the Second World War,

considered the source of every wretched irrationalism. The unpronounceable avant-garde is the other side of the idle talk of mass society. The welding together between neo-avant-garde and bourgeois-capitalist order has become organic and explicit after having been, for the historical avant-garde, only implicit and indirect.

4. Today the fundamental forms of the historical avant-garde are no more than simple expressive instruments, mere modules serving contemporary expression and communication. In the literary forms of the new avant-garde, I cannot make out novelties that are substantially different from those developed by the European avant-gardes of the first 30 years of the century. (I would certainly not say the same thing for the plastic arts and music.) Or rather, there is a novelty, and it is fundamental; it is one that Sanguineti had programmatically intuited a dozen years ago when—borrowing from Paul Cézanne—he addressed to me a phrase that he would later repeat many times, even though, I would suggest, he would come to contradict it for the sake of *propaganda fide*; namely, that the avant-garde had to be turned into an art as durable as that of museums. This is exactly what I then did not fully grasp and which I am now articulating: the only real difference between the neo-avant-garde and the historical avant-garde consists, when it does, in the former's almost exclusively ironic and 'pseudo-classical'[7] use of iconographic, verbal and psychic material which in the major historical avant-garde was often still 'tragic' and in the direct lineage of Romanticism.

Let me explain, while sparing myself the repetition of a demonstration I have carried out one too many times. If the power of 'denunciation' in avant-garde artistic expression has diminished to the point that it only subsists in country districts,[8] in culturally-underdeveloped zones; if the apologists of the avant-gardes are themselves forced to postulate some kind of automatic renaissance of the power of opposition from within integration (but are we not dealing with the force of contestation that is implicit in *any* work of art?), this is because the 'tragic' dimension of the avant-garde (its agonic-catastrophic aspect) has lost and is losing relevance in favour of the 'ironic' moment (parody, mockery, irreverence). The latter is clearly, if not absolutely, prevailing; not only in all the forms of cut-up or 'visual poetry' but also in the great majority of compositions in verse or prose that are based on the use of found and clichéd expressions or of micro-citation. In the past few years, all the forms of sarcastic, humorous, pataphysical, epigrammatic, mad, jocular literature, which aim to deconsecrate communicative and persuasive language (duly inspired by Breton's anthologies of 'black humour') have experienced among us an expansion unprecedented in previous epochs: cabaret and polemical songs, genres that were almost unknown in Italy, seem to have turned into placid democratic institutions (like birth control and divorce will soon be . . .). That then seems to be the province—I mean the *domaine*—of the recent avant-garde.

In our second half of the century, the successive waves of the avant-gardes—from expressionism, imagism, Futurism and Esprit Nouveau to Dadaism, surrealism and so on, to more recent years—have overlapped, eroding and hollowing out many of the forms that have nonetheless accompanied our century, namely, 'critical realist' narrative and post-symbolist poetry. But by 1930, all of this had already taken place, with the *oeuvres* of Chaplin, Picasso, Klee, Mondrian, Kandinsky; of Proust, Joyce, Kafka and Musil, and the major works of Brecht, Breton and Éluard. The works and creators which came after, that is, in the last 30 years, probably don't have anything to envy from the works and creators of the first three decades of the century. Groups instead have much to resent, since those were not only instruments of literary warfare but also veritable workshops of forms.

5. Cesare Cases has recently returned to the theme of the avant-garde, declaring its experience to be 'valid and meaningful, to the extent that it put its finger on the sore point, namely, the inadequacy of the humanist legacy when it comes to understanding the demands of the present, the abyss being dug under the feet of civilization'.[9] But this 'gesture' of the avant-garde—as Cases himself recalls—should be interpreted with the old (or even timeless, as the inevitable idiot might say) voice of Lukács: 'The deeper and more genuine these experiences, the more decisively they break the concrete and sensible unity that is the premise and foundation of every aesthetic creation'.[10] In other words, the valid and meaningful experience of the historical avant-garde consists in having broken, along with the foundation of *aesthetic* creation, the veil that got in the way of glimpsing the abyss; it consists in having imperiously demanded its own end, its own overcoming in subversive and revolutionary praxis. Otherwise, what would be the point of 'putting its finger on the sore point'? If the humanist legacy has fooled us—deceiving us into thinking that we could come to stably possess it, when instead that possession is now everyone's or it is no one's—the avant-garde polemic against that legacy is valid to the extent that it corroborates, and not just in words, the end of the poetic and artistic institution (in bourgeois-capitalist society, needless to say).

But this is not the path of the so-called new avant-garde, which, in effect, truly differentiates itself from its predecessor, I repeat, in this and this alone. As I have already said, the novelty is in the renunciation of intransigence and practical transgression. To the degree that some representatives of the Italian avant-garde retread the steps of Breton, they inevitably end up accepting (albeit to an extent obviously aggravated by the intervening time) the compromise between surrealist action and poetry that was the *felix culpa* of the best of the 'faithful of love'[11] in the earlier groups and the miserable downfall of many epigones. Their political intransigence is not worth much, either in theory or in practice; to the degree that it doesn't touch the real and fundamental problems of the contemporary world, using them as sheer ornament for its own exhortations, it is inoffensive. Among the avant-gardists, those who institutionalize derision and fatuousness and situate themselves on the 'right' are far more coherent. The latter, it seems to me, have correctly concluded that the avant-garde is 'a simple adjustment of art in the age of technics' (Cases denies this, and obviously so do I for the historical avant-garde but I think it true of the recent arrivals); they have understood that their grandfathers' discoveries must be systematically applied as a relatively innovative system of signs, but no longer with the pretence of overstepping the literary-artistic institution. From this point of view, the more recent trends in structuralist formalism (e.g. Roland Barthes), by accentuating the idea that literature (also criticism and the human sciences more generally) is but a function of language—or better, precisely by restoring the values of 'rhetoric' of a classical-medieval type—help to unmask the double-dealing of neo-surrealist extremism; they constitute themselves into what they in fact are, namely, the bodyguards of a formalism that in its nominalist essence is ultimately 'traditional', and can easily welcome into its fold the frivolous collage, stories based on paradoxical logic or baroque amplification, neo-orphic or electronic poetry or what have you.

To put it more succinctly, the historical leap between the avant-garde of 1905–30 and the contemporary (Italian) one is—contrary to a commonplace of the contemporary debate—the jump between an 'open' phase of expression (and social struggle) and a 'closed' one (in Europe).

6. 'And I led him back to the silent stable' [*E lo riportavo nella stalla silenziosa*].[12] I think this well-known verse of Sanguineti, which speaks of a 'sizeable tail! frigid whip! oh muscle! oh fist! penetrating' [*consistente coda*! *frigida frusta*! *oh muscolo*! *oh pugno*! *penetrante*] can be understood, through its genital metaphor, as allegorizing the vicissitudes of the avant-garde. The 'penetrating fist' has been led back to the stable. In other words, back to the terms of the institution. Personally, I think a stable to be a very useful thing—but also the consciousness of the stable. And, I repeat, here lies, when it does, the only difference between the avant-gardes of the past and the new ones. Or rather, the new ones are not avant-gardes. They are literary groups that manage as best they can; they are writers who make it and writers who don't, brilliant or silly, mediocre or talented, etc. Obviously, as reader or critic, I take into consideration various authors who in the past 10 years have written in the modes of the avant-gardes—and some of them or their works into high consideration. In the end, I think the whole operation has been useful. Better still, absolutely beneficial, a technological upgrade; an introduction of new machines which may have caught by surprise the literary trade unionists hitherto used to the old style of lyrical agitation, but which makes new problems emerge, at a more advanced level—the problems that come after welfare and affluence, the *cafard après la fête*.[13] And, where I think neither respect nor consideration is due, this generally concerns rationalizations, ideologizations, pseudo-critical activities. This is very much the opposite of what we usually hear from those who praise the ideological and critical intelligence of our avant-gardes but gaze suspiciously upon their 'creative' texts; the latter are, sometimes, interesting and even alive—which is a lot—while the critical-ideological bric-a-brac is almost invariably at a frighteningly low level in terms of its crudeness, eclecticism, second-hand interpretations and, often, simple ignorance or wrong-headedness. The nonchalance of more than a few pamphleteers of the neo-avant-gardes would be a virtue if it weren't of the kind possessed by dogs, notoriously lacking every human respect or shyness in crossing a boudoir or a morgue, a musical theatre or an anatomical one—in brief, the virtue of innocence. It is difficult to avoid a twinge of compassion when we think that, years back, many of them had denounced the manoeuvres of the dirty old men of the establishment, designed to circumvent them and kill them with kindness. That's how it should have been. Swallowed by the quicksand, they quibble over their deeds of succession and think about the times when they themselves were younger and their bibliographies a little shorter.

7. It is worth remembering that today there is no substantial difference between mass culture and elite culture. Not, or, rather, not only because of the homogeneity between the producers of the one and the other, or between their respective addressees, but also because of the similarity of structures.

In this respect, I think that the research direction proposed by Barthes is right; it anticipates a homology, emerging from close analysis, between the assizes of so-called 'bad literature' or 'mass literature' and those of so-called 'good literature'—starting with the avant-gardes. Of course, this does not mean that the apparent distinction can disappear; it is far too necessary for the industry. Nor that the exchanges, the linguistic borrowings between one sector and the other have particular value or should raise special fears or alarm. We are in the presence of an ambiguity that only praxis, that is to say, use can resolve. To say that, at least in the West, the distinction between elite literature and culture and mass culture does not exist can in fact be used to affirm that class distinctions are either becoming extinct or being introjected, so that in every one of us there would now coexist the boss and the servant, the capitalist and the exploited, the producer and consumer of subculture; this reactionary use of indistinction omits the real argument: it is not at all a matter of separating or reuniting or mixing the messages originating in so-called mass culture with those coming from the other 'high' culture but, rather, of observing in what context, in what fabric of values these messages come to intervene. This amounts to recalling the impossibility for the only culture that exists for us (that of capitalism) to produce a coherent pedagogy. At the same time, it means reaffirming the identity—already lived by the Soviet and Chinese revolutions—between socialist revolution and generalized pedagogy, for all and by means of all; the only authentic 'mass culture' if there ever was one.

A more attentive consideration of the development of literary forms and expressions in the rest of the world should perhaps have suggested a different policy to the promoters of Italian neo-avant-gardes. One has the impression that, when it comes to the neo-avant-garde, the mediation of publishing has offered a distorted reading grid or interpretive key. Yet this is a phenomenon that does not take place just in Italy, as testified by some impressive (in terms of basic vacuity and eclecticism) roundtables published by French or German journals on the problems of the avant-garde, the novel or the new poetry. One has the impression that the will to be up to date, adapted and deprovincialized has been mistaken not in its goal but in its means—means that are indeed voluntaristic. As people used to say in Florence, with force you can't even make vinegar. There was a belief that one could adapt oneself to a condition—that is, to the legacy, the repertoire of the historical avant-gardes—without grasping that this could be done only on condition of erasing, as they used to say of the lion in the Middle Ages, 'one's prints with one's tail', that is, without creating 'movements'. Publishing and commercial demands exerted pressure, of course, to follow the path of noise, of 'movement', of the 'group'; so one was forced to conjure up or exhume all the theories (surrealist and Dadaist) that mixed together action and expression, gesture and speech and so on; circumventing them with the notion of the open work, visual or technological poetry, with exhibitions, soirées and other demonstrations of activism. Without realizing that—in the whole world—a capital dislocation had taken place. On one side, the formal innovations of the avant-gardes had become part of the repertoire, so that new expressions could happily accept, before even being born (instead of feigning they were being forced into it, amid cries and gesticulations), that market–museum or museum–market that had belonged to them since the times of Homer; on the other, actions-works had found other forms, they had become behaviours of the masses or at least of ample strata among the populations of the West—in beatnik habits, in political neo-anarchism, relatively unreachable by those who still wish to think of themselves as 'writers' or 'artists' in spite of it all. Some of course had grasped that delay and that error; and, taking their distance from their more fatuous and 'hot-headed' peers, they soon sought out the coldness of the specialist. But the pleasing *image*[14] of the local neo-avant-garde couldn't be discarded so easily. It was a trademark, a brand, bought at no small expense. Besides, if certain misunderstandings are allowed to persist for so long in our country, this is because, as everyone knows, of the uneven development and stratification of our economy. It doesn't matter that books and journals circulate throughout the peninsula, an avant-garde periodical printed in Chieti or Treviso, or the cultural debate on the future of literary language hosted by the Circolo Salvemini of Mazara del Vallo or in the House of Culture of Rovereto are situated in a context that is so different from that of the so-called major cities, they fulfil such different functions that they end up receiving—from those forces which precisely in the provinces and in the minor centres are often more intelligent, prepared and generous—a justification and meaning that they otherwise wouldn't have; also because of the enduring indolent presence of positions that are not only backward but also reactionary. So until there are circles, associations or art galleries to set up, the commercial salesmen of technological, neo-Dadaist, visual, electronic, etc. literature will have work to carry out, high-school students to promote or perturb, ladies to scandalize, dignified priests to conquer ('Let the new artistic tendencies adequate to our times be recognized by the Church'—Pastoral Constitution *Gaudium et spes*, par. 62).[15]

8. A few years ago, Viktor Shklovsky told me that when interest in and research about formalism in literary criticism (of which he was, as everyone knows, a major promoter in the 1920s, between Revolution, Civil War and the New Economic Policy) returned in the Soviet Union, some younger scholars had rediscovered, so to speak, those same methods of work, not without the support of recent technologies, electronic equipment and mathematical formulae. On the occasion—I seem to remember—of a public debate in Moscow crowded with students, after the contribution of one of these formalists, Shklovsky, having been asked to speak, would thus have declared: 'I am pleased to hear some of our positions confirmed. Our ancestors, the Scythians, always used to deliberate twice: the first time drunk, the second with a clear head. Well, you are repeating sober what we, 25 years ago, said, for the first time, drunk.'

This jest, insolent to the point of generosity, applies to the grandchildren of the historical avant-gardes. That said, if honestly practiced sobriety has its merits. In the world shaped by today's industry, the soul of wine no longer sings in the bottles, as in the time of the poet who first mocked the used of military terminology as applied to politics and letters.[16] In years closer to us, the death of Dylan Thomas due to acute alcoholism already seemed out of step with reality, out of time. The drugs from New York or California are a social phenomenon before they are a tool of literary levitation. 'Is it sobering? Can it be read in the morning?', with these words Brecht—who came from the historical avant-garde but did not remain in it—left precious advice for the new avant-gardes and us.[17]

Four Postscripts

1. So the two avant-gardes are in the end just one. The new one is to the previous as . . . (the adult to the youth?) But why keep looking? It is enough to recall, as I have already said, the rise in irony and the fall in the contest (the market–museum relationship wasn't born all of a sudden, it developed over at least half a millennium). Delirium has turned into a delirium of immobility. But we will be asked why the forms of the historical avant-garde have had such meagre fortunes in Italy. This is an important question, since it reveals numerous misunderstandings.

A superficial answer would indict the delay in industrial development. But what of the Russian avant-gardes? The Spanish ones? What of Bulgarian, Bosnian, Saudi Arabian, Martiniquean surrealists? There is no force in the world that in the 1930s could stop a group of intellectuals from Bucharest or Oviedo, Krakow or Alexandria from enjoying a projection of Luis Bunũel's *Un Chien Andalou* or publishing a review of automatic writing and essays on Sade. The answer is a different one—the historical avant-gardes had their moment of success in Italy, after a fashion. It may not have been iconoclastic and cynical or gallant or perverse or rebellious; but Futurism was not only Marinetti, it was also Palazzeschi and Ungaretti;[18] and *Lacerba* was not merely an Italian journal. And this was true even later, in some formulae of the literary *Novecento*.

2. One of the usual sophisms of the apologists for today's avant-garde is to begin with scrupulous distinctions between historical and non-historical avant-gardes, between this group and the other, this tendency and that sub-tendency; except, when it comes to the perorations, to forget all these niceties and defend oneself by defending one's great-grandparents (who can very happily do without it) or, better still, to exploit the dumbest of arguments—that of the ordinary incomprehension that accompanies the new, and its inevitable glory, etc. Dumb because it occludes how much of that new was not, and often for good reason, ever understood; and it blackmails its contemporaries with unverifiable descendants. As far as this question is concerned, even the most intelligent and unprejudiced frequently fall into using the argument from novelty: 'How could it be', we often read, 'this is an argument from 30, 50 years ago', or 'that's how people wrote before the war' and the like. The prejudice at work in this way of speaking (I won't say of reasoning, that would be too much) should be obvious to anyone.

3. The idea that art in general (not the avant-garde) is a response to the transformation of human relations into things (reification) and therefore a way of conserving or preserving the human image—so that, as Schiller thought, from the copy we would one day be able to reconstruct the original—is indeed an idea from the age of Goethe. And what I sometimes hear discussed as the constitutive or coexistent moments of the avant-garde, the heroic-pathetic moment and the cynical one, appear to me as nothing other than two loci assigned by Romantic culture—tragedy and irony. Both transformed, of course, in the course of a century and a half but not really changed in their essence: which is, to be a response to a condition made of man as a commodity.

4. On more than one occasion, I think, Sanguineti has tried to establish a relationship between commodification and the avant-garde. The latter would be relative to the economic conditions in which the history of bourgeois art develops and reaches maturity and, more precisely, to the socioeconomic relations reflected in the art market and in the pseudo-class of intellectuals. But we are told that because this is indeed a pseudo-class, it is not possible to infer any necessary relationship between class and the avant-garde. This would be *proven* by the lack of correlation between the avant-garde and the *political positions* of its components.

In this way, through this three-card trick, the class character of the avant-garde is cleverly dissolved at the very moment that, with conspicuous stress on socioeconomic relations, you make a show of being terribly 'Marxist'.

As we should know, *class* character does not at all correspond to *political* character. The common example of the 'political' divergence between Russian Cubo-Futurism and Italian Futurism only means that the political application of the ideology of the two groups was divergent (following an equivocalness typical of the *intelligentsia*); it does not in any way mean that there wasn't a profound affinity (or at least that the affinities didn't prevail over the differences) between the artistic and literary ideologies that found inspiration in the two movements which, after all, were flowers on the branch of the general ideologies of the European bourgeoisie, whether Italian or Russian.

But it would be best not to insist on this point. On the one hand, there is a desire to put the avant-garde in relation with commodification (otherwise where would the 'Marxism' go?), not to fall into the swamp of an undifferentiated, ahistorical and cosmic 'alienation'—dear also to the avant-garde, but to that of the 'right'. On the other, one doesn't want to give up on the stash of good conscience drawn from the 'neo-avant-gardes' of the so-called socialist countries; one doesn't want to give up on the pleasure of being on the side of Revolution and of Progress . . . Quite a mess, in any case.

1966

Notes

Originally published in *Avanguardia e neo-avanguardia* (Giansiro Ferrata ed.) (Milan: Sugar, 1966). Fortini is echoing the title of an essay by Lucien Goldmann (on whom see 'Deus Absconditus', pp. 311–18 in this volume), 'Les deux avant-gardes', *Médiations* 4 (1961), published in Italian translation in *Le due avanguardie e altre ricerche sociologiche* (Paolo Fabbri ed.) (Urbino: Argalìa, 1966). [Trans.]

1 André Breton, *Manifeste du surréalisme* (Paris: Editions du Sagittaire, 1924). [Trans.]

2 Roland Barthes, *Criticism and Truth* (Katrine Pilcher Keuneman ed. and trans.) (London: Continuum, 2007), p. 9. Translation modified. [Trans.]

3 See Jacques Lacan, 'Le séminaire sur la lettre volée', *La Psychanalyse* 2 (1956): 1–44. [Trans.]

4 Ibid. Translation modified. [Trans.]

5 Here Fortini employs the terms *Ottocento* and *Novecento* not only as chronological markers but also as periodizing, cultural categories, for which there are no equivalents in English. [Trans.]

6 A reference to Benedetto Croce (1886–1952), philosopher, historian, politician and a dominant influence on Italian cultural and intellectual life. [Trans.]

7 *classicheggiante* [Trans.]

8 *pagi*, an ancient Roman territorial administrative category, from which the term *pagan* (*paganus*) originates. [Trans.]

9 Cesare Cases, 'Prefazione' in Walter Benjamin, *L'opera d'arte nell'epoca della sua riproducibilità tecnica* [The Work of Art in the

Age of Its Technological Reproducibility] (Turin: Einaudi, 1966), p. 15. [Trans.]

10 Georg Lukács, *Il significato attuale del realismo critico* [The Meaning of Contemporary Realism] (Renato Solmi trans.) (Turin: Einaudi, 1957), p. 41. [Trans.]

11 *I fedeli d'amore* refers to the group of vernacular poets associated with Dante; most influential among them was Guido Cavalcanti (1250/59–1300). [Trans.]

12 Edoardo Sanguineti, 'Erotopaegnia' (1960), *Segnalibro. Poesie 1951–1981* (Milan: Feltrinelli, 2010). [Trans.]

13 Literally, 'the hangover after the party'. [Trans.]

14 *Image* is in English (or French) in the original. [Trans.]

15 'The Pastoral Constitution on the Church in the Modern World' was one the constitutions resulting from the Second Vatican Council. It was promulgated by Pope Paul VI in 1965. [Trans.]

16 Charles Baudelaire, 'The Soul of Wine' [L'Âme du vin] in *The Flowers of Evil* (James McGowan trans.) (Oxford: Oxford University Press, 1993), pp. 215–16. [Trans.]

17 Bertolt Brecht, 'The Doubter' in *Poems 1913–1956* (John Willett and Ralph Manheim eds) (London: Methuen, 1987), p. 271. [Trans.]

18 Aldo Palazzeschi (pen name of Aldo Giurlani) (1885–1974), poet and novelist, distanced himself in the 1910s from futurism's pro-war stance; Giuseppe Ungaretti (1888–1970), leading figure in twentieth-century Italian poetry—his collection of war poetry, *Allegria di naufragi* (Florence: Vallecchi, 1919; 2nd EDN, *L'Allegria*, Milan: Preda, 1931) is regarded as a turning point in Italian literature. [Trans.]

VII

Avant-garde and Mediation

1. Of course, the new avant-garde is capable of 'profoundly demystifying' all the remaining illusions and claims inherited from the historical avant-garde. Anyone is capable of irony about anyone else. Today's avant-garde would simply be continuing the literary tradition which, ever since Balzac at least, has placed the artist, the writer and his activity at the centre of its discourse (thus rendering explicit a moment implicit in any artistic making). Of course it is possible to document the self-destructive instinct of the recent avant-garde. But let us ask: What does 'destruction' mean? What do these 'negations' negate? If we do not make the activist and naturalist mistake (with its other inevitable magical-mystical face) of *immediately* linking praxis and theory; if we do not identify (as do most of the French godfathers of the new avant-garde) 'reality' and 'discourse', we should be able to see not only that poetic and artistic discourse differs from practical-political discourse but also that the first will not negate or destroy much of anything *as such*, namely, qua poetic and artistic discourse. Instead, all its tormented and ironic negations will compose a form, the hated and inevitable 'artwork'. The practical-political function of works of poetry—their aptitude to legislate the world—no doubt exists, but only at the end of a path that differs from that of practical-political discourse. As everyone knows, there are two forms through which the literary ideology of our century has sought to escape that fate of practical impotence—the first equated all literary work to action (the surrealist or existentialist doctrines of commitment), the second eliminated the problem by reducing every artistic or literary fact to communication or information.

Therefore, to say that the historical avant-garde 'preserved, by repudiating it, the sacredness of art' amounts to saying that the authors—the surrealists in particular—while deriding the tradition of the poet-demiurge continued both to demand, from the verbal–formal operation, a magical efficacy and to identify speech and action. Now, it does not seem to me that the new avant-garde has overcome that claim, even if it intended to do so. That is clear from the way in which it continues explicitly to take on a function of protest, negation, etc. (and nourishes itself on current affairs). It is the environing social reality that has overtaken the new avant-garde; it is the cultural habitat of advanced capitalism that no longer leaves any margin for the 'revolt' of artists and writers. Other is the power of negation and new birth that belongs to *every* work; in that sense, the orientation that can be drawn from the late Vittorini or from Philippe Sollers in France—that strenuous experimentalism which shares only its scientific horizon with the Revolution—would obviously be more correct, albeit superfluous. How can we not frequently discern, among those who debate these questions, a 'corporatist' defence of arts and letters, which is becoming stronger, the more it would seem that their interests impel them to contest 'the existing state of things'? We are even told that 'the death of art would strongly contribute to the definitive legitimation [. . .] of the existing state of things'—where it should be noted that 'the death of art' does not necessarily mean the death of 'any art' but, perhaps, just that of the art produced by the avant-garde groups of the industrially developed countries, like the 'state of things' is the one that 'exists' only in one part of the world, and it is contested there too. Why indulge in the myth of 'modernity', where 'life' and 'death' would only pertain to forms accepted as 'modern'? To modify the state of things is a meaningless pursuit if among its multiple elements we do not delineate a hierarchy of priorities, values and instruments. It seems to me, in the end, that the great works of literature and art have a capacity to genuinely disrupt the dominant ideologies not so much because of how they contest the usual and the banalized, not only because of their capacity to break outdated formal schemas, but especially (or at least, also) because of their profound untimeliness and their ironclad[1] conclusiveness which no 'open' or 'interminable' or 'polysemic' or 'informal work' can escape. That is because formality lies in their etymology, in their nature as enormous *morphemes*. In this sense, it is useless to declaim against the sacredness of art (I have done so for 30 years) because the most desecrated and desecrating, humble and makeshift work of art appears, thanks to its own *conclusion*, like an artifice 'charged with values' which always silently alludes to something, to a possibility that is not only never the same as the possible-future of the politician, but is also in relation to it frequently—in the most precise sense of the word—*untimely*. It is this way of making himself the bearer of a strategic design which is often unknown to him, in an anachronism that some circumstances can even beat the most acute of politicians, which explains why the poet has always been likened to the priest, be it in scorn or praise, and why both (rightly) bother the politician. It is one thing to fight the arrogance or haughtiness or simple silliness of priests and poets when they make themselves the arbiters of kingdoms and crowns or threaten the daggers of Tacitus[2] (a necessary struggle if you are persuaded of the decisive primacy in the present of political action); it is another to delude oneself that a wilful gesture or a supplementary and programmatic negation is enough to escape from priestly or literary 'shame'.

2. I am criticized especially for what I asserted in the essay 'Two Avant-gardes', to wit, that both avant-gardes, that of the first quarter of the century and the recent one, place themselves outside the category of mediation. In the mature Lukács, and in my essay, the Hegelian notion of *Vermittlung* (mediation) would have been substituted with 'in-betweenness'[3] or equilibrium-in-contradiction.

The art of the avant-garde, which is immediacy and negation, would instead be situated before *Vermittlung*.[4] It would constitute—in its historical form—the 'Great Refusal' of the 'power of facts' which is affirmed by a reifying society. Today, the new avant-garde, conscious of the capacity for integration and commodification of the society in which it lives, would also negate that 'Great Refusal', and would, as a 'wager', go to the edge of silence. Many assertions contained in this thesis would deserve a detailed discussion (for example, how it interprets the development of Lukács's thought).[5] However, I will restrict myself to one point.

Having observed that I borrow from Lukács 'the criticism [. . .] according to which irrationalism is envisaged as the refusal of the dialectic and as the opposed-complementary pole of a purely formal rationality', my interlocutor resorts to a hypothesis which, in other circumstances, I had advanced with regard to Lukács: The 'essayism' to which the then young Hungarian writer devoted himself was the metaphor and anticipation of the category of mediation, which would have gradually assumed in his work the features of the Party and the Typical. As Tito Perlini writes, 'It is clear that [. . .] the category of mediation as *conciliating intermediate element* stands in Lukács as the escape from an unresolved and unresolvable conflictuality, as the evasion of tragedy.'

Much of the ensuing argument derives from this thesis—faced with historical necessities, Lukács (and, albeit in another form, the undersigned) would have capitulated in favour of a 'just middle', of a 'shrewd and precarious balance', the apparent remedy for 'tragedy'. Perlini adds:

> The avant-garde as radical negation is not the rejection of the category of mediation but its premise. It is not mediation that precedes negation, which would reject its wisdom in order to move towards an irrational and abstract refusal of existing reality; it is negation that posits itself as the originary moment in a process of totalizing mediation. The conflict that avant-garde artists are involved in cannot

> refuse mediation for the simple reason that it is situated before mediation and not after it. It is immersed in an existential sphere that precedes the exercise of mediation; it is therefore *immediacy*.

But what else was I trying to say? The criticism that Lukács makes of the avant-garde (which I partially reprised) is precisely that it is a mode of art and literature that *immediately* poses contradictions (form–content, subjective–objective, arbitrary–necessary, rational–irrational, psychologism–naturalism). I should have simply added that modern semantics and linguistics have provided us with the possibility of registering the degree to which these contradictory elements were merely juxtaposed and the degree to which instead these mediated contradictions were marked by vital tension and elasticity, all the way down to the level of the linguistic microcosm. The negation that Perlini attributes to the avant-garde ('immersed in an existential sphere', etc.) is *a* negation, not Negation *itself*; it is negation in the register of will or persuasion. The paradox of the avant-garde—which is 'integrated' and doesn't want to be—is that of not having accepted incarnation (this is always the sin of spiritualism . . .), of refusing what is here termed as 'compromise' (which Perlini connotes as ambiguous and contemptible) and which is, very simply, the work in its objectivity. It seems to me that there is a confusion between the aims, programmes and polemics of the avant-garde (which I will agree, for ease of argument, to call 'radical negation' while always keeping in mind that we are dealing with an ideological, philosophical, political and ethical negation—and not a literary or artistic one) and the works of that same avant-garde; but this is possible only if we wholly accept the premises of the avant-garde—which, following surrealism in this respect, refuses not only the distinctions between literary genres but also between the moments of life, and is, as Breton suggests, the search for a place where contradictions stop being perceived as such. In fact, to posit contradictions flat out is the same intellectual act as negating them with equivalent immediacy . . .

'Reality is negated in its empirical immediacy in order to be reaffirmed through mediation'. Sure. Artistic and literary creation is nothing other than *one of the ways* in which one 'reaffirms', at a higher level, a reality negated in its empirical immediacy. It is an intermediary (others are possible) between reality 'in its empirical immediacy' and the successive and superior non-immediate 'reality', the one that the presence of artworks (in the case in question) helps to determine, to reveal. In this sense, it is very true that the avant-garde ignores mediation because it places itself 'before' the moment of denial. But, if it stops there, it is not; it freezes in its negation. Or, if it is, it mediates (expresses) itself in forms other than artistic-literary ones. The motto whereby the surrealist act par excellence would be to go down to the street with a revolver in hand and start firing into the crowd suggests a certain attitude of negation, and if nothing else it negates the life of one's neighbour; but it evidently cannot be considered more poetic than any other act, except to the extent that others objectify it; for example, through a cinema lens inserting, say, the detonation of the shots, the fall of the bodies, the dance of the shooter into a predetermined rhythmic framework. Anarchy is not a sub-clause of surrealism but, perhaps, the other way around. Meanwhile the marquises have continued to go out at five o'clock, in spite of Valéry and Breton's disgust for that famous opening line.[6]

What here is termed as 'balance' or 'flight from a torn reality' alludes, more simply, to the flight from youthful aestheticism and the tragic posture. Here we do not wish to justify the political thought of the older Lukács; only to recall that he is right when he admonishes, for example, that the conflict between capitalism and socialism will never present itself as the struggle between good and evil on the fields of Armageddon; in other words, the fundamental contradiction of an age masks itself with a contingent host of secondary contradictions. Here I do not wish to justify the taste of the Hungarian critic; only to recall that Proust, for example, is not

Pathos der Mitte despite being the very opposite of the immediacy of any of his contemporaries in the historical avant-garde.

Let me add here that my personal torments, my biographical 'tragedies'—which have given succour to very lazy attitudes about what I write and have written—should not be of interest to anyone; not, or so I hope, to the critics of my verses. One should not be excessively indulgent with tragedy. One the most widespread prejudices of our time is that the negative, on its own, is more or better than the positive—contradiction than agreement, despair than hope, the unconscious than the conscious, evil than good and so on. How many times have I heard people repeat, with barely changed words, one of Gide's most facile remarks, namely, that '*c'est avec les bon sentiments qu'on fait la mauvaise littérature*'.[7] I firmly believe that any excessively swift assent to the negation, contempt or devaluation of the-world-as-it-is—especially coming from intellectuals and the young in countries such as ours—can hide within itself, unchecked, an agreement with that reality, a filial dependence; and that it is necessary to have been conscious of the uniqueness of life, the value of the world and the positivity that accompanies even the worst decadence, oppression or corruption if one wishes authentically to negate the latter's *present* figure. To put it otherwise, you will not know who your enemies truly are if you do not know, in the same moment, who are your friends. Institutional, romantic or avant-garde negation lives, no doubt, in individual tragic heroes. But few—even among them—escape the aestheticized payback.

3. It would make little sense for me to presume to lecture on dialectics if the argument did not in the end have another meaning and another objective. Whether or not the historical or new avant-gardes refuse the moment of mediation is of interest, to my mind, only in order to judge whether the new avant-garde has its own legitimacy and authenticity, whether it interprets the needs that from today look towards tomorrow. In the conclusion of his text,

Perlini sees the greatest value of the new avant-garde in its wager at the edge of silence and its ironic-tragic attitude, provided it does not turn into suicide. This last observation grounds what is ungrounded in many avant-garde arguments. These usually list all the reasons why it is impossible or pointless to write, paint and so on. But they conclude that some solution must be found, because everything can be accepted but not that one ceases to write or paint. And when they discuss this or that country which made or is making its socialist revolution, they worry that no 'voice' should be abandoned or unprotected, and they want to see how things are with cinema or painting or theatre or lyric poetry in Cuba, China, Hungary or North Korea, and they draw from them the omens for the fate of those countries. As far as I'm concerned, I think that much depends on the hierarchy of values or priorities that a society assigns itself. Unfortunately, most leaders of contemporary socialist revolutions have lodged in their heads the idea that the fine arts and poetry should be, with all their flourishes, a kind of proof of revolutionary achievements. With the excellent results that we know. Art can very well die because in history it truly dies a thousand times, and I know nothing more scandalous than the plaint over burnt libraries or antique bronzes melted into cannons. Alfred Jarry's famous retort—'*Nous vous en ferions d'autres*!'[8]—should be our reply to those who fear the end of artists.

4. I will not follow here the example of my courteous critic whom—having set out my opinions with such exactitude and excessive praise—in the process of disputing a non-decisive point ends up negating their whole substance; namely, the thesis of the meagre relevance of the so-called new avant-garde.[9] With the passing of time and the confirmation of the flimsiness of any literature that has only itself and the drama (or comedy) of its self-negation as its object, I have become much more aware—and thank my critics for it—of the crucial demands that (recent or historical) avant-garde poetics have advanced, and which it is important to safeguard. Here

I can only allude to this because it is not the object of this note; but I think I have now understood how two directions almost always present in the development of literatures presented themselves even in literature of surrealist provenance (a term which for me implicates many of the motivations of the avant-gardes). The first aims at *conclusion* by stressing the self-sufficiency of the operation on language, and thus to close in on itself, in keeping with a mode that presupposes as already given—in the environing socio-historic complexity—the possible integration of its own discourse, the localization of its own microcosm (until yesterday, we could find it, for example, in some of the poetics linked to the French group around the journal *Tel Quel*: Revolution at the level of language is parallel to political revolution, etc., everyone should do their own job, the integration of the different moments is delegated, in the final analysis, to power). The second tends to perceive the insufficiency and limits of its own 'specialization'; it refers its own interpretation and future to something other than itself, it cuts across genres and so on, exercising a sort of vicarious function vis-à-vis the organic functions of a society in its throes; a society whose contradictory outline can be glimpsed in the present, coming undone. I have the impression that this second direction is the only salvageable meaning of the obstinate formulae of Vittorini, when he insisted so strenuously on 'science' and 'rationality'; even though he would, most certainly, have been horrified by the 'romantic' echoes elicited by this second tendency—to which he belonged. Well, this 'opening out' of a work, not only to a plurality of interpretations but also to the other-than-itself, this being unfinished despite its formal conclusion (a trait all masterpieces share), so that the discourse may continue in philosophy, in science, in praxis—this is the precious and contradictory legacy that from Romanticism traverses the avant-gardes and reaches us.

5. What has been called—inaccurately and with critical one-sidedness and obtuseness—postwar 'neorealism' originated in the consciousness of an open predominance of the future over the present, in an awareness of how the social forces that pushed for a transformation of the national community delegated (or appeared to delegate) to literature and the arts some of the (ethical and political) functions that should have belonged to a new society. The more that transformation was gradually realized, but in a direction other than the one aspired for, in the shape of stabilization—not only national but European—the more literary tendencies reaffirmed their autonomy or self-sufficiency (as they had done, in an entirely different context, in the 1930s). First (in the period 1950–56) by taking up a reflexive and self-critical consciousness concerning what in the previous period had existed as hope and immediacy; whence the ironic and elegiac character shared by our narrative and poetry from those years and, at the same time, the strong desire for formal 'completeness' (in Cassola, Bassani, Calvino and Pasolini, to name just a few) that could counter the previous chaos of authors and their society. Then, in the following decade, after the transformation resulting from the domination of industrial development and consumption, and by the definitive incorporation of our capitalism into European and world capitalism, the 'corporatist' autonomy of literature took on—in the new avant-garde and its critical language—a sectorial social function. The social ghetto, which it has both endured and chosen for itself, has led it to the mystified conviction of a possible unlimited and informal revolt. In this sense—if not in the more vulgar sense, itself not devoid of truth, which was employed in the polemics of the past few years—modern capitalism has furnished much modern art with the metric grid, the rhythmic cage that the compositions of the avant-garde thought they had rid themselves of or which, when it suited them, they thought they could reconstruct at their own subjective whim. The consciousness of commodification has led to the mythologems of the semi-death and semi-suicide of art, to the conceited ravings of those who think they can save themselves from the swamp of objectivity with a private act of will. In that period, which is immediately behind us, I had the occasion to warn those who, in their refusal or fight against the current socioeconomic structures, were reluctant to accept the objectively 'conservative' component of any artistic expression. I reminded them of how protracted the struggle was, in the name of past or future of revolutionary participation, against the two camps—opposed and yet complicit in their extolling of 'life'—that triumph in the present. On the one hand, the orphic-aristocratic and spiritualist camp, and on the other, the technocratic-subversive and scientistic one.

In the years closer to us, it seems that the reality of class conflict, as recognized on a global scale, together with choices that are no longer either national or European in scope (which now penetrate the everyday aspect of each existence, no matter how remote from them it may appear), can once again propose that figure of substitution—or, as they say, of protest—which we were familiar with a quarter of a century ago. We can already notice its symptoms and make out its first documents. If contemporary criticism cannot avoid being a criticism of tendencies or trends, our task is not to race behind the periodic oscillations of taste but to transpose their curves into a discourse whose own tendency is not sectoral but global, not specialistic but universalizing. We thus risk ideologism and superficiality, but always with the aim of identifying, and of reading between the lines, the fundamental contradiction which alone gives the right value and weight to the existence of subordinate contradictions— to those figures of mediation to which works of poetry also belong.

1968

Notes

Original publication: 'Avanguardia e mediazione (risposta a Tito Perlini)' [Avant-garde and Mediation (Reply to Tito Perlini)], *Nuova Corrente* 45 (1968). Tito Perlini (1931–2013), philosopher and specialist of the Frankfurt School and the work of Lukács. Fortini's essay is a reply to Tito Perlini, 'Avanguardia e mediazione (a proposito di un saggio di Franco Fortini)', *Nuova Corrente* 41 (1967): 69–84, itself a critical response to the essay 'Two Avant-gardes', included in this collection. Quotations in this chapter are from Perlini unless otherwise noted. [Trans.]

1 Exaggerating (but certain 'overcomers' should heed the Kierkegaardian warning, from the final pages of *Fear and Trembling* [1843]) and extolling this 'retroverted' aspect, tragically denied the future and contemptuous of beggarly hope, some have wished to contest all the literature of our century which contains, in a Lukácsian sense, a *terminus ad quem*, that is, a perspective. Of course, there is a frequent temptation to believe that skill and perhaps even genius is positioned on the 'right'. But it is a facile temptation: Every word of skill and genius is to the right of the activist and to the left of the philistine. Those critics will also have to keep silent about all those authors, including great ones like Brecht, from all tendencies, even ones as important as surrealism, who do not fit that schema. What Vittorio Saltini has recently written is probably truer than one may suspect—that the group comprising the 'sacred monsters' of the twentieth century (Proust, Joyce, Kafka, Musil; I would make an exception for Proust, still imperfectly understood) now appears concluded and distant to the new generations, and that one should go back to speaking of authors from remoter periods—even from those bourgeois eighteenth and nineteenth centuries which Vittorini, shortly before his death, refused with a gesture as broad as it was ineffective.

2 In Book II of the *Annals* of Publius Cornelius Tacitus (56–117 CE), the Roman senator and historian recounts the suicide of the Emperor Otho: 'Towards evening he quenched his thirst with a draught of cold water. Two daggers were brought to him; he tried the edge of each, and then put one under his head. After satisfying himself that his friends had set out, he passed a tranquil night, and it is even said that he slept. At dawn he fell with his breast upon the steel'.—*The History of Tacitus* (Alfred John Church and William Jackson Brodribb trans) (London: Macmillan, 1873), p. 70. [Trans.]

3 *medietà* [Trans.]

4 Perlini, writing with with reference to Hegel (no doubt correctly), affirms that in the dialectic the moment of Negation is situated *after affirmation* but before *mediation*.

5 Lukács is so universally under attack, since forever and by everyone, as to make his defence entirely superfluous. Nothing is truer than the observation that the 80-year-old Lukács today pronounces banalities or defends mistakes and testifies to the limits and faults of the revolutionary generation that was already more than 30 years old in 1917—even though I cannot but wish for myself and my critics that in 20 or 30 years we shall enjoy the same lucidity as the one manifest in the 1967 preface to *History and Class Consciousness*. But we're not talking about hormones. And what seems to me truly strange is to accuse the Lukács of the period following his early masterpiece of a kind of moral and intellectual capitulation, of a Mannian *Pathos der Mitte*, of the 'bitter wisdom of one who has overcome or, rather, repudiated the phase of youthful illusions'. In the past, I too shared this psychological and moralistic interpretation. Not for nothing did I address, on 23 October 1956, this epigram to Cesare Cases—I won't apologize for the self-citation—while the monument to Stalin fell and Lukács appeared to have interpreted, at the Petöfi Circle, the demands of the Hungarian youth: 'The object objects, Georg returns; and there falls / the idol of essence. Too late! / Existence already bloodies the streets.' [Published, in a somewhat different form, as '27 ottobre 1956', *Avanti*! (18 April 1957).] But today I know that, though I can judge Lukács's political position during the Stalinist period, it is fruitless for me to ask whether that was a concession to the 'middle way', a renunciation of 'youthful illusions' as my critic ironically notes (if youthful illusions appear to be illusions, one should give them up), when two generations of revolutionaries let themselves be killed while repeating, with Trotsky and Lukács, 'right or wrong, my party'. Something more important than the moral or intellectual coherence of a philosopher was at stake: namely, the fate of Soviet socialism, what would survive of it in our world, or if it would. Therefore—and I hope no one thinks I'm so stupid as to want to draw comparisons, but simply because my work was also under discussion—it matters little if I've managed to be biographically coherent, contradictorily laying claim to the legitimacy of poetry as anticipation and 'affirmation of the absent' and denouncing it as the ornament of a ruined society; what will matter more is what of the present figure of the world will transpire from

me, and how, to those who will come after—and, why not, even in verse.

6 It is said that Paul Valéry once explained his inability to write novels to André Breton by saying he could never write a sentence like 'The Marquise went out at five o' clock'. [Trans.]

7 'It is with fine sentiments that bad literature is made'.—André Gide, *Journals, Volume 4*: *1939–1949* (Justin O'Brien trans.) (Champaign, IL: University of Illinois Press, 2000), p. 44. [Trans.]

8 'We will make you some other ones!' These are the words that Jarry allegedly addressed to the lady who was lamenting the risk to the lives of her tots in the garden adjoining the one where the poet practiced his shooting.

9 At least as far as the Italian neo-avant-gardes themselves are concerned, the dispute now seems both concluded and corroborated by the facts; and this entire discussion appears, I concede, rather superfluous.

VIII

Written and Spoken

1. Writing and Intonation. We know that the written word does not signify the spoken word. It is a graphic language that declares something about a phonic language. In each is reproduced the relationship between the two. There is a 'written' degree of the spoken and a 'spoken' degree of the written. But graphic aids able to signify intonation are scarce; whence the supplement offered by written syntax and by particular figures of discourse. Where the expressive intention is strongest there is a greater use of orthographic and typographic signs and figures become more frequent. Where communicative intentions are the strongest the importance of intonation declines. (Works of poetry are also attempts to extend to an entire complex organism the metaphorical imitation of the kind of complex affective intonation that in its particulars characterises every passage from the spoken to the written.) Even if they abound with suggestions for intonation some pages of poetry benefit from a visual-mental reading. Intonation has been entirely transferred to the writing; that is why any recitation of those poems cannot fail to be an interpretation and new creation which can either be accepted or cause irritation. That is the case with Belli's sonnets.[1] Pages that instead cloak expression in a communicative guise tend to diminish the traces of intonation as much as possible; those who read them out aloud will only accord them a minimum of expression and will speak 'like a printed book'. That is the case with Leopardi's prose writings.[2]

I say this much because class borders penetrate the written just as they do the spoken. Privilege is not written language or the writing of language but a given degree of formality and organization of spoken or written language when it becomes inseparable from the dominant ideologies and especially from the structures that ground them. Let us not confuse the class situation with the situation of privilege. The hand of those who touch upon the relations between class and language should be nimble.

2. Subsistence Levels.[3] I have been writing in Italian for several years and I am convinced that something can be done in order to improve its written usage. But we need to know what kind of writing is called for. That of poetry and narrative tends to take revenge on any partisanship. Language is its material more than its instrument. It is rare that it furnishes generalizable results. Poets can be useful to language if they are not—or rather not only—considered as poets. Petrarch and Manzoni are models of language independently of their poetic truth. That truth will only serve as the vehicle for linguistic influence.

We may instead imagine interventions into a whole welter of forms of writing from journalism to essay writing. These pages belong to them. Such interventions comprise the largest percentage of the words read by our fellow citizens in the school textbook and the newspaper article just as in works of history or advertising copy. Essay writing is communicative and expressive. With its ambiguous form it contests every separation. It is not thinkable outside an objective social context but it possesses the percussive force of subjective declarations. It is prose.

These various kinds of writing can endure the precepts that manuals of good writing no longer impose. But they should. It is possible to learn how to write clearly and usefully. If one does not want to one should stay silent or be very inspired.

I open a dictionary and notice that besides particular expressive intents or technical necessities it is three-quarters full of words and examples unfit for use except with irony or shame. But irony and shame have in practice become lifeless stylistic flourishes. One should try to work with a subsistence level of language—a lexical minimum—that is to say with poor and vital words. Use two words instead of one if that one word is too antiquated or folkloristic or too modern or rare. Prune the wings of grammar. Condemn the oblique cases of relative pronouns. Discard the excess of tenses and modes. Shift writing's centre of gravity onto syntax. Wager on the expressive possibility of syntax while simplifying that of the sentence. Rooting out incidentals and parentheses is a worthwhile battle. Thrift makes good politics. This advice is centuries old. The novelty lies elsewhere. The sector of language to be truly reformed is that of the structures of argument. Are the modes and sequences and connections of exposition facts of language or not? You never come across a text that deals with them. Every novice speaks about linguistics. You cannot find anyone discussing logic. The average essay or comment piece seems to be written out loud; a parvenu use of quotations and unnecessary technical terms. Among those younger than 50 it is difficult to find essay writing that does not indulge in humanistic cadences or burden itself with colourful minutiae. Sergio Solmi[4] and Calvino—almost alone in this—know how to write their essays so as to make themselves understood. Disgust with dull late-Crocean writing has led to the spread of a language that floats countless technical terms on a fluid emotive inattentive background immune to any possible control or test—not unlike much narrative and poetry. Sometimes imposed by profit and more often by notoriety haste disguises itself as inspired freedom. Then it feels shame and learns some nice scientific expression. In this way it thinks it can distinguish itself from its fathers the literature professors.

Why should the commentary and review or the article and essay not look for their rules? Why should they not also be constructed on the basis of an idea of their addressees as 'addressees of ideas'? The contempt for the reader matches the certainty of impunity. With the applause of their dissolute teachers most find newspapers to publish them and an audience to appreciate them. Foreigners laugh at our literary journals. France in the past few years has not had much to be happy about but even an artificial page such as Starobinski's[5] shows a disciplined handling of the connections between sentences together with that play of counterweights which like the whole art of rhetoric is a virtuous homage of vice to virtue. The crude jargon of much of our militant literary criticism would indeed be preferable if it really wanted to be crude and not very delicate instead.

A reform of the contemporary forms of writing also entails a repression of genius. Their practical necessity should be subjected to control. If there is no censorship it must be invented. Let formal coherence and clarity be respected as eminent virtues. A Russian poet from the last century once wrote 'a poet not necessarily; a citizen you needs must be!'[6]

Let us stop flaunting the rights of the lifelong public veneration of one's own ignorance in the name of a well-turned-out novel or poem. The first who should deal with these questions of language should be the specialists. We should listen to them especially if they are boring. We just need to warn them about the frequent temptation to practice coquetry with literary flourishes and their wish to appear as good social company.

To systematically select vocabulary and explore syntax in this way can only be done by one of those groups of control and reciprocal advice that in the history of our letters have sometimes not been lacking. With access to our present means of broadcasting one of these could even carry out considerable modifications in the linguistic consciousness of one part of society. Equally or more important is the other operation: to restore dignity—that is to submit to public criticism so that they may become practicable and therefore coherent with their ends—the forms of the literature of communication and persuasion. This is the old dream of seeing writers apply themselves to the real and decisive cruxes of written language. A critical note or a school textbook just like a newspaper article or a collection of essays must be correctly executed. All the better if they can then also be intelligent and new.

The author learns where he can. To make these lines brisker he has omitted all the commas—the first exercise for those interested in calisthenics.[7]

1965

Notes

Originally published in *Rinascita* 22(5) (30 January 1965). *Rinascita* was the official journal of the Italian Communist Party. [Trans.]

1 Giuseppe Gioachino Belli (1791–1863), poet writing in Roman dialect. Admired by Gogol and Sainte-Beuve. [Trans.]

2 Giacomo Leopardi (1798–1837), poet, essayist, philosopher and philologist. His *Canti* contain some of the most beautiful and complex poems in the Italian language while his vast collection of reflections and aphorisms, the posthumous *Zibaldone* (only recently translated into English), alongside his 1824 *Operette morali*, sets out a unique naturalist and pessimist worldview which influenced, among others, Friedrich Nietzsche. In the essay 'Passage to Joy', Fortini discusses Leopardi and his foremost Marxist interpreter, Sebastiano Timpanaro; see pp. 360–7 in this volume. [Trans.]

3 Literally, 'the vital minima'. [Trans.]

4 Sergio Solmi (1899–1981), essayist, poet and specialist of Leopardi. Founded, with Giacomo Debenedetti, the literary journal *Primo Tempo* in 1922. Father of Renato Solmi (1927–2015), translator of Adorno and Benjamin, with whom Fortini collaborated in *Discussioni*. In 'Solmi' (*Saggi ed epigrammi*, p. 1181), Fortini likens Sergio Solmi's poetry to that of Antonio Machado while noting the Italian poet's 'more obscure attraction for the obscure'.

5 Jean Starobinski (1920–), Swiss literary critic, whom Fortini met in wartime Switzerland.

6 See Nikolai Nekrasov, 'The Poet and the Citizen' (1856), translated by Philip Nikolayev. Available at: https://www.facebook.com/RussianPoetryInTranslation/posts/233897150083018 (last accessed on 9 May 2016). [Trans.]

7 *volteggio a corpo libero*, a wordplay on the gymnastic disciplines *volteggio* (vault) and *corpo libero* (floor exercise, literally, 'free body'). [Trans.]

PART II

The Condition of the Guest

I

Radek's Hands

1. There exists a short film documenting an intervention by Lenin at a congress of the Third International. Three members of the Italian delegation—Bombacci, Graziadei and Serrati[1]—can be made out behind Vladimir Ilyich. Recognizable by his beard and heavy lenses is also Karl Radek. In another shot, just as Lenin has finished speaking, Radek turns to him laughing, then stretches out his hands on the papers that cover the table before him.

I have had the opportunity to compare two copies of the same film. The second was worked over by Stalin's censors. A stain covers the faces of our socialists. As for Radek, sentenced in 1938, his face has disappeared—but not the hands. They move about next to Lenin's.

I recall having seen in Ravenna the signs of a purge from 14 centuries ago.[2] Theodoric, a Goth and an Aryan, commissioned the mosaics in Sant'Apollinare Nuovo. Thirty years later, the Catholic Justinian rededicated that basilica to Saint Martin of Tours, 'hammer of the heretics', and ordered the expunging of the images of Theodoric and his court, depicted in the act of leaving the Palatium. Replacing them with curtains and architectural motifs, the mosaicists of the archbishop Agnello overlooked some traces of the figures. The *damnatio memoriae* has left on the columns hands suspended in mid-air like those seen fluttering about in séances.

One wonders whether these are merely two botched jobs; then, about the legitimacy of our singular repulsion or immoderate attention. But can we really speak of carelessness?

Are we to suppose that the functionaries of the Exarchate or of the Soviet film industry were not zealous enough? To notice those hands, you need to know that they're there; would none of those praying in Sant'Apollinare have asked what they were and to whom they belonged? By comparison with the tenacity shown in other circumstances, in other damnations, the inconsistency here is manifest. Besides, when Stalin expunged the names of his enemies from books, the *operatsiya* often scraped the paper, perforated it, exposing itself; in the meantime, in the archives, someone made sure that the documents would be preserved. Radek himself physically survived his execution in effigy. The guilty verdict was exoteric. Even when it killed, it was making a gesture. Memory, more than destroyed, had to be execrated. Silence was a supplement of fear, not a premise of the verdict.

It is not hard to detect something ambiguous and repulsive in the attention that is generally paid to these cases, protracting historical agonies, emblematic of the 'mystery' of the vanquished, so many affective identifications and projections, substitutes and euphemisms of every violent death—of every death. They conceal by evoking, meaning, they conceal all the better, the myriad who have left behind neither hand nor shadow—commoners, biological matter. The silences, or the cursory mentions, of death in Marx refer back to Hegel and his terrified sarcasm about the 'Absolute Master'.[3] Until recently, modern Marxism has always feigned not to be disturbed by those silences.

At least here in Italy, to those fingerprints of chopped hands which the sequence of rehabilitations embodies, to the impossibility of justifying every 'before' with an 'after' and of bringing to a close without any salutary anxiety the debits and credits of half a century of socialist revolution, some socialists and communists have responded (yet again) by grasping at the arguments of others, taking as true the very ideologies of their foes, whose falsity they had elsewhere unmasked. They have accepted their rival's pessimism about the possibility of navigating the current historical straits except through a generalized technocracy; they have extolled, as a new socialist path, the economy of competition and the 'sporting' ethics that accompanies it, and they have called this 'modern Marxism'.

2. Many continue in good faith to defend—without knowing from whom—certain humanist values which are but the surface aroma of social democracy. But a modern social democracy cannot in practice be anything other than technological and scientistic—so they realize, or they should, that within it humanism becomes a topic for Sunday sermons. And from the enormous heap of the human past they are barely able to predict what the eyes of electronic calculators can already see: a future mapped out by industry's need for biological survival.

Besides, all the recent pronouncements against Marxist humanism and historicism[4] seem to share a great if not inordinate haste. The haste is great enough not to tolerate the tortuous patience of historical movement; it proposes to us the (reformist) movement from societies of historical traction (or class societies) to culturally fuelled ones (or societies of functions). We are promised that this passage will be less painful than the political one because it subdivides every problem into ever-smaller and more distinct parts.

But that haste is not great enough. It leaves time for individual rage and indignation. Look at the interminable proliferation of harmless rebels in Western culture. It does not even have the strength to tighten the spring of the only revolt that is effective because it is true, *the one that does not trigger one life at a time* but, rather, expresses and distributes itself steadily in the revolutionary behaviour of whole social groups.

Those who wish to see human conditions transformed, *and to be transformed by them* in turn, see in historical change a step for moving from history to metahistory, from class society to communism—to one of the possible modes of the relation between human beings, which is also defined by a different collective perception of time, a different kind of memory. Contrast this with the massive intimidation campaign of 'progressivism' against any hypothesis of the end of history—allowing the latter to be cultivated only in the gardens of decadence.

Those who instead wish to *direct* transformation and thus *not to be transformed* by it (enlighteners and technocrats, all the way up to contemporary planners and their assistants); those who basically wish to exert power over men by means of things, deny both existence and necessity to that narrow passage, to that long moment incessantly pursued; they deride it as religious or pre-scientific. Alternatively, in the very midst of duration, they tend to turn the hard, obstinate demand for a death of history, the thirst for immediacy—which a poet once called 'co-created', inborn[5]—into a garden city that is either aesthetic or scientific, and often more the former than the latter, just like the positivism of a century ago. Today the fading of the drive towards the other and the different is augured by contemporary ideologies as a way of expanding the buffer zones, the limbos that only secure knowledge of the eternity of the system can create. The imbalances necessary to the maintenance of the profit regime will continue, but remotely, at the edges of the geographical, historical and moral West; and deep in the mines of our separate egos where that part of our internal people, comprising the helots and the unformed, labours away.

History—toil, death—would remain a kind of military service, a tribute, for the 'disadvantaged' strata, peoples and individuals, the depressed regions in each of us.

Once again we have to choose. Like in 1943, in 1947, in 1956. And all the signs of the times are ambiguous. We must face up to the ridicule directed at insufficiently motivated great syntheses. Once again make like the 'poor man' who has no time to wait for the learned to gather all the data.

3. For example, there is a tendency to classify as a single phenomenon (independent of social structure) the primacy that Americans and Russians are said to grant to science and technology, and their meagre sensibility for the dimension of history. What does this tendency mean? No doubt, it is also the first stage in a process of neurotic repression of difference, and of ideological insurance against all the risks of the West's devaluation. It implies the idea that technologies determine consciousness, not the social structure as organization of property and class relations. But doesn't that common and banal idea in part allude to a deeper truth, obviously neither willingly nor knowingly? In the so-called socialist universe, couldn't the simplifying empiricism of the Soviet youth, and even the abstract ideologism and voluntarism of their Chinese counterparts, be interpreted as premonitory signs, as beginnings of the end of the protracted cycle of society 'fuelled by historical coal'? As the entrance into that narrow passage or gorge that Marxism had indeed spoken of? Into the long corridor of transition? Instead of reading that empiricism and voluntarism as 'delays' and interpreting them as the sign of the past (as they regularly appear to the Western observer)? And in the most advanced capitalist countries where technology turns everything, even history, into mere news, prohibiting us from experiencing it as an exodus through the desert and towards a goal, are we to consider the silent areas and buffer zones that history must not disturb, the meadows of the universities, the new cloisters of the soul, of science, art and eroticism, far-removed from the shouting of legionnaires—everything that the capitalist universe generates and permits within its own expansive movement—only as irrationalist exuberance, the point of honour of a dishonoured society? Or could these tendencies—antipodal and symmetrical to those we call socialism, imitating it like the sneer imitates the smile—not *also* be paradoxical confirmations, distorted returning echoes of what has, in spite of everything, started to take place where the premises (and not just the productive ones) have been established for the communism to come? Could we not also classify them among those anticipations that capitalist development cannot help generating, only to repress them, positing all the themes of the future and offering all the solutions, but rigged as mere individual or statistical possibilities, and never brought forth as collective necessities-freedoms?

In the meantime—an everyday experience even in random conversations—the advice and practice of looking to the contemporaneity of human societies rather than to their temporal succession and opposition has become more widespread in the West. Ethnological rather than historical eyewitnesses step forward. There is a desire for the new generations to remain on the hither side of history, never to think they can move beyond it, not even escorted by the religions, which are certainly capable of 'adapting to the times' to the degree that they can identify new and real worldly forces, but which are proportionally incapable of eschatological violence, and always cultivating the cardinal or human virtues more than the theological ones. Scientistic-conservative ideology disjoins history from finality, progress from history, society from progress, man from society and, finally, function from man.

The ethnological optic proposes a global market for the values of each society, based on equal rights; but in such a free trade area, one would actually be impelled to treat values irreconcilable with the fundamental value of capitalism (in part accepted by some socialist societies as well) which is founded on production and consumption and, therefore, on differentiating between societies that are industrially more or less advanced, more or less backward. The contradiction cannot be resolved with goodwill or cultural exchanges; this is proven by Africa's recent defeat at the hand of neocolonial methods. It can only be resolved by the destruction of the hierarchy of values that is grounded on production and consumption while in theory heralding the equality between societies. In other words, it can be resolved by the destruction of property and production relations that support that order of values. (That is why the history of the failed revolution in the European West is also to be found in the unwritten history of commercial agreements between socialist countries, and of the priorities reflected in those agreements.) Did the revolutionary socialist traditions say anything else? Obviously everything has conspired to make us forget what is meant by 'the last are the first'. *We have forgotten that the 'last' are those who live the double identity of the recognized and the non-recognized, the human and the inhuman,* oppression and freedom; and that this double citizenship really makes you stateless. The 'proletarians' are the border fighters, not those who abide within the sociological boundaries of their class. Class consciousness is also consciousness of the *other* class—bilingualism.

4. The double character of every 'sign of the times' is thereby confirmed; the call for synchronicity has two *opposed* meanings depending on the context in which it is uttered. There is a part of the world, of every society (of every human being?) in which the possibility of the withering away of history is achieved only through the fiercest subordination to historical necessity. It is, literally, a Long March. Chinese socialism and the socialisms of the underdeveloped countries, in their demand to exist and be considered as the *contemporaries* of Soviet socialism, in the name of values that cannot be calculated in tonnes of grain or steel, do not refuse a certain parallelism between productive progress and socialist progress, between 'science' and 'truth'; but they supplement it with some questions that are radical, ancient and in part forgotten, directed towards the outcomes of a century of socialist struggle. Questions (*Which* is the end of history? *Where* does it end?) that, because of their energy and insistence, are already in part their own answer: 'We want it to end'.

In another part of the world, in another part of every society (of every human being?), the call for the synchronicity of values serves instead as a 'democratic' erasure of reality, the transference upon societies and peoples of the myth of the equality of individuals-citizens, a silence on the end and the ends of history. Public silence and, inevitably, private prayers: 'Let your kingdom come'.

That is why we must urgently rid ourselves of that century-old low historicism, oscillating between exhortation and productivism with its familiar capitalist pedigree, which has long been the dregs of the European lefts and still stirs in official Soviet language. *This must be done in the name of the absolute tendential synchronicity of the present and past worlds and of our existences within it, a synchronicity that has to be conquered and which begins to exist in the assertion of the contemporaneity of all the living.* We must leave behind the moral insanity induced by the current phase of capitalism, which has also affected Soviet (and Italian) communism. The Chinese factory worker, the black South African miner and the insurgent Venezuelan peasant *are not our past. They are our present.* Or rather, to the extent that they are the clearest figures of passage and mutation, they are our future—they occupy a place to which we have yet to arrive.

5. The notion of history as a continuum and perpetuum devoid of qualitative leaps generates scientism, technological optimism and reformism. History withers away but only as a standpoint. Man no longer knows what he lives towards.

The notion of history as duration and intermittence, as the alternation of the quantitative and the qualitative, as refusal of continuity entails finalism, perspectivism, it prepares for the end of history as we know it. And to the extent that this history is already exhausting itself, man no longer needs to know towards where he lives because he lives it.

6. After a century, the end of global revolution—which didn't just seem but had truly been deformed and distanced—once again appears in all its clarity. It is that beyond of our days which already exists. It is to be found in the end of the societies powered by history, that is, of the societies founded on class conflicts. But the passage to the beginning of that end has not been the operation of consciousness-culture, the work of those 'educators' of whom Marx spoke, who in their turn 'must be educated'. It is manifest in that long or very long temporal operation called revolution in which part of human society and of man already lives, albeit with pauses and ebbs—and which only partially recognizes itself in the emblems of its own flags. That revolutionary operation, in the form of institutions and human beings ever-more alien to those we knew until now, works to restructure what the class struggle against the institutions of past and present, undoes and negates bit by bit—given relationships of men to one another, given hierarchies of ends, a given 'history', with its miserable brevity and length, counted in a few thousands of our years.

With its refusal of utopia, Marxism showed that it was ashamed of itself. Suppressing its own eschatology, it accepted to be the highest expression of bourgeois thought.

We can now understand why our desire to be appalled in front of Radek's face and those hands suspended on the wall in Ravenna should be judged a decadent sentiment. Because it comes from a Christianity that has lost its power and faith in the edifying inevitability of worldly injustice and the futility of power itself—this went from the medieval *Ubi sunt*?[6] to Bossuet and Baudelaire shaken by the eminent dignity of those who 'have never lived at all'.[7] Because it originates in a bourgeoisie or a secularism which has lost its powerful assurance in the redemptive justice of progress and the pedagogical energy of historiography, that horror of ours really expresses the loss of a perspective. It indicates such a weak force of necessity (or such an uncertain consciousness of it) as to make us accept a truncated and frightened freedom. It suggests we forget every other perspective with the help of biological melancholies or the ethos of specialization and probity. In other words, through those artistic or scientific attitudes, entirely valid in themselves, which nonetheless ratify the system or delay its expiry by no longer putting it to the test.

7. Who could have foreseen that in only two or three generations we would have found ourselves—peoples classes individuals—faced with the surge of such sudden memories, with the spreading of such deep oblivions? Or better, how could we have predicted that the social and geographical areas of memory and forgetting would have shifted so rapidly? Against the notion of history as a continuum, as memory of the past and unidirectional process—which has always presented the socialist revolution with its 'language of slaves'[8]—we must reaffirm the paradox of the simultaneous reality of *duration* and *intervals*.[9] The end of history as end of class struggle and unity of the human species will enact the only possible conservation of the past—the one that destroys it as past and makes it present. This is the real resurrection and survival of the dead and the only final justice: the transparency of objects and bodies, the perceptibility and untrammelled usability of the infinite 'dead labour', awaiting resurrection, that the world is. The end of historical alienation, which we have already begun to live, will also be the end of historical memory as spectral and persecutory memory, as *guilt*; it will also be the end of hope as *compensation*. The future tense nevertheless hides from us the 'sacramental' and 'figural' character possessed by certain (in themselves complete) virtualities or ages or intermittencies of the present, that have been termed 'recomposition of the class' by Marx, 'groups in fusion' by Sartre, heirs to the 'general will' and the 'communion of the saints'.

The terror we feel when faced with injustices from the tears of Dostoevsky's young girl[10] to the hands of the betrayed and the universe of the dead—a terror that is mystical to the extent that its effect is annulment or suspension of the real—is also born from the necessary inability to imagine a life and an activity different from the ones known to us. Or, even though we imagine them, to want them. If 'history is nothing but the activity of man pursuing his aims' (Marx), that terror is one with the doubt that man can *really* begin to pursue ends other than those which until now appeared to have been his or at least those of the great majority of human beings; in other words, to live an objectively and qualitatively different history than the one lived until now. The narrow path to that objective difference is marked by the intensity of the 'intermittencies', that is, of the concrete revolutions of our time. But if the industrial proletariat was, for the duration of an epoch, the consciousness of the rest of the world, it is not certain that it necessarily must be that today, or that other strata or classes will take on that role *beside that class which is defined by the degree of denial of essence to which it is subjected by the other classes.* These are the 'underdeveloped', in the strict and figural sense, the oppressed and the exploited insofar as they don't exploit or oppress anyone else and know themselves as such, in that 'ought' that is class consciousness. They exist everywhere, even in those (Soviet) structures that the work of 'incarnation'—namely, the creation of the productive base for socialism insofar as it actually submits to the hierarchy of values grounded on production and consumption—seems to have condemned to generating an enormous volume of 'false consciousness' as its by-product.

Only the 'underdeveloped' part of ourselves, that is to say, the part that is not recognized in reality, contains (and is) the consciousness and truth of the part that is recognized. The latter is recognized, in daylight, by its peers; it conspires to oppress, repress and omit the servile part, it 'plays the game' exactly like the great planned industries and the reformist trade unions. *Only where we don't oppress or exploit ourselves and others dwell the forces capable of not letting us 'lose our life'.*

Every fraction of life and every word that wishes to be true must embrace a useful consummation, a destruction-fulfilment, a here-and-now; immediacy, as we know, is not only what must be overcome, without it there would be nothing to overcome. At the same time, life and word must cry out the desire for an avenging survival. Only hands that have survived incinerated bodies will be able to terrify Balthazar's animated dinner guests and herald the ruin of empires.[11] *With history against history.* 'When the creature will rise again', when the age of simplifiers without memory will carry out or is already carrying out (innocently and thus all the more completely) our vengeances, 'death will be surprised and nature too'.[12] But the advent (or recognition) of that age will not be (or is not) given except for those who through history will have brought (or are bringing) upon themselves contingency, causality and toil.

1963

Notes

Originally published in *Questo e altro* 4 (4 July 1963). [Trans.]

1 Nicola Bombacci (1879–1945), founding member of the Italian Communist Party, he became a supporter of Mussolini and was executed by partisans, his body hung in Piazzale Loreto along with that of the Fascist dictator; Antonio Graziadei (1873–1953), economist and founding member of the Italian Communist Party, from which he was expelled in 1928, to be readmitted in 1945; Giacinto Menotti Serrati (1874–1926), leader of the Italian Socialist Party, who led its left wing to fuse with the communists in 1924. [Trans.]

2 While working for Adriano Olivetti, Fortini wrote the introduction to *Mosaico di Ravenna* (Ivrea: Olivetti, 1957). [Trans.]

3 'These individuals who have felt the fear of death, of their absolute master, again submit to negation and distinctness, arrange themselves in the various spheres, and return to an apportioned and limited task, but thereby to their substantial reality'—G.W.F. Hegel, *Phenomenology of Spirit* (A.V. Miller trans.) (Oxford: Oxford University Press, 1977), p. 361.

4 I am thinking, for example, of structuralist methodologies and their various expressions. In France, in anthropological (Lévi-Strauss), psychoanalytic (Lacan) and literary and linguistic (Barthes) research. Regarding Lévi-Strauss I am referring especially to that part of the *Conversations with Claude Lévi-Strauss* by Georges Charbonnier (Paris: Plon-Juillard, 1961; John and Doreen Weightman trans, London: Jonathan Cape, 1969) which tells us about 'cold' or 'mechanical' societies, as studied by the ethnologist, against modern 'cold' or 'thermodynamic' ones. The author is categorical in this regard; for him, 'culture' is the ensemble of relations which, in a given form of civilization, human beings entertain with the world whereas 'society' is the ensemble of relations that human beings entertain among themselves. From this distinction, which sets itself decisively against Marxist thought, derives the idea (which does not avoid a reference to Arthur de Gobineau) that modern civilizations live on internal and external conflicts as 'imbalances' necessary to produce progress. 'It is conceivable that, for modern societies, progress and the achievement of a great degree of social justice might depend on transferring entropy from society to culture. This may seem a very abstract way of putting it, yet I am only repeating Saint-Simon's statement that the problem of modern times is how to effect the transition from the governing of men to the administration of things. "Government of men" corresponds to society and increasing entropy; "administration of things" corresponds to culture and the creation of an increasingly varied and complex order' (p. 42).

It might seem inappropriate, when it comes to the thought of Lévi-Strauss, to refer to such peripheral remarks. Yet we should not forget that they find confirmation in the anti-historicist polemic of *The Savage Mind* (1962). Bolstered by their great authority, they communicate in France and modern Europe the old dream of an exit from history through science and the replacement of class struggle—as agent of revolutionary transformation—with research departments controlled by the established powers. And, I would add, they also find confirmation in other disciplines. I leave the classification of these observations of mine to those who need a label in order to know whether they are 'for' or 'against'. I restrict myself to noting how the intelligence of Barthes (employing tools analogous to those that Lévi-Strauss calls 'structuralist', and moreover doing so with considerable legitimacy, ever since the notion of structure has become, rightly or wrongly, the trademark of a school of linguistics and then of critical method) does not escape the ideology and positivist standpoint of 'functions'. The continual reassertion that literature is a 'deceptive' system of signification, an intransitive language destined to recite the real, a language 'for itself' that is 'constitutionally reactionary' and so on, is absolutely important, even though—for a certain Italian tradition—it is far from new. Except that this notion of literature does not derive from, or is not framed by, the horizon of a totalizing drive or a kind of circularity, and the disenchantment that grounds it is a disenchantment of brief moment and little weight once one does not believe, or no longer does, in the first or transitive 'meaning' which must be undercut and overturned. In other words, the same word ('literature') covers both the linguistic fact that draws the uninterrupted power of its significations from the contradiction between communicative intention and linguistic form, and the one which in fact does not seek to communicate but only to confer upon practical everyday communication a set number of distancing formulae (literature in the sense of the 'good manners' that Croce spoke of). To put it otherwise: you cannot ideologize innocently, and it is not by chance that Barthes arrived at his current structuralism from a meditation on Brechtian *Verfremdung*; 10 years—and what years—have passed in the history of the Fourth and Fifth Republics, and the *sens deçu*, the disappointed meaning in which the French critic sees an ineliminable moment of literature, is also the great historical disenchantment of the *gauche*; except that the ideological coordinates (and then the cultural ones: the inevitable compromises of the critic of contemporary literature, who must after all speak of this or that author and be invoked as a sponsor for this or that literary or publishing operation and so on) tend to omit certain connections, to make historical inquiry superfluous, even about the immediate past, and to preclude the future: they institutionalize depoliticization. This is the difference between the positions of Barthes and those advanced below [see the section entitled 'Beyond the Social Mandate' in 'The Writers' Mandate and the End of Anti-Fascism', pp. 247–62 in this volume].

'It seems that today we accord a half-aesthetic, half-ethical privilege to openly disappointing systems, to the degree that literary *research* is ceaselessly brought to the limits of meaning; it is, in short, the frankness of literary status that becomes a criterion of value: "bad" literature is the one which proclaims a good conscience of fulfilled meanings, and "good" literature is on the contrary the one which struggles openly with the temptation of meaning.' So says Barthes ['Literature and Signification', *Critical Essays* (Richard Howard trans.) (Evanston: Northwestern University Press, 1972), pp. 262–82; here, p. 270, translation modified]. Even the famous dove that wanted to fly in the void struggled openly against the 'temptation of meaning'. [A reference to Immanuel Kant's remark: 'The light dove, in free flight cutting through the air the resistance of which it feels, could get the idea that it could do even better in airless space'—Immanuel Kant, *Critique of Pure Reason* (Paul Guyer and Allen W. Wood eds and trans) (Cambridge: Cambridge University Press, 1998), p. 129.] What is bracketed here is the fact—invoked in many other occasions—that literature is not just 'bad' or 'good'; it is a system of signs that also signifies itself; and those who struggle against the temptations of meaning do not thereby struggle against the meaning of literature itself, against its 'specialty', like one struggles against the Angel and like all great works struggle. The point is this: that for Barthes literary honour affirms itself by fighting at the borders of meaning while for us it does so by fighting at the borders of literature itself. His dialectic only operates internally to formalized functions. Is it because of despair? Pride? Self-defence? I don't know. As far as I'm concerned, I would like the lacerations of the 'human body' to be very visible, for no false or facile humanism to mask them, not in order to institutionalize them but to make the violence of the scandal (like one speaks of the 'scandal of the cross') cry out.

5 A reference to Canto 2 of Dante's *Paradiso*: *La concreata e perpetua sete / del deiforme regno* 'In-born in being, our perpetual thirst / to reach the deiform domain'—Dante Alighieri, *The Divine Comedy 3: Paradiso* (Robin Fitzpatrick ed. and trans.) (London: Penguin, 2007), p. 14. [Trans.]

6 From the Latin *Ubi sunt qui ante nos fuerunt?*, 'Where are those who were before us?', a recurring phrase in medieval poetry where it indicates a meditation on mortality. [Trans.]

7 A reference to Baudelaire's poem 'Le Crépuscule du soir' (Dusk): *Encore la plupart n'ont ils jamais connu / La douceur du foyer et n'ont jamais vécu*! (But most of them have never known the call / Of friendly heart, have never lived at all!)—Charles Baudelaire, *The Flowers of Evil*, pp. 194–5.

8 See Ernst Bloch, 'A Glance at Slave-Talk' in *Atheism in Christianity: The Religion of the Exodus and the Kingdom* (J.T. Swann trans.) (London: Verso, 2009), pp. 2–3.[Trans.]

9 'What characterizes revolutionary classes at their moment of action is the awareness that they are about to make the continuum of history explode'. And: 'We know that the Jews were prohibited from inquiring into the future: the Torah and the prayers instructed them in remembrance instead. This freed them from the spell of the future. . . . This does not imply, however, that for the Jews the future became homogeneous, empty time. For every second was the small gateway in time through which the Messiah might enter'—Walter Benjamin, 'On the Concept of History' in *Selected Writings: Volume 4, 1938–1940*, (Howard Eiland and Michael W. Jennings eds) (Cambridge, MA: Harvard University Press, 2006), pp. 389–400; here, p. 395, 397 [translation modified].

10 A reference to *The Brothers Karamazov*, where Ivan asks Alyosha: 'Tell me straight out, I call on you—answer me: imagine that you yourself are building the edifice of human destiny with the object of making people happy in the finale, of giving them peace and rest at last, but for that you must inevitably and unavoidably torture just one tiny creature, the same child who was beating her chest with her little fist, and raise your edifice on the foundation of her unrequited tears—would you agree to be the architect on such conditions?' —Fyodor Dostoevsky, *The Brothers Karamazov* (Richard Pevear and Larissa Volokhonsky trans) (London: Vintage, 2004), p. 245. [Trans.]

11 A reference to a tale in the Book of Daniel, about the Babylonian king who hosts a banquet where he serves wine out of golden vessels

stolen from the Temple in Jerusalem, whereupon a disembodied hand inscribes some premonitory verses on the wall. The expression 'seeing the writing on the wall' comes from this parable. Rembrandt's painting *Belshazzar's Feast* has this allegory as its subject-matter. [Trans.]

12 A quotation from the thirteenth-century Latin hymn *Dies Irae*, whose influence recurs in Fortini's work. [Trans.]

II

The Writers' Mandate and the End of Anti-Fascism

(a) *Brecht and the Origin of the Popular Fronts*

1. In Italy, between 1945 and 1953, and again in 1956, there was much discussion on the relations between cultural and political activity. In particular, the theme of the status of the writer and the artist within a socialist political perspective, party or country elicited some notable contributions. No Italian intellectual could remain aloof from that debate,[1] which went through stages determined by national and international events—the polemic over the demise of the journal *Il Politecnico* (1947), Zhdanov's theses on art and literature (1947), the publication of the works of Gramsci (1948–51) and of Lukács (1953–56), the debates on commitment[2] (1945–47), the cultural front (1948), neo-realism (1946–50) and socialist realism (1955).

These debates generally involved finding an answer to the question of what the cultural leadership function assumed by the Communist Party in our country was or could be. They faded out when, *de facto* if not *de jure*, the Communist Party ceased to lay claim to what it had instead practiced during the preceding years; but especially when (as a result of a process that took place between 1957 and 1962) it became apparent that almost all Italian writers had come to accept, along with the framework of parliamentary democracy and the existing institutions, the privatized forms in which the culture industry was organized.

If we are to understand some of the recent discussions on realism and the avant-garde, or the development of our literary culture over the last two decades, it is necessary to take a closer look at the limitations of the debates of the postwar years and the reasons behind them. I am convinced that it is not possible to decipher the meaning of the present without criticizing the ideological and political terms within which these debates took place, and without assessing the radical deficiencies in the way Italian culture, as it emerged from fascism, understood or thought it understood the terms of what had been the most important turning point of the past 30 years in the relationship between revolutionary intellectuals and writers and the working-class movement. Such an enquiry is historical, and therefore political. The lack of information on this question among young people is terrifying. Before getting a chance to apply their own informed judgement to the criticisms of knaves and fools, the young are forced to nourish themselves (has this always been the case?) with too many deficient by-products. In recent years, for example, the fashion among the heirs of the Italian left seems to have been the concoction of acceptable 'avant-garde' formulae, particularly where this involved exhuming models that had formerly met with the death penalty. The 1920s (in the Soviet Union, Germany or France) are 'reprised'—not for the sake of giving a new interpretation to the (often very) great artistic and poetic achievements and values of that period, but in order not to make a bad impression in the debate over peaceful coexistence and to show that, before the *mésalliances* of social realism, one knew how to hold one's position.

The responsibility that can be ascribed to those intellectuals who, between 1945 and 1956, either could not or would not look back over the immediate past of the class struggle, and remained satisfied with the assertion of their own anti-fascism, resembles that which the Italian intellectuals of the 1930s bore towards the generation that was about to leave school and enter the war.

When the history of Italian Stalinism is finally written, it will document the repression that between 1944 and 1948 targeted a nonconformist revolutionary culture which, however uncertainly and confusedly, was nevertheless beginning to take shape; it will make clear the extent to which the intellectual weakness of those who emerged from Fascism (our weakness) was objectively complicit with certain moral weaknesses and with the cultural policies of Stalinism, polemicizing with it from the right and thus from radical-liberal rather than Marxist positions; when this has been done, we might acquire a less mythical vision of certain projects, such as neo-realism in cinema, the *Politecnico* journal and so on. But it is already possible to argue that the postwar horizon was in a way blocked, at first spontaneously and then artificially, by the immediate past of Fascism and the blinding expanse of ruins and massacres. Besides the political calculations of its leaders, a kind of self-defence drove the intellectual left (authors, publishers, journalists, ideologues) to find mediated precursors in the immediate past—in other words, in the anti-fascist tradition. The boundaries of that viewpoint (as evinced, for example, in *Il Politecnico*) were the Popular Front in France, the Spanish Civil War, the New Deal. Beyond, two indeterminate decades, the ones which from 1937 stretched back to 1917. It is no accident that after the fall of Fascism we had to wait 20 years for the publication of a history of the Spanish war in Italian. And, to confine these observations to the position of writers: Didn't the whole discussion on commitment and non-commitment basically take place between a generic anti-fascist left under the guidance of the Communist Party (so much so that, between 1950 and 1955, someone like Lukács could still appear as a dogmatic extremist, a man who wanted literature in chains, etc.) and the idealist and Catholic tradition? There is no need for me to recall how many were in agreement back then, united in presenting a complex, varied, open, critical and generally all-purpose 'left' formula, in which one nevertheless spoke *parum de Deo, nihil de principe*[3]—or rather, little about the princes and not at all about Stalin.

The notes that follow are intended as working hypotheses.

2. During the period of what Lukács calls 'ideological decadence' (roughly, the second half of the nineteenth century), the intellectual body of the bourgeoisie split into several parts: organic and apologetic intellectuals (for example, Taine), progressive scientists (Darwin), artists and writers who confined themselves to an objective contestation of the capitalist reality represented in their work (like Guy de Maupassant) and oppositional authors (Rimbaud). But the bourgeoisie did not on the whole revoke the social mandate it had previously entrusted to writers. Their function as organ of universal conscience, characteristic of the *Aufklärung*, persists among the intellectuals of the age of democracy. Even if this function is in fact mystified, the advocates of socialism set themselves the task of realizing it. The entire misunderstanding over 'progressive' naturalisms and scientisms derives from the continued acceptance within European social democracy of a status for the man of letters and the artist, the one that had been articulated by the ascendant bourgeoisie. Between 1890 and 1915, in the inconclusive struggles of nationalities against super-national empires and against authoritarian and anti-democratic involution (in Germany, France, Italy and Spain), the socialist intellectual continued to draw sustenance from the illusion of a continuity of progress, beginning with the French Revolution and carried on by the Garibaldian and Mazzinian wing in Italy, and later by socialism (De Amicis, Cavallotti, Bettini, Rapisardi[4]), and in France by the democratic-Hugoist tradition. For, however great the tensions and conflicts, the national alliance had not yet been broken; it could be broken only in those countries where the bourgeoisie was very weak and pre-bourgeois survivals correspondingly strong—in Russia, or among the oppressed nationalities and, to a lesser extent, in Italy. In practice, the intellectuals and writers who were, or felt themselves to be, in conflict

with society in that quarter century did not even pose for themselves the problem of 'separation', that is to say, the problem of the 'Party', except in Eastern Europe. In Russia, the impetus of 80 years of intellectual and working-class struggle was such that at the end of the century, when the Social Democratic Party is formed, that division takes place, accompanied by a debate on the participation and commitment of the intellectuals, and there are splits among the latter (brilliantly portrayed by Maxim Gorky in the *Life of Klim Samgin* series) of an intensity unknown in western Europe even at the time of the Commune, and whose contemporary equivalent in the West took the typically 'backward' form of the Dreyfus Affair. What was going on in Italian literature and culture, as mirrored in the periodicals of the time, is eloquent testimony to this. As for the 'historical' avant-gardes, especially in the century's first decade, whether they belonged to an aristocratic and aestheticizing 'right' or to an anarchic and destructive 'left', they shared a rejection of the cultural terms of socialist discourse precisely because of the way it presented itself as a humanitarian, rationalist, optimistic and exhortatory tradition. The 'break' (in the form of avant-garde 'decadentism') with the realistic and naturalistic-veristic traditions of the European bourgeoisie was the mystified and ideological anticipation of a revolutionary 'break' that was failing to take place, but it was also the authentic expression of that shattered reality which social democracy instead regarded as subject to continual change. It is no accident that the 'historical' Parisian avant-gardes (and to differing degrees those of Munich and Vienna, as well as certain milieus in the Moscow and Petersburg avant-gardes) adopted habits and lifestyles copied from the anarchist underworld, living, as the phrase goes, 'on the fringes of society'. The aristocratic avant-gardes—people like André Gide, Robert Musil and Alexander Blok—were not all that different from Guillaume Apollinaire, Pablo Picasso and Vladimir Mayakovsky, living among *voyous* and *apaches* in the colourful *anar* world. What was unimaginable in the western Europe of the two decades before the First World War was a relationship between writers and the workers' movement comparable to the one that will be globally manifest, following the example of the Soviet Union, in the two decades from the October Revolution to the outbreak of the Second World War.

3. The problem of a 'spiritual homeland' (the phrase again is from Lukács, and follows the admission that, with Stalinism, the Soviet Union could no longer perform that role for intellectuals in the West) is not only that of a real separation from the national bourgeois community but also that of the achievement of an integration into the proletariat and thus into its 'vanguard'[5]—the Party. This problem was posed for Western writers only after the experience of the First World War and the immediate postwar period (and even then, just for a few of them[6]). In other words, the overwhelming character of the armed revolution and civil war in Russia created the conditions in which, at least temporarily and in spite of factional conflicts, the heirs of progressive humanism, the decadents and the avant-garde innovators managed for some years to cohabit in a shared acceptance of revolutionary reality. In the West, however, the cohabitation took place between capitalist society, social-democratic formations and revolutionary ones, with the result that for a pretty long time—roughly up until the world economic crisis of 1929—the theme of the relations between revolutionary organizations (and ideologies) and artistic and literary avant-gardes (and their ideologies) posed itself in an unprecedented way. The misunderstandings were immediate and destined to become tragic. For such a relationship can be non-formal and non-institutional only in the creative act, through the mediation of the 'language of art' and when it becomes an originary and direct relationship between the class and the poet without intermediaries. (The names of Sergei Yesenin, Isaac Babel and Attila József spring to mind here.) It is also inevitable, however, that the superstructural function of literature, its 'institution', should enter into conflict with that other aspect of the superstructure—the political organization of the

proletariat, namely, the Party. There begins a fierce dialogue of the deaf. It is an 'investiture contest' that simultaneously reveals and conceals a point of theory and praxis which is immeasurably important and has been hidden from us, both in Russia and western Europe, by the terms imposed upon us by 30 years of anti-fascist struggle.[7] Writers and artists demanded from the political organism not only mediation vis-à-vis an audience but also an institutional 'social mandate', a 'situation', a status. But this the political organism could not grant, for to do so would have meant renouncing some of its jurisdiction and prerogatives; it would also have meant confessing the error of having wished to anticipate *in* the Party something that can only be the aim *of* the Party. Besides, the political organism demanded of writers and artists that they should be the consciousness or reflection—the conscious reflection—of an order of reality that the political organism did not have the tools to bring to life. What was demanded, indeed, was not so much a propaganda function as one of revelation and discovery. But the formal character of artistic and literary expression is such as to render all contents ambiguous. So the Party—thinking it can satisfy, in all their naivety, the demands of the writers and artists themselves—before it resorts to salaries or deportations, rushes to their aid with contents, that is to say, with thematic proposals. But these, even when they are accepted, give rise to unforeseen formal results. Hence a conflict that is permanent and, to the extent that its real terms are mystified, useless.

4. The real conflict that the visible conflict frequently masked may be summed up as follows: The Party is the entity which, by its presence, points to the overcoming of 'specialisms'; it is the collective Prince and the collective philosopher *in potentia*. Now, to the extent that through their power over the word they preserve the spiritual power 'to bind and to loose', intellectuals (and in particular writers and artists whose activity is not reducible to a specialism) actually deny the unique power that the Party claims for itself. They mimic

the role of the priestly caste (in their cowardice as much as in their martyrdom). The Party claims the right to exercise *now* the function that it will perform only when it is dissolved as a Party in the classless society and in the homeostatic circulation of its components. The writer inserts himself into that *vacatio* and makes of himself a prophet disarmed, a tribune of 'values' not synchronous with the political present. The Party cannot allow the duality of powers, because that would constitute either a regression to liberal agnosticism or the positive beginning of its own withering away. It therefore demands deference—and gets it. But consciousness escapes it. The greatness of the Party lies in its refusal of the distinction between sacred and profane history: '*homo* homini deus'. While the greatness of the poet is to be found in his reaffirmation, 'so that this time may pass': 'homo homini *deus*'.

5. In the period of history we are summarizing here, the (biographical and poetic) case of Bertolt Brecht is of exceptional importance. The opposition of Brecht to Lukács, observable in our latitudes for a decade or so, is now a matter of popularization (or vulgarization, indeed vulgarity); but it symbolizes well enough the contradictions we have been talking about. And as my own discourse has no claim to be the historical-critical study that Brecht's work requires, we can still make use of that opposition.

It has become de rigueur in Brechtian criticism to establish a chronology and a description of the shift from the pre-Marxist to the Marxist Brecht. But what remains to be done, or to be made known in Italy, is a history of German Marxism in the Weimar period; it is extraordinary, for example, that the determining role of men like Fritz Sternberg and Karl Korsch in Brecht's ideological formation should be a recent discovery.[8] I think it is possible here to advance a hypothesis. We should start by rejecting two convenient pictures. The first is that of a Brecht enduringly attached to 'extremism' and its 'unrealistic' consequences—some verbal reservations aside, this is Lukács's fundamentally negative formula, but it is also present positively in the enthusiastic and tendentious interpretations of Brecht by the neo-avant-garde. The second is that of a Brecht who, throughout his various phases, remained on the right path—this is the auto-apologetic interpretation of the clerks-literati. What emerges as more plausible, both from a reading of the texts and by reference to the history of contemporary events, is that the study of Marxism (roughly between 1927 and 1929) produced in Brecht a radical change of position towards the bourgeois cultural inheritance. The fundamental difference is that whereas for the early 'avant-gardist' and 'subversive' Brecht, experimenting along with Erwin Piscator, 'tradition' means the bourgeois cultural tradition—something either to be rejected or to be used as a rag box or as junk thrown up on the flea market of global history—the Brecht of the phase going from *The Threepenny Opera* (1928) to *The Measures Taken* (1930) appears to belong to a current of Marxist thought that has cast off almost all anarchistic components of the avant-garde and is trying to trace a thread of tradition and an order of references which is not merely that of the golden age of the bourgeois and Jacobin achievement. It could indeed be claimed that even if we did not know about the influence of Korsch (not to mention many other possible influences), it would still be possible to read Brecht's poetic work as a rejection of the universalist-Jacobin component of Marxism or, rather, an acceptance of that component only in close conjunction with others—with the pre- or proto-bourgeois medieval and baroque inheritance (Germany between the Peasants' War and the Thirty Years' War) or with extra-European elements. Whence his predilection for wise sayings, proverbs, apologues, 'China'—and for the class supporting that entire inheritance, the peasantry. The Brechtian ideal is that of an Age of Science fashioned by the hands of people who like their roast geese, whether they be the hands of 'peasants' or of 'bourgeois in their ascendant phase'. The world of the future is for him, at one and the same time, atheist-rationalistic and rich in psycho-physical 'wisdom'. Lukács instead always retains a Eurocentric or, rather, Germanocentric attitude. It is the *working* class that is the heir to the universities, and it is the Soviet functionary of the First Five Year Plan, who in Lukács's eyes stands in for the (vanished) Russian working class, for whom one must reopen the way that leads from Lenin to Marx and from Marx to Hegel. From *The Measures Taken* onward, Brecht is instead especially sensitive to 'backward' forms of elementary, colonial or semi-colonial exploitation. We should not be surprised if his mythical Far East ends up actually coinciding with the prose of Mao Zedong.

What's more, Lukács's mistake does not appear to be the one for which he has been so often castigated, in his own country and here, which is in fact his greatest claim to fame—his struggle against mechanicism and positivism. If anything, it is the political and historical error (confirmed and aggravated by his most recent writings) of having believed that, from the time of the Popular Fronts (1934–35) onward, 'bourgeois-critical' intellectuals allied to the Communists in the struggle against fascism would have been able to furnish the (already Stalinized) working-class movement with elements of Hegelian Marxism that had been present in the Soviet Union in the early years of the revolution, in struggle with other tendencies such as that of Alexander Bogdanov. Lukács's theses triumphed too late, in the tragic and derisory formulae of 'socialist realism', and were imposed by sovereign command and government decree at the time of the establishment of the Union of Soviet Writers (1934), when Communist parties were crushed everywhere between the fascist offensive and internal bureaucratization. To have raised the banner of socialist humanism in the Europe of the 1920s; to have, as it were, spoken of Goethe to the Red Army soldier with his 'bloody and empty hands' to whom Brecht had dedicated one of his early poems—this is Lukacs's great honour. His error is to have believed that the image on this banner could survive the five-year period that begins with the assassination of Sergey Kirov (December 1934) and ends with the German-Soviet Pact (August 1939).

So the emblematic opposition changes face. Brecht is not the 'avant-garde' that Lukács had thought he was. Lukács is not the Philistine that Brecht believed him to be.

6. Another aspect of Brecht's importance—theatrical activity, which puts the work in direct, physical contact with its recipients, seemed more than any other literary form to choose its public, or at least to mark it out, and to define the social place of the author. Piscator's memoirs formulate the question with precision: For whom does one act? To whom are the performances of the 'Political Theatre' destined? But his book gives only a faint intimation of the answer. To understand what is at issue, one must keep in mind the whole complex universe of German communism and socialism and its 'cultural' organizations. Quite apart from the audience statistics, there is no doubt that the aims of Piscator's political theatre (for the purposes of this article, this can stand as the representative of a particular conception of theatrical commitment) were those of a proletarian public, a specific 'class' public. In other words, as the figure of Brecht gained prominence and as he began, along with his study of Marxism, to create his major works in parallel to the rise and victory of Nazism, so too was German communism increasingly constituting itself as a society within society. German communism tended to present itself as a new society, with all its attendant superstructures. Hence, among other things, its sectarian characteristics. It had partly inherited, and partly imitated, the cultural organizations of the social-democratic tradition, just as later it was to produce the mirror image of the armed formations of the Nazi Party. Throughout the Weimar period (and increasingly so, as one moves closer to Hitler's triumph), the process of progressive separation of the writer from the united bourgeois-democratic community (and therefore from the German democratic and enlightenment tradition) is brought to completion, a process that had been triggered, for the West, by October 1917. What certain groups in France, notably the surrealists, tried to accomplish by joining the Communist Party, was immensely more significant in Germany to the degree that the KPD was a larger party and had far wider support from intellectuals and writers who shared or sympathized with its positions. This confirms the truth of Walter Jens' observation (approvingly quoted by Lukács), that the whole of German literature in the 1920s is dominated by the theme of the interpretation of Soviet experience and the attitude to be taken towards it. Writers close to the revolutionary movement drew themselves into the 'circle of those who were below and struggling', looking for a task, a function, a *mandate*. Brecht portrays himself as one of 'the wise and friendly, angry and hopeful',[9] though it is not hard to point out how anachronistic, and indeed medieval, such a portrayal of the revolutionary writer is. Brecht does better in another poem of the same year (1939), when he speaks of the 'Danish thatched roof' and says that 'Yellowed books, fragmentary reports / Are my sources'.[10] (The fact is that, in reality, Brecht lived both functions—on the one hand, the compiler of a message that had to go 'under their sweat-soaked shirts / Through the police cordons',[11] the scribe whom the tumultuous Ciompi forced to put their truth down on paper; on the other, the mission of the man whose words to himself are: 'That's something you're doing for yourself; make it / Exemplary'.[12]) In 'Motto to the Svendborg Poems', from which I quoted above, the situation of the 'outlaw' with all its problems of double citizenship and double identity, is expressed as literally intolerable, and it explains why, for many, the Communist Party, even more than vanguard of the proletariat, acted as a society within society, a state within the state, an emanation of the Soviet state and a concrete anticipation of socialist society in which the writer could feel himself fully integrated. The violent victory of Nazism, depriving the writer even of the appearance of a society, left him with the choice of either integrating himself in the party as representative of Soviet power (and therefore, as it soon became clear, in a bureaucratic role) or facing the void. But what about those who accepted neither the 'humanist' illusions of the democratic anti-fascist fronts nor the idea of a return 'home', as one witnessed with the majority of English intellectuals after the Spanish War? On the eve of the Second World War, a number of writers finally discovered what the working class should have known for at least a hundred years—that they had no homeland. This elementary truth, although etched into the pages of the *Manifesto*, had been regarded as little more than a phrase and interpreted only in a simple anti-nationalistic direction. Accusations of cosmopolitanism or worse awaited anyone who spoke the truth—that the homeland of the best had now become the death camps. That is why the responses of leftist German intellectuals to the Nazi victory are of exceptional importance. As I mentioned with the example of the theatre, in no other European country did the errors and strengths of the communist movement create within bourgeois capitalist society such an illusory anticipation of a proletarian state and had therefore carried to its ultimate consequences the process of bringing intellectuals and writers closer to the political organization of the proletariat. All this, needless to say, in a characteristically 'German' manner, in the sense in which Marx uses the word—that is to say, in a formal, idealistic and therefore paradoxically literary manner, that of one who has everything *except* power. So, all that will be left by way of testimony of the age, amid the rising reality of the physical slaughter of political and trade union cadres, will be the literary and poetic word.

7. There is no need to clarify how Brecht's work was at the same time a product, an expression and an overcoming of the condition I have been describing. Suffice it to say that if, from about 1930, it became practically impossible *anywhere in the world* to venture a positive formulation of the relation of writers and artists to the revolutionary parties, this was to a large extent due to the fascist weapon of capital and the pressure of the class enemy which drove the country of 'socialism in one country' into false consciousness.

In this connection it is very striking to find in the essays of Lu Xun, alongside a deliberate revolutionary commitment, this consciousness of a paradoxical condition. In a 1927 essay, commenting on an article by Radek about the suicides of Sergei Yesenin and Andrey Soboly entitled 'Artists without Fatherland', Lu Xun writes:

> Any revolutionary poets who have ideals and illusions before the revolution are likely to suffer the fate of crashing themselves to death on the reality for which they have sung paeans of hope. Yet, if the reality of the revolution does not pulverize the illusions or ideals of such poets, then this revolution is nothing but empty talk. Yesenin and Soboly should not be blamed too much, they had fulfilled themselves by singing an elegy for themselves. They used their own deaths to prove that the revolution had been going forward.[13]

And, in a talk at the Military Academy of Huangpu in the same year, he has an identical reaction to the one which Brecht will have 10 years later in Spain. Lu Xun: 'I would rather hear the thundering cannon. . . . A poem cannot frighten a "master of war", but a cannonball can overthrow him. I know people who think that literature has a great influence on the revolution. For my part, I doubt it'. And Brecht, in his speech in Madrid in July 1937: 'If culture is something inseparable from the whole productivity of a people, if one and the same aggressive intervention can rob people of both butter and the sonnet, if culture is something so material, what must be done for its defence? . . . [It] must now be defended with material weapons'.[14] Let us recall that on the same occasion the official communist spokesman (Paul Vaillant-Couturier) said this instead: 'Remain writers. . . . We do not want to make a corporal of a man whose voice can move an army'. That statement touched on a bitterly important point. For the writer whose 'voice can move an army' is in fact the bureaucrat of letters, the specialist in propaganda, integrated in mystification. But the writer who (like Ludwig Renn, a fighter in Spain who at the same Congress said, 'I offer you this pen as a present') has no great belief in the influence of literature on the revolution and who, despite his militancy, bears witness to his divided condition thereby points, through his own destiny and his own work, to an unresolved and possibly unresolvable question of doctrine and action in the revolutionary movement; he cooperates with that movement 'as an intellectual' with a force that, at the very least, matches that of his most inspired and solitary poetic creations.

8. Lukács's struggle against what he now calls sectarianism—and defines as the tendency to reject the moment of mediation between principles and practical action—has led him to claim that the anti-fascist struggle was a strategic mediation of the fundamental conflict: 'Not only can there be an opposition between any absolutely necessary tactical action and general theoretical and universal-historical principles, but such an opposition can occur even within our own strategy.' Or again: 'The contradiction whereby our strategy and tactics were not determined by the fundamental opposition of the epoch, the opposition between capitalism and socialism, but by the one between fascism and anti-fascism, was a real historical contradiction, an expression of the real historical movement.'[15] The same thesis is repeated in the postscript to the 1957 book *Mein Weg zu Marx* (My Path to Marx), where Lukács recalls that at Wrocław, in 1948, the theme of his intervention was the unity and dialectical distinction between yesterday's enemy (i.e. Nazism) and today's enemy (i.e. imperialist reaction). Furthermore: 'While in the second half of the 1920s the struggle against fascism had become the central problem, Stalin did not grasp its significance for another ten years.' This was an age, he adds, in which 'the formation of a unitary front, and indeed a front of all the democratic elements, had become a vital question for the future of human society.' Finally, in a recent text on the Sino-Soviet debate (1963) he notes that although he still believes the 1939 Molotov–Ribbentrop Pact was correct, 'it was a serious error for the Communist parties of the West [i.e. the French Party] to have seen in Hitler's attack against their homelands an imperialist war of the old style and, contrarily, their own governments and not Hitler, as the real enemies.'[16]

At this point, one cannot help observing that between 1934 and 1935 Stalin enacts—and gets the other communist parties to follow suit—precisely those policies that Lukács was calling for, except by the time he does it Hitler is already in power. Likewise, we can observe that the policies of the Popular Fronts, coherently pursued throughout the decisive years from 1935 to 1939 and throughout the Spanish War, concluded—as I see it—in a series of defeats, the greatest of which was precisely the outbreak of the world war.

Given all that we have said about the main tendencies in revolutionary literature between 1918 and 1933, Lukács's interpretation of the politics of anti-fascism, particularly in his recent writings, is obviously of extreme importance. These tendencies can be reduced to three. The first regards the perspective of revolutionary culture as the realization of the best of bourgeois humanism; it aspires to reconnect itself with that humanism across the caesura of 'decadence' which can take the form of avant-gardism, psychologism, aestheticism or naturalism, creating separations on both synchronic and diachronic planes. The second is represented by the 'historical avant-gardes' which proclaim rupture with all the cultural forms of the immediate past, salvaging only a long list of precursors and initiates that culminates in surrealism. The third tendency corrects the first and the second, and tries to link with a tradition that is both beyond bourgeois humanism and outside the European tradition. Now it is more than likely that there exist a whole series of relations between the way one sees one's own position in the present (i.e. in the revolutionary workers' movement), the way one sees one's attitude towards the past (i.e. tradition), and the way one is to interpret an historical event of the magnitude of fascism.

Here the a posteriori justification of the Popular Fronts proposed by Lukács, when tested against what happened in the field of cultural politics (and the Paris Congress of 1935), proves to be driven by the same contradictions of which he accuses Stalin. Lukács does not tell us that the Popular Fronts were a necessity imposed by the struggle against fascism, though they did not succeed in avoiding the greatest malediction, namely, the war; and, in particular, that the intellectual convergences of the time proved of limited value in the struggle against fascism and were largely negative in their effects on socialist struggles. Instead, Lukács depicts both the fronts and these convergences as revolutionary victories.

As late as 1933, through the mouth of Georgi Dimitrov, fascism is considered the armed organization of the bourgeoisie; and Nazism, in Leon Trotsky's words, as 'Thiers riding an armoured car'. But when the 'sectarian' theses of the KPD are replaced by the slogans of the Popular Front, the antithesis fascism–anti-fascism comes to occupy the entire historical horizon (this is because there is no longer any internal movement within the Party and it can only move 'like one man'). As a result, the writer and intellectual are faced not only with the problem of a *political* alliance with social-democratic or liberal forces prepared to join the fight against fascism but also with that of seeking intellectual convergences (whether because of opportunism or bureaucratic convenience, either way there are phrases in the texts of 30 years ago which reek of lies). But where are these convergences to be found if not in a definition of fascism as 'the enemy of every civilization'—meaning bourgeois civilization too? If fascism is indeed linked to capital, but by its pathological and monstrous features, as an enemy of the human race and if from 1935 onward the desire not to 'frighten away' writers and intellectuals 'of good will' with Marxist slogans comes to dominate (10 or 15 years later, this fear will still be at large in our own country), then the only ground on which a meeting is possible is that of the most insipid social-radical 'humanism', the same cultural ground that produced aesthetes and decadents in art and literature. Lukács is thus reluctantly driven into the illusory pursuit of the last gold-bearing veins of 'great realism'. Innovators, avant-gardists and the like become acceptable only if they are prepared to repeat, under the shade of the Popular Fronts, the same innocuous gestures of revolt they had carried out under the shade of governments of national unity or of the right.

The truth that the fundamental historic conflict between capitalism and socialism takes different forms at different times has been unjustifiably extended to define the tasks, functions and responsibilities of the revolutionary writer. If at this point we recall the phrase of Goethe's that Lukács himself quotes in his recent comment on the Sino-Soviet debate—adding that there can be no 'co-existence' between ideas and that '[c]ultural accomplishments of high value have to exact autonomy in their own sphere'—we are once again brought to the central tragic point of this half-century long story. Up until now it has been impossible for the party of the proletariat and of the revolution to articulate within itself, in an organic way, the tension between the order of truths of the 'short term' and those of the 'long term', between the superstructural area of political will and that other superstructure which belongs to the writer and poet and touches on historical, philosophical and scientific 'knowledge'—with the consequences we are all familiar with.

(b) *Palais de la Mutualité, 1935*

The First International Congress for the Defence of Culture, otherwise known as the Congress of Anti-Fascist Writers, held in Paris in 1935, now seems like just one among those politico-cultural congresses of which there were so many in the years immediately prior and even more in the years that followed. Despite the scope of its debates and the claim advanced by some that it was 'the most important event in the history of culture since the Great Encyclopedia', the majority of the 2,000 participants did not seem to believe in the efficacy of their own declarations.[17]

The value of this congress—which I want to discuss in relation to both the text by Brecht reproduced as an appendix to this section and the two other sections of this essay—stems from the fact that it was a conclusion and a beginning. It brought to a close a series of encounters between a number of European anti-fascist writers and intellectuals and their counterparts from an already Stalinist Soviet Union; encounters that had begun some years earlier under different conditions. It also established a type of relationship between the writer and the Party and between the writer and Soviet power that corresponded to a political formula for cultural alliances and that remained more or less unchanged for over a quarter of a century. It must therefore be seen as a major step in a process that involved us all until very recently—the evolution or involution of individual positions in relation to the contingent ideological stances of political or party authorities.

If we consider the complex and contradictory directions taken by the Soviet cultural leadership in the years between the death of Lenin (1924) and the expulsion of Trotsky (1928), and even more in the following period which saw the consolidation of the formula of 'socialist realism' (1932–34), and if we then situate these events alongside the development of western European fascisms and the world economic crisis of 1929–33, we get the impression that the progressive liquidation of the literary and artistic avant-gardes in the Soviet Union, through the affirmation of a poetics of 'socialist realism' and 'revolutionary romanticism', was paralleled in the West by an increasing awareness on the part of anti-fascist intellectuals and writers of their political responsibility. While in the USSR ideological and political control on writers grew progressively more severe, reaching its apex in the purges that followed the assassination of Kirov in 1935 and again in the trials of 1936–37, in the West, and particularly in France, an increasing number of writers from the humanist tradition, becoming aware of the threat posed by fascism to the values of the liberal-democratic tradition, readied themselves for the hypothesis of the Popular Front. In France there already existed, for example, the journal *Europe*, edited by men like Charles Vildrac, Georges Duhamel, Marcel Martinet, Jacques Mesnil, Boris Souvarine, Charles Plisnier and Fritz Brupacher, who cannot be dismissed as mere intellectual mouthpieces of the SFIO.[18] It is true that between 1927 and 1933 the anti-socialist polemic of the communists was quite virulent. But the organizer of the pacifist anti-fascist congress held in March 1929 in Berlin (still on social-democratic positions) and also of the international congress against the war in Amsterdam from 27 to 31 August 1932 is the very same Henri Barbusse who, three years later, will organize the great congress of intellectuals in Paris; while among the promoters, in both cases, we find Maxim Gorky and Romain Rolland. Meanwhile, from 1925, a journal like *Clarté*, founded by Barbusse after the war on pacifist positions was becoming, thanks to the work of a group of writers including Jean Bernier and Marcel Fournier, the base from which the surrealist group could move towards direct participation in politics. For example Éluard and Breton joined the PCF in 1927, but during that year they continued working for *Clarté* whose stances were so out of line with official party positions that its reporting on Moscow and China—of decisive importance at that moment—was signed Victor Serge. Later Serge was to be deported by Stalin and his case will come up, as a 'scandal', at the 1935 Congress itself. The conflict which the Congress was to witness had therefore been in preparation for at least eight years.

In March 1932 (that is to say, even before the Amsterdam pacifist congress), the so-called EAR (*Association des Écrivains et Artistes Révolutionnaires*) was formed, leading to the founding of *Commune*. This journal first appeared in July 1933 and featured a very significant editorial board. Alongside Rolland and Barbusse, representatives of the anti-militarist tendency and inheritors of the radical socialist spirit who had rallied to communism, there was Gide while the PCF was represented by Vaillant-Couturier. (Later Gorky's name was added, though clearly only in an honorific capacity.) The administrative editors were the 'young men', Louis Aragon and Paul Nizan. This composition already suggests a 'popular front' formula, even though in the pages of the magazine one could still criticize a manifesto issued by the *Comité de vigilance des intellectuels antifascistes* and signed by 1,200 people, including Rolland himself, perceived as rallying the workers to unity on an excessively indiscriminate basis. But then came the attempted fascist coup of 6 February with a fire-fight on Place de la Concorde, and the first months of 1934 saw the political organizations taking steps towards the formation of the Popular Front. By the second half of the year, the Front was already a reality, although its definitive sanction, involving all the communist parties, came only in the following year.

In the USSR, meanwhile, the movement took what appeared to be an opposite direction. Following a decree of the Central Committee of the CPSU(b) of 23 April 1932, preparations were carried out to allow the convening, from 17 August to 1 September 1934, of the first Congress of Soviet writers. This congress formulated the notion of socialist realism and founded the Union of Writers, and was thus an instrument which (with the complicity, though it is not clear how wilful, of Gorky) was to consign Soviet literature into the hands of the bureaucracy for a quarter of a century.[19] It is interesting to note that in the June issue of *Commune* there appeared an article signed by Pavel Yudin and Alexander Fadeyev entitled 'Socialist Realism: Fundamental Method of Soviet Literature', followed by the 'Projected Statutes of the Union of Soviet Writers'.

The second half of 1934, as we have already mentioned, witnessed the continuing spread and success of the new formulae of the 'fronts'. In August, for example, socialist and communist Italian émigrés proclaim their pact of unity of action. On 18 September, the USSR was admitted to the League of Nations marking the beginnings—in keeping with the revision of Soviet foreign policy—of a rapprochement between the Soviet Union and France which led to Pierre Laval's visit to Moscow in the first half of 1935 and the signing of the Franco-Soviet Treaty of Mutual Assistance (2 May).

On 10 June, 11 days before the opening of the Congress, Trotsky, expelled by the Daladier government in honour of the new alliance, leaves France and writes the following in an open letter to the French workers:

> Two years ago, *l'Humanité* used to harp daily: 'The Fascist Daladier has called the social-Fascist Trotsky to France in order to organize, with his assistance, a military intervention against the USSR'. . . . Today, as everybody knows, these gentlemen have made an anti-Fascist 'people's front' with the 'Fascist', Daladier.[20]

It should be noted here that the new political line of the Comintern, which was explicitly formulated in its 7th congress in July–August 1935 (in which Togliatti played a major part), encountered considerable resistance in the German Communist Party. In January 1935, a resolution of the Politburo of the Comintern criticizes the KPD for its sectarian position. There follows a purge of the leadership, starting with Fritz Heckert, leader of the party after Thalmann's imprisonment. On 19 January, the order is given to break off the ongoing negotiations between the KPD leadership and the exiled social-democratic left and to start negotiations directly with the leadership of the Social Democrats (first steps are taken on 11 February, leading to an abortive meeting in August). Meanwhile, on 30 January, the new Central Committee of the KPD passes a resolution approving the policies of the Popular Fronts.

This heavy-handed intervention of the Comintern helps to explain, to my mind, Brecht's temporary refusal to rally to the new positions, which is implicit in his speech at the Congress.

The biggest delegations, alongside the French, were the one from Soviet Union (which had never before sent such a large contingent of writers to the West) and the one composed of the German émigrés. The speeches dealt with the relationship between culture and the nation, between creation and freedom of thought as well as with the problem of modern humanism. The French group included, besides Barbusse (who wrote very tendentious accounts of the Congress in *L'Humanité*), Gide (who had gone to Berlin the year before with André Malraux to request the liberation of Dimitrov but who the following year, after his journey to the USSR, was to break with the Communists), Malraux, Aragon (who three years before, at the Kharkov Congress, had already begun his separation from the surrealists), Julien Benda, Jean Cassou, Jean Guéhenno, Paul Vaillant-Couturier, André Chamson, Jean-Richard Bloch, Georges Friedmann and Paul Nizan. The Soviet delegation, apart from the 'Parisian' Ilya Ehrenburg (who on the eve of the Congress was slapped in the face by Breton on the Boulevard Montparnasse for having described the activities of the surrealists as 'pederastic'), included Alexei Tolstoy, Nikolai Tikhonov, Vsevolod Ivanov, Isaac Babel, Mikhail Koltsov, Boris Pasternak, Fedor Panferov, Alexander Shcherbakov, Vladimir Kirshon and another 10 or so writers, either less well known or members of other non-Russian nationalities. (Two years later, at the Second Congress,[21] Mikhail Sholokhov and Alexander Fadeyev will join the new delegation, while Babel, Pasternak and Ivanov will be absent.[22])

Among the Germans, there were Heinrich Mann, Johannes Becher, Gustav Regler, Max Brod, Erich Weinert, Anna Seghers, Egon Erwin Kisch, Waldo Frank, Klaus Mann and the ageing critic Alfred Kerr. Musil, still little known, was also present and was indeed on the presidential platform at the first session. And, arriving from Svendborg in Denmark, the 'little country' he will talk of in his speech, there was Bertolt Brecht.

One day it would be useful to provide a detailed study not only of the 10 sessions of the Congress between 21 and 25 June but also a reconstruction of the days leading up to it, particularly as concerns the discussions between René Crevel and the Congress organizers who refused to allow Breton to speak (his speech was eventually read out by Éluard) as well as Crevel's subsequent suicide. Nor was there any shortage of dramatic episodes and violent polemics during the congress itself. Nonetheless, I feel that the main concern of an inquiry such as this should be focussed on trying to identify those mental attitudes, formulae and watchwords that for a long time thereafter enjoyed a worldwide circulation and became veritable ideological schema of our century. As far as our present interests are concerned, we should note a clear desire on the side of the communists (at least the Soviets and the French) to play down but, at the same time, to not ignore the presence of an opposition generically referred to as 'Trotskyist'. This can be seen, for example, in a declaration signed by the whole Soviet delegation and published in the official Comintern bulletin, or in the following comment from *Commune*: 'The pettiness of some Trotskyists and the petty-bourgeois attitudes of some of the surrealists have provoked universal contempt and pity, for example, the attempts by Mme Paz and by Plisnier to sabotage the unity of writers from 35 countries under the pretext of defending the counter-revolutionary Victor Serge'.[23]

Naturally, the vast majority of contributions, coming as they did from non-Marxist writer-intellectuals, came down on the side hoped for by the Communist organizers; they supported just those interpretations of the fascist phenomenon that Brecht rejected. The official party representatives rubbed the point home. Vaillant-Couturier even uttered this extraordinary statement: 'In the struggle between barbarism and culture, culture is faced with the problem of winning over the majority.' And a few lines further: 'We offer to everyone a minimum programme for the defence of culture compatible with everything that can survive within it of old-world influence. . . . Patience is the greatest revolutionary virtue'.[24] Tristan Tzara, who was obviously brought in to 'execute' the hated Breton, declared in his speech that intellectuals were threatened by two extreme positions, one of which was the 'ivory tower' while the second was devoted 'in the name of some sort of revolutionary leftism of a clearly anarcho-idealist stamp, to criticizing social action down to the smallest detail and thus to rejoining in a roundabout way the enemies of the revolution'. Tzara goes on, alternating blackmail and threats: 'The poet who places his production above his existence, places himself in the camp of reaction. But the poet who, though he may be ready to give his life for the revolution, ends up throwing a spanner in its works under pretexts that range from outmoded aestheticism to post-revolutionary philosophy, such a poet, I say, must be driven out of the revolutionary community that is taking shape'.[25]

There were very few contributions to the debate that were not generically humanistic or aligned on the positions of communist tactics or in declared opposition to them.[26] Among these we should mention (besides John Strachey and Georges Friedmann) the 30-year-old Paul Nizan who seems to be at least a decade in advance of many more authoritative participants.[27] Polemicizing with Benda, Nizan affirms that humanism is great only when it is unfaithful to purity. The civilization that the communists aim to create is both a continuation of existing civilization and a break with it. It accepts from the Western tradition everything that indicts the world and puts itself forward as a demand for totality. Rejecting every humanist mythology, 'our attitude is neither a continuation nor a break: it is a selection.' Further: 'the problem of the writer is posed within a humanism that involves both the conquest of the earth on the part of all mankind and the conquest of the highest degree of consciousness and humanity by each human being'. In a letter written by a Petersburg worker to the editors of *lskra*,[28] one can read the following:

> We have written to *lskra* so that it may show us not only where to begin but how to live and how to die.
>
> *In this world where each of us is prey to solitude and war, the affirmation of communal values is possible only among those who are engaged together in a common struggle* [I emphasize this phrase of Nizan's since here he comes closest to Brecht's position]. . . . A day will come when men will be able to accept their destiny. . . . But today we are still

> speaking only in the name of a humanism that is limited both because it rejects the world and because it implies hatred; and in which the only value prefiguring our future is the voluntary fraternity of men committed to changing life.

In this context, Brecht's intervention[29] can be considered from two angles: it is the expression of a temporary dissent from the new line of the communist movement; but it is, above all, the objective expression of a condition of the revolutionary writer (symbolized by his exile in a Danish house), which differed from that expressed in the opposition between 'socialist humanists' and Trotskyist 'avant-gardes'.

At the opposite extreme from the frontist bloc were the surrealists, as expressed in Breton's speech read out to the Congress by Éluard (a couple of years later it would be reworked in the declaration of the *Fédération internationale de l'art révolutionnaire indépendant*, the 'Manifesto for an Independent Revolutionary Art' signed by Breton and Diego Rivera, though co-written by Trotsky and Breton). The surrealists treated figures like Gorky, Barbusse, Rolland and Mann as prehistoric fossils, viewing themselves as the most coherent anti-fascist writers. The surrealist thesis affirmed an anti-capitalist, anti-fascist, anti-Stalinist struggle to 'change life' (in Rimbaud's phrase), and thus a revolt against fatherland, family, religion, police, etc. Whence their insurgence against what they considered to be an abandonment of the Leninist call to 'turn imperialist war into civil war' and against everything in Stalin's Russia that smacked of restoration of the family, of hierarchies, of the army, etc. About the significance of these theses I have written at length elsewhere.[30] What interests us here is the absence in their position of any mediation (whether theoretical or practical, ideological or political) between an analysis which is, once and for all, taken as a given (the discourse on 'property relations' or revolutionary prolegomenon) and a literary or artistic practice understood as an immediate appropriation of the future in the present and as a practical aid to the transformation of the world. It is to them, but *only* to them, that one can apply the criticism that Lukács directed—under the heading of extremism—at everyone who at the time opposed the formulae of socialist realism. In the surrealists, but not in Brecht, there is total refusal of all tactics in pursuit of a strategy that dwells on the horizon like a true 'bad infinity', becoming the accomplice of immobilism.

Brecht instead does not follow his discussion of *Eigentumsverhältnissen* or property relations with any 'cultural' or 'literary' slogan other than that of 'specifying or helping to bring about social conditions which will make barbarism superfluous'—in other words, executing the most coherent political action. The experience of Hitler's rise to power and of emigration revealed to him the need to renounce 'classical' fullness and the 'solid ground beneath their feet' which both 'socialist realists' and 'progressive humanists' claimed to have or feigned having. He knew that, in Europe at least, Marxism was not capable of overcoming the antithesis between the 'here and now' and the 'long run', between the cry of revolt and the power of patience. The integration of intellectual and artistic labour within the working class in advance of the revolutionary leap had become mystified, it was posited now *only* for the purposes of antifascism. This was the endpoint of the numerous incarnations of an old dream of intellectuals and poets, that they could live and work, so to speak, in a room of the 'house of the people', integrated into a kind of society that had hollowed itself out a space within the society of the ruling class, no longer as orphans, no longer speaking two languages, no longer burdened with a double identity . . . This will, or this hope, had probably found in the intellectual left of Weimar Germany and in Brecht's own work (particularly between 1929 and 1933) its most coherent and intense formal expression. But (and here the argument would require a lot more evidence) the very formula of didactic theatre, and the very theory of the alienation effect and its resistance against identifying actor and character prove just how precarious and hard to sustain was the aim of an artistic expression by the class for the class, in a situation where the class did not exercise power over society. *In a nutshell, we can suggest that those theories and the living contradictions that were introduced into Brechtian theatre during the Weimar period may be seen as a transposition and reflection of the dual class character of the audiences, a social duality of the public.* It is irrelevant whether Brecht remained faithful to his artistic ideology or whether he occasionally abandoned it in order to burn some 'Aristotelian' incense at the altar of the Party. The point is that after two years in exile Brecht issued a political call to arms and gave counsel on how to 'write the truth'. In other words, Brecht advances techniques for the class struggle and tries to fuse his own vocation as an artist with that of the revolutionary copywriter. But he remains well aware of the need to reject the sterile materials and padding with which some were trying to fill the 'essential void' in the proletarian condition. 'Let us talk of property relations' means the exact opposite of the French slogan of *engagement*. In reality, in Spain (and later in the Resistance), and precisely on the basis of the anti-fascist myth, the intellectuals and poets of the 'left' will find for the last time a 'home' and temporary 'society', a prefiguration or premonition. In Italy, for obvious reasons, this would remain true for a few more years.

Today, when the condition of 'internal émigré' is the only possible condition for the intellectual who has not given up on the socialist perspective, the invitation to talk about 'property relations' and descend to the nether regions where 'a minority has anchored its pitiless domination' contains a hard prophecy and a directive which is all the more difficult to carry out to the extent that the last 25 years seem to have made the invitation derisory, because it is obsolete. 'Property relations' and 'pitiless class domination' are no longer hidden and there is no need to descend into hell to find them. As Brecht hinted elsewhere, that domination is programmed for 10,000 years.[31] No longer being able to tell hell and heaven apart, or good from evil, is the surest proof that you are in hell, which is evil at peace with itself.

Appendix

Bertolt Brecht's Speech at the First International Congress of Writers for the Defence of Culture (*Paris, 1935*)

Comrades—without wanting to say anything particularly new, I should like to say something about the struggle against those powers which at present are striving to smother in blood and filth Western culture or, rather, such remains of culture as a century of exploitation has left alive. I should like to draw your attention to a single point, about which, in my opinion, we must be extremely clear if it is our intention to fight these powers effectively and fight them to the end. The writers who, in their own body or in the body of others, experience the atrocities of Fascism, and are outraged by them, are not automatically as a result of this experience and this outrage in a position to fight these atrocities. Some may think that it is enough to describe these atrocities, particularly when real talent and real anger are at work to make the description effective. Such description is important. Atrocities are taking place. This must not be. People are being struck down. This must not be. What further discussion do we need? Let someone stand up and fall upon the torturers. Comrades, we need to discuss.

Someone perhaps will stand up; that's not too hard. But then we must fall upon the enemy, and that is harder. Our anger is there, the enemy is identified. But how do we bring him down? The writer may say 'My task is to denounce wrongs', and he can leave it to his readers to act against them. But then the writer will have a strange experience. He will discover that anger, like pity, is something that exists as a quantity. It is available as a quantity and it is released as a quantity. But the worst of it is that where more is released it is because more has been needed. Comrades have said to me: When we first announced that our friends had been killed, there was a cry of outrage and offers of help. That was when a hundred had been killed. But then when thousands were killed and there was no sign of an end to the killing, silence spread and little help was offered. This is how it is. 'When crime becomes frequent it becomes invisible; when suffering becomes unbearable, the cries of the sufferer become inaudible. One person is killed and the bystanders faint. That is natural. When massacre comes falling like rain no one any longer calls out halt'.

That is how it is. What is to be done about it? Is there no way to stop people turning their faces away from atrocities? Why do people turn away? They turn away because they can see no way to intervene. People do not dwell on the sufferings of others when they have no means of helping. One can stay a blow when one knows when it will fall, and where it will fall and why and to what purpose it will fall. And when one can stay the blow, when any possibility, however slight, exists of doing so—then one can have sympathy with the victim. One can also do it at other times, but not for long, and not for all the time that the blows are raining on the victim. So we must ask: Why does the blow fall? Why is culture being thrown overboard like ballast, those remains of culture that we still possess? Why is the life of millions of people, of the majority of people, being impoverished, stripped naked, nearly or even totally destroyed?

Some of us would answer the question in this way: Out of brutality. They believe that they are experiencing a terrifying outbreak among increasing sections of humanity, a monstrous occurrence with no knowable cause, that has appeared suddenly from nowhere and will perhaps, with luck, disappear into nowhere, a violent emergence of long repressed or slumbering instinctual barbarity.

Those who answer in that way are of course themselves aware that such an answer does not go very far. And they also feel that one should not grant to this brutality the status of a natural force, of an unconquerable power from hell.

So they speak about the neglected education of the human race. Something there has been passed over or could not be done in a hurry. Lost ground must be made up. Goodness must be set against brutality. The great words must be invoked, the exorcism that has worked before, the immortal concepts, love of freedom, honour, righteousness, whose efficacy is proved by history. The exorcism is applied. And what happens? The proof of its brutality is offered by Fascism in the form of fanatical celebration of brutality. Accused of fanaticism, it answers with the celebration of fanaticism. Charged with offences against reason, it proceeds complacently to put reason itself on trial. Fascism too finds that education has been neglected. It hopes itself to influence minds and captivate hearts. To the brutality of its torture-chambers it adds that of its schools, its newspapers and theatres. It educates the whole nation and educates it all day long. It has not all that much to offer the great majority, but it can offer education. It has no food to offer, so it educates people to self-restraint. It cannot get production working properly and it needs wars, so it educates people for physical courage. These are ideals, demands to make on people, sometimes they are even high ideals, noble demands. Now we know what purpose these ideals serve, who is doing the educating and who the education benefits, which is surely not the educated. But what of our ideals? Even those of us who see the root of the evil in brutality and in barbarism, speak, as we have said, only of education, only of intervening in people's minds, certainly of no other intervention. They speak of education in the direction of Good. But Good will not emerge spontaneously from the demand for Good, from Goodness under all conditions, even the worst, just as Brutality did not originate from Brutality.

I do not believe in brutality for brutality's sake. One must defend humanity against the accusation that it would be brutal even if brutality were not good business. My friend Feuchtwanger is witty but wrong when he says vulgarity comes even before self-interest. Brutality does not come from brutality, but from the business that can only be done with its assistance.

In the small country where I live conditions are less terrible than in many countries, but every week 5,000 prime heads of cattle are destroyed. That's bad. But it is no outbreak of sudden blood-thirstiness. If it were, then things would not be so bad. The destruction of beef cattle and the destruction of culture do not have barbaric instincts as their cause. In both cases, a part of the stock of laboriously produced commodities is eliminated because it has become a burden. In view of the starvation that reigns over four-fifths of the world, these measures are doubtless crimes, but there is nothing wanton about them, nothing at all. In most countries of the world today, we have social conditions in which crimes of every kind are highly rewarded and virtue is expensive. 'The good man is defenceless and the defenceless man is beaten to death, but with brutality one can get everything one wants. Vulgarity has set itself up for 10,000 years. Goodness needs a bodyguard, but finds none.'

Let us beware of simply asking people to provide this bodyguard. We too must be careful not to demand the impossible. Let us not expose ourselves to the reproach that we too came to people with an appeal to humanity to do the superhuman and virtuously to suffer appalling conditions, conditions which can be changed but which should not be changed! Let us not talk just about culture!

Let us have pity for culture, but let us first have pity for humanity! Culture is saved only when humanity is saved.

Let us not be carried away to the extent of asserting that people exist for culture, not culture for people! That would be too like the practice of the markets, where the people are there for the cattle, not the cattle for the people.

Comrades, let us reflect on the roots of evil!

A great doctrine, which is seizing hold of ever-greater masses of people on our planet, which is still a young planet, says that the roots of all evil lie in our property relations. This doctrine, like all great doctrines, has seized hold, above all, of those masses who suffer most from existing property relations and from the barbaric methods by which these relations are defended. And it is being realized in a country which covers one-sixth of the surface of the world and where the oppressed and the property-less have seized power. There no destruction of foodstuffs takes place and no destruction of culture.

Many of us writers, who are experiencing the atrocities of Fascism and are outraged by them, have not yet understood this doctrine and have not yet discovered the root of the brutality that outrages them. For them, the danger exists of treating the horrors of Fascism as unnecessary horrors. They hold to their property relations because they believe that the horrors of Fascism are not necessary in order to defend them. But the maintenance of the dominant property relations does require cruelty. Here the Fascists are not lying. They are telling the truth. Those of our friends who are as outraged as we are by the horrors of Fascism but wish to maintain existing property relations, or are indifferent whether or not they are maintained, cannot carry on the struggle against this spreading barbarism long enough or strongly enough because they cannot specify; and help to bring about the social conditions that will make barbarism superfluous. Those on the other hand whose search for the roots of evil has led them in the direction of property relations, have plunged deeper and deeper, through an inferno of deeper and deeper lying atrocity, until they have reached the place where a small section of humanity has anchored its pitiless dominion. It has anchored it in that form of individual property which involves the exploitation of their fellow men and which they defend with tooth and claw. In the process, they are quite willing to sacrifice a culture which no longer helps to defend them and is no longer any use to defend them, and to sacrifice utterly all those laws of human coexistence for which a despairing humanity has struggled so long and so bravely.

Comrades, let us talk of property relations!

This is what I wanted to say about the struggle against the spread of barbarism, so that it would be said here too, or so that I too should have said it.

(c) *Beyond the Social Mandate*

1. These past years have pointed towards the fusion between industry and society (which should not be regarded as either total or irreversible); the road, which in the past had appeared difficult but clear, towards a socialist management of common life, has become almost invisible; the gap between the essence and appearance of society has narrowed. And it seems as if we must consume away what remains of our life in the recognition of a seemingly compact surface lacking in footholds—a world in which one can do nothing but live yet which deprives of meaning any kind of death. If all that is true, then it is absurd (and reprehensible) to engage in any nostalgic or rebellious attempt to restore to the writer the social status inherited from Romanticism which made him into the voice of national conscience or the historian of private life. Equally impossible and consolatory is the return to the mandate and status that the working-class movement offered to the writer, whether (over a long phase spanning the nineteenth and twentieth centuries) as inheritor of the mission of bourgeois enlightenment, or (over the years from 1935 until very recently) through the formation of the anti-fascist fronts. As for the 'socialist' countries, although they continue to go through the motions of the writer-functionary, everybody knows that the writers who really count are all 'Western' writers. I won't speak here about China and the Third World since the environmental and cultural parameters there seem so different from our own.

What hypotheses, then, are being formulated today about the legitimacy of literature? Some say that, in our societies, much of the communication traditionally performed by literature has been absorbed by particular scientific disciplines—cue no end of quotations from the fields of psychology, anthropology, sociology and so on. But this haemorrhage has been going on since at least Herodotus' day, and everything to be said about the uselessness of literature had already been said in the polemics of the early eighteenth century. For all that literature has not ceased to exist. More often today the argument turns to the death of art, not in the properly Hegelian sense of the phrase but as the end of a certain idea of poetic art. Alternatively, we are offered the idea of a 'death and transfiguration', namely, the recuperation of the forms of mass communication—perhaps not forgetting but certainly underestimating the fact that the real multiplier of mass media lies in the perpetual formation of commodities for elites or indeed in the formation of consuming elites. Alternatively again—and this is the case with the more intelligent recent manifestations of linguistic and structuralist formalism—one salvages from the wished-for death of the notions of 'art' and 'poetry', that is, of 'values', the notion of 'literarity' defined as a particular operation performed on l anguage, an activity that never gives answers but always only raises questions: signification suspended but infinitely decipherable, inexhaustible ambivalence, articulation and so on and so forth. This remains a kind of communication but a paradoxical one, radically intransitive but nonetheless capable through its bare presence, of contesting reality. Even in this hypothesis, however, the denial of the recognizability or visibility of a social function is implicit—except for that of a master of ceremonies or shaman.

How can it be denied that in our countries the literature of denunciation or of the rupture with society has become a genre like dramatic verse or the historical ballad? Such literature may employ the methods of sarcasm or invective or lament. It may make people cry—or laugh. But what can an adult do with those tears or that laughter? At most this literature becomes a lightweight, provisional weapon. In any case, what interests us here most is the fact that the literature of denunciation, demand or protest can no longer have any serious relationship with the organizations of the workers' movement, be they parties, associations or movements. What's more, in relation to the new and growing (though still barely visible) forms of a new workers' movement, literature (as 'poetry' or 'form' or 'value') cannot but remain extraneous, precisely due to its essential propensity to confirm the domination of the owners of conscience and consciousness—the 'owners of God'. The relation between literary expression and revolutionary movement is a relationship of the type indicated by Marx when he called the proletariat the heir of classical German philosophy. The revolutionary class, as matrix of future society, is the bearer of poetic truth, which is why that truth cannot but be partially off limits for it in the present. Besides, poetry does not fool around. It really does allow the future to be consumed in effigy, the god *sub specie*, the wheat still green. It can even go so far as denying the future itself, turning it into the 'eternal'.

It is clearly pointless then to try and distinguish between denunciation, demands, appeals to novelty, etc., either at the level of contents or of forms. Safeguarding the relationship between sociopolitical progress and the progress of expressive forms? That was the illusion of the avant-gardes, and Trotsky's too. No doubt, stylistic innovation is related to social transformation, but it is a relation expressed over the 'long run'. In other words, whatever cross-section one chooses to make of the poetic object, the degree of translatability of the work from its own order of existence to that of knowledge-for-praxis has become minimal. I say 'has become' because this was not always the case. But the more the area of active social mystification expands, the harder it becomes to make a tendentially universal use of poetic truth. The old, much-derided claim that capitalism is necessarily the enemy of art can be interpreted in this way: *Poetry necessarily belongs to an order of values analogous to the one for which the capitalist order is a systematic, organized and inevitable obstacle.*

Once the social mandate of which Mayakovsky spoke has come to an end, poetry either retreats entirely into the private sphere or carries out some honourable ideological services. In the best of cases, thanks to a duality inherent within it as a vital tension, it fulfils both functions. This is the case with much of Brecht's later and often wonderful lyric poetry. Seen from one angle, it performs an ideological task while viewed from another it remains rigorously private. Especially when it clothes itself in historical allusions.

2. What would seem to be the strongest objection to what has been said so far? The one that would denounce the separation—reasserted here—between literature-as-fact and poetry-as-value as a spiritualistic and aristocratic residue, further denying the existence of any qualitative difference between forms of communication besides a merely territorial or regional one. In response to such an objection, there is not much to be said. If anything, one might counter that reasoning of this kind casts doubt on the very notion of a qualitative leap and therefore on that of revolution itself. Certainly the use of poetry as a value has been a class use and it carries the ugly marks of its most recent historical usufructuaries, of bourgeois and capitalist culture. It is also true that, with its formal power of disenchantment, poetry, in spite of it all, has continued to ask questions of reality and not merely to act as its disguised confirmation. But everything that I have been saying about the history of half a century of relations between poetry and revolution makes it impossible for me to relapse into the illusion of an 'other' poetry. It is inevitable that revolutionary action, once liberated of its Aeneas complex—its haste to rescue the idols of a city in flames—should adopt the stance of certain Russian revolutionaries of the last century ('a pair of boots is worth more than Shakespeare') or the negations of a Tolstoy. And what are these if not the echoes of the most coherent formulae of the fighting bourgeoisie of the eighteenth century, which can still be heard in the memorable 'Digression' with which the second volume of Manzoni's *Fermo e Lucia* begins?[32]

3. In fact, the consumption of poetry-as-value continues and can only be carried out within existing cultural modes. To think that one can escape the ambiguities of this usage by simply denying poetry-as-value is equivalent, as I have said, to denying the very possibility of revolution. For the current reduction, which is empiricist, of all poetry-as-value to the level of literature-as-fact does not belong to the 'violences' of history of the kind mentioned above but is a pure and simple 'fall in value'. It does not bracket one truth in order to emphasize another, but it keeps alive on corporatist criteria one sector of expression precisely by accepting its demotion to the status of a sector. The fact that, across the communist world, proletarian poetry of an immediately persuasive and emotive type continues to be promoted—and that one insists on calling it by the same name employed to designate poetry-as-value—is a matter of cultural policy that does not concern us here and whose origins we have already discussed. What I wish to get across instead is that our distinction (which is an aristocratic distinction, because although the poet must be democratic, poetry, if it is not to be literature, cannot but be aristocratic) should not be used as an alibi to evade the problems of the vast area that comprises literature and its institutions. Here in Italy, the possible field of action for writers and critics in relation to literary institutions remains large despite our dogged reluctance to occupy it. It is no accident that proposals to intervene in the management of certain literary and cultural institutions are either deformed or passed over in silence by the established powers, and, above all, by the Communists. For although the autonomous control of cultural organizations is ultimately impossible without a transformation in the rest of society, it can operate as an immediate practical-political or, rather, 'syndical', proposal whose effect is to unmask the futility of a whole series of sublime laments and literary disputes. Writers and critics who have registered the end of the social mandate have not for that reason deprived themselves of an area of possible 'civic' activity. It remains open to them to devise models of critical writing, of essayistic language, of written information, of the organization of literary inquiry and research, of translation or editing in the ambit of literary disciplines. And to do this without the pretension that these models compete with those that already exist—precisely because one knows that revolutionary reality, when it emerges, will be such as to render even the most generous models unrecognizable.

4. (Advice to the few. No point hurrying to identify the nuclei of resistance or the new areas of ossification forming themselves in our social fabric. The labour of 'recognition' must be prudent because it is desperate. We are guilty of not having despaired enough. Of not having really abandoned the belief that we could see with our own eyes what is, by definition, not visible—a first step taken by our country towards communism. It would have been preferable to have conceded defeat, to have adopted the tones of futility and sarcasm, thus bearing witness to the fact that our rational deference was directed at something more lasting than the few decades at our disposal. Today, instead, separation and clandestinity (or seriousness) are forced upon us by the merciless persuasion of our years. One feels 'outside' one's century. If only that were so! At the margins—that's where we find ourselves.)

5. The sundry tendencies of critical formalism (semantic, structuralist) are in accord with a whole interpretive tradition when they recall that poetry (or, as they say, literature) is powerless to directly intervene in the transformation of the real. It should be noted however that while these theories of criticism tend to accentuate the specificity of literary language, its 'literarity', and thus to isolate it from any contamination—to the point of falling into line with a number of classical autonomistic or mystical theses—they are also forced by their own anti-historicism (or by an historicism that denies every finalism) to reject any notion of value. Accordingly, they extend to the entire field of literature a conception of linguistic operations whose validity applies in reality only to a more definitive order which can more strictly be called *poetic*. In practice, however, these tendencies—with their ideology of non-communicativeness (that is, of coded communication)—extend from creative literature

all the way to ornamental literature, implicating critical language, essayistic language and even (if not principally) the world of conversation and rhetoric; save, of course, to rescue from ambiguity and ineffability so-called science, that is to say, a (differently) formalized language. (Whereas it is not only legitimate but also necessary, in the name of a 'religious' or historical goal, to reject the facile illusions of easy communication between people. There is nothing more repulsive than doctrines of incommunicability and the impossibility of persuasion that see themselves as 'atheistic' or as denying any historical teleology. Under their posture of tragic and heroic stoicism, they are commanding a caste hierarchy based on a kind of snobbery of the spirit.)

6. But might not the literary use of language, its formalization, the exercise of its 'signifying and yet deceptive nature' (Barthes), be a metaphor for a mode of human existence? As Lukács has shown, from Romanticism to the present, the increasing importance attributed to poetry and art has to be seen in relation to the extension of the process of reification in every other sector of human activity. I refer here to the essay on 'Reification and the Consciousness of the Proletariat' in *History and Class Consciousness*, and in particular to 'Section II.3'[33] and the extraordinary footnote[34] where Lukács alludes to the reactionary degeneration of the notion of 'organic growth': 'Here it is only the structure of the object that need concern us: namely, the fact that what would seem to be the high point of the interiorization of nature merely implies the abandonment of any true understanding of it'. If, particularly during the last century, poetry and art became 'form and structure' this is precisely because they appeared as a kind of 'second nature'; namely, as the only kind of action that has apparently not yet been invaded by the sclerosis of reification—proof of the spectral legitimacy of formalist theories. But the humanist tradition, exemplified for Lukács by Goethe and Hegel, introduces into the Marxist perspective the ending (or, better, the conservation-overcoming) of alienation and the restitution of man to himself as the ends of communism. In other words, the capacity, individual and collective, increasingly to make oneself, to be self-determining, to form past, present and future. This 'superhuman' capacity, however, not only excludes any 'squalid pride'[35] as its servile hymn but also surpasses man only to the extent that it deepens his fundamental contradiction. Now the praxis-consciousness which is the end of Marxist 'history' is nothing other than the 'dream of a thing' that men would have always harboured; it is, in other words, *the formative faculty oriented towards life*, the ordering of life in view of the goal, *which is precisely what is proper to works of art*. The 'formalization' of life is the victory over the merely praxic use of it to which we are subjected by alienated labour. By way of further proof: What is aestheticism (or for that matter any individual ethical-religious 'edification') if not the illusion of being able to pre-empt a privileged formalization of one's *own* life?

I say aestheticism because the work of art or poetry is not (and this is entirely to its credit) anything more than the metaphorical prophecy or prophetic metaphor of that formalization. The formalist notion of poetry—that it is the organization of an ambiguous lie in order to tell an ambiguous truth—finds its historical legitimation in the extreme petrification of humanity. Unfortunately, the partisans of the doctrine use it in a conservative way, situating poetry as a 'section' of a universe entirely composed of 'forms'. What one should do instead is take the formalist methodology literally, so as to restore poetry to its circumscribed and therefore tragic dignity. In this conception—at least for those who presuppose that a history has an end—poetry is the point of intersection of clock time and historical time (or, as a religious person would say, the profane and sacred orders). Poetry—like those fragments of meteoritic iron that lie on the earth and remain iron but 'signify' a different origin—manifests itself as fractions of 'orientated time'.

7. In what sense is the poetic work a prophetic metaphor for the formalization of life? The elements that make up the artwork stand

in definite relations to one another and establish between themselves a system of tensions, ranging from the simplest to the most complex. Although one might say the same thing about any living reality, it is not a question of affirming a homology between the two systems (or a vitalist use of art, as in I.A. Richards, where art is the presence of a model', legitimate and relevant though such a use may be). Instead, what must be affirmed is that the definitive manifestation of the tensions internal to the work of art is to be found in its formalness, and that this formalness can indeed be felt in the work as such but it is not imitable or reproducible in the real life of the single individual but only in the context of a human society and its modes of association. Consequently, although there is an insurmountable gap between poetic formalness and real formalness, and although the experience of the latter is sufficiently served by the normal, impoverished and imperfect formative activity of our lives, art and poetry continue to reiterate their proposal of a definitive 'imitation' of themselves. This proposal bursts the bounds of our present formative capacities by silently pointing to an absence, and, simply in so doing, heralds the demand that these capacities be augmented—not quantitatively but in a qualitative leap.

8. In confirmation of the correctness of the analogy advanced herein, we can note that both in poetry-as-value and in life-as-form are present simultaneously the richness of meanings and possibilities and their radical insufficiency. The working class is coerced into the practical employment of its own life, into the performance principle, into immediately useful labour. Insofar as it is the revolutionary class, or 'true' negation, it acts objectively to abolish the 'informality' of its own existence and of existence in general, and thus to 'formalize' life. Though this means discovering and practising the inexhaustible richness of life—life's potential to redeem history—it also means, precisely in order to dominate the existent, the need to discover it as such, as illegitimacy, precariousness, insignificance, 'useless passion'. Well, then, poetry's formal nature also foregrounds both the potentially infinite richness of its modes and its own futility and instability (even at the linguistic level), the fact that poetry is always an ode to dust.

9. So the class which is necessity (and the movement that represents it) *cannot* establish the same kind of normal relations with poetic formalization as those entertained by its class antagonist, who claims to be and in fact is in possession of itself and therefore is form. Poetry is enjoyed especially by the dominant class, not only for the vulgar empirical reasons that immediately spring to mind but also because the opposite could be the case only in the other (or future) world. The light of poetry is the *metaphorical* light of an *integral* formalness and as such infinitely exceeds the real but partial formalization represented by the dominant class. Hence (and this belief is rooted in the epochs and ideologies that equate progress with the extension to the dominated of the formative capacity of the dominant class) poetry *seems* to be addressed to the dominated and oppressed. But it only seems so. For in practice they can enjoy it only insofar as they partake, to a greater or lesser degree, in the culture of the rulers and can thus share for a moment in their illusion of universality, in mystification. And poetry makes us complicit in this. This 'reactionary' figure of poetry is something that the Romantics and post-Romantics knew all too well, as Rimbaud demonstrates. When the likes of Barthes say that literature 'releases a question . . . gives the world an energy [*donne du souffle au monde*] . . . permits us to breathe', they unwittingly make clear why for revolutionaries one must never let the world breathe.[36] The 'world' must choke. Lenin (so the anecdote goes) could not bear to listen for long to Beethoven's music which told people *uselessly* what they might become.

10. The revolutionary class can also be defined as the class capable of rejecting the continual 'proposals of essence' addressed to it by the culture of capitalism, that is, by culture. It chooses itself practically against 'truth', its own informal reality against the legitimacy of form, the negation that negates against the negation that collaborates. Anything but irrational or vitalistic, coerced as it is into the rationality of capitalist production, it is revolutionary precisely to the extent that the pressure of need and performance allows it no ought other than that of acting to reduce need and performance. Its existence is defined by its need to 'search for the East by way of the West', to aim at freedom and essence by way of necessity and inessentiality. It is this paradoxical placement that makes it apparently so difficult to locate. Its movement may be slow, almost unverifiable, bradyseismic.[37] But from time to time it blocks the path of the 'conscious', as the Carrier does the Merchant in Brecht's *The Exception and the Rule*. And when it occupies the streets and public places it provokes the cry 'is this not the son of the carpenter?'[38]

The magical and vital delusion of form, the disillusion of contradictory meanings, the shifting relations between levels and sign-signifieds within formal boundaries, all this is poetry, and when understood it makes life hang on an ephemeral form. Ulysses has to have himself tied to the mast, the oarsmen have to have their ears blocked or they will not reach their goal. But for those who have no goal to reach because they think they have already reached it, the same songs are heard as a delicious thrill, a presage of death that sharpens the pleasure of being. They pay the Sirens to sing at their banquets. Yet there is a lofty lesson that poetry can teach to the class of negation and to those who lead it. It can introduce the healthy suspicion that the class struggle that is fought to abolish classes leads to a higher and ineliminable contradiction—the one we have already alluded to, between a limitless capacity to manage life and its limitless infirmity. This is exceptionally important, even essential, as it can help to free the revolutionary movement from its infantile optimism, its elementary and ever recurrent progressivism. Perhaps the greatest thing that poetry can teach that movement today is the readiness to grasp the magnitude of the nothingness that accompanies positive action.

11. The owning class can experience every poem as a poem of the present. Disillusion is in fact the greatest confirmation of its existence. It is an operation, formerly magical-religious and today 'artistic' which, informing it of the (partial) void, in fact confirms the (partial) plenitude of power. The part of us that believes in its self-ownership needs to believe that poetry models its own modelling capacities. A capacity which, within its class limits, is real enough. But that which in poetry really transcends class limits is converted into 'religion' or separated into a specialism. Conversely, the dominated class—or the part of us that knows only mere existence and penury—will continue, as it does at present, to consume poetry. It cannot help doing this, because its face is turned towards 'culture' as a power-promising form. Dominant culture is continually presented to it as its possible essence. But it will be forced necessarily to experience poetry as not-contemporary, as a formalization of the existence of others. Alternatively, it will not be able to avoid minimizing and indeed entirely passing over the formal nature of poetry, precisely because it manifests itself as a trick, as a pointless idol. Is this perhaps not the explanation for the spread of the didactic-emotive use of poetry on the 'left' (that old habit)? And of the necessary demotion, on the 'left', of poetry-as-value into literature-as-fact? But this is the *correct* response of revolutionary negation to poetry; except that the leadership of the workers' movement, precisely qua leadership, takes over from 'culture' the notion of poetry-as-value and projects it onto the didactic-emotive literature which it cannot help promoting. Past Soviet and present Chinese propaganda is right to talk of the novelty of this sort of literary production compared with that of pre-revolutionary times, but it is wrong when it uses the same category to define it. Paradoxically, an inverse process is taking place simultaneously in the other camp. The formal use of poetry, its use as a metaphorical fulfilment of existence is, albeit in a degraded form, the use transmitted by the elites down to the culture industry. The culture industry *preaches* the formal use of poetry as a supplement for religion.

For their part, the ideologists of the elites themselves want poetry to be mere literature and formalization to be a property of all human activity; they preach a 'secularism' of art (and life) whose practical role is to quench with magic and superstition, as strong as any drug, that thirst for irreality and emptiness without which the owning class cannot enjoy the taste of power and domination.

Where does the complication and entanglement of these relations come from? It is only the complication and intricacy of class relations in an historical phase that has stripped them of their appearances, reducing them to substance, to the relationship of 'naked domination'—at a level infinitely deeper and more recessed than that to which 120 years ago the *Manifesto* claimed that the bourgeoisie had reduced the vestiges of the picturesque medieval world.

12. We have simply tried to register the historical end of certain 'figures'. We have known for some time that writing is literally impossible. That the writer can only *das Leere lernen, Leeres lehren*,[39] learn the void and teach the void, is no less true just because every child knows it. The important thing is not to take this as an easy consolation, not to reach an accommodation with present conditions, that is all. There are those who go around talking of a 'renewal of the mandate', confusing the rhythm of history with that of publishing. No doubt, if someone wants to write, nothing can stop them. Poetry is impossible, yet at this moment there are people writing real poetry. That the voice of the poet is not there to move armies, to comfort or enlighten, our enemies know this as well as us. We can leave them to their illusion: that if we say the same thing, it really is the same thing. Nor should anyone complain that the separation recorded here is equivalent to suicide. As we have said before, an enormous field still remains open to literary discourse, to the latter's *usefulness*. Of course, this counts for those who are convinced of the end of every visible fatherland and have renounced every 'house of the people', all human warmth, that is to say, any public, any life even, but are waiting for it to be restored to them, in the knowledge that it will be brought back only by the order of communism, by the 'real movement which abolishes the present state of things', by visible and invisible organs that make themselves 'formatively', operating on the basis of the availability of man to himself—and all this in the course of the day-to-day conflicts in which communism is illuminated and obscured. The writer we speak of must simply be capable of one thing: to distinguish, at least as far as the eye can see, life from the work; and to do so in terms of a classic teaching which the figures of commitment had rubbed out. The inner forces which he calls upon in order to achieve his own work will not forgive him of any unjustified transfer of privileges and priorities from the work to life. If the latter can lay claim to the devotion of commitment, the former can feed only on renunciation. The joy, the manifest joy, and the vitality of the work, will come, when it comes, in Mozartian guise: the kind of joy that terrifies.

13. (The nexus dialectic-certainty . . . tends to be replaced by the more fragile and problematic nexus of dialectic and hope. . . . But the problem of certainty, or that of the concrete modalities of transition, is essential to theory. . . . Where and to the degree that this [class] consciousness is slow in manifesting itself, or expresses itself in alienated form, Marxism enters into contradiction with itself and ends up, whether or not it likes it, by taking on speculative characteristics.' [Renato Solmi, 'Introduction' to the first Italian edition of Theodor W. Adorno, *Minima Moralia*, Turin: Einaudi 1954, pp. *lix–lx*.]

'It could be claimed that in Benjamin religious symbolism, the theological image of redemption, is the Archimedean point of hope. . . . But the issue here is not to stress the theoretical fragility of this support or its incompatibility with the real forms of thought and collective emancipation. . . . It would be wrong for critics to take his paradoxical formulations literally.' [Renato Solmi, 'Introduction' to the Italian selection from Walter Benjamin, *Angelus Novus*, Turin: Einaudi, 1962, p. *xxxvi*.]

Note has been taken. Take note.)

14. If it is true that the *literary use of language is homologous to the formal use of life which is the aim and end of communism*, then it is possible cautiously to suggest a direction or dedication to those nearest to us who intend to be writers: Try to create in the literary or poetic work a stylistic structure whose internal tensions are a metaphor for the internal tensions and structural tendencies of a human social 'body' moving on a revolutionary path towards its own 'form'. This is the theme derided by the 'new believers', the theme of 'perspective'. But in the poetic work, the metaphor or, rather, the allegory of the 'human social body' will have to rest entirely on formal-linguistic elements, thereby legitimating the use of the analytic instruments of semantic or structuralist criticism and the formalist tradition in general—but only on that condition.

And if it is true that the *class is the instrument which tends to make the formal use of life possible*, combining, in that use, pessimism and optimism, making that use possible beyond itself—if in its struggle, proud of the bruises left by its chains, the class appears to move away from that finality and to assert itself only as particularity and immediate existence; if, when it is silent and degraded to the level of a mere sociological category, it appears on the other hand to be approaching that finality by taking on the 'forms' proposed to it by the owners of consciousness—if all this is the case, then we can also add that it is possible to write as if there did exist in front of us, in its integrity, that weapon of the class which we call the Party. What I mean is that it is possible to write in its presence, not by its mandate, free of the illusion that the poetic function finds shelter within it. I say 'as if it existed' in order to imply that today the problem for the intellectual or 'man of culture' (who as such would no longer have a place in the Party) is not that of recreating or reforming the party, still less that of making it a prefiguration of communist society, but of *recognizing* the party when and where it takes shape, *if* it does so here or in any other part of the world, but without making mistakes in reading the order of stars and the hour of departure.

15. Is it possible that the 'proletariat', the 'working class', the 'revolutionary class' do not exist and have never existed? That they are only images of something else to which we cannot or will not give a name?

It is possible. And although such an admission would not necessarily deprive of value the homology we have proposed between poetic formalization and the tendency towards formalization of human reality in history, which could always materialize in other ways, it would deprive us of value. It would leave us naked and silent, not merely dead but unborn. For Christianity, the formalization of life takes place in cooperation with Grace and outside of time. Whereas modern historicism denounces the idea of an end of history as illusory, even the idea of a qualitative leap in history, and, therefore, the idea of the end of the 'prehistory' which is our own.

There is a risk here, and it must be run; an ancient wager, and it must be accepted. If 'this history', the history around us, has neither aim nor end, then inexistence is already closing in to receive and annihilate the form we give to a poem, a form scarcely less imperfect than the one we are attempting with a few comrades and no illusions, to give to the illuminated area of our life. Honour will have counted for nothing, without truth. But the opposite may hold too, that honour bends truth towards itself, and holds it.

1964–65

Notes

This essay brings together four pieces originally published separately: Section (a) 'Brecht e l'origine dei Fronti Popolari', *Giovane critica* 4 (July–May 1964); Section (b) 'Per un discorso inattuale' [An

Untimely Argument], *Quaderni rossi* 3 (20 June 1963); while Section (c) is an amalgam of 'Mandato degli scrittori e limiti dell'antifascismo. La fine del mandato sociale' [The Writers' Mandate and the Limits of Anti–Fascism: The End of the Social Mandate], *Quaderni piacentini* 3 (17–18, July–September 1964); and 'Al di là del mandato sociale' [Beyond the Social Mandate], *Rinascita* 22(11) (13 March 1965). This translation is indebted to the version of 'The Writers' Mandate and the End of Anti-Fascism' published in *Screen* 15(1) (1974) (which omitted a number of Fortini's notes), from which I have taken the translation of Brecht's speech [Trans.]

1 See the bibliography (*Politica e cultura*, 1945–55) edited by s.c. (Sergio Caprioglio) in *Ragionamenti* 2 (November–December 1955): 16–17. For a facsimile reprint of the journal, see *Ragionamenti 1955–1957. Ristampa anastatica* (Maria Chiara Fugazza ed.) (Milan: Gulliver, 1980).

2 *impegno* [Trans.]

3 Medieval expression suggesting that one 'speak little of God and not at all about the prince'. [Trans.]

4 Edmondo De Amicis (1846–1908), author of *Cuore* [*Heart*, 1886] and *Primo Maggio* [*First of May*, published posthumously in 1980] started his writing career as a military journalist; Felice Cavallotti (1842–98), writer and politician, fought with Garibaldi in the war of independence; Pompeo Bettini (1862–96), poet, novelist and translator into Italian of the *Communist Manifesto* (1892); Mario Rapisardi (1844–1912), poet and follower of Mazzini. [Trans.]

5 *avanguardia* [Trans.]

6 In Italy, the 'meaning' of imperialist war is almost completely lacking: I don't know of a single study on this question, which could prove vital. Consider the scarcity but especially the vantage point of poetic and literary testimonies. The limit of consciousness is to be found in the combination of stoic endurance with existential (Giuseppe Ungaretti), patriotic-democratic (Piero Jahier) or Christian (Clemente Rebora) elements. And we never, or almost never, hear of the others, the 'enemies'. Missing, even at the level of simple condemnation, is something akin to the books of an Henri Barbusse or, 10 years later, an Erich Maria Remarque—not to speak of Brecht. The case of Emilio Lussu's beautiful book *A Soldier on the Southern*

Front, written in 1936, is exemplary: Lussu's book owes its quality precisely to his decision not to alter the relative youthful unconsciousness of himself as a captain in 1916 in light of the political consciousness of 20 years later. 'The erosion undergone by the interventionism that was his starting-point does not attain the ideological overturning of the premises'—Mario Isnenghi, 'La guerra sconsacrata di E. Lussu', *Quaderni piacentini* 19–20 (1964): 70.

7 Though it is customary to apologize for quoting oneself, I don't think I need to apologize for recalling that in 1956, with an article in *Il Contemporaneo* (later published in *Dieci inverni* ['Politicità e autonomia della cultura', pp. 249–55]), I had brought to a close the attempts, which had lasted for a decade, to go beyond the ridiculous freedom-authority dilemma—that is to say, autonomy of the intellectual primacy of the Party—which all sides had employed to rock us to sleep. This conclusion was not historical or philosophical but pragmatic: it suggested that so-called autonomy could only be justified and guaranteed by self-organization. It is not fruitless to note how much those observations of mine (which at the time, as often happens, I shared with some friends) harboured a grave mistake, the same one which this text attributes to German Communism in the Weimar period: to hope for institutional 'prefigurations' of the tools of cultural work in a socialist society. What's more, 1956 witnessed the liquidation of the little there was. The entire thrust of the present text should be understood as a correction of that earlier mistake.

8 I refer to the text by Siegfried Melchinger, 'Brecht and Politics', *Neue Zürcher Zeitung* (25 January 1964); and to that by Wolfdietrich Rasch, 'Bertolt Brechts marxistischer Lehrer' [Brecht's Marxist Teacher], *Merkur* 188 (October 1963): 988–1003. The bibliography on Brecht's work grows by the day and our Germanist friends (I am thinking especially of Paolo Chiarini and Cesare Cases) have to work hard to keep us abreast. I certainly cannot critically evaluate the information carried by these publications. What I can say is that the intellectual figure of Brecht is emerging from them if not radically altered, at least very unlike that of a decade ago. Melchinger's essay, which is very rich in references, is also a review of recent writings on Brecht; it deals in particular with Brecht's relations with

Sternberg, who published his own memoirs of the relationship in *Der Dichter und die Ratio* (1963). Brecht regarded him as his first 'teacher'. Rasch's article is of enormous interest because it not only contains the testimony of the widow of Karl Korsch (the well-known sociologist and philosopher, professor of law at the University of Jena, expelled from the party in 1926) but also quotes at length from Korsch's correspondence with Brecht, telling us of the close relations between the two, who lived side by side during their Danish exile, as well as of their continued correspondence during their emigration to the US.

It seems that the publication of an Italian anthology of Korsch's writings is forthcoming (rather curiously, in Delio Cantimori's university course of 1946–47 on the 'Interpretazioni tedesche di Marx nel periodo 1929–1945' [German Interpretations of Marx in the Period 1929–1945], now in *Studi di storia* [Historical Studies] (Turin: Einaudi, 1959), pp. 139–237, Korsch's name is mentioned together with Lukács's, then the examination of Korsch's work is announced twice but it never follows). Among my own friends, those who have read the work of Korsch—which, having been published the same year as Lukács's *History and Class Consciousness* (1923), was attacked along with it by Communist orthodoxy (it is called *Marxism and Philosophy*, and was republished in 1930 in an expanded second edition)—either don't speak of it or say that it's not worth much. It would not be the first time that a mediocre thinker proves decisive for a poet. But see in *Arguments* [Paris, Issue 16 (1959): 24–8] some theses by Korsch on Hegel (first published in *Der Gegner* in 1932) and on Marx (1950), presented by Kostas Axelos and Maximilien Rubel. They can now be read in the appendix to the French translation of *Marxisme et philosophie* (1964). [In English, see Karl Korsch, *Marxism and Philosophy* (Fred Halliday ed. and trans.) (New York: Monthly Review, 2009). The two texts indicated by Fortini can be found in English translation as 'Theses on Hegel and Revolution', appendix to Karl Korsch, 'A Non-Dogmatic Approach to Marxism', *Politics* (May 1946): 151–4; and 'Ten Theses on Marxism Today', *Telos* 26 (1975): 40–1.] I will only point to the concluding thesis on Hegel and revolution: 'The attempt made by the founders of scientific socialism to salvage [*Hinünberrettung*] the high art of dialectical thinking by transplanting it from the German idealist philosophy to the materialist conception of nature and history, from the bourgeois to the proletarian theory of revolution, appears, both historically and theoretically, as a transitory step only. What has been achieved is a theory not of the proletarian revolution developing on its own basis, but of a proletarian revolution that has just emerged from the bourgeois revolution; a theory which therefore in every respect, in content and in method, is still tainted with the birthmarks of Jacobinism, that is, of the revolutionary theory of the bourgeoisie.'

9 Bertolt Brecht, 'Literature will be scrutinised', *Poems 1913–1956*, p. 344.

10 Brecht, 'Motto to the Svendborg Poems', *Poems 1913–1956*, p. 320.

11 Brecht, 'Literature will be scrutinised', p. 345.

12 Brecht, 'Washing C.N.', *Poems 1913–1956*, p. 290.

13 Lu Xun, 'Zai Zhonglou Shang' [On the Bell Tower], quoted in Lin Yü-Sheng, 'The Morality of Mind and the Immorality of Politics: Reflections on Lu Xun, the Intellectual' in *Lu Xun and His Legacy* (Leo Ou-Fan Lee ed.) (Berkeley: University of California Press, 1985), pp. 122–3. [Trans.]

14 Bertolt Brecht, 'Speech at the Second International Writers' Congress for the Defence of Culture' in *Brecht on Art and Politics* (Tom Kuhn and Steve Giles eds) (London: Methuen, 2003), pp. 170–1.

15 Georg Lukács, 'Der Kampf des Fortschritts und der Reaktion in der heutigen Kultur' [The Struggle Between Progress and Reaction in Today's Culture], *Aufbau* 12(9) (September 1956): 761–76.

16 Georg Lukács, 'Reflections on the Sino-Soviet Dispute' (Lee Baxandall trans.) in *Marxism and Human Liberation: Essays on History, Culture and Revolution* (E. San Juan Jr. ed.) (New York: Delta Books, 1973), p. 81 [translation modified].

17 *Commune* 23 (July 1935).

18 *Section Française de l'Internationale Ouvrière* [French Section of the Workers' International], the official name of the French Socialist Party from its foundation in 1905 to 1969. [Trans.]

19 For a disillusioned testimony, and a broader reflection on these congresses of writers, see Klaus Mann, *The Turning Point: The*

Autobiography of Klaus Mann (Princeton: Markus Wiener Publishers, 2007), pp. 285–8.

20 Leon Trotsky, 'An Open Letter to French Workers', *The New International* 2(5) (August 1935): 148.

21 Among the best-known writers and men of culture participating in the Congress, besides those of the French, German and Soviet delegations, *l'Humanité* recorded Martin A. Nexö, Karin Michaelis, Aldous Huxley, Mike Gold, John Strachey, E.M. Forster, Eugenio d'Ors. Gaetano Salvemini spoke on behalf of Italian anti-fascism (on the evening of the 24th), declaring his opposition to a common front between an anti-fascist culture with liberal-democratic origins and a communist one—thus eliciting (according to the communist newspaper) the applause of the Trotskyists. The young Ambrogio Donini made a significant intervention in which, among other things, it was said that: 'Official fascist culture comprises all the elements, all the typical lineaments, all the old motifs which in these last 40 or 50 years in Italy have accompanied the cultural development of the dominant class'. Alongside D'Annunzio and Papini, Croce is pointed out (along with Gentile) as representing the culture responsible for fascism. Croce, 'in a society based on the sufferings of the immense majority, took on as his task the ideological justification of that reality'. In this intervention, Donini considered Alberto Moravia's *The Indifferents* [*Gli indifferenti*, 1929] as a sign of the formation of an anti-fascist literature.

22 The First Congress, the one that concerns us here, concluded with the foundation of an international bureau of 121 members presided over by André Gide, Henri Barbusse, Romain Rolland, Heinrich and Thomas Mann, Maxim Gorky, E.M. Forster, Aldous Huxley, George Bernard Shaw, Sinclair Lewis and Selma Lagerlöf. The Second Congress took place in the midst of the Spanish Civil War, from 4 to 8 July 1937 in Madrid and Barcelona and from 16 to 17 July in Paris. The Presidium comprised Rolland, Malraux, Benda, Bloch, Aragon, Heinrich and Thomas Mann, Feuchtwanger, Hemingway, Shaw, Rosamond Lehmann, Forster, Alexei Tolstoy, Sholokhov, Antonio Machado, José Bergamín, Martin Andersen Nexö, Lagerlöf and Guglielmo Ferrero. In the *Bureau International*, German literature was represented by the two Manns, Feuchtwanger, Ludwig

Renn, Regler, Brecht, Becher, Willi Bredel, Kisch, Seghers. Italy was represented by Ferrero, the Count Sforza and Ambrogio Donini. The US by Hemingway, Sherwood Anderson, Eugene O'Neill, Van Wyck Brooks, Fannie Hurst, Langston Hughes, Carl Sandburg, Malcolm Cowley, Mike Gold. Nâzım Hikmet was nominated for Turkey. For Chile, Pablo Neruda; for Cuba, Nicolas Guillén; and for Peru, César Vallejo.

(Gramsci had died four months before; he was entirely unknown for those who, like the undersigned, were 18 years old at the time. Donini's intervention announced the presence in the studies and writings of Gramsci, but 'especially in his letters from prison', of 'an absolutely unique power of thinking, of style and of humanity' and called him 'the foremost Italian of the century'.)

23 See Victor Serge, *Memoirs of a Revolutionary* (Peter Sedgwick, with George Paizis trans.) (New York: New York Review Books, 2012), pp. 370–1.

24 *Commune* 23 (July 1935): 1263.

25 Ibid., pp. 1233–4.

26 The monotony and vacuity of many of those declarations is briefly alluded to in the memoirs by Klaus Mann cited above [see p.267n19]. The text by Wolfdietrich Rasch mentioned earlier reproduces a passage from a letter that Brecht sent from Paris to Karl Korsch—who had already been excluded seven years before from the KPD—in which the poet mocks the Congress intellectuals and in particular Heinrich Mann, who would have preventively submitted to the *Sûreté* [the French national police] the text of his own intervention on the freedom of the writer . . .

27 Paul Nizan, 'Sur l'humanisme', *Europe* 151 (15 July 1935): 452–6.

28 Official organ of the Russian Social Democratic Labour Party, edited by Lenin, and published between 1900 and 1905. [Trans.]

29 Brecht's speech under the title *Eine notwendige Feststellung zum Kampf gegen die Barbarei* [A Necessary Observation on the Struggle Against Barbarism] was published in *Neue Deutsche Blätter* 11 (6 August 1935): 341–3, in Prague, as indicated by the *B. B. Bibliographie* by W. Nubel, under the heading C-268. It was not reprinted until 1957. The translation in the appendix to this essay is of the version in Notebook 15 of the *Versuche*, the last of the series,

published posthumously under the editorship of Elisabeth Hauptmann (Berlin: Suhrkamp Verlag, 1957). The Italian translation appeared in *Quaderni rossi* 3 (Milan, June 1963): 114–18. [The translation here follows the one included in the first translation of Fortini's essay in *Screen*. A version of Brecht's speech can also be found in *Brecht on Art and Politics* (Tom Kuhn and Steve Giles eds) (London: Bloomsbury, 2015), pp. 147–56.]

30 Franco Fortini, *Il movimento surrealista* (Milan: Garzanti, 1959), pp. 21–49.

31 'The oppressors move in for ten thousand years'. 'In Praise of the Dialectic'. [Trans.]

32 *Fermo e Lucia* (1821–23) is the first version of Alessandro Manzoni's masterwork *I promessi sposi* [The Betrothed], first published in 1915 under the title *Gli sposi promessi*. [Trans.]

33 Georg Lukács, *History and Class Consciousness* (Rodney Livingstone trans.) (Cambridge, MA: MIT Press, 1971), pp. 173–81. [Trans.[

34 Ibid., p. 214n47. [Trans.]

35 *fetido orgoglio*—an expression from Giacomo Leopardi's poem *La Ginestra* (Broom). [Trans.]

36 Roland Barthes, 'Literature and Signification' in *Critical Essays* (Richard Howard trans.) (Evanston: Northwestern University Press, 1972), p. 267. [Trans.]

37 A seismic phenomenon involving multiple moderate earthquakes in between volcanic eruptions, with uplift or subsidence of the Earth's surface, manifest in the Phlegarean Fields near Naples. [Trans.]

38 Matthew 13:55.

39 A quote from Goethe, *Faust II*. [Trans.]

III

In Defence of the Idiot

In *Quaderni piacentini* (Issue 28, p. 160), the *Cronaca Italiana* column mockingly quotes from the letter of a certain A.Z. to *Vie Nuove*,[1] where he has a go at the *beats*, contrasting them with himself:

> Ready to do my part, but with a degree in chemistry, working in the countryside to fund my studies, without long hair or dirty clothes, making mistakes, suffering, bettering myself. Without easy girls in miniskirts to give me strength, but with the fiancée whom I love and who really gives me strength, whom I respect because she deserves respect, who knows that I don't believe in God and that I'm a communist and who doesn't hate me because of it. I am ready, but with work, with study, with the advice of the old and the young, with honesty, etc.

Scanning these lines quickly (amid the boreal problems and thoughts besetting us, what can be the importance of comrade A.Z.?), I felt that something didn't ring right. Deterred from trying to defend such an unsavoury character, from seeking an approval that the young should certainly deny me—if the commonplaces about them are true—I stubbornly believe that this could be a decent occasion to touch on some themes for further reflection, and not just on matters of style.

What do we deride in this character? Not so much the young Italian-style revolutionary, the 'conformunist'[2] mass produced by the last decade of involution of the workers' movement. In other words, the result of a miseducation for which we too have been responsible due to the caution, slowness and indiscipline of our resistance. In brief, not its political meaning but its cultural and psychological components, the rhetorical crudity, the sexophobia, the expressive inability, the auto-didacticism, the bragging . . . But what are these if not some of the class connotations of the *new* petty bourgeois, that is to say, the signs of the (rearguard) resistance that the new proletariat opposes to the 'cultural' forms of advanced capitalism, to its own definitive colonization? Provided we accept that, beyond Catholic or social-communist virtuousness, the culture of advanced capitalism aims—at least in Italy—at demoralization and ideological disarmament, technological cynicism, consumerism and finally at the destruction of many of the ideals paraded by A.Z.

The backwardness of our 'idiot' should not be confused, as hurried observation might instead suggest, with that classic philistine petty-bourgeois narrow-mindedness that gets on the nerves of many of our peers whom a long tradition has made slaves of an intellectual attraction or enthralment with the elegance, largesse and immoralist generosity of the great bourgeoisie and the international ruling classes with their high and low courts of libertarians, artists, outlaws and suicides. It stems from it, relates to it; consider his 'progressive' library, with over 'one thousand volumes' (his grandfather had a similar one, between 1890 and 1910, like his great-grandfather, the pharmacist Homais[3]). But the difference lies in the fact that he is the child of the industrial transformation of Italy in the past 15 years or, if you prefer, of the lag of that transformation in comparison to other more modern states; he is the child of 15 years of Christian-Democratic and Togliattified schooling. Now, what is that new Italy that has grown up around us, if not the matter, object and subject of any possible state or revolution here among us? Let's look at him, the hateful 'idiot'. Let's replace some books in his library, some sentences in his arguments. Let's even swap the party-membership card in his wallet. The substance stays the same. Repellent, inhuman, disheartening? Yes, for us—and never did this *us* define us so negatively. *But not for anyone truly in possession of the urge and capacity for the political, the sense of the possible and the concrete.*

Descendants of the Voltairean *petit troupeau*[4] and the Gidean adolescents that books and films have been parading before us for half a century, they (meaning, many of us) forget that the 'idiots' are the (legitimate) absolute majority of humanity, because they are those who from scarcity (of every kind), disorder (perhaps of a well-ordered type), ignorance, and the unnecessary contradiction between individual needs and ethics desired by the bosses strive towards a better material condition, a rational order, a knowledge; and towards another species of contradiction, perhaps the one between everybody's needs and everybody's ethics. After all, it is with and for the 'idiots' that one makes those revolutions about which so much has been said that our heads have run dry. They do not know what Nietzsche knew, even if (out of too much love for his own fate) he didn't overcome it in the only direction possible, that of political action—namely, that the philistine's moralistic criticism brims over with philistinism. In the end, the laughter about the 'idiot', the blissful certainty that we enjoy the approval of strong spirits is moralistic, and in the worst way. They feel superior to the 'idiot'. And they are. But in a strictly classist sense—as a 'superior' class. Not in the name of a thought or an action that knows how to simultaneously voice the apologia of greatness and humility; which is, at one and the same time, absolutely aristocratic in what concerns values and absolutely democratic in what concerns human beings, dares to use the 'words' (that is to say, the limits) of morality, knowing that it will have to destroy them. Which makes room for the 'idiot', knowing that the world *needs* (in the strictest meaning of the term) him too in order to diminish, if at all possible, universal idiocy.

The strong spirits who deride the 'idiot', in so doing dream of the mythical place where supreme-bourgeois culture would celebrate with an invisible 'workers' science' a wedding as dizzying as that of bees. They do not know that it really exists, that place. Yet it is not a place of union but of permutation. It admits no spectators, only actors. Within it all are protagonists and often—as entire generations, entire classes—victims.

'Within the scope of their sensibility [of Italian literary populists] there is still place for a *positive* conception of the modern world where honesty, purity, goodness, naivety and sacrifice can be considered essential forces of human coexistence', writes Asor Rosa, with a diabolical glint in his eye.[5] Indeed, there is still room. When the Bolshevik revolution took to affixing the adjective 'socialist' to an institution or a value (socialist heroism, socialist justice, socialist tribunal and the like) it was no mere gesture. It meant that those institutions or values now had to move in a context that would change them radically. They became living examples of the ought. In this sense, it was absolutely true that the conscious worker had to battle the nationalism and patriotism of his own (bourgeois) country while defending with arms the 'fatherland of the proletariat' as well as his own, if the latter was socialist. 'Honesty, purity, goodness, naivety and sacrifice' not only can but, rather, must be considered 'essential forces of human coexistence' because they really are the reasons for which people fight for communism. *'Values' are a fiduciary circulation guaranteed by a collective political intentionality, by the actions of the group that accepts them.* In this sense, Lenin's phrase is rigorously true: What is moral is useful to the revolution. The error of our 'idiot' is not that he believes in those values but that he does not know that 'only if socialism is defined as the extreme and demystifying phase of bourgeois contradictions, can it be the bearer of those values in a socialist manner'.[6] He does not know it appeals to those values which are justified only to the extent, matched by a political conduct that fights capitalist mystification, they express a 'state of objective non-freedom and condition of subalternity'[7]—in no way an individual fact. So it is not because of what he says that he is an 'idiot' but because he writes it in *Vie Nuove*. In other words, he is an 'idiot' because he entrusts his beliefs to a mystifying political context.

He is purged of his private 'idiocy', so to speak, to the precise degree that he is a victim of dialogical conformunism. As we know, the everyday ideology of today's Italian communism (or at least of broad sectors within it, the outcome of more than a decade of pedagogical activity) has ended up creating an ever-more complex series of mediations and contradictions between the exercise of certain (moral, civic) virtues and the struggle for the destruction of the international capitalist order. Or rather, it has stabilized that contradiction into a political tradition. Given that the advanced forms of capitalist ideology themselves appear to liquidate the very 'values' that only yesterday they treated as their own, it may seem as though the contradiction is positive. But that's not actually the case; paleo-bourgeois values (sexual repression, work, fatherland, 'culture', etc.) are dried leaves or 'gathered flags' (according to the image dear to Stalin)[8] when they are not reasserted in a horizon of real (i.e. political) overcoming, not only of neo-capitalist laxity and cynicism but of these values themselves. You can't correct A.Z. by showing him the positivity of the *beats* or of miniskirts, the compatibility of non-repressed sexual mores and the struggle for communism or the opportuneness of suppressing close relatives, or by improving and updating the composition of his library. He can be corrected only if one can make him understand the itinerary of his virtues and the point at which their force of impact fades, the buffer that snuffs and cancels them. *That point is a political point.* The political channels that should convey those desires and virtues are blocked. Those who know don't act and those who act don't know. Among A.Z.'s personal proclivities to commitment and sacrifice and the global struggle for communism, there is no longer any relationship. Lives become literally pointless, or make up fictive, intermediate ends for themselves.

Sartre once observed that many became surrealists to upset their fathers. *Familles, je vous haïs.*[9] For 30 years they've been telling us that (Soviet and later Western) communism has restored or defended typically petty-bourgeois values. One would like to know from where, from what summit, those who repeat this refrain speak. Gide lamented that, in the USSR, in 1934, pederasts were sent to forced-labour camps and he was right. The snag was that they were about to do this especially with the communists. But men of letters were interested in ending the family, in the free use of bodies, basically in 'public mores', and not in what sustained and determined them. The surrealists sang of Violette Nozière, patricide and attempted matricide.[10] They applauded the kicks aimed at the poor, blind violinist in *Un Chien Andalou*. Later, the luxurious pages of *Minotaure* magazine would carry stinging images of bloodied corpses on the streets of Mexico City with commentaries by Breton, or photos from an institute of forensic medicine of the victims of the greatest rippers from the end of the nineteenth century.

Thinking about what was then beginning and has continued until today, one is almost minded to ask the heirs of those revolts the same question a French dame in a railway carriage was reported to have asked of a well-endowed exhibitionist: *Et alors?*[11]

You need to be able to look your parents in the face. 'The infantile error, common to almost all men, but which should always be avoided by he who puts himself forward as a leader or a teacher, consists in not being able to look one's parents in the face, that is, in believing oneself free from one's family tradition, whether at school or on the streets'.[12] To have a non-neurotic relationship with one's fathers is probably very difficult; but it implies, or symbolizes, the relation with class, with reality. *He who wishes to speak to others or in their name*—as we have been taught by psychoanalysis and were taught before that by the history of intellectual and political minorities—*must already have been 'spoken' by others, must be the living support of communication, the proof of its paradox. To communicate, in this sense, is to choose comrades for oneself, positioning oneself with them within the order of time.* Recognizing or electing 'fathers' is the only way to have the right to 'sons'. Nothing in common with complaining about the petty infamy of contemporary Italy. This is what makes the beautiful cries of so many friends, and our own too, so sterile and strident as well as confused. And it is what makes so useless, by dint of its barehanded sincerity, the 'compulsion to repeat' of Pasolini, who now discovers the America of the New Left, instead of explaining better to himself and to us what he has made and made believe, how and to whom, in the last 10 years, with films, poems and articles—notwithstanding that these remain among the best of the intellectual production of this country which, though it may sometimes summon him to the courts, more often provides him with honours and means of subsistence.

It is time to have done with those puerile historical compendia of the idiocy of the left, which have taught us to groan at the fact that, for example, when Charles Baudelaire's *Les fleurs du mal* was being printed in 1857 we were still waiting for the poems of Giosuè Carducci in Italy. They incessantly give birth to unsullied dreams of Russias, Chinas, Americas, arch-angelic Proletariats. They lead us to accept an 'idea of progress' which, in the final analysis, is derived from its industrial and technological variant. They distract from the part assigned to us—which is that of our country, not as a 'national road', but as the space and body of action, as its incarnation.

Why should our boreal thoughts, used to ranging from the Far East to the Bronx, care about comrade A.Z.?

Because there is a council of prudence here to be gently unfolded. And it is this: *Every gesture or phrase or reflex or sneer of intolerance towards others*—and the more so, the less relevant, responsible or dangerous its target—*risks being matched* (when one believes or fools oneself that one is serving a truth before serving an action) *by a movement of complaisance and tolerance towards oneself*—and the more so the less coherent, generous and lucid its target. That complaisance and tolerance manifest themselves above all with regard to those who, because they share our opinions, seem closer, almost extensions of ourselves, and they tend to turn them into the members of a sect. In fact the (contradictory) movements of the sectarian are twofold; not only that of purifying the group from any supposed incoherence but also that of co-opting into it whomever swears to its credo, regardless of their character or the nature of their works—as Dostoyevsky's *Demons* teaches us. The most tenacious sects are those that base themselves on intellectual privileges whether true or false—that is to say, false, if they are privileges. This can range from the great Enlightenment masonic lodges of bourgeois society all the way to the most miserable erotic-artistic cliques. To call those distant from us 'idiots' risks habituating us to refrain from doing so with those who are closer and perhaps deserve it; it accustoms us to exclude the practice of 'fraternal reprehension', to avoid inevitable and salutary disagreements, the disagreements of 'communication'.

We all engage in inadmissible and often shameful indulgences towards men and books when they seem to believe the same things that we do, even if the degree of that belief, its level, appears to us vulgar or inferior. There are cases—more frequent than we think, even among the most delicate dispositions—in which, having confused the respect for truth with the respect for oneself, one accepts and applauds the fact that others repeat or interpret those truths provided they do so at a level *inferior* the one at which we have partaken in them or expressed them, only if they are, or appear to be, a little inferior or base. This is an instance of intellectual demagogy more dangerous than that of politicians because, being less obvious, it cannot do without the aristocratic thrill of power.

The more they preach the end of 'values' the more they rattle off lists of 'counter-values'. They too, by which I mean those who laugh about comrade A.Z., 'sweat morality from every pore', as Brecht said.[13] That inevitable servility of theirs, that pitiful duel in the dark, makes them so likeable that I'd clasp them and the 'idiot' in a single embrace. They tend to confuse—a venial sin if there ever was—their own personal universe of tastes and mores (and the perceived and presupposed one of their peers across the world) with a 'progress'. When the only progress that we should hold dear is the one that makes the intellects more rigorous and the wills more inflexible for emancipation towards communism, if this word still means anything.

1967

Notes

Originally published in *Quaderni piacentini* 6(29) (January 1967). [Trans.]

1 A weekly linked to the Italian Communist Party, founded by Luigi Longo, and published between 1946 and 1980. Pasolini had a column in *Vie Nuove* between 1960 and 1965, where he answered readers' letters. Pasolini's articles were later collected in *Le belle bandiere. Dialoghi 1960–65* (Gian Carlo Ferretti ed.) (Rome: Editori Riuniti, 1977). [Trans.]

2 *comunperbenista* [Trans.]

3 Refers to the character in Gustave Flaubert's *Madame Bovary* (1856). Flaubert delineated Homais as a representative figure of the new bourgeoisie. For example, he is not well educated but is a self-proclaimed exponent of Voltaire. [Trans.]

4 A reference to Sainte-Beuve's remark on Voltaire: 'Voltaire is against masses and misunderstandings; as far as reason is concerned, the masses appear to him as naturally stupid; he believes that good sense is only to be found among a small number of people and it's enough for him if one tries little by little to increase the small flock [*le petit troupeau*]'—Sainte-Beuve, *Les lumières et les salons. Anthologie* (Pierre Berès ed.) (Paris: Hermann, 1992), p. 178. [Trans.]

5 Alberto Asor Rosa, *Scrittori e popolo. Il populismo nella letteratura italiana contemporanea* (Rome: Samonà e Savelli, 1965), p. 270. [See English translation: *The Writer and the People* (Matteo Mandarini trans.) (London: Seagull Books, 2016); for a new, expanded Italian edition, on the book's 50th anniversary, see Alberto Asor Rosa, *Scrittori e popolo 1965. Scrittori e massa 2015* (Turin: Einaudi, 2015).]

6 Edoarda Masi, 'Note sulla fine del progresso', *Quaderni piacentini* 5(27) (1966): 13.

7 Ibid.

8 Stalin had declared that the communist parties should 'pick up the banner of democratic freedoms' that 'the bourgeoisie had dropped'. [Trans.]

9 'Families, I hate you.' A famous phrase of André Gide, from his 1897 prose-poem, *Les Nourritures terrestres* [The Fruits of the Earth] (Paris: Gallimard 1921), p. 72. [Trans.]

10 Refers to an infamous Parisian murder case from 1933. The surrealists published a collective volume in her defence and praise, *Violette Nozières* (Bruxelles: Nicolas Flamel, 1933), with texts by André Breton, René Char, Paul Éluard, and art by Salvador Dalí, Max Ernst, Alberto Giacometti, René Magritte and Hans Bellmer, among others. See Sarah Maza, *Violette Nozière: A Story of Murder in 1930s Paris* (Berkeley: University of California Press, 2011). [Trans.]

11 And? [Trans.]

12 Giacomo Noventa, 'Terzo manifesto di una filosofia classica' (1937), *Nulla di nuovo e altri scritti* (Franco Manfriani ed.) (Venice: Marsilio, 1987).

13 'Exploiters constantly preach morality to their workers. But while their preachers coerce the workers to behave morally, the circumstances coerce them to behave immorally. In their struggle against their oppressors, the workers sweat morality from every pore.' —Bertolt Brecht, *Buch der Wendungen* [Book of Changes] in *Werke—Band 18: Prosa 3* (Frankfurt: Suhrkamp Verlag, 1996), p. 152. Translation from Markus Wessendorf, 'Brecht's Materialist Ethics between Confucianism and Mohism', *Philosophy East and West* 66(1) (2016): 122–45; here, p. 134.

PART III

Of Some Critics

I

Reading Spitzer

Cesare Cases' essay follows quickly on the heels of the Italian translation of some of the Viennese scholar's most significant writings.[1] It is a Marxist critique of the claim to present the work of some stylistic critics as total criticism.

For Cases, the polemic between Leo Spitzer's idealism and the anti-sentimentalism of the neo-positivists is merely a civil war. The limits of stylistics would be exactly the same as those of contemporary aesthetics with respect to the three major problems that aesthetic subjectivism has failed to solve: the degree of *effability* of the individual, the *knowingness* of artistic activity and the *genesis* of the work.

Having reaffirmed the primacy of a criticism grounded on a philosophy, for Cases stylistic inquiry will be legitimate as the philological propaedeutic to criticism, or as the exemplification and confirmation of the results attained by criticism through other means.

The questions of method posed by the translation of Spitzer's book (I am not concerned here with his analyses) fit into a debate that has been busying some of our scholars for half a century. Here it will be considered (in order to briefly explore only one of these questions) in relation to Cases' essay, among the first in Italy to handle a set of problems that will increasingly make demands on scholars of literature and critics schooled in Marxism. If the translation of Spitzer is a sign of expansion of stylistic criticism outside of academic milieus, we can only hope that Cases' essay will elicit further studies on the part of so-called militant criticism.

Aside from some excesses of polemical partisanship (the accusation of theology levied at Spitzer, even if it is grounded should not, for example, imply that the wish to remain within the work must be interpreted as a *unio mystica*[2]), we can agree with the kernel of Cases' theses—namely, that the scientific pseudo-objectivity of the stylistic critics is often reduced, by the pressure of their inevitable prejudices, confirming traditional judgements rather than innovating upon them.

But let us limit ourselves to the second of the problems that, according to Cases, stylistics would leave unresolved—the one of the knowingness of artistic activity, the keystone of stylistics. According to Spitzer, we find in the poet a knowingness of meanings pertaining to logic and content while his unknowingness, which always concerns *form*, would, once identified as such, be the clue to other, truer contents. But, Cases replies: Why does 'unconscious formal will' sometimes contradict the chosen content, and sometimes not? Subjectivist aesthetics has no answers on this score. If we suppose instead that the writer works up an objective reality, we must be able to imagine him as *artistically* conscious (that is, in his formal activity) of that reality even if he is not conscious philosophically, politically and so on. This is Lukács's famous thesis—the 'triumph of realism'. For Spitzer (according to Cases), the artist knows what he thinks but not entirely what he does; and in his doing he reveals, unknowingly, something other than what he thought. For Cases (and Lukács), he always knows what he does even though he doesn't always know what he thinks, or his thinking is mistaken. Where ideological self-consciousness fails, the 'higher honesty' of the artists would come to the rescue. And it is clear that the point of contention concerns the notion of 'knowledge'.

In brief, for Cases (and for Lukács), contradiction, when it exists, will be cognitive (we could call this aesthetic intellectualism, by analogy with the ethical kind); for Spitzer, it will merely be psychological, belonging to the *individuum*. The first resembles logical or ethical inconsistency; the second, a slip.

Bet let us now try to ask Cases whether the criterion of artistic validity (the last and first of the problems) lies in the degree of adequation to (or *reflection* of) objective reality (mimesis of nature or history) or instead in the modes and degrees of *elaboration and combination* of data. (Do we need to note that when we speak of 'reflection' and of objective reality, we do not mean anything inert and passive; and that objective reality *is not* sensible immediacy? But when we speak of the modes and degrees of elaboration and combination of *data*, with this last word we mean to refer to the set of elements and signs which, taken one by one, are indeed the elaboration or combination, or the signs of an experience, but they are aggregated and combined with one another precisely as 'parts of discourse'—from 'that branch of the lake of Como' to the element called 'Renzo', or the one called 'plague in Milan' and so on).[3]

In the first case, the judgement about the adequation of a work of art (the judgement of 'verisimilitude') will be relative not to artistic knowledge but to scientific, historical and other types of knowledge of objective reality possessed by the critic or the writer. I know (or think I know) what is a shipwreck, a bout of jealousy, the experience of a young man on the battlefield and I will thus be able to judge, without overstepping my competences, the adequacy and verisimilitude of Book Five of the *Odyssey*, Book Two of the *Recherche* or Book One of the *Chartreuse* . . . But it is easy at this point to note the most severe consequences of this heteronomy (which in truth is experienced by every critic or reader of poetry). One of those consequences is that the gap between the cognitive-discursive and the synthetic cognitive-expressive register (which is the work of poetry) is, in practice, often surreptitiously filled with aesthetic prejudice or ingrained aesthetic knowledge, so that the degree of adequation of a given artistic fact will not only be adapted to a reality gathered in snatches of 'life' (or history, or science, or philosophy, or philology) but also to remnants of previous artistic 'organizations'. This is proven by much critical objectivism or classicism—and by classicisms in general, which are inseparable from 'models'; but also by the limits of Lukács's theory, with the familiar consequence of a possible critical sterility. There exists no reader (and certainly no critic) who besides, or along with, having a set of non-artistic experiences and knowledges does not also bear an artistic 'past', an artistic 'memory'. And there is nothing strange in the fact that, at least in Western culture of Renaissance origins, the 'truth' of classicist or rationalist poetics has almost always been compatible with dogma, canon, rhetoric.

In the second case (of elaboration or combination), the criterion of validity of the work will no longer exclusively reside in 'verisimilitude' but, rather, in the margin of positive non-adequation; that is, in the margin of (apparent and contingent) unreality, in its unprecedented interpretation of the real. Where earlier, the critical eye was cast only on similarities, now it will turn to differences (and the sum of differences is the supreme difference, the dream of absolute autonomy). Balzac tells us something different about the France of Louis Philippe's time and the *homo franco-gallicus* of the first half of the nineteenth century than what a historical or scientific inquiry could offer us. And the difference is not only formal. It is something that, in order to be partially verified, has had to unfold in time its virtualities (the determinate phase of bourgeois society, etc.), just like the events that narrate the story. But it does this in a way that does not stop being a creation (unlike historical narration), that is to say, it is substantially incommensurable and irreducible to the elements, familiar to us, of the real it elaborates. In other words, the convergence between scientific, historical and other knowledge of the real, on the one hand, and artistic knowledge, on the other, is merely the necessary starting point to discern the specific difference of the latter. The criterion of value will be found in the tension between conversion and divergence. The more the artwork will appear to say the same truths as scientific, or historical, etc., knowledge, the more the differences will manifest themselves. The work lives (in the precise sense of 'work', namely, artistic execution, not document; and of 'living', namely, possessing communicative-expressive efficacy) in proportion to the tension between historical-critical judgement, and its resistance to that judgement (its apparent 'unreality'). Now, what is the last instance of this tension? It is the 'real' which fuels the two different forms of knowledge. Both refer to it. But what is the experience of that 'real', if not praxis?

Every reading is a confrontation between the sign–signified nexus that lies on the page and the 'cultural' totality of the reader. But we cannot say that the latter resolves the former into itself like a reduction of the unknown to the known. What is usually called the inexhaustibility of the artwork does not seem to reside in the plurality of meanings of the poetic word or, as some say, in its different possible readings, but in the circular motion the work establishes with a part of itself which is relatively reducible in different terms; in a word, translatable. I speak of circularity because with time what seems clear becomes obscure again, just as other parts or aspects of the work come into the light. 'Form' itself is transmuted.

The famous mystery of artistic survival remains, but alters its features when, instead of looking (in keeping with Marx's observations[4]) for those aspects of the art of the past that live on despite the disappearance of socioeconomic structures, we look to what no longer lives—to the price of survival. If it is superstructural, and thus, in the final analysis determined by praxis, every episode of artistic knowledge can—even beyond the zone subjected to the mutations of fashions and tendencies—suffer an erosion, an impoverishment, phases of relative aphasia and finally of death and resurrection caused by structural upheavals. Worse comes to worst, Jupiter dies and the poet's hymn dies with Jupiter. The survival of Greek art (to stay with Marx's example) was guaranteed by a formidable cultural relay, from Horace to Canova, which allows Lord

Elgin's flayed marbles to speak to us. (In the intervals of this relay, feudal peasants calmly melted down pagan bronzes.) And it is the absence of that continuity which means we do not perceive proto-Chinese, or Indian, or pre-Colombian art as *normale Kindheit*[5] and why these need or demand, in order to be understood, a leap outside the classicist tradition.

To reiterate, Spitzer's man is essentially Freudian man and his relationship between conscious and unconscious is subjective, or partakes of a sociological-scientific objectivism; while Lukács's (and Cases') man has class-alienation as his unconscious. In the latter, the stratification of the real determines internal stratification, the mystery of libido is nothing but an allegory of the mystery of history. And, if Marxist self-consciousness is a necessary moment and an authentic progress (grounding Cases' criticism of the bad objectivity of stylistic criticism and his demand for an explicit partisanship), it is also true that just as only praxis, and not self-consciousness, defeats neurosis, the 'mystery of history' is not dispelled by reading either *Capital* or the entire bibliography of Marxism, but only through action aimed at revolution, and solely to the degree that action modifies the world. It is understandable that Cases (still in a Hegelian manner, and like many Marxists) seems to want literature and art to always remain a little beneath philosophical and historical criticism, save to raise the red disc of 'science' when that criticism underlines the autonomy of art a little too emphatically. The struggle against autonomy always conceals the tendency towards a one-way heteronomy. It is understandable because in this way one tries to 'open' in the 'discursive' direction what in the highest works of art we feel is 'closed', self-satisfied, consumed in effigy.

In fact, the prophetic character—apostolical but conservative—of all great works of poetry makes them intimately contradictory. In the act through which they reveal the alienated characteristics of the real with extraordinary energy, they overcome them, but only in hope, utopianly ('in words'), thus confirming them. One wants to ask whether it is not possible to apply what Marx says of religion to art as a whole or, better, if many difficulties experienced by Marxist aesthetics and the 'artistic politics' of the workers' movement did not actually derive from the unconfessed fear of the consequences of a similarity taken to its limits, of the enormous cave deserted by so-called irrationality . . . [6]

The artwork does not exhaust itself in criticism. It is not mediated by historical or philosophical thought. What it has to become, it directly is; educating us to discern and order the world according to its formulae, through a continuous 'proposal of being' that calls for transformation. The work of poetry stands before us. Apparently, it doesn't ask for anything.

> We must therefore acknowledge those people to be entirely right who declare the Beautiful, and the mood into which it transports our spirit, to be wholly indifferent and sterile in relation to *knowledge* and *mental outlook*. They are entirely right; for Beauty gives no individual result whatever, either for the intellect or for the will; it realizes no individual purpose, either intellectual or moral; it discovers no individual truth, helps us to perform no individual duty, and is, in a word, equally incapable of establishing the character and clearing the mind.

So says Schiller.[7] But he adds right away that 'precisely by this means something infinite is attained'. And, to the extent that it is the very notion of 'beauty' which has changed between Schiller and us while remaining in line with the reflections I've just quoted, we can add that the work of art and poetry *appears* charged with potential and not actual energy because it unites the apparent contingency of an object of nature with the latent violence of a human intentionality. That ancient Greek who was found embracing the Aphrodite of Knidos was right. Through its presence alone the work of poetry proposes that the world measure and structure itself in its image and resemblance. Contrary to the aestheticism which thinks it can abolish the distinction between form and life, the work of art and poetry—as the metaphor or model of remorse or hope—looks at life from afar. It does not point to anything outside itself. That is why aesthetic consummation is necessarily a failure; that is why the movement emerging from the image of art and poetry is paradoxically a movement of disobedience to that appearance, of detachment from those eyes of Medusa. However, we find its type of metaphor and model in praxis; the two different, incommunicable languages structure themselves in analogous ways, they are articulated in similar figures. Finally, the thoroughgoing transformation of human relationships, in the registers of history and praxis, appears as the fulfilment of a silent intention of the greatest works of poetry.

For these openly 'romantic' hypotheses Spitzer's *Zirkel im Verstehen* is both necessary and insufficient.[8] That is because it tends to exhaust the work of poetry in a motion from the circle to the centre and the centre to the circle, when it instead harbours a centrifugal component, a 'love of perdition',[9] both towards the pre- or post-poetic—without which it would not exist—and towards the historical erosions of linguistic context which no philological surgery can compensate and no critical genius can do more than describe.

1955

Appendix

Two Letters from Spitzer

After the publication, in the first issue of *Ragionamenti*, of the preceding article, I received a letter from Leo Spitzer. My reply was followed by his. I would have liked to continue the correspondence; but when I started on my reply, which I reproduce here, I became aware of the impertinence of lecturing a man like Spitzer and left my reply unfinished and unsent. In Spitzer's texts I have simply corrected some spelling mistakes and omitted, as in my own, some private references.

Baltimore, Johns Hopkins University
23 November 1955

Dear Mr. Fortini,

I have read your review of the article by Mr. Cases and I take the liberty to make a few observations.

Contrary to your heading (L. Spitzer . . . Cases . . .), you criticize Cases, not me, or only that 'me' which you have glimpsed through Cases' words. This approach seems to me inexact: you do not have a direct knowledge of my writings, only a 'reflected' knowledge.

This is what makes you say that 'Spitzer's man is essentially Freudian man'. The truth seems to me to be the following: I myself related my first investigations into the criticism of style to a Freudian influence, but it also seems to me true that, little by little, I rejected the Freudian framework (style = deviation from normality, etc.). In my Italian volume one can easily see that today my criticism is inspired instead by the literary tradition that determines the style of the writer. And this stylistic tradition is something objective, perhaps due to that 'cultural relay' of which you speak so well; but in the end we can say that a given ode by Claudel, say, is conceived according to two traditions that are combined with each other; those of the Renaissance ode and of hymnology. You may dislike this analysis of the action of the past on the present, but there must be someone (the philologist, I believe) who deals with such influences.

There are other things in your article that I don't grasp fully, no doubt because of a lack of knowledge of Marxist aesthetics. The artwork, according to you, is a 're-elaboration of the real' and is parallel to (but different from) history and science. I am struck by the fact that you exemplify with Balzac, that is, with one of his *novels*, what you intend by the reproduction of a given historical, social, etc., reality. But what does a poem like the one that every

German would probably declare the most excellent written in his language—Goethe's 'Über allen Gipfeln ist Ruh'[10] —have to do with social history? Will one say that the evening feeling that comes close to the idea of a placid death is the result of a social alienation? That the association 'evening-death' is due to certain conditions either not recognized or falsely interpreted by Goethe? That in a different environment Goethe would not have thought of death? Therefore, there must be 'atemporal' feelings on which your structure or superstructure, whatever it may be, cannot bite. If you say, with my absolute agreement, that the artwork educates 'to discern and order the world according to its own formulae', that poem appears to me to educate us to see certain analogies between the natural phenomena proper to man and nature, and this attribution can naturally be referred to certain ideas of the eighteenth century; but to my mind the efficacy of the poem still resides precisely in what cannot be attributed to that century alone.

I do not know how one can attribute to me the general idea that 'the artist knows what he thinks but not entirely what he does'. Perhaps one of my studies may have given this impression. But I know that when I demonstrate that Claudel organized his ode on a kind of skeleton articulated around the repetition of the word *grand*, it is implicit that he did not do this unawares.

Perhaps I have not understood your article correctly, but it seems to me to follow a 'second hand' idea of my writings, of which I am the last to deny the contradictions and weaknesses. But even Mr. Cases has conceded in his letters to me that many times he went beyond the reality presented by my writings. You will understand that when one sees himself being treated as a *tête de turc*,[11] the Turk would at least like to be represented as a *true* Turk.

Please accept my greetings and thanks,

Leo Spitzer

Milan, 28 November 1955

Esteemed Professor,

[. . .] Let me admit right away that I committed an error or at least exaggerated in affirming that 'S.'s man is essentially Freudian man'. That 'Freudian' is no doubt false when it comes to your more recent work. But I must agree with Cases (following pp. 50–1 of the first instalment of his essay, *Società* 1, February 1955) that the *ideological patterns*[12] you utilize tend, in what concerns history and culture, to order themselves into a *Geistesgeschichte.*[13] We are more inclined to inquire into what socioeconomic structures were not only at the root of Christian hymnology or the Renaissance ode, but also which were at the root of Claudel's *mens*; to ask ourselves what class determinations operated in Claudel so as to lead him—through a series of mediations that became, but originally were not just 'cultural'—to look for that inheritance (the Renaissance ode and hymnology) rather than another. I don't contest that the action of the past on the present must be the foundation of any authentic critical inquiry; but of the whole past and, therefore, also the past of socioeconomic structures. And, in the example at hand, to what extent does Claudel relive those two cultural inheritances nostalgically, also because they correspond to types of socioeconomic relations that he would have desired and which the world around him instead increasingly destroyed?

As for the Goethian example, it is clear that we are not dealing with the mere association 'evening-death' but with a particular passion and agitation, painful and necessary, and with a death-rest that no doubt echoes Christian death (and the 'sleep' and 'good night' of Protestantism, which follows upon active daytime pessimism, more so than Catholic death) but which rules out every survival and tends to identify with the Great Whole, with Nature, obeying a cosmic law. And I would say that the poet here has marvellously signalled both the Christian legacy—the *pilgrim's progress,*[14] the end as peace and haven, etc.—and his detachment from it, that is to say, the acceptance of the end as a 'just' norm, not as the consequence of sin, and at the same time (with the double meaning of *Warte nur* . . . , signifying, I believe, 'wait' and 'wait for yourself', 'pause' and 'you will see') the slight, ironic advice to give time and nature time, not to hurry peace along with the same agitated thrust with which one lived the day of *Streben*.

'Atemporal' feelings? According to you, that Goethian lyric (I omit here a discussion of whether it is legitimate to discuss it critically without connecting it to the rest of Goethe's lyric *oeuvre*) 'appears to me to educate us to see certain analogies between the natural phenomena proper to man and nature, and this attribution can naturally be referred to certain ideas of the eighteenth century; but to my mind the efficacy of the poem still resides precisely in what cannot be attributed to that century alone'. According to me, I would say, its efficacy lies in the specific difference between its form and other possible forms of a generic feeling of 'evening-death'. The 'project of being' contained therein is not 'think the evening as peace-death' but 'fashion yourself a mind and a heart capable of reading *Gleichnisse*[15] in every natural object, but quickly, immediately; making it so that the dialogues with your conscience are surrounded by the same silence and blankness that surrounds my words. Let the syntax in your mind·be similar to the syntax of these verses; learn that euphemism is not hypocrisy but is truer than the true'.

In sum, you can deduce from those verses an image of man, or at least a silhouette, which exists in time and in history; faced with it, our attitude can be one of consent or refusal, we can feel it as confined to its century, or instead as alive for us or, rather, as an omen of a humanity to come, for us or for others. If such a comparison is legitimate, then Goethian man—who, alone in his evening forest, having carried out his *Tagewerk*, his day's work, looks at death-rest with scarcely a breath (*kaum einen Hauch*) of regret for the farewell—is actually much closer to us than the Baudelairian man who feels the ecstasy of a desperate solitude in the night. Needless to say, inasmuch as we remain inhabitants of horrible cities spawned by industrialism and the artificial multiplication of needs, we still feel or at least comprehend the Baudelairian night. But inasmuch as we—us 'Marxists', at least—wish for a real humanization of nature and a naturalization of man (this is Marx, *Economic-Philosophical Manuscripts of 1844*, Manuscript I, *Alienated Labour*; via Hegel, Goethe would have understood perfectly), Goethe's 'bourgeois' proposal is closer to us and our future than the desperate 'rebel' proposal of the French victim of the Industrial Revolution. The admiration in which that lyric was held by a century or more of German philistines is more proof of its historicity; I fear that what they loved was the pathetic appeal to death, the 'spiritual aroma' that allows, after a day spent making money, to feel oneself as a noble soul close to the little birds. And that if the past two generations of cultured and semi-cultured Germans really wished to express their feelings about death, they would have instead resorted to quotes by Stefan George or Rainer Maria Rilke...

It would therefore be an unforgivable foolishness to say that the feeling and the nexus 'evening-death' are tied to a particular social structure or alienation; it is instead possible, and to my mind necessary, not to limit the chain of mediations to *ideological patterns* but to see what lies behind them—meaning, not only how the latter are in the final analysis determined by the modes and relations of production but also how the evaluation of ancient or modern artworks is strictly inseparable from the judgement and wish that we make about humanity, today. That is the sense in which I paradoxically ended my piece, saying that the 'truth' of the artwork is practical action . . .

Baltimore, 2 December 1955

Dear Doctor Fortini,

Our correspondence appears to follow an identical pattern to my correspondence with Cases: first I read things in print that are, or seem to me, exaggerated, then I learn from immensely (really, undeservedly) courteous letters that perhaps there was an error of detail, but on the other hand . . .

But, to get things in the open, I will say this about your Marxist interpretation of Goethe: personally, I don't have the least inclination to forbid a criticism of Goethe that would show the nefarious facet of his place in the history of Germanism (and I would probably agree with you, and have in fact expressed similar ideas about the philistine or pharisee *Goethekult*). But when we analyse one of his poems, everything that is outside the text must be excluded; we must make the presuppositions of the text our own: if it is pastoral, let us become shepherds; if it is a critique of industrial life, let us become critics of industry; if it is Catholic or Buddhist, let us for a moment become Catholics or Buddhists. So that a Marxist or anti-Marxist criticism only finds its place after the 'literature class', or outside said class. First we must understand the poem according to its data. Everything that you explain about 'Über allen Gipfeln' seems to me the confusion of a poetics with a sociological analysis, which is possible only after the former. When I read 'Über allen Gipfeln', I don't need to know anything about 'Goethian man', about his *Tagewerk* ('biographical fallacy'!),[16] his *Streben*,[17] the false idealism of Germans who pretend, after a day of making money, to be close to the little birds, 'quickly' to find parallels between nature and man . . . All of this is irrelevant—*allotria*, to use Croce's term.[18] Were you to contradict me, I would say that you do not conceive of art as a 'disinterested thing' in the Kantian sense—and then 'aesthetic criticism' can no longer exist, only 'ideological criticism'.

Therefore I believe that great poetry is atemporal—like mathematics. In that field no one would dare to invoke a Jewish prejudice, or a bourgeois-Christian or a socialist prejudice and so on. Why should we act differently when we are dealing with poetry which also creates modules that once created remain with humanity, with its 'eternal patrimony'. In effect, that feeling of evening-peace which you describe so well (not Christian, but 'natural') is an achievement, whatever its origin may be, for everyone, even for a factory worker coming home tired from his work. And the Claudelian ode too is an achievement even if Claudel himself in other works proved to be a propagandist of a bad sort. And if a factory-worker poet, a true artist, were to paint the evening as the death inflicted by human meanness, I would be ready to read his poem with reverence as an achievement. Is that not how we read Kafka's 'poetry'? And you must concede that in the University there needs to be a place (a Chair?) where poetry is explained as poetry, not as a thing that must first be 'accepted or rejected' but as what must absolutely be 'first accepted'—and then to think of other things, of moral or social consequences, etc.

I understand very well that [. . .] a young man desires a total renewal of the cultural atmosphere. But just as I'm sure you do not think it is necessary to renew 'bourgeois mathematics', so I cannot see why the atemporal works of bourgeois poetry must be drowned in 'causal' criticism, alienating us from poetry which in a certain way has no 'causes'. Because Plato was an arch-conservative in political matters, should we not be able to rejoice in the poetry of the *Symposium*?

But perhaps you think that poetic fantasies like all the ones I have enumerated are not in keeping with the current climate, with the urgencies of life today? But if one wishes to forbid such fantasies, how are we to avoid the 'captive mind', the authoritarian prescription of morality and taste? I believe that both you and our friend Cases don't want to reach these final consequences! All my best wishes

Leo Spitzer

Milan, 1 January 1956

Esteemed Professor,

[. . .] I understand very well why you would oppose a poetic analysis of poetry to a sociological analysis. In other words, to pick an example, why you oppose your 'stylistics' to analyses, say, of the kind made by Lukács. With the provisos advanced by Cases, I understand; between those two modes of criticism there really is such a difference of method that we may discuss their respective validity but we certainly cannot confuse them. What instead I do not understand is how you can end up calling *allotria*, in the Crocean sense, the very historicity of language. You say that one 'must understand the poem according to its data'; I have no difficulty in conceding this, at least in this context, and what you have chosen to call my Marxist interpretation of 'Über allen Gipfeln' was certainly 'sociological', meaning that it presented what to my mind were the results without presenting the stylistic itinerary. And yet I open your book of essays and read that all of your analyses take their cue from—and how could they not?—a philological reading thoroughly saturated with historicism. You will concede that in order to make the presuppositions of the text itself our own, as you say ('if it is pastoral make ourselves shepherds', etc.), we need, at the very least, to understand what we are talking about and at least know, as I think Croce himself says faced with the first verse of the *Furioso*, that the knights whereof it speaks are not those of the Order of the Crown of Italy and that the weapons are not the kind you could buy at the corner gun shop. As soon as you write: 'Here *flamme* is not one of the usual, conventional linguistic preciosities of court theatre . . . ' (your unforgettable pages on *Phaedra*!), you will admit that the reader eager to follow you must at least have some knowledge of these worn and conventional *Kenning*, no?[19] Well, suppose for a moment I had been so daring or so foolish as to attempt a stylistic reading of 'Über allen Gipfeln', clearing my mind of all the sociological prejudices, ignoring all the banalities about Goethe that I have impertinently repeated in my previous letter. I would probably have tried to detect consonances and dissonances, coquetry with 'normality' and double entendres and so on and so forth. *That* language, if observed very attentively, would have disclosed its historical essence, would have defined itself as what it 'is' starting from what it 'is not'. Alas, I can't manage to see how this 'literature class' could radically differ from a subsequent 'sociological literature or *allotria* class'. In sum, I have always thought and still think that reading 'inside the text', a 'stylistic' reading, should lead to—if carried out with all the rigour of which you are a master—the same results as a criticism that starts from 'the outside'. Was it not you who taught us that we must constantly move from the centre to the periphery and vice versa? Far be it from me to believe that poetry (whether or not bourgeois) must be drowned by a 'causal' criticism, or to believe that I should not enjoy the poetry of the *Symposium* because Plato was an arch-conservative. Or rather, precisely because we maintain that art and poetry are the expression of a conception of the world tied to a class and a historical moment, we think we know that they are not its mere passive reflections, and we are therefore certain that the poetic force of Plato prevails over his own political views. We believe then that poetry is never 'reactionary' and retrograde, but this does not mean that we should not also evaluate 'sociologically' the pre-poetic world, the sentimental and ideological 'material' of an author . . .

Notes

Originally published without the Fortini–Spitzer correspondence as 'La critica stilistica' [Stylistic Criticism] in *Ragionamenti* 1(1) (September–October 1955). [Trans.]

1 Leo Spitzer, *Critica stilistica e storia del linguaggio* [Stylistic Criticism and History of Language] (Alfredo Schiaffini ed.) (Bari: Laterza, 1954); and Cesare Cases, 'I limiti della critica stilistica e i problemi della critica letteraria' [The Limits of Stylistic Criticism and the

Problems of Literary Criticism], *Società* 1 (1955): 47–63, and *Società* 2 (1955): 266–91.

2 The mystical union of the individual with the deity. [Trans.]

3 Alludes to Alessandro Manzoni's novel *I Promessi sposi* [The Betrothed, published in 1827]. 'Quel ramo del lago di Como' [that branch of the Lake of Como] is the first line of this novel. [Trans.]

4 See Karl Marx, *Grundrisse* (Martin Nicolaus trans.) (London: Penguin, 1973), pp. 110–11. [Trans.]

5 Normal childhood (German). An allusion to Marx's phrase, 'The Greeks were normal children'; ibid., p. 111. [Trans.]

6 Roland Barthes has recently confirmed in what sense literature is 'constitutively reactionary':

> Each time we valorize or sacralize the real (which has hitherto been the custom of progressive ideologies), we realize that literature is only language, and a second language at that, a parasitical meaning which can only connote the real, not denote it: logos thus appears irremediably severed from praxis. . . . But also each time we write ambiguously enough to suspend meaning, each time we proceed as if the world signified though without saying what, then writing releases a question, it troubles what exists, though without ever preforming what does not yet exist, it gives the world an energy: in short, literature does not permit us to walk, but it permits us to breathe.

See 'Literature and Signification', *Critical Essays*, p. 267 [translation modified]. Here, immediately after my agreement, I only need to add that the notion of literature (which I here take to mean institution, moment of being, modality of language) does not coincide with the one of 'poetry' or 'art', which I have employed more often. The latter retains a criterion of value; it is in the register of value that conservative or reactionary ambiguity of the work hides, in its *being-already*, in its (appearance of) completeness, in its being which 'enjoys itself in itself'. Luckily the artwork, no less than God, needs men.

7 Friedrich Schiller, *On the Aesthetic Education of Man* (Reginald Snell trans.) (Mineola, NY: Dover, 2004), p. 101.

8 The circle . . . is not a vicious one; on the contrary, it is the basic operation in the humanities, the *Zirkel im Verstehen* as Dilthey has termed the discovery made by the Romantic scholar and theologian Schleiermacher, that cognizance in philology is reached not only by the gradual progression from one detail to another detail, but by the anticipation or divination of the whole—because 'the detail can be understood only by the whole and any explanation of detail presupposes the understanding of the whole'. Our to-and-fro voyage from certain outward details to the inner center and back again to other series of details is only an application of the principle of the 'philological circle'.

—Leo Spitzer, 'Linguistics and Literary History' in *Linguistics and Literary History: Essays in Stylistics* (Princeton: Princeton University Press, 1948), pp. 1–29; here, pp. 19–20. [Trans.]

9 Refers to the title of the novel *Amor de Perdição* (1862) by the Portuguese Romantic writer Camilo Castelo Branco. [Trans.]

10 J. W. Goethe, 'Wanderer's Nightsong II' (1780), also known as 'Ein gleiches' (Another One). [Trans.]

11 French expression denoting a scapegoat, after the attraction in nineteenth-century French fairs, where visitors would test their strength by punching the effigy of a turbaned man. [Trans.]

12 In English in the original. [Trans.]

13 The history of spirit or mind. [Trans.]

14 In English in the original. [Trans.]

15 Parables, allegories or similes (German). [Trans.]

16 In English in the original. [Trans.]

17 Striving (German). [Trans.]

18 See Réne Wellek, *A History of Modern Criticism: 1750–1950. Volume 8: French, Italian, and Spanish Criticism, 1900–1950* (New Haven: Yale University Press, 1992), p. 195. [Trans.]

19 *Kenning* is a figure of speech in Old Norse, and later Icelandic and Anglo-Saxon poetry. It can be found in *Beowulf*, in expressions such as *seġl-rād*, 'sail-road' or *swan-rād*, 'swan-road'. [Trans.]

II

Mimesis

The more the selection of texts, the critical pretexts and transactions present themselves as dictated by chance, the more in Erich Auerbach's work the history of Western literary realism is dominated by a precise tendency. In the book's final chapters, the recovery of the 'great world' in the microcosm of psychology occurs (when it does) in the modern narrators under review thanks to sudden simplifications of sociohistorical reality. Likewise, in Auerbach's work, the passage from the examination of the fragment to the cultural and historical synthesis takes place only thanks to the *a priori* of sorts that governs, like an iron framework, the whole book.

This is the hypothesis of the pagan age of separation of styles that is followed by the Christian or 'figural' age. In the latter, the 'sublime' and 'modest' styles unite—as in the prose of the Gospels—only to separate anew in the West of the Renaissance and the absolute monarchies, and to conjoin again in the Romantic and modern epoch, thanks to the serious treatment of the events of everyday life.[1] But this movement of *solve et coagula*[2] is accompanied for Auerbach by an ever-greater deepening of the realistic vision. We thus have a twofold relationship: one between the works (or the individual authors under examination) and the ideas or images that contemporary culture had of 'reality' (assuming it had them); and the other between these works or authors and the idea of reality or realities that we and our environing culture possess.

It follows that for Auerbach the work is:

(a) the synchronic literary equivalent of a conception of the real based on determinate ideologies (moral, religious, etc.);
(b) the anticipation of future ideologies; and,
(c) in a subordinate manner, an original and direct interpretation of a reality, more 'real' than the others because it is confirmed by contemporary science.

(It should be noted than when he speaks about the sciences, Auerbach tends to mean the so-called human sciences—sociology and psychology in particular.) Owing to the second and third features, he is certain that there is a parallelism between the scientific conquest of an ever-more adequate notion of reality and its literary representation—ultimately, two parallel *progresses*.

We can now understand why the convergence between Auerbach's progressive sociologism and Marxism is only apparent. The notion of decadence does not belong to Auerbach's viewpoint. The arrival point of *Mimesis* is not represented by the great French novelists of the nineteenth century (who nevertheless made it so that 'the tragic, the grave, the problematic appears in . . . everyday life',[3] introducing the life of the people 'in the depths of the workaday world and its men and women'[4] alongside 'a serious representation of contemporary everyday social reality against the background of a constant historical movement' of classes[5]) but, rather, by those contemporary authors for whom 'the random moment . . . concerns the elementary things which men in general have in common',[6] with the attendant 'fragmentation of the exterior action . . . reflection of consciousness . . . stratification of time'.[7] Auerbach even goes so far as to say that this valorization of the most elementary aspects of our life, 'comparatively independent of the controversial and unstable orders over which men fight and despair',[8] foreshadows a unity of humankind. The optical aberration is so obvious here that there's no need to insist upon it too much: a period (no doubt extremely important) of the literature of the imperialist age is mistaken for the entire literary development of the modern age; all the contrary, and often crucial examples spanning opposite tendencies (Mann, Kafka) are forgotten; and, most importantly, Auerbach suggests that a social and political problematic is absent among the writers under consideration, when it in fact exists as the anarchic-existential claim to the instant and the immediate—the humble tragic everyday.

Faced with a work which it is not hard to read as that of a master, a certain unwarranted dissatisfaction could overtake a reader confronted with the lack of the deliberate coquetry which, instead, impresses the sign of invention upon all of Spitzer's essays, for example, and turns them into the site of an encounter between a method and a taste. In Auerbach, stylistic analysis, in the strict sense, seems to be both less determinant and less despotic; focused more on the syntactic structures than on the vocabulary and the grammatical modes, it shades imperceptibly into the analysis of contents. That work of high linguistic microbiology that in Spitzer leaves one stupefied, dazzled and perplexed is rare in Auerbach; on the other hand, the social framework of tastes, tendencies and conflicts within which the personality of the writer under examination unfolds, when it is convincingly argued, does not appear new or at least not rich with new insights. Above all, it seems insufficient—as though the author were hastening to conclude his race through the centuries. If one intends to engage in sociological reconstruction, why not then reread or rewrite those works that our fathers and grandfathers would entitle, say, *Cervantes and his World* or *The Age of Racine*, which at least brim with data and information?

In the preface to the Italian edition of *Mimesis*, Aurelio Roncaglia[9] replies to Cases' objections against the claims to autonomy of stylistics that the circularity of understanding (for which what is presupposed doubles as the result) belongs to every interpretive experience. But when, in his Epilogue, Auerbach praises historicism as the 'perspectivism' of judgement 'which makes it possible to accord the various epochs and cultures their own presuppositions and views . . . and to dismiss as unhistorical and dilettantish every absolute assessment of the phenomena that is brought from the outside',[10] and then practices that 'perspectivism' extensively in his work—now recommending to the reader the originality of Dante now that of Saint-Simon or Stendhal—from what presuppositions and points of view does he draw that 'line of ideas' denominated as 'realism' which furnishes his book with its read thread? Ultimately, one will have to concede that it is not possible to draw it out of distant centuries, but at most from the decline of the Romantic age. In fact, Auerbach himself has an answer, generously affirming his situation, his connection to the present, the awareness that *Mimesis* 'does not conform to changes in expert opinions. It has to do with a version of the thought, which was formed by me around 1940'.[11] In short, Auerbach has two registers at his disposal: one is the notion of objective, scientific or scientistic, realism; the other is a historicist perspectivism or relativism. Yet one has the impression that the two do not overlap or encompass, that they are instead juxtaposed. In other terms, the notion of reality employed by Auerbach is indeed borrowed from the human sciences more than the physical or natural ones but it nevertheless remains positivist in kind.

What's more, realism (as the artistic application of ideologies concerning reality) advances in tandem with, albeit on a different path, realism understood as the direct artistic recording of a reality independent from extra-artistic ideologies. It is clear why Auerbach falls into the facile paradox of thinking that the progress of realist literature is in truth the progress of the scientific–historical interpretation of reality, such that the poorest student at the polytechnic would be more 'advanced' than Galileo, and any journalist deftly employing tropes and images that were once the original inventions of authors from bygone centuries should be considered from the standpoint of 'realism' to be more 'realist' than Cervantes. As I have said, the two formulations of realism are in tandem; in truth, literature appears here as a formal institution of ideologies, a part and a reflection of them, almost never the direct interpretation of reality, that is, the *source* of new conceptions of the world.

What Auerbach refuses to provide is a criterion for going from fact to value or, better, for constituting a given order of facts as value. This is because he seems to ground the value of a poetic expression on its capacity to exemplify rather than to establish an advanced conception of reality.

It is not enough to affirm that the subjectivity of the starting point finds its outcome in the objectivity of stylistic inquiry, nor that prejudice has as much of a right to exist as the conclusive judgement, resting on the research that overcomes and realizes that pre-judgement. Even if we do not wish to repeat here, echoing Cases, that the 'circularity of spirit' is only a vicious circle, it remains the case that precisely that pre-judgement will need to be subjected to criticism, that is to say, to the 'point of view' chosen by the critic. For example: to affirm openly, as we do, the heteronomy of every judgement of artistic *value*—meaning, that at the basis of every critical reasoning lies an ineliminable extra-aesthetic prejudice—will only make sense if we simultaneously agree to discuss the soundness of the pre-judgement, namely, in our case, to discuss the validity of that 'conception of the world' which includes an immediate socialist perspective. It's really not clear why the critic should benefit from the same 'respite'[12] or tolerance enjoyed by writers and artists when it comes to the possible divergence between intentions (or 'conceptions of the world') and results. Furthermore, we have always thought that the forbearance one encounters both in idealist criticism and in the Marxist criticism of Lukács is offensive. The 'triumph of realism' shares with the Crocean idea of the irrelevance of the 'structural' elements of poetic creation the tendency to underestimate intentional (and not just final) ideological structures as essential components of artistic unity. And the true and great artwork is—even more than Lukács's declarations suggest—a correction of its own ideological premises or, rather, a 'truth' in the order of knowledge. This is why the work of a poet can be a decisive objection against the thought of a philosopher (and vice versa)—an assertion more easily accepted than practiced. For us the religious and imperial conceptions of Dante, like the tsarist and slavophile ideas of Dostoevsky, are true (and therefore not mere regressive negativity in contrast with the more advanced ideologies of their time) by dint of the level at which they are lived and expressed; and the Christianity of Alighieri or Dostoevsky is incommensurable with the prevailing Christianity of their time, at least as much as their poetry is incommensurable with that of a Jacopo Alighieri[13] or of any other Russian slavophile or mystic of the 1870s. No 'overcomer' of Christianity who does not possess at least the genius of Dante is superior to his Christianity, just like no author of a socialist society will be superior to the reactionary slavophilia of a Dostoevsky or the evangelical humanitarianism of a Tolstoy just because the society in which he lives is superior to the one in which the two great Russian writers lived. And if that much is true for the writer, why should it not be all the more true for the critic, from whom we have the right to demand a full explanation as to the prejudice that governs his method?

[What then is my prejudice? That the 'semantic coherence' of the literary work is not its value, but only an index of its value. That value is relative—let's hope we are making ourselves understood!—to the degree of pedagogic and psychogogic power of the work; we should add right away that what is at stake is a pedagogy and psychogogy towards a humanity or a way of being human that we consider *superior*, in other words, more valid than another. Clearly, this criterion of validity is openly extra-aesthetic and moralistic. For us today, such a way of being human is the one proposed by or underlying a socialist civilization or humanity, by which we mean the overcoming of the public and the private, of bourgeois egotism and altruism, of the contradictions between manual and intellectual labour and so on.

The *specific* pedagogic and psychogogic power of the (literary) work is given precisely by its *indirection*, its metaphorical character, therefore by its not being a logical-scientific discourse. Put even more simply: what *distinguishes* artistic discourse from another discourse it its tendency to semantic coherence (the other side of its formal self-sufficiency), but what *founds* its value lies outside it. The artistically weak or failed work is the one that does not tend to overcome itself, that is self-satisfied, that does not measure up to time and corruption, and that therefore decays and grows silent all the more quickly. Even the works of remote civilizations still live on as the schema or skeleton of a tension or a demand unrealized within history, an unkept promise. For Auerbach, the advance of the artwork is the advance on successive interpretations of the real and (to simplify, let me push the paradox) the best is the one which has glimpsed first a notion of reality that will become banal centuries later; the 'figural' character of Medieval art stings Auerbach with nostalgia because the modern world no longer appears to him to strive for that relation between terrestrial and celestial affairs. But all the art that still speaks to us is 'figural', it is an object which, emerging from the space and time that delimit it, demands its own withering away as an object, its own metamorphosis into living human beings.]

In a review of *Mimesis*,[14] Cases sees the paradox of Auerbach in the 'fact that he has carried out an investigation into European realism without in the end believing in reality'. I don't think that is exact; 'reality', for Auerbach, is the one of contemporary non-Marxist science, which is difficult to term as 'idealist'.

The paradox of Auerbach may instead be this: while Lukácsian criticism is almost exclusively the criticism of 'masterpieces', which envelops and implies the 'minor works', Auerbach's is the criticism of the 'minor works' or the reduction of the greatest writers to 'minor' ones, their decomposition into so many distinct moments that can belong to the so-called great synthetic personality as much as to time, fashion or taste. For him, an obscure dramatic Medieval text is equivalent to Dante, and I note a dangerous aestheticism à la 'imaginary museum' in his manner of relishing, for example, the crude Romanic puppets of a Gregory of Tours. One has to ask oneself what Homer and Shakespeare really have to do with this 'history of forms'. The correspondence between positivistic objectivism (history of forms, of culture, etc.) and anti-historicist subjectivism or, better, the inevitable jump from one to the other, could not be more obvious. Yet the doubt lingers as to whether the antidote can be represented by Lukácsian objectivism. The German and the Hungarian are both equally given to illuminating the object of their studies according to a perspective with the difference that Auerbach, exiled in the midst of the war of extermination, wishes for a condition in which the 'little world' of tragically everyday humble life—in its miserable and sublime immediacy—empties and absorbs the 'great world' which has turned into the theatre of inhuman insanities. He sees in the stocking of Woolf's *To the Lighthouse* a secular equivalent of Abraham's little donkey, of which he speaks in the first chapter, as the point of intersection of the instant and the eternal. While Lukács, precisely because he is a Marxist, does not believe in anarchic redemptions. So it is not because of psychological differences but because of historical perspectives that we live through a schism in criticism, which is *une et indivisible* according to Gianfranco Contini. Nor will it be healed until we are told through what mediations, through what phenomenology of reading or stylistics *a parte lectoris*,[15] a *Hamlet*, for example, without ceasing to be 'representative of the inner crisis of feudalism' (according to Lukács and Cases) may be able to represent other crises—our own.

This one insistent objection will not be silenced by the formula that makes the present into the outcome of the entirety of the past.

It is not only by conscious or unconscious 'memory' that the works of the past move us, nor simply because of our similarity to that past, but also because their unresolved tension continues to give a form to our own. And our dissimilarity from that past, perceived along with similarity in a unitary form, pushes us by individuating us to look to our future for a solution to that tension and to our own; in short, an achieved dissimilarity or an integral adequation.

1956

Notes

Originally published as 'Arte e società' [Art and Society], *Ragionamenti* 2(5–6) (May–August 1956). [Trans.]

1 'In our study we are looking for representations of everyday life in which that life is treated seriously, in terms of its human and social problems or even of its tragic complications.'—Erich Auerbach, *Mimesis: The Representation of Reality in Western Thought* (Willard R. Trask trans.) (Princeton: Princeton University Press, 2003), p. 342. [Trans.]

2 'Dissolve and coagulate', a major principle of alchemy. [Trans.]

3 Auerbach, *Mimesis*, p. 246.

4 Ibid., p. 444.

5 Ibid., p. 518.

6 Ibid., p. 552.

7 Ibid., pp. 552–3.

8 Ibid., p. 552.

9 Aurelio Roncaglia (1917–2001), philologist and literary critic. [Trans.]

10 Auerbach, *Mimesis*, p. 573.

11 Ibid., p. 563.

12 Fortini uses the term *comporto* which refers in Italian labour law to that duration of time for which workers can keep their job if they are on maternity or sick leave. [Trans.]

13 Jacopo Alighieri (1289–1348), Dante Alighieri's son and composer of the encyclopedic poem *Il Dottrinale* (1328). [Trans.]

14 Cesare Cases, 'Il paradosso di *Mimesis*', *Il Contemporaneo* 3(27) (7 July 1956): 8. [Trans.]

15 On the side of the reader. [Trans.]

III

Deus Absconditus

1. Lucien Goldmann's book, like most of his sociological work, is a treatment of the notions of totality and *vision du monde* (world-view); it is about their application in the study of Pascal and Racine but it is, especially, the proposal of an interpretation of Marxism. This proposal is openly ideological in nature, and consists in the effort to establish a passage from Pascal's 'tragic wager' to the Marxist dialectic. It is also a variant and robust reprise of the numerous anti-providential (and anti-scientistic) responses of the non-Stalinist left to the ideologisms of the past 20 years. Goldmann is adamant in marking his distance from existentialism; the 'sense–non-sense' that would lie at the core of Sartre or Merleau-Ponty's thought appears to him as an abdication in the face of the ever-resurgent demand for reason and lucidity that belongs to tragedy and the classical spirit. Against the ambiguity of romantic drama or of tragedy as 'gloom', Goldmann stakes a claim to the heroic obduracy of the spirit of tragedy, in the Pascal–Kant–Marx–Lukács lineage. For these thinkers, contradiction is no longer scandalous—it is institutional. According to Goldmann, the true tragic lesson is to be found in the pages of the 'sane' and balanced Marx, not in those of the great troubled consciences of the nineteenth century or among the 'heralds of the storm'.[1]

2. For Goldmann, Marxism is a thought which affirms that no value must be recognized and accepted unless this recognition is grounded in an objective and positive knowledge of reality, namely, in a 'practice in accordance with historical progress'. This knowledge includes social life, and therefore differs from every knowledge of the scientific-deterministic or 'legal' kind—and it is inseparable from action. Hence the impossibility, for the Marxist, to demonstrate the *necessity* of historical progress; and hence the inevitability of an initial 'wager', an act of Marxist 'faith', the recognition of a super-individual reality as the supreme value that must be realized in history. Ethics claims to ground ahistorical value, sociology to collect judgements of fact independently from judgements of value; for Marxism, instead, *every* meaning is historical and history has *one* meaning. The meaning is its end: a classless society, the becoming explicit of inter-individual humanity.

This raises a problem. If we don't accept for human facts the absolute determinism of physical laws, every behaviour is objectively a *choice* between different possibilities. But if only successive choices—that is to say, the direction of history itself—are able to guarantee the validity of the preceding choices (herein lies the 'risk' of the wager), then the very end of the 'wager' or of the revolutionary project will change with every subsequent behaviour. If the historical realization of communism is at the same time the end and the means, intermediate ends modify the End and the object of the 'wager' will not be the realization of the End but, rather, the addition and succession of particular ends will not radically alter its nature. And if that is the case, then the repudiated existentialism returns; wagering on an absolute *but* historical future means wagering on the outcome of choices present and to come—staking the future day by day.

3. Goldmann's existentialism, even if disavowed, could not fail to introduce the problem of time into Marxism; this is decisive both in its positive aspects (prediction) and in its negative ones (the tyranny of hope). What is this future, this terminus of historical progress? An end. Not any progress whatsoever but *that* progress. And we make it, with individual actions. But which among these actions are in accordance with historical progress? Which constitute it positively and which negatively? For the Calvinist, success would have been the index of election. For the Marxist militant who does not wish to wallow in his good conscience, the only possible guarantee of the political-moral 'correctness' of action is the past conquest, and enjoyment of the end—an absurd hypothesis. What then? Knowledge-action will concern 'partial totalities', conventionally severed from the distant future. But at this point it will not be possible to invoke the mere repetition of the initial 'wager', the appeal to Grace or the existentialist impetus—'choice', 'risk', permanent conversion. *The results must be tested, verified.*

4. This is the point at which the twofold face of the mediating demiurge, the Party, comes onto the scene. On one side, as concrete super-individuality, guardian of the end, it amortizes historical risk and responsibility, doling out preventive absolutions; it is both a church and the celebration of historical mysteries. On the other, it is the organizer of *tests* and *revelations* (which are themselves actions). Tests and revelations imply *predictions* and *communications*. But this remains the universe of the near past, the past imperfect, the present and the near future. It is a dramatic and not a tragic universe; it is a universe of needs, as ephemeral as a truffle hound's sense of smell. The need for communication diminishes instead in proportion to the distance from the verifiable horizon. The young Lukács cited by Goldmann rightly reminds us that the solitary man can have brothers, but not comrades. It is no accident that Goldmann evokes the 'Jansenist' perspective of the Marxist when the Marxist future seems to demand the 'wager', when fraternity appears to be the only value capable of surviving the conditions that have dispersed the comrades. But we do not need to insist on this familiar reciprocity of faith and works.

5. On this terrain, dialectical relations become pure paradoxes or antinomies. Everyday experience presents us with untested parties-mediators, instruments of communication without communication, the superimposition of 'materialism' (statistics, objects, production) and 'idealism' (bureaucratic nominalism, 'wooden languages'). Moreover, the tragic impetus can stem from the negation of the future as much as from its affirmation. We can also add that, in the modern world, the tragic bearing of the believer of Port Royal[2] has become objective and commonplace. A vast crowd of brokers of nothingness—we ourselves—behold their own acts, incessantly fleeing into the horizon without ever witnessing their 'return', or at least without 'recognizing' them, that is, without any vital response. The ignorance of the mechanical destination of the individual component ejected by the machine is matched by the ignorance about the recipients of ideological labour, from which producers suffer to the point of aphasia. This gives rise to communities of retreat, false echoes and social integrations so perfect in their imitations of truth they can fool the most expert eye.

We realize that the critique of mystified society (i.e. the critique of ideological mystification) runs the risk of becoming shrouded in a fog of contradictions. All existential 'presentism' in its many variants (Catholic, historical, libertine, anarchist, etc.) contains the assertion of the positivity of the particular and the immediate as well as the anxiety-ridden accentuation of the tragic character of existence. It is opposed to Marxist 'futurism'[3] in two different and opposite ways, countering the implacable appeal to a future that must be realized with the image of happiness, of *bonheur* (and thus preaching the socialism of distribution against the socialism of production, consumer goods against heavy industry, etc.) but also laying claim to the existential absolute, the refusal of mediations and of 'facticity' against those organisms of intersubjectivity (the Party) that 'futurism' creates in order also to diminish and mediate the unbearable urge towards the future. Inversely, Marxist politics oscillates between the obscuring of the future, when it establishes the institutes of class solidarity, and an appeal to that same future when the difficulties of the present can only be overcome with a *supplement d'âme*.

6. I think Goldmann gave such little prominence to those forms in which, according to him, Marxism would have conserved and overcome the tragic vision, not only because this was not the object of his work but also because the ideological movement—the 'passion' of the book, its true centre—was the tragic refusal of worldly life. Goldmann's discourse is thus important, notwithstanding its inevitably undeveloped character, precisely because it again raises, in the act of negating them, the questions of a Marxist ethics.

'Society is necessary', 'Society is death'. 'Value cannot be embodied immediately', 'Values must be embodied immediately'. 'I cannot be right without the others', 'Even alone I can be right'. These antinomic pairs cannot be rhetorically mediated, the tension between them must be genuine. But we can't rest content with a pendulum movement that would betray the dialectic itself. If ethics can only be based on historical duty, and behaviour can ultimately only be grounded on action, the latter demands a system of tests. We can say that the tests form the base of *predictability*, an intermediate zone of clarity between the absolute present and the absolute future of the wager. And we can add that perhaps never has prediction begun to shape the possibility of a different kind of destiny as in the modern world, eliminating the conditions of 'depraved faith'—namely, the dream of an instantaneous and absolutely private communication—and eschatological hope, or despair. To have his tragic freedom protected from the compromising mediation of society, man does not need to be *effrayé* by the silence of infinite spaces; to say no to the Great Animal of the present, he does not need to 'wager' on a communist advent at the borders of history, at the border of the predictable and the unpredictable where the circle of light of associated life ends and the clearing of the not-yet and no-longer-human begins, man can—or rather, now must—

constantly question the pact that ties him to his group, class and nation (and to his very species), in a movement of successive and responsible refusals and acceptances which excludes the 'wager' without thereby eliminating the risk. Like that blessed hermit from Siena who had withdrawn to the desert, the 'Accona Desert' outside of any human society but not so far away that he could not still see the distant communal tower of his city on the horizon, and return to it—when pestilence appealed to his piety—to act and die.

7. The true protagonist of Goldmann's book is Phaedra. The book advances towards Racine, and through Racine towards the analysis of *Phaedra* the most persuasive reading of a tragedy. We could almost say, notwithstanding the scholarly apparatus, that *The Hidden God* really originated in the need to recognize and account for *Phaedra*. Goldmann is less convincing precisely when he wants us to believe that Marxism has sublated tragedy. In fact, his tragedy or tragic *vision du monde* is that of Phaedra, though of a Phaedra hidden by much sociological eloquence.

It is also necessary, if easy enough, to observe a contradiction between affirming the need for a 'total' critique and limiting oneself to delineating the ideological schema of Racine's tragedies—which thus end up almost becoming plays by Sartre. Racine's so-called form (you could call it his melody, the timbre of his *Dämpfung*,[4] his 'sweetness') is essential in order to grasp the ideological schema. There would be no tragedy, no 'refusal of the world' if, in the same gesture, the world were not offered up; if the world and hope did not, at every moment, envelop the tragic characters in the sinuous wave of sweetness; if, so to speak, the flute of elegy did not always call to them, did not incessantly invite them to exit the scene, *loin du regard de Dieu*.[5] In this sense it is advisable, having read Goldmann, to reread Spitzer's Phaedra. How inadmissible is Spitzer's interpretation, which sees in Theseus the hero of baroque *desengaño*, and how plausible instead that of Goldmann, making it all the more necessary to engage in a 'stylistic' reading after, or alongside, the ideological one.[6]

I repeat that the meaning of *The Hidden God*, which I think is summed up in Phaedra, is Marxist in a deep sense that is concealed, as it were, by the author's sociological dialect: contradiction, monstrosity, illegality, evil—they all demand citizenship in the world of the living, once again. In each and every one of us there is a part that is the daughter of Minos and Pasiphaë, of the contradiction between reality principle and pleasure principle. The wretched, and the wretched parts of humanity, want to be accepted; contradiction wants at the same time to be lived, overcome and posed again.

Engels' English working class could, at the time, embody total 'refusal'. Too many things have changed since. It is unlikely that unionized workers across the social-democratized half of Europe feel themselves to be *les damnés de la terre*. The historical *monsters* are elsewhere, in other continents. But there is an *Unterwelt* among us, in us, everywhere, where the world of Theseus causes the death of Phaedra—murderers in seedy hotels, psychotic wards, suicides in the depressed areas of every nation and individual.

It will be said that this *n*th effort to graft existentialism onto Marxism is a rearguard battle. That's likely. But, whenever the oxygen levels in a society drop beneath a certain threshold, questions that can be calmly called 'ethical' pose themselves anew. 'Totality' is never as evident and peremptory as when reality appears broken in a broken mirror.

1956

Notes

This comment on Lucien Goldmann's *Le dieu caché. Étude sur la vision tragique dans les Pensées de Pascal et dans le théâtre de Racine* (Paris: Gallimard, 1955) [English translation: *The Hidden God: A Study of Tragic Vision in the Pensées of Pascal and the Tragedies of Racine* (Philip Thody trans.) (London: Routledge, 1964)] was originally published in *Ragionamenti* 2(8) (December 1956–January 1957), as 'Goldmann: "Visions du monde" e marxismo' [Goldmann: "World-views" and Marxism'], and in French as 'La "vision du monde" chez Lucien Goldmann', *Arguments* 1(3) (April–May 1957). Fortini would later translate *Le Dieu caché* with Luciano Amodio: *Pascal e Racine. Studio sulla visione tragica nei Pensieri di Pascal e nel teatro di Racine* (Milan: Lerici, 1961). [Trans.]

1 *Annunciatori della tempesta*—probably a reference to the Italian translation of Maxim Gorky's 'Song of the Stormy Petrel' (1901). The expression was also used in the 1920s by the libertarian communist Luigi Fabbri and by Mussolini. [Trans.]

2 A reference to *La logique, ou l'art de penser*, also known as the *Port-Royal Logic*, published anonymously by the Jansenist theologians Antoine Arnauld and Pierre Nicole in 1662, with the likely collaboration of Blaise Pascal. This text is a key reference in Goldmann's *The Hidden God*. [Trans.]

3 *avvenirismo* [Trans.]

4 A term employed by Leo Spitzer to describe Racine's way of softening his characters' utterances. [Trans.]

5 Far from the gaze of God. [Trans.]

6 Leo Spitzer, 'The *Récit de Théramène*', *Linguistics and Literary History* (Princeton: Princeton University Press, 1948), pp. 87–134. [Trans.]

IV
Lukács in Italy

1. *The Reception of Lukács's Work in Italy*

Our aim is not to critically review what has been written on Lukács in Italy but to simply consider some attitudes taken by certain sectors of Italian culture towards the Hungarian thinker. But we should say what we think from the outset: a reading of the work by Lukács published in Italy should make it possible to conclude that his questions are not different from those of the Marxist tradition; that they owe their value and importance not from being uttered by a scholar however pivotal to the culture of our century but, rather, because they merge almost entirely with the questions that contemporary history and social consciousness raise for each and every one of us.

It should be noted that the order in which Italian translations of Lukács have appeared has contributed to some misunderstandings.[1] What's more, many or most of us lacked the cultural–historical background necessary to situate their author. Weimar Germany and the Vienna of his youth were largely alien to the formation of the guardians of our literary culture. That perspectival shift had yet to take place that now allows us to see the Vienna of the young Lukács, rather than the Paris of the time, as the place where the decisive currents of contemporary culture were forged. Since Lukács's major philosophical and historical works remain unpublished in Italian, he has been regarded principally as a literary critic. In the end (in keeping with that dismissive haste that manifests itself in our country every time certain foreign cultural personalities make their appearance), it was believed that his essays on Balzac or Dostoevsky had these authors as their primary focus, or that the *Short History of German Literature* was really a short history of German literature.

Let us recall that, in the first few years after the war, the demands for renewal led—in what concerns the problems of literary creation and criticism—a generic affirmation of new contents as well as to the figure of the politically engaged writer and critic. Those demands quickly took two divergent directions which survive to this day. On the one hand, polemicizing with the Crocean tradition and with the hermetic-spiritualist literature of the 1930s, there was an effort to recover the intellectual, literary and artistic experiences that fascism had at least partially removed from Italian culture. These can be gathered under the generic name of the avant-garde (French surrealism, German expressionism, the American novel, Spanish poetry) and they must, of course, be considered alongside their philosophical and ideological premises. Everything that was deemed innovative with respect to the Italian tradition was related not so much with Marxism, conceived as an organic form of economic and philosophical thought, as to the generically innovative demand with which the political parties of the Left had been imbued by the Resistance and the events of the immediate postwar period. To transpose a term from the language of politics to that of literary and critical tendencies, this was a 'frontist'[2] and therefore eclectic attitude which referred to other political and cultural 'fronts': the pacifist and subversive front in Germany and France after the First World War, that of the Spanish war and the international front of resistance against Nazism and Fascism.

On the other hand, adopting the theses that Soviet and international communism had already canonized, there was an increasingly distrustful perception of the identification between avant-garde and democratic thought, and an effort to recover an authentic Italian progressive and democratic tradition as well as to introduce the themes and models of Soviet 'socialist realism' to our country.

Coexistence and, later, conflict between these two tendencies and their obvious political implications preceded the appearance of Gramsci's *oeuvre*: between 1948 and 1950, when the initial volumes (including *Letteratura e vita nazionale* [Literature and National Life]) come to be widely read, the divorce between the two tendencies has already been consummated, and the distinction between generically frontist or 'progressive' writers and Marxist intellectuals or writers is consolidated. The tensions of the Cold War and Zhdanov's theses determine a particular interpretation of Gramsci's 'national-popular'; but in keeping with the two simultaneous tendencies of the communist cultural policy of that period, while efforts are made to unite the secular-democratic tradition and Marxism, along the 'Southern' line of national Hegelianism (De Sanctis,[3] Spaventa,[4] Labriola,[5] Croce–Gramsci)—presented as the 'open legacy' of the Italian revolution—there is a tendency to oppose, in congresses and party publications, an international front of 'socialist realism' against the old and new avant-garde, depicted as corrupt and corrupting.

It is in that climate—and I'm not speaking of the thought of a few specialists, who in any case also experienced, more or less willingly or consciously, the pressures of the positions of the moment—that the first translations of Lukács's works into Italian see the light.

In *Il Politecnico* (Issues 33–34, 1946) one could already read an excerpt of a few pages—on Kleist and Fontane—from *Short History of German Literature*, published in instalments in *International Literatur*; and in the last issue of the journal, Number 39, from a year later (December 1947) a part, to be continued (it was not), of *The Destruction of Reason*. It is interesting to note that those pages come with a prefatory note in which it is affirmed that 'Giorgio Lukács is today the greatest living Marxist theorist', with reference to that work (*History and Class Consciousness*) that Lukács had already repudiated and to the 'masterful monograph on Hegel' (*The Young Hegel*), only to conclude on a critical note. We may be forgiven for spotting Elio Vittorini's pen behind that note, which declares that Lukács's 'intransigent critique of irrationalism [is] more a "front notebook" than a "prison notebook"'. We can also discern the germ of the opposition between Gramsci and Lukács, which has since been amply explored. But we can say that these texts, like some other contributions appearing in *Studi filosofici* (let it be noted, in passing, that Antonio Banfi[6] held Lukács in low esteem), went mostly unnoticed. Nor was much greater attention granted to the volume *Goethe and His Age*, which came out two years later, in October 1949; especially, I think, in the wake of Croce's sneering review.[7] Lukács's visit to Italy, the appearance of those texts in various journals and the translation of his book on Goethe must also be related to the fact that in those years, as Istvan Mészáros writes, the activity of the Hungarian philosopher had taken on a quasi-official character, 'identified with the Party's cultural policy'. But the turn of 1947–48 and the consolidation of cultural Zhdanovism, with the launch of a violent polemic against Lukács that culminated in his self-criticism, halted the diffusion of his thought within Italian and French Marxism; so much so that the only book of his translated before 1957 by an openly communist publishing house was a collection of essays on Soviet literature (Editori Riuniti, 1955) which had been released in East Berlin in 1943; and which Lukács, by his own admission, wrote as a political *pensum*.

The first work by Lukács that was really noticed by a scholarly audience was the *Essays on Realism* (1950); and, three years later, the collection of essays *Marxism and Literary Criticism* (1953).

At the time, the *Essays on Realism* were related to the most noteworthy examples of Italian Marxist aesthetic reflection, namely, Gramsci and Della Volpe.[8] Let us also recall, among the reviews, an especially warm piece by Giampiero Carocci[9] in *Belfagor* (September 1950). But the impression was that the interest for Lukács was particularly alive in the Milanese milieu, around Remo Cantoni's[10] review *Il pensiero critico*; a study group met to discuss my presentation on the book which Armanda Guiducci[11] reviewed in the journal. Guiducci would then return to the theme with several essays in various reviews; her essay 'Estetica e Marxismo: G. Lukács' remains to this day the most accomplished expression in Italy of the 'liquidation' of Lukács's aesthetic from the standpoint of a methodologism with neo-positivist features, inspired by Anglo-Saxon critical literature. I will not discuss these writings here at any length. The polemic between Cases and Guiducci, triggered by the aforementioned essay, is familiar enough not to insist upon it.[12] The debate on Lukács's aesthetic had mutated into a general debate on Marxism and neo-positivism which I neither have the intention nor the capacity to join, even if I concur with many of Cases' thesis (though I remain anything but persuaded by the validity of his arguments in favour of dialectical materialism). However, I must note that the polemic fully confirms the idea that it is impossible to debate Lukács's critical methodology without involving, as we have already observed, the entire edifice of Marxist thought. Today there is no longer any critical exercise or methodological effort worthy of the name that does not contain within itself, whether explicitly or otherwise, the acceptance or refusal of the Marxist 'conception of the world' in the sense given to this expression by Lukács himself. It is also evident that contemporary commentaries on Lukács's positions figure mainly as historical curiosities. There is a habit of associating his name to the adjective 'metaphysical', and this liquidation sees the convergence of communist and catholic writers, post-idealists and neo-positivists, men of letters and philosophers, poets and philologists. But a coincidence must be noted: the discredit into which Lukács's thought appears to have fallen (and which, if an easy prophecy is permitted, the publication of his major philosophical work will not remedy) is parallel to the widespread discredit of Marxist thought and the long dormancy of the Italian workers' movement. It's easy to say, but it must be said nonetheless—with the crisis of 1956, conversions to theoretical reformism (the practical kind was always at work) have spread with lightning speed, causing a formidable change in the tone and language of commentary, especially of the literary kind. Since the situation seems devoid of (political) prospects, it is only natural that the large majority of Italian writers and critics have in fact accepted it. The classic opposition between (political) 'realism' and utopianism poses itself again; and the choices are as precarious as ever, namely, between the deceptive voices of 'historical necessity' and the equally deceptive ones of 'social conscience'.

2. *Some Critical Writings on Lukács*

We have already mentioned the properly political reasons that hindered the incorporation of Lukács's thought into Italian Marxist culture. But there were far deeper ideological reasons. Lukács's work came into contact with Marxist debates exactly when political and cultural leaderships started to become conscious of the 'ideology of the monopolies' (as they called it), that is, of the massive introduction of a cultural problematic and 'material' that was the latest direct response of neo-capitalism to Marxism. Hence, Lukács appeared as the nemesis of that neo-realist 'tendency' that prevailed within the communist left in Italy and beyond; but also as a relatively ineffective thinker when it came to countering neo-positivistic imports, due to the Hegelian origins of his Marxism. Besides other precise political motives (like the energetic stance against Lukács taken by some Soviet cultural leaders, like Fadeyev), today it is clear that Lukács's thought could not be accepted either by a national-popular Stalinism, with its formulae about 'revolutionary romanticism' and the like, or by the 'reformist' wing of the Italian left, and even less so by some 'extremist' minorities that were naturally drawn to a literary and artistic avant-garde with its roots in surrealism or expressionism.

In this sense, it is interesting to turn to two articles from 1953[13] by Carlo Salinari[14] and Valentino Gerratana.[15] In Gerratana's text, we find the first formulation of a distinction between realism as method and realism as tendency that has recently been reprised.[16]

Gerratana contests Lukács's claim that realism is a method first and foremost, and what he sees as the related proposal of immutable norms and canons. He deems both 'formalist' and dangerous the idea that the transition to a different cultural tendency—when it fails to attain in the individual artwork the aesthetic level of the preceding tendency—should be considered as a regression. The reasonable objection that a 'tendency' consists of numerous (and not necessarily artistic) elements, some of which may be 'progressive' even when the work is artistically worthless, did not cross Gerratana's mind. For him, it was a question of defending Soviet literature and art as well as the literary and artistic tendency which, at that moment, was dear to the Italian communist leadership. According to Gerratana, Lukács would have been wrong to consider aestheticism and naturalism, literary subjectivism and objectivism as equivalent; while it would be necessary to save naturalism, at least in part, as the condemnation and unmasking of social ugliness: 'to concentrate all firepower on naturalism . . . is only grist to the mill of formalism'. Amid this firing and grinding, the most relevant criticism chides Lukács for the idealist character of his dialectic of phenomenon and essence: 'the phenomenon becomes appearance and hides the essence when it is cut off from the objective process of which it is a moment, and is reduced to a simple subjective process adopted as a criterion of the nature of reality'.

In other words, 'art . . . reflects . . . some essential aspects of reality at a given historical moment and not because it grasps the real in its totality'. (This kind of retail historicism, so to speak, can be found in Gerratana's aforementioned argument in 1959, and it is another way of confirming his sympathies for naturalism.) Salinari's piece, while warm towards Lukács the critic, agrees with Gerratana in condemning as idealist Lukács's formulation of the phenomenon–essence relationship, and accuses the Hungarian philosopher even more severely for lacking 'a precise and concrete analysis of the involution of capitalism in its various national contexts, and its ideological, cultural and moral consequences'. It cites against him Engels' critique of Paul Ernst, who wanted to define the petit-bourgeois Ibsen on the basis of the general concept of petit-bourgeois rather than analysing the concrete situation of the Norwegian bourgeoisie. But when all is said and done, Salinari concludes, we do better to hold on to De Sanctis and Gramsci.

Six years later, these theses have not changed substantially and the charge of insufficient concreteness and inadequate attention to particularity continue to be levied at Lukács from Marxist quarters. We encounter it again in Salinari's introductory talk at the 1959 conference on the problems of realism in Italy, as well as in Gerratana's intervention.[17] If the method–tendency distinction was passed from Gerratana to Salinari, the latter gave the former the citation from Engels' letter. Nonetheless, some innovations should be noted. First, Salinari openly contests the triadic character of a materialist dialectic, calling upon a Kantian and Crocean dyad, thus eliminating the Hegelian and Lukácsian category of the 'particular'; while Gerratana, quite strangely, dubs as 'sociological' the criticism that does not highlight the specific characteristics of the determinate capitalist society to which the artwork refers but only the generic features of capitalist development.

Lucio Colletti's intervention instead defends Lukács's position on this point.[18] The 'historicism' of local and particular historical situations has little in common with Marx's materialist historicism; Lukács's critical *oeuvre* cannot be understood if we don't take into account the fact that he works on a socioeconomic formation—the development and decline of capitalism—which is, to borrow Engels's expression, a 'long period'.

Whether the periods are long or short; the historicism, retail or wholesale, my impression is that these distinctions fall short of Lukács's thought. No reader will have failed to be struck by the schematic character of the correlations that Lukács establishes between socioeconomic evolution and literary works. I don't think this is enough to condemn the preponderance of a 'speculative' mentality. We should emphasize, contrary to appearances, a constant refusal in Lukács to consider an artwork a 'document' or a 'passive mirroring'. If Lukács seems to disregard the mediations that move from socioeconomic structures to the literary work, dealing with elementary indications (reserving the most properly 'sociological' and detailed comments to works that he does not consider to be great and accomplished artworks) this is because he always maintains the artwork's character as 'cognition', and thus its absolute dignity as a microcosm, an original interpretation of the real. Unlike stylistic critics, he is not interested in reconstructing the individual or even the *mens* (as Spitzer does) through the text. Nor does he bother about locating parallels between the artist's notion of the 'real' and the one held by the coeval culture, or by our own (as Auerbach does). He stays 'within the work' only to the degree that it allows him to identify the major elements of conflict and translate them in philosophical-historical terms. The feeling of frustration of the 'literary critic' faced with Lukács's critical *oeuvre* is in this sense justified. One often has the impression that the artistic universe for Lukács is a pretext for his historical-philosophical allegory, and that our lament is akin to that of the Goethean Wagner:

> *Mir wird bei meinem kritischen Bestreben*
> *Doch oft um Kopf und Busen bang.*
> *Wie schwer sind nicht die Mittel zu erwerben,*
> *Durch die man zu den Quellen steigt*!

To which Faust, now alone, responds with some famous lines in which we can find, more than might be expected, a key (at least a psychological one) to understanding Lukács:

> *Wie nur dem Kopf nich alle Hoffnung schwindet*
> *Der immerfort an schalem Zeuge klebt . . .* [19]

And yet almost unnoticeably, notwithstanding the resistances and criticisms, between 1954 and 1956 Lukács's influence in Italy only grew. In retrospect, it was indeed helped by the climate of the 'thaw'. It was an often unconfessed but very obvious influence: some (like Salinari) spoke of an imminent transition to 'realism' in literature and the arts. In that period, one really had the impression that, having definitively liquidated second-rate literary neo-realism, overcome (or nearly so) the stubborn programmatic remainders of a naturalist or avant-gardist kind, and assumed a more reflexive attitude vis-à-vis Soviet literature, Lukács's notion of 'great realism' permitted not only a rethinking of the literary and critical vicissitudes of the past 30 years in Italy and a definitive break with the cultural roots of our decadentism but also allowed one to consider the literature of the nineteenth-century bourgeoisie in a different light, replacing the decadentist schema with another kind of reading. That was a great wasted opportunity for Italian Marxist culture (and not the only one). Not only could the greatness of Tolstoy or Balzac be grasped once again, one also discovered the possibility of understanding, say, Baudelaire or Manzoni differently. Lukács suggested a perspective on the European nineteenth century that in Italy had hitherto remained closed, after De Sanctis' synthesis and Gramsci's influential insights. Authors and periods that the culture of idealism and hermeticism had kept in the dark or hidden were visible once again: I'm thinking of Heinrich Heine and Gottfried Keller,[20] Alexander Pushkin and Heinrich von Kleist. There's more: Lukács's teaching led us back to the sources of classical German thought, forcing us to return to, or to read for the first time, Goethe or Schiller or Lessing. For the first time, the meaning of certain great dormant works, like the *Meister*, became clear to us; the angle through which we read Hölderlin changed; and it was possible from that vantage point to try again to understand Swift, Cervantes, Shakespeare.

What some of us had dimly intuited in the years of our aestheticizing or hermetic formation, and had not found in Croce's Dante, Shakespeare or Ariosto; that sense of the richness and complexity of human experience and of its alienation from history, which had shaken us in our personal biographies as well as in the pages of Marx; that possibility of 'becoming adult', realizing and conserving transformed youthful 'existential' individuality—all of this, notwithstanding the extremely slow pace of historical evolution (and the involution of the political conditions in our country) was also spread through Lukács's teaching. Today it would be difficult to document how Lukács's books catalysed those demands for a whole swathe of our 'left' culture. But they can be found in the literary polemics of those years (for example, on Vasco Pratolini's *Metello*, 1955), or in the ones about film (for example, on Luchino Visconti's *Senso*, 1954), and in more than a few pieces appearing in the journals *Società* (I am thinking in particular, as revealing a certain mood, those of Ippolito Pizzetti and Paolo Chiarini, not to mention Cases),[21] *Officina* (especially Francesco Leonetti, 'Il decadentismo come problema contemporaneo', 6, April 1956), and *Ragionamenti*. In the latter, the theme of Lukács returns with particular insistence, from its very first issue.[22]

In *Ragionamenti* (Issue 5–6, 1956) you can find a study by Luciano Amodio ('Der alte Lukács' [The Old Lukács]),[23] which to my mind is the sharpest of those that appeared before Adorno's most recent essay.[24] Amodio clearly frames the relationship between Stalinism and Lukács, and he synthesizes all the most serious criticisms about the lack of relation between background and figures, 'like a Greek frieze', in Lukácsian criticism: the lack of a reflection on the moment of technical–artistic 'reproduction'; the paucity of relations between totality and the moment of expression; the aestheticizing and insufficiently articulated character of the polemic against the division of labour; the incapacity to reduce decadence, the avant-garde, bourgeois 'progress' to the status of moments . . . Amodio, aided here by a piece by Goldmann from 1950 (now collected in a recent volume by Gallimard[25]), with great precision has noted the permanence, in the Marxist and Leninist Lukács, of the utopian element; that element (with all of its ascetic-aristocratic and sacrificial resonances), which had already been foregrounded—as Goldmann tells us—in an old polemic between Lukács and Ernst Bloch, the philosopher of the *Principle of Hope* (1954–59) provides one of the most solid footholds for the current polemic which accuses Lukács of harbouring metaphysical residua. Cases, in the biographical essay on Lukács ('Lo scoiattolo e l'elefante' [The Squirrel and the Elephant], *il Contemporaneo*, 21 April 1956)—which according to Lukács is an intelligent interpretation of his conversions and self-criticisms—tries to show that as he moved from his youthful pessimism (during which he contrasted the integrity of the Greek *epos* with the Christian-bourgeois epoch of 'absolute sinfulness') to the 'Luciferian' catastrophism of the Marxist neophyte of *History and Class Consciousness*, finally to arrive at the most recent phase of this thinking (decadentism still appears as radical evil but empurples the West with its rays, 'omen / of a more serene day', due to the real prospect of socialism), Lukács was progressing straight towards *objectivity*. Amodio—in agreement with the undersigned—emphasized instead the secret permanence of the 'tragic vision', which, in his early writings, had made Lukács a precursor of Heideggerian existentialism. After having rightly recalled that 'Lukács's greatness stems from that phenomenology of artistic forms that his dialectic is able to deduce from historical reality, above all, "genres", ' Amodio concludes:

> Reification *today* is only undone by artistic *anticipation*; the principle of *Humanität* is the Godly gaze before which the tragedy of the old Lukács unfolds; it is the infinite for which the content, intact, reverses its meaning . . . but only in art can reality present itself as identical and reversed; the formal act as the *contemporaneousness* of utopia.

This conclusion is very close to Adorno; we will, in fact, encounter this conception of art as de-reifying precisely in Adorno's recent essay against Lukács. I don't think we have the right simultaneously to exalt and to liquidate the thought of Lukács by making it retreat entirely into an allegorical universe. And yet it must be said that his Olympian stance, especially in the recent autobiographical writings and the prefaces to the works recently translated in Italian (one of his weaknesses has always been that *imitatio* of Goethe), with his unchanged faith in 'socialism' about which—between the 20th Congress and the firing squads in Budapest—he is careful not to provide any particulars ('right or wrong, my party'[26] he told us in May 1956; never had his 'party' so resembled an invisible church), reveals itself as the latest mask of an 'existential' tension. We do not have the right to say 'socialism' in the same way as Lukács who has been living in socialist countries for over a quarter of a century, for better or worse. Our task is to formulate the how and wherefore of socialism—that is why we are affected by the 'ascetic' or 'tragic' moment in Lukács, and why (ready to be accused of metaphysical speculation) we are not prepared to trade it either for the well-integrated anxieties of the latest avant-garde or for the neo-Enlightenment patience of contemporary Italian literary reformism.

At this point we should note, briefly, that Galvano della Volpe's recurrent polemic against Lukács seems to us more legitimate when it challenges his Hegelianism, that is, the acceptance of Hegelian logical categories (singular, particular, universal), than when it accuses him of aesthetic intuitionism. From the reading of the works of Lukács that are known to us, in particular the recent *Prolegomena to an Aesthetics* (1957), we think it is possible to refuse the idea that the expression 'to sensibly intuit', used by Lukács in his 'Marx and Engels on Aesthetics'[27] can be honestly understood in the usual sense accorded to it by idealist-Crocean thought. Even Cases in *Marxismo e neopositivismo* (p. 50) after having recalled, with Lukács, that the rational–irrational antinomy, which we continue to employ too often and superficially 'belongs to the problematic of the philosophy of decadence', writes: 'Hegel and his epigones never understood the *Anschauung* which is undoubtedly the gateway to art as a Crocean "intuition" polemically juxtaposed to the understanding'.

Independently of this historical and interpretive question, it should be noted that Della Volpe's refusal of the Hegelian categories adopted by Lukács corresponds to his own adoption of the notion of 'semantic coherence'. Now, awaiting a more precise treatment of this notion or critical instrument (and on this point Della Volpe's thought should absolutely not be confused with that of the many anti-Lukácsians), it should be noted that, in the hasty applications of intellectual journalism, investigations into 'semantic coherence' continually risk falling into the well-known prejudice of stylistic criticism—namely, the reading of 'signs' at their simplest level (lexicon, syntax, 'figures') while appealing instead for the 'verification' of macro-signs (characters, situations, 'world-views', ideological conflicts) to an outside of the work; in other words, precisely to those ideological universes in the face of which no pre-constituted neutrality can be maintained. In Lukács on the contrary, because he presupposes the objective unity of the historical real, the confrontation between 'artistic reflection' and 'historical-scientific reflection' leads one to define that work as 'great', which has forced so much of the *Totalität* into its own microcosmos as to be, at least to a very large degree, self-sufficient. In other words, semantic self-sufficiency can be obtained only on the condition that one remove or bracket the ideological features (in the Marxist sense) of expression and communication and, condemning as metaphysical the notion of 'totality', unify them under the notion of the 'sign'; while the (relative) self-sufficiency of the work, in Lukács's sense, derives from its being the *tendentially total representation-interpretation of sociohistorical relations within artistic typicality* in keeping with a cross-section that cuts through all the mediations that take us from socioeconomic structures to the ideological superstructures borne by languages.

In January 1954, Pietro Citati published an interesting note on the part of Lukács's *oeuvre* that had been published in Italian.[28] It sums up the favourable attitude, with some provisos, of an entire non-declaredly Marxist sector of Italian literary criticism. Having outlined the resemblances between the thought of Gramsci and Lukács (dialectical tradition, anti-positivist polemic, importance of the structure–superstructure nexus), Citati presented Lukács's greatest effort as directed towards saving the structure–superstructure relationship from Soviet conformism through the well-known thesis of the 'triumph of realism' and 'uneven development'. Yet Citati's article follows a double movement of agreement and refusal: in the first moment, Lukács is seen as the preceptor of a 'novel to be written', the theorist of a poetics whose test is exclusively historical-political; later, Citati affirms that this poetics is in fact an aesthetics, that realism is not a style but that style is poetry and he precariously tends to draw similarities between Lukács and Croce, thus anticipating the more recent, neo-empiricist anti-Lukácsian arguments (without noticing how the category of the typical or the particular, interposed between the singular and the universal allows Lukács a historicization of artistic forms that is denied to Croce's absolute and eternal Poetry). Citati here ignores that the tendential coincidence is not so much between literary criticism and aesthetics as between literary criticism and history, aesthetic and historical judgement. He observes—a theme constantly reprised by Lukács's critics—that his 'preponderant nineteenth-century taste', maturing between Tolstoy and Balzac, would mean that the critic or reader of 'Shakespeare or Petrarch, Racine or Proust would find in this aesthetic only blunted instruments or obstacles to the comprehension of poetic texts', and that 'having been born to defend the dialectic, along the way this culture ultimately morphed into a teaching by precepts, an immobile classicism'.[29]

But Citati's most relevant contribution is to be found in the last two paragraphs of his article: first, when he underscores the importance of putting art to the test of represented reality; second, when he points to some examples of schematizing monotony in Lukács (his polyvalent formulae); third, when—apparently in contradiction with the first part of the article—he sees in Lukács the development of 'some aesthetic instruments marked by a substantive anti-historicism', absolutely ill-adapted to explain the phenomena of contemporary art. In a lively and almost impulsive form, we find here the major themes of future anti-Lukácsian polemic: the idea of a 'test'[30] is accepted, but in the name of a pluralism or eclecticism of viewpoints (critical empiricism) rather than that of an acceptance of 'reflection'; there is a gesture towards a sociological elaboration of Lukácsian 'simplification', a path that will basically be Goldmann's; above all, we encounter a defence of the art of decadentism and the avant-garde, in the name of a passionate comprehension. This fails to recognize that Lukács's challenge demands a response on the terrain of politics, that is to say, of socialist 'perspectives'; merely condemning his misunderstanding of Proust or Kafka is not enough. Another characteristic trait of Citati's article is the intelligent indication of the most brilliant moments in Lukács's writings (the essays 'Narrate or Describe?' and 'The Intellectual Physiognomy in Characterisation' in particular), without however drawing adequate consequences or further developments from them.

A unique example of coincidence between partisan communist criticism and idealist-derived criticism is to be found instead in an essay by Pier Luigi Contessi.[31] While Contessi traces, in Lukács's work the tendency to a 'cultural and political mediation' between the communist world and the West, with reference to the writings of Banfi and Caretti,[32] he accepts the reservations about Lukács's Marxist orthodoxy expressed by Banfi, Della Volpe and Gerratana, chiming also with Salinari's preference for Gramsci.

And, again in *Il Mulino*, we find a very precise exposition of the *Prolegomena*, penned by Renato Barilli.[33] He attributes the criticism of the literature of the avant-garde to Lukács's refusal of some 'fundamental components of modern civilization' (Bergsonism, pragmatism, Gestalt psychology, psychoanalysis, etc.), whose literary pendant would be represented by the avant-garde. Of course, to the extent that the horizon of Lukács's scientific culture—formed precisely during the period and in that part of Europe where that civilization was vibrantly developing—is limited by the taboos of the Stalinist period, it lacks the possibilities for expanding its taste; but it does not make much sense to reproach a philosopher for what lies at the very centre of his reflection, considering that in *The Destruction of Reason* Lukács subjected those components of modern civilization to scrutiny. To my mind, in order to understand Proust or Kafka, Joyce or Musil, one need not be a Bersgonist, a believer in *Gestalttheorie* or an advocate of psychoanalysis. Lukács's aim is to evaluate, not to classify. He does not want to *understand* a writer in order to stretch the limits of his own taste or judgement but only to identify, in certain authors, some of the values to which he has chosen to accord particular importance.

Barbèri Squarotti has dealt with Lukács on several occasions. In one of his most exhaustive articles[34] it would seem that he has accepted the most widespread image of Lukács, that of the ideological propagandist. While he's ready to accept the transition between the bourgeois realism of the beginning of the nineteenth century and realism, he refuses the one between naturalism and decadentism-avant-gardism, without realizing that for Lukács the roots of these changes lie in modes and relations of production, which is to say, in the case in question, in the evolution of capitalism into imperialism. That is why constants are far more important than variables which are often reducible to 'contrasts, innovations, stylistic-formal struggles among tendencies', as Lukács himself tells us. In Squarotti's article, there is also a refusal of Lukács's 'general schemas' in the name of neo-philology, of the 'concrete' and so on. This leads him to a dichotomy between the realm of historical judgement and that of 'values', which we hope he would be able to resolve once he discerns within this dichotomy the typical reflex of the ideological condition of a class. This dichotomy is not so much 'existentialist' as, on the one hand, scientific-positivist (historical judgement as philological–stylistic–sociological judgement) and, on the other, Christian-spiritualist ('value' judgement as ethico-aesthetically ineffable). The development of this second component, by laying bare all the *Misère* of the present 'cultural' situation for Squarotti, should push him to evaluate the ethical-political meaning of the attitude of those who dispatch Lukács so that he may join Hegel in the cemetery of 'dead dogs'. We have reason to think that he has already reconsidered his views. A point about which Squarotti is correct concerns Lukács's notion of a 'socialist perspective'; he criticizes the contingently political meaning of 'socialist transformations of the economy' and 'socialist political regimes'. It is absurd, of course, to treat that notion so reductively and not to recognize it as the 'world-view' corresponding to a very general ethical-social perspective on humanity which is opposite or historically subsequent to others—more often than not, this is the sense in which Lukács speaks of socialism. There is no doubt, however, that in *The Meaning of Contemporary Realism* (1957) and other more recent writings, there is an intentional ambiguity, a verbal cunning that dangerously doubles as political and philosophical alibi; an unsavoury residuum of 'Aesopian language'.

3. *Adorno on Lukács and the Privilege of the Reader*

One of the aspects of Lukács's thought that is most often subjected to criticism is the accusation of one-sidedness and (which amounts to the same) lack of perspective—turning his criticisms of avant-garde literature against him. This thesis is repeated in *The Meaning of Contemporary Realism*. Let us recall here one of its synthetic formulae:

> [S]ince the avant-garde . . . portrays . . . deformation without critical detachment . . . it may be said to deform deformation further. By attributing deformation to reality itself, the avant-garde dismisses the counter-forces at work in reality as ontologically irrelevant. It is easy to understand that the experience of the capitalist world does produce, especially among intellectuals, *angst*, nausea, a sense of isolation, and despair. A view of the world that *excluded* these emotions would prevent the present-day artist from depicting his world truthfully. The question is not: Is *x* present in reality? But rather: Does *x* represent the whole of reality?[35]

Now, all the defences of avant-garde literature and decadentism penned in Italy, which are not just synthesized but powerfully framed by Adorno's essay, either deny:

(a) that, in what concerns particular works or authors included by Lukács under the broad notions of decadentism or avant-garde, the accusation that they make all really-existing counter-forces and counter-tendencies disappear is legitimate by demonstrating, for example, in some major writers (such as Proust or Musil) the depiction of antitheses (entrusted to situations more than to characters, to stylistic instruments more than to recognizable 'perspectives'); meaning, that they affirm

(b) that literary representation is, in its own right, the 'counterforce' apparently absent from the figuration of the negative (this is argued, for example, by Adorno); or

(c) that the artistic completeness of a work requires its internal dialectical completeness; or finally

(d) (and finally, these are obviously the apologists for the banalized negative) they affirm 'that reality is the whole of reality'.

We do not intend to subject Adorno's essay to a detailed scrutiny, which it certainly merits, but we cannot fail to note that, alongside an unpleasant stylistic and moral inelegance, there are some glaring distortions. Despite the fact that the likes of Goldmann make explicit references to Lukács's early work, it is not true and cannot be affirmed that Lukács's European fame today is predominantly linked with those writings. How can one refer to a type of judgement about modern art that could be traced via a whole series of historical precedents all the way back to Goethe, as a 'Soviet verdict'? How can one attribute to Lukács the denial that solitude is 'historically mediated solitude, not ontological solitude',[36] when it was Lukács who saw in the doctrines of solitude the ideological expressions of a given society? Similarly, when Adorno writes 'even what Lukács considers to be a solipsism and a regression to the illusionary immediacy of the subject does not signify a denial of the object, as it does in bad epistemologies, but rather aims dialectically at reconciliation with the object',[37] how can we not retort that Lukács struggles against the poetics of decadentism as an advanced form of anti-socialist ideology and not against the profound insights of *represented* (i.e. poetic) solipsism, and that he contests it as bad epistemology because it leads one astray from possible aesthetic results?

This is just a sample of the counter-arguments that should be levied against a patent polemical deformation of Lukács's thought.

It is more interesting, however, to recall a passage from Adorno's essay that implies the attitude which we classified above under heading 'b':

> The object is taken into the subject in the form of an image rather than turning to stone in front of it like an object under the spell of the alienated world. Through the contradiction between this object that has been reconciled within an image, that is, spontaneously assimilated into the subject, and the real, unreconciled object out there in the world, the work of art criticizes reality. It represents negative knowledge of reality. In analogy to a current philosophical expression, we might speak of 'aesthetic difference' from existence: only by virtue of this difference, and not by denying it, does the work of art become both work of art and correct consciousness.[38]

We can object to this thesis—which the dream of art as anti-physis, anti-history, anti-life, a 'saving sign', and is not exempt from a lucid veneration of horror—that it attributes the capacity to criticize reality and by that token to be 'correct consciousness', to the *formal* character of the so-called work of art, namely, to its being an artistic form, and not to a particular degree of 'excellence' of that formality. Now, though every artistic form criticizes Reality, the object that it reconciles with the image ('the unreconciled object out there in the world') differs depending on the work because of the different levels, the complexity, etc., of reality 'reconciled within the image'. To be more precise, the artwork does not criticize Reality but *a* reality which it at once evokes, formally reconciles within itself and contests. Whence a historical hierarchy of 'realities' and 'works'. Perhaps unwittingly, in that formulation Adorno corroborates the formalism and pan-aestheticism of contemporary taste; the optical illusion of the imaginary museum inhibits him from seeing that Lukács's choice, his 'antho-logy', does not stem from mere limits of taste but follows from a choice of values, which is to say, of priorities. Against the naturalism and sociologism that classifies and preserves everything, Lukács once again poses his lapidary questions: What is *important* for men, today? Which reality has the right to a priority, to be reconciled in form and contested in exteriority? In the eyes of the critic, if not the poet, are these not matters of ethics, aesthetics and politics?

Even more interesting is the position that we indicated above in the formulation in under heading 'c'. It is expressed in another part of Adorno's essay:

> The substantive content of a work of art can consist in the accurate and tacitly polemical representation of emerging meaninglessness [in this case, of 'society totally in the grips of the culture industry'], and that content can be lost when it is stated positively and hypostasised as existing, even if this occurs only indirectly, through a 'perspective'.[39]

Granting that Adorno here voices a possibility, where the zealots of avant-garde literature would have preferred instead a resolute affirmation, we should ask ourselves what is implied by the notion of 'tacitly polemical representation'. I think it is relatively obvious, beyond the concrete and limited terms of the question, that every expression—in our case, every literary expression—is situated, in all of its parts and as a whole, in relation to a sociohistorical context, whose specific articulation depends on its origin as well as its destination: this is what we customarily call its cultural or ideological or linguistic *habitat*. No doubt the work—whether by resonance or opposition, silent consent or silent polemic—calls upon one or more ideological complexes, one or more conceptions of the world, in the very act whereby it conveys or is such a conception. We can thus say that the work institutes two different orders of relations and tensions: one towards the outside, which is its servitude and its historical freedom; the other towards the inside, that is, towards its own elements. These orders can, of course, metamorphose into one another but sometimes they can be distinguished, and clearly so.

Now, what is a 'tacitly polemical' representation if it is not a representation that entrusts its own reasons to its silence, to the unsaid; that is, to the interpretation or supplementation provided by the reader? Preterition, like irony or sarcasm, invokes something essential which is kept quiet. We could even say that formal novelty often corresponds to this need for abstraction, the need to make the scandal of absences shine forth. But when cultural contexts are transformed or broken, when the ratio between consent and dissent is altered, or when the principles that are yet to be confirmed or combated are extinguished or modified in the consciences of their addressees, it is then that we know that the chance for a text to survive depends either on the long hard road of historical philology and reconstruction or—and this is what concerns us here—on that kind of authentic interpretation which is furnished by inner tensions, by represented contradictions.

In light of these observations, I think we can begin to understand the reason behind Lukács's demand for 'counter-forces' and 'perspective'. Lukács is, let us not forget, an intellectual of bourgeois formation who chooses the socialist camp, convinced that it is the negation and guarantee of a reconciliation of man with himself; and who experiences, ever since the moment of his Marxist conversion, that growing contradiction between communist universalism and the creation of socialism in one country. Day after day, Lukács lived through the real or apparent death of humanist postulates in the conflict between the bestiality of Nazism and Fascism and the implacable hardness of Stalinism. His work appears as the greatest effort to safeguard, through his age and our own, an inheritance that is essential for socialism, namely, the 'classical German philosophy' whose heir, according to Marx, is the international proletariat; an effort that was well worth the masses[40] and self-criticisms, the *pensum* on Soviet literature, the NKVD prison, the 'Aesopian' style, the countless attacks and the half-light in which Lukács is living out his final years. He is situated in a society whose cultural fabric is objectively different from that of imperialism, even if it antagonistically complements it, but which has an even deeper change as its horizon.

The tendential onesidedness of contemporary literatures—the avantgardist–decadent writing and that of a Stalinism 'without conflict', as it were—cannot but appear to Lukács in the register of both polemic and apology, as 'tacitly' complicit with the forces that need to be countered. The classic (contrary to one of the commonplaces of anti-Lukácsian criticism) appears to him as the opposite of classicism; the latter relies on a cultural-social consensus, in taste and ideology while the former rises above taste and ideology in the depiction of conflicts. For Lukács, the 'masterpiece'—let us accept that element of philistinism in his taste, these are not the limits that matter here—is doubly self-sufficient because of the (relative) autonomy of the artwork, and because it contains all the superstructural or ideological elements required for its own interpretation. In effect, its 'test' or 'verification' is not provided by the determinate cultural context from which it emerges and within which it operates but, rather, by the historical schema of the whole phase of social evolution which that 'masterpiece' interprets. That is the sense in which a few years ago I could write that Lukács apparently looks to the artwork simply for the confirmation of truths already discovered by Marxist inquiry. I was wrong. Today, I see that we are not at all dealing with a parallel between, say, the historical reconstruction of the society of Louis Philippe and the novels of Balzac, but between the latter and the historical interpretation of an entire phase of the evolution of modern man, in which the France of Louis Philippe is but a moment. Nor are we dealing with a mere quantitative difference: Lukácsian 'simplification' is based on questioning *every* sociologism. In other words, Lukács (who has dealt with 'minor' authors, and who would be wary of calling into question the usefulness of meticulous reconstructions and historical inquiries; who is in fact, above all, a historian) has too great a sensibility for the 'city in flames' not to demand from both himself and us a choice about what can be salvaged. With the word 'inheritance', he is telling us the same thing as with the word 'perspective'; he demands from us a 'whence' and 'whither' that are not chronological but also ethical: 'a reality . . . can neither be known nor lived in its unity and fullness without living and recognizing in being (in every moment of becoming, which necessarily gives itself the form of being) its origin and its goal.'[41]

If that is so, the demarcation between the notion of 'realism' of someone like Auerbach and that of Lukács, or even between the whole of the sociology of culture and Lukácsian Marxism could not be clearer. At this point it is worth noting that the real or potential circulation of certain works and tendencies of the Western avant-garde in the communist world does not contradict but, rather, confirms what we have said about the meaning of Lukácsian 'perspectivism'. To the extent that, for example, the antecedent Stalinist reality or the fear of an atomic war were interpreted by the (manifest or latent) ideology of new Soviet authors in terms analogous to the ones that belonged or belong to bourgeois Western culture, for those works too the 'privilege of the reader' will be operative—by which I mean the reader's capacity to supplement the onesidedness of particular texts. I call the 'privilege of the reader' what Lukács terms as the 'triumph of realism': the superior honesty of the authentic author—in this hypothesis, the Soviet author—

will overcome the ideological weakness with which he is or will be forced to confront the representation of reality by a recent tragic historical past; and the reader will recognize a truth that the author did not know he had posited, or at least not with that aim in mind. To the extent that the typical phenomena of contemporary industrial culture spread through the Soviet world, the 'the accurate and tacitly polemical representation of emerging meaninglessness' will be reasonably successful. But that is precisely why it is possible to assess the enduring validity of the 'humanist' and 'aristocratic' elements of Lukács's theses (elements that can also mutate into apocalyptic or tragic ones): greatness is the tendency towards totality; the perspective of the *Integrität des Menschen*[42] as disalienation, etc., and as consciousness of social integration is never seen as an integration of *functions*, in a typically technological and neopositivistic way, but as an integration of *individuals*. In short, the category of decadence in Lukács undoubtedly possesses a precise historical meaning; it is legitimate and necessary to investigate it further, to strip it of every moralistic connotation and (especially by criticizing Lukács's idea of 'character'), to evaluate all the great works of decadentism in which conflict is represented without giving undue significance to the lifejacket-concept of critical realism —Lukács's least felicitous. At the same time it will be necessary, in a certain sense, to retrace Lukács's spiritual itinerary in reverse so as to understand it and draw from it all possible lessons, asking ourselves whether it is not in fact the case that the result was, notwithstanding his conversions, the one that Goethe envisaged as 'the deepest happiness of the personality—the bringing to ripeness of one's early tendencies'.[43] In Lukács, these stemmed from the violent consciousness of the opposition between 'life' and 'not life'. We need to ask ourselves whether totality and partiality, alienation and integrity, realism and anti-realism are not to this day objective elements of our existence, whether we are not, above all, called upon not to mediate them too easily, not to mask them, not to lay them out in the optimistic 'plane geometry' of reformism.

4. *Some Conclusions*

The paradox harboured by Lukács's positions and their criticisms (by Adorno, for example, and not a few Italian scholars) is that if we compare those positions to the present political, cultural and literary situation in Italy—but this is very likely also true for other literatures, and not just for capitalist western Europe—they end up proposing a moral and mental attitude that could appear to be the opposite of the one they seemed to suggest a decade ago. To the Italian reader, in the final years of Stalinism, Lukács appeared as a Marxist thinker who transposed—not without rigidity and harshness—the principles of the class struggle and of historical and dialectical materialism into the field of aesthetics. His entire teaching was committed to battling the doctrines that separated literature and art from social life as well as from historical and scientific thought, so much so that (at least for critics formed in idealism or spiritualism) his essays appeared nothing more than evidence of sectarian insensibility for the values of poetry. Croce himself feigned horror upon reading that the vicissitudes of *Faust I* reflected a phase of the conflict between feudal leftovers and bourgeois ideology. Today the situation seems inverted. From every corner, whether we're dealing with neo-philologists or neo-positivists, neo-Marxists or official Marxists, arguments against Lukács, and particularly against his notions of decadentism and avant-garde, reproach him for adopting an abstract, monumental and 'anti-historical' canon, and for desiring a literature (and a criticism) relatively separate from the vicissitudes of contemporary society and current cultural circulation.

If what we have been arguing until this point is true, then Lukács—especially in his most recent writing—continues, of course, to advance the socialist perspective and its necessity. But, at least to the extent that this perspective is no longer bound by Stalinist simplifications but tied to the complex institutional and political transformations currently at work in the countries that lay claim to socialism—in other words, at a time when it has again become difficult to distinguish between historical embodiments of socialism and socialist demands that are very far from having been realized (especially insofar as the meaning, possibility and direction of a socialist perspective have been obscured in the West and particularly in Italy)—then Lukács's proposal can seem like (or indeed be) a call to detach oneself from contingency, from participation, from 'cultural struggle'; in short, from a partisan 'tendency'. In a situation such as the present one, the following two formulae do not only contradict current habits but also seem to suspend and almost bracket the contemporary forms of ideological and cultural dispute:

(a) The formula of artworks of great complexity, as self-sufficient as possible, encompassing the conflictual elements of present history and of its perspective, and thus unsuited in their 'realism' for both kinds of 'denunciation' (the avant-garde one, which demands a reader who is basically complicit with the denounced reality, and the naturalistic-revolutionary one, which demands a reader who basically partakes in the anticipated ideals).

(b) The formula of a criticism which is also largely self-sufficient, produced by critics-writers or critics-philosophers, conceived as the living prefiguration of an overcoming of passive specializations which are ideologically enslaved to structures removed from criticism.

The radicalism of these formulae can even appear as ascetic and not just aristocratic, metaphysical and not just historical. And yet, the question mark they hang over us cannot be brushed aside. Is a socialist perspective on the contemporary world still valid? If the answer is yes, then what can be the meaning of a cultural action that does not refer to the real forces that work or can work towards that perspective? In the domain of culture, which is to say, of truth, is every reformism a contradiction in terms, or not? But, as we know, it is the notion of 'culture' itself—highlighting as it does the elements in common to different specializations—which our adversaries reject. That is why I insist: Is it not an opportunistic pretence to write literary or critical works which, though in their recognition of the relational, communicative, 'rational' and 'civil' moment they may represent a progressive antithesis to the literature of escape and of gastronomic or intuitionist-stylistic criticism, can nevertheless only operate within the very narrow boundaries traced by the culture industry and the neo-capitalist management of intellectual production? This does not mean that one should dismiss action aimed at renewing our literature and criticism; it means taking our distance from the situation. Affirming that stylistic renewal stems from a renewal of contents, and immediately adding that it is only the result of a renewal of culture, can lead to two separate but simultaneous mistakes: on the one hand, a formalism of 'contents', the stylization of a mere taste or fashion (Arcadian themes and minor romanticism are its historical examples in Italy); on the other, a 'cultural renewal' exclusively entrusted to ideological formulae, in the worst case, or to particular results and contributions that only renew culture by confirming the existing system, in the best. I don't want to suggest that this kind of activity is sterile or useless but that it *tends to consider present social relations and the fundamental ideological bases on which they rest as basically unchangeable*, at least as far as our gaze can reach. It thus objectively tends to corroborate them, limiting itself to a kind of 'constitutional opposition'. An activity of renewal that congratulates itself for being revolutionary when it is objectively reformist, which counters the so-called 'mysticism' and 'intuitionism' of the twentieth-century avant-gardes only with the 'subsistence levels' of ideological nourishment, without framing them in terms of what Lukács calls 'the great problems of human progress', obviously has nothing to do with Marxism, and should draw the relevant consequences.

Therefore, it seems to us that the real 'useable' meaning—in the sense that one speaks of 'useable space'—of Lukács's method can be extracted only if we translate in terms of our current needs and requirements notions like 'realism' and the 'typical', as well as Lukács's periodizations, and his notions of 'progress' and 'decadence'. In other words, only if we supplement and correct everything that in his history of the literature of bourgeois civilization could be considered as schematic, or, as we have said, allegorical; if we recover all the crucial values of so-called decadent literature which harbour within them the same conflictuality and tendency towards totality that Lukács praises in the masterpieces of realism; if we extend and supplement his notion of character; if we signal the possibility of employing certain methodological connections with reference to literary expressions, like poetry, that Lukács seems to neglect. And, finally, if we contest where necessary Lukács's 'scientific' horizon like one contests the notion of 'science' held by Marxism in the Stalinist period. Yet, what appears to us solid and precious in Lukács's work is precisely what his critics wish to deny him: the unshakeable demand that we measure ourselves against the highest dimensions of human history and the greatest possibilities of mankind; that we renounce appearance to preserve the substance that can change us, our work and the society that is inseparable from our work and from us.

1959

Notes

Originally published in *Officina* 2 (May–June 1959). [Trans.]

1 *Goethe e il suo tempo* [*Goethe and His Age*], a collection of essays first published in the 1930s, was published in German in 1947 and in Italian in 1949 (Milan: Mondadori); the volume *Saggi sul realismo* [Essays on Realism] appeared in May 1950 (Turin: Einaudi), comprising writings from the 1934–39 period, with the exception of the essay on Dostoevsky (written in 1943) and 'Tolstoj e la letteratura occidentale' [Tolstoy and Western Literature, in 1944]; *Il marxismo e la critica letteraria* [Marxism and Literary Criticism, orig. *Karl Marx und Friedrich Engels als Literaturhistoriker*], a collection of studies from 1936 to 1940, was published in 1953 (Turin: Einaudi);

La letteratura sovietica [Soviet Literature] (Rome: Editori Riuniti, 1953) contains essays written in the postwar period, between 1949 and 1951, as well as an earlier essay on Gorky; March 1956 saw the publication of the essay collection *Thomas Mann e la tragedia dell'arte moderna* (Milan: Feltrinelli) [Thomas Mann and the Tragedy of Modern Art; see the English-language collection *Essays on Thomas Mann*], which ranges from a youthful piece (1909) to the preface to the Italian edition, dictated in August 1955; in the same month is published the *Breve storia della letteratura tedesca dal Settecento a oggi* (Turin: Einaudi) [Short History of German Literature from the Eighteenth Century to Today, orig. *Skizze einer Geschichte der deutschen Literatur*], composed 11 years prior, in the last year of the war. January 1957 sees the publication of the translation of an important conference held by Lukács on 28 June 1956 at the Political Academy of the Hungarian Workers' Party, 'La lotta fra progresso e reazione nella cultura d'oggi' [The Struggle Between Progress and Reaction in Contemporary Culture, orig. 'A haladás és a reakció harca a mai kultúrában' / 'Der Kampf des Fortschritts und der Reaktion in der heutigen Kultur']; in September 1957, *Il significato attuale del realismo critico* (Turin: Einaudi) [*The Meaning of Contemporary Realism*, Renato Solmi's translation was the first appearance of the text, which was published in West Germany in 1958, as *Wider den missverstandenen Realismus*, Against the Misunderstanding of Realism], with a 'Preface' from April, and the *Contributi alla storia dell'estetica* (Milan: Feltrinelli) [Contributions to the History of Aesthetics, orig. *Beiträge zur Geschichte der Aesthetik*] (compiled in one volume in 1954), with a prefatory note dated 'Budapest, May 1957', are printed. The *Prolegomeni a un'estetica marxista* [Prolegomena to a Marxist Aesthetics] (Rome: Editori Riuniti, [October] 1957) also feature a preface, significantly dated 'Bucharest, December 1956'. Two of Lukács's major philosophical works appeared in Italy after the original version of this article: *La distruzione della ragione* [The Destruction of Reason] (Turin: Einaudi, 1959) and *Il giovane Hegel* [The Young Hegel] (Turin: Einaudi, 1960). Further publications include the volume on *Realisti tedeschi del XIX secolo* [German Realists in the Nineteenth Century] (Milan: Feltrinelli, 1963), which includes some of Lukács's finest critical essays, and two important early writings, *Teoria del romanzo* [Theory of the Novel] (Milan:

SugarCo, 1962) and *L'anima e le forme* [Soul and Form] (Milan: SugarCo, 1963). A consideration of the numerous writings published after 1959 on Lukács would be noteworthy, since their focus is primarily on the main philosophical works of the Hungarian thinker. In the meantime, his major work, *History and Class Consciousness* (1923), is only available in a French translation of doubtful accuracy. Twenty years will not suffice for Italy's cultural and intellectual sensibility to fully grasp Lukács's work. [*Storia e coscienza di classe* was published by SugarCo in 1967.]

Among Lukács's writings published in Italian periodicals we should recall, on account of their significance (beyond what is probably his first piece translated into Italian, namely, the essay on 'Rosa Luxemburg, marxista' published in Issues 14, 15 and 16 of *Rassegna Comunista*, organ of the Partito Comunista d'Italia, in 1921), the essay 'Che cosa è il marxismo ortodosso' [What is Orthodox Marxism?, 1919], translated from *History and Class Consciousness* and published in *Ragionamenti* 2(10–12) (May–October 1958), and the autobiographical essay 'La mia via al marxismo' [My Path to Marxism] in *Nuovi Argomenti* 33 (July–August 1958) which includes some pages written in 1953 and a *Postscriptum* published in Japan and written in 1957. The 1953 essay opens with a thesis that Lukács's whole life has sought to demonstrate: 'The relation to Marx is the touchstone for every intellectual who takes seriously the elucidation of his own conception of the world.'

2 The formula is admittedly drawn from polemics, but we repeat it here precisely because we're speaking of tendencies, and thus of formulae.

3 Francesco De Sanctis (1817–83), foremost Italian nineteenth-century critic and historian of literature. Named by Garibaldi to the position of Director of Public Instruction; also served as Minister of Education. He authored a history of Italian literature (*Storia della letteratura italiana*, 1870–71), considered by literary critic René Wellek to be most accomplished history of any national literature, and was used as a model by F. O. Matthiessen for his *American Renaissance: Art and Expression in the Age of Emerson and Whitman* (1941). [Trans.]

4 Bertrando Spaventa (1817–83), philosopher and uncle of Benedetto Croce. His interpretation of Hegelian idealism was formative for both Croce and Giovanni Gentile. [Trans.]

5 Antonio Labriola (1843–1904), Marxist philosopher, influenced by both De Sanctis and Spaventa. [Trans.]

6 Antonio Banfi (1886–1957), Marxist philosopher and PCI senator. [Trans.]

7 Benedetto Croce, 'George [sic] Lukacs, *Goethe und seine Zeit*', *Quaderni della critica* 5(14) (1949): 110–12. [Trans.]

8 Galvano Della Volpe, 'I presupposti critici di un'estetica materialistica' [The Critical Presuppositions of a Materialist Aesthetic], *Studi filosofici* 2 (April–June 1947): 97–111. [Galvano Della Volpe (1895–68), Marxist philosopher, known for his critique of Hegelianism, his inquiries into communist conceptions of freedom, and his writing on logic and aesthetics. He discusses Della Volpe's *Critique of Taste* (1960) in 'Traduzione e rifacimento' [Translation and Recreation] in *Saggi ed epigrammi*, pp. 831–5. Fortini mentions Della Volpe's support for the journal *Ragionamenti* in *Un giorno o l'altro* (p. 278), which also includes a letter from Fortini to Della Volpe, accompanying a copy of his poetry collection *Poesia ed errore* (p. 224). [Trans.]

9 Giampiero Carocci (1919–), historian specializing in the nineteenth and twentieth centuries, strongly influenced by Gramsci. [Trans.]

10 Remo Cantoni (1914–78), philosopher and student of Antonio Banfi, founder of *Studi filosofici* and *Il pensiero critico*. [Trans.]

11 Armanda Guiducci (1923–92), philosopher, literary critic and feminist anthropologist, founded the journal *Ragionamenti* in 1955 along with Fortini, Luciano Amodio and Roberto Guiducci. [Trans.]

12 Cesare Cases, *Marxismo e neopositivismo* [Marxism and Neo-Positivism] (Turin: Einaudi, 1958); Armanda Guiducci, 'Estetica e Marxismo: G. Lukács' [Aesthetics and Marxism: G. Lukács], *Passato e presente* 3 (1958), pp. 261–94. [See also Armanda Guiducci, 'Eterodossia e ortodossia: Lukács' in *Dallo zdanovismo allo strutturalismo* (Milan: Feltrinelli, 1967), pp. 47–106.]

13 Carlo Salinari, 'Marxismo e critica letteraria in un libro di Lukacs', *Rinascita* 11 (1953): 620–4; Valentino Gerratana, 'Lukács e i problemi del realismo', *Società* 9(4) (1953): 137–54.

14 Carlo Salinari (1919–77), literary critic and partisan (arrested by the Nazis along with Luigi Pintor in 1944). [Trans.]

15 Valentino Gerratana (1919–2000), philosopher; edited the first complete critical Italian edition of Gramsci's *Prison Notebooks* (*Quaderni del Carcere*, 1975). [Trans.]

16 Carlo Salinari et al., 'Problemi del realismo in Italia', *Il contemporaneo* 11 (1959): 3–59.

17 Included in 'Problemi del realismo in Italia', *Il contemporaneo*. The conference was held at the Istituto Gramsci, 3–5 January 1959. [Trans.]

18 Lucio Colletti (1924–2001), Marxist philosopher. A student of Galvano Della Volpe, he built on the latter's critique of Hegelian Marxism in *Marxism and Hegel* (1969), and strongly influenced the theoretical debate on Marxism in the New Left both in Italy (through his journal *La Sinistra*, 1966–67) and in the Anglophone world (through the *New Left Review*). He eventually broke with Marxism in the 1970s on both political and philosophical grounds, becoming a member of parliament for Silvio Berlusconi's Forza Italia party in the 1990s. [Trans.]

19 'I fear with my critical endeavour / My head and heart may come to grief. / How hard the scholars' means are to array / With which one works up the source'. 'Hope never seems to leave those who affirm, / The shallow minds that stick to must and mould'—Johann Wolfgang von Goethe, *Faust I* (Walter Kauffman trans.) (New York: Anchor, 1963), pp. 107, 111. [Fortini's translation of both volumes of *Faust* was published in 1970 by Mondadori, and reprinted in 1994 and 2010.]

20 Gottfried Keller (1819–90), Swiss poet and writer. [Trans.]

21 Ippolito Pizzetti (1926–2007), critic, translator and landscape architect; Paolo Chiarini (1931–2012), Marxist literary critic and translator, specializing in Brecht and modern German literature. [Trans.]

22 Franco Fortini (on Spitzer and Lukács, Issue 1), Armanda Guiducci (on Galvano della Volpe and Lukács, Issues 1–2; on the *Short*

History, *Thomas Mann* and *Soviet Literature*, Issues 5–6); Thomas Münzer (on *History and Class Consciousness*, Issue 9); as well as the piece by Amodio and the already cited translation of 'What is Orthodox Marxism?'

23 Luciano Amodio (1926–2001), Marxist philosopher and critic. He co-founded *Ragionamenti* with Fortini, with whom he had already collaborated in the journals *Politecnico* and *Discussioni*, and with whom he translated Goldmann's *The Hidden God* into Italian. For his philosophical work, see Luciano Amodio, *Storia e dissoluzione: L'eredità di Hegel e Marx nella riflessione contemporanea* [History and Dissolution: The Legacy of Hegel and Marx in Contemporary Thought] (Macerata: Quodlibet, 2003). [Trans.]

24 Theodor W. Adorno, 'La conciliazione forzata. Lukács e l'equivoco realista', *Tempo presente* 4(3) (1959): 178–92. English translation of the original German essay: 'Extorted Reconciliation: On Georg Lukács's *Realism in Our Time*', *Notes to Literature, Volume One* (Shierry Weber Nicholsen trans.) (New York: Columbia University Press, 1991), pp. 216–40. [Trans.]

25 Lucien Goldmann, 'Georg Lukács l'essayiste' in *Recherches dialectiques* (Paris: Gallimard, 1959), pp. 247–59. [Trans.]

26 In English in the original. [Trans.]

27 Published in Italian in *Il marxismo e critica letteraria*; and in English in *Writer and Critic and Other Essays* (London: Merlin, 1970), pp. 61–88. [Trans.]

28 Pietro Citati, 'Tre libri di Lukács' [Three Books by Lukács], *Lo Spettatore italiano* 1 (January 1954).

29 In the past few years, however, Citati seems to have reversed this perspective, as we can see from his dismissal of Lukacs's *The Meaning of Contemporary Realism* (1957), a book which he said is, at best, only good for the Soviets.

30 *verifica* [Trans.]

31 Pier Luigi Contessi, 'Questioni di estetica e materialismo dialettico' [Questions of Aesthetics and Dialectical Materialism], *Il Mulino* 32 (1954): 408–22.

32 Antonio Banfi, 'A proposito di Lukács e del realismo in arte' [On Lukács and Realism in Art], *Realismo* 18 (January–February

1954): 6; Lanfranco Caretti, ' Il marxismo e la critica letteraria' [Marxism and Literary Criticism], *Itinerari* 5–6 (1953): 73–5.

33 Renato Barilli, 'Lukács e gli scrittori dell'avanguardia' [Lukács and the Writers of the Avant-Garde], *Il Mulino* 79 (1958): 354–60.

34 Giorgio Barbèri Squarotti, 'Arte e società [Art and Society], *Questioni* 4(1–2) (1958).

35 Georg Lukács, *The Meaning of Contemporary Realism* (John and Necke Mander trans) (London: Merlin, 1963), pp. 75–6. [Translation modified: the Italian translation has *avanguardia* where the English term is 'modernism', and *deformazione* instead of 'distortion'.]

36 Theodor W. Adorno, 'Extorted Reconciliation: On Georg Lukács's *Realism in Our Time*', p. 229.

37 Ibid., p. 224.

38 Ibid., pp. 224–5.

39 Ibid., p. 226.

40 Fortini is playing on Henri IV's supposed declaration upon renouncing Protestantism and taking the French throne: *Paris vaut bien une messe* [Paris is worth a mass]. [Trans.]

41 Lukács, *The Meaning of Contemporary Realism*, p. 54 [I have retranslated the passage directly from the Italian as the English variant has drastically compressed the passage and stripped all the philosophical terminology: 'It is something which cannot be measured or understood until its stages have been experienced as a movement from and towards a certain goal'.]

42 Human integrity. [Trans.]

43 Georg Lukács, *Essays on Thomas Mann* (London: Merlin, 1964), p. 99.

V

The Young Lukács

In 1910, when Georg von Lukács published *A lélek és a formák* in Hungarian (the following year saw the publication of its German translation: *Die Seele und die Formen*), he was a 25-year-old man with a degree in law and a position at the Ministry of Public Education, already known for having won a literary prize for an important study—the *History of the Development of Modern Drama*, which would be published two years later.

The importance of *Soul and Form* has been elucidated on several occasions by Lucien Goldmann; according to him, the main theme of these essays (which only appear to have as their object: Rudolf Kassner, Søren Kierkegaard, Novalis, Theodor Storm, Stephan George, Charles-Louis Philippe, Richard Beer-Hofmann, Lawrence Sterne and Paul Ernst) is the inquiry into the 'dynamic signifying structures' that Lukács calls 'forms' of the different modalities privileged by the relation between the human soul and the absolute. Goldmann tells us that this notion of 'form' came to the young Lukács from Wilhelm Dilthey. But for Dilthey, 'forms' had a historical character while for Lukács (probably under the influence of Husserl's writings) 'forms' were atemporal. A step backward from Dilthey (I am still paraphrasing Goldmann) in effect becomes the condition for a step forward.

One of those forms or 'signifying structures' is particularly prominent in this work, namely, the 'tragic' vision, recovered through the relations between 'individual', 'authenticity' and 'death', in the ambit of the ultimate irrelevance and inauthenticity of worldly existence. With this reprise of themes that belonged to Pascal and Kant, the young Lukács goes far beyond the position which at the time belonged to German philosophy, largely anticipating Heidegger's thought and placing himself among the forebears of modern existentialism. That is the nub of Goldmann's interpretation. To which we must not forget to add the enormous importance of dramaturgy (Ibsen), the novel (Mann) and symbolist lyric (not to mention other authors of the nineteenth century such as Kierkegaard and Dostoevsky) for those who wished to rediscover the paradoxical universe of tragedy.

But living 'tragically' amounts to dying.[1]

In a text that would deserve to be quoted at length,[2] Thomas Münzer tells how already in the 1912 essay 'On Poverty of Spirit' (which Max Weber had especially praised), Lukács affirmed that death can only be escaped if knowledge is transformed into action; we would already be close to the Marx that the young Hungarian, retracing the milestones of German classical thought, encountered after the Kant of *Soul and Form* and the Hegel of *The Theory of the Novel*, and who in the war years would have spurred him to write *History and Class Consciousness*.[3]

And yet, Goldmann underscores a very important contradiction in the young Lukács. It is true that a logical progression takes him from 'true life' (or a life lived tragically) to the overcoming of the tragic *impasse*, to taking the standpoint of history—and thus of the one which, among historical 'concrete totalities' or classes, is the 'class of the producers' (in other words, moving from the Epos and Tragedy to the Novel . . .). But in another essential text from *Soul and Form*, namely, 'On the Nature and Form of the Essay' which serves to introduce the others, the author—in contradiction with the last chapter on the tragic, but not with his later thinking—defines the essay as an autonomous form between philosophy and literary expression. The objects-occasions of the essay are actually realities and values complementary to those of truth and error. The essayistic operation is the 'form' of every 'ironic' discourse in which one says one thing to imply another. We are, accordingly, beyond the peremptory choices of tragic 'form'. From the very beginning of his activity, while he experiences and expresses the tragic instant and tragic atemporality, Lukács also chooses himself as an *essayist*, refusing 'death' and accepting the register of intermediate discourse. The question and hypothesis is therefore the following: Is this intermediate discourse, this 'form' that is essay writing, not a metaphor or anticipation for what in Lukács's later thought will be the fundamental category of *mediation*? In his political choices, critical activity and aesthetic meditation, it will take a variety of names: the Party, the concrete universal mediating between the 'ought' of class consciousness and action ('organization is the form of the mediation between theory and praxis'); the Typical, the poetic mediation between the universal and the particular. The anti-fascist struggle 30 years ago and the struggle for peace and coexistence just yesterday were for Lukács concrete embodiments, born of History's mediating cunning, of the fundamental conflict between capitalism and socialism, which cannot be fully experienced as such because gazing on it directly, as with the tragic Godhead or the sun, would strike down the incautious. It seems likely then that while in Lukács's thought there is a unidirectional sequence—the 'extremist' one—that takes him from the 'tragic vision' to party discipline (historical factors like biographical ones are relatively unimportant for such a development), it is countered from the start by another line of thought that theorizes mediation, treating it as a principle of conduct. While, according to the first sequence, Lukács can always repeat (as I heard him do in May 1956), 'right or wrong my party'[4] (that typical motto of absolute choice), according to the second he can engage in self-criticisms, that is, in something which differs greatly from the pure and simple acceptance of discipline and of its paradox—inasmuch as these self-criticisms are, so to speak, 'essayistic' interpretations, an 'ironic' form of praxis in the course of which one says one thing to say another and the speaker's register both is and is not that of his listener.

If this hypothesis is in any way grounded then Lukács's mistake—in its own right both coherent with his principles and inevitable—was that of having censored his entire *oeuvre* up until *History and Class Consciousness*, including that part in which one could sift the 'extremist' elements of his thought from the 'essayistic' ones that were destined to make his survival possible. In so doing, he could give the impression—like a father whose misplaced mercy leads him to spare his son the ordeals of youth—that the great historiographic themes of his mature work had not in fact been experienced by someone who had spent his season in the hell of 'decadence' and made such a great contribution to it but, rather, by someone born adult.

This may help to explain why Lukácsian 'realism'—in the different acceptations of the term, critical, political and ethical—started to lose its power of persuasion when socialist history, with the end of the Stalinist period, appeared to leave behind a reality consisting of absolute and tragic choices. The latter demanded to be read and governed not by a thinking based on the method of 'all-or-nothing' but by dialectical mediations; while, with the generalization of techno-scientistic attitudes and the devaluation of ideological ones (in other words, of judgements on the present and the past on the basis of the future) absolute conflicts *appear* to have departed from the world stage to retreat into interiority and the private.

The young and less young who are irritated by the mask of the sublime philistine worn by the older, mature Lukács will do well to read the young Lukács. They will learn about the fundamental aspirations to totality and revolutionary apocalypse that structure his later work as historian and critic. They will also be able to recognize how many biased idiocies have been written against that work in these past few years. And they will be able to ponder what kind of readings and what writerly taste, as subtle as they were severe, lay at the origins of an author and teacher who in later years explicitly tried to 'write badly'; that is, to renounce flashy elegance along with the possibility that—as he once remarked—scintillating quotations could be drawn from his writings. This is the writer which the know-it-all ignorance of much of our wizened or barely pubescent avant-garde has seen fit to accuse of mediocre or awkward taste. A different argument, one spoken in friendly confidence, would be required for some readers or scholars of Lukács who seem to have been born, so to speak, after everything was settled—already wise, objective, realist, deft overcomers of the tragic and of extremism. They think it suffices that someone else lived through and wrote about that 'prolonged stay' in the vicinity of death, that tarrying (*Verweilen*) which according to Hegel alone grants the magical force to bear the weight of death. Reading or rereading those pages will also prove useful to them.

1963

Notes

Originally published as the introduction to Georg Lukács, *L'anima e le forme* [Soul and Form] (Sergio Bologna trans.) (Milan: Sugar, 1963). [Trans.]

1 The Italian reader might recall that precisely between 1909 and 1910 (the year that sees the first appearance of two works by Kierkegaard in Italian) Carlo Michelstaedter, two years younger than Lukács and like him a citizen of the Austro-Hungarian Empire, was developing his only philosophical work as a student in Florence. In *Persuasion and Rhetoric,* he opposed these two forms to each other, and the abiding (*menèin*) of the hero within essence to the fatuousness of the inessential everyday. Michelstaedter killed himself in his hometown of Gorizia on 17 October 1910, the same month in which Lukács wrote that letter to Leo Popper from Florence, 'On the Nature and Form of the Essay', which opens *Soul and Form* and features an implicit attempt to overcome the tragic identity of life

and death (as found in the thinking of Michelstaedter, no doubt unknown to Lukács). There, as though thinking of that 'figure' of Werther he was leaving behind, Lukács writes: 'Neither living nor dying are adequate means to express what is essential in life'.

For Lukács's later attitude, it suffices to recall the testimony of Victor Serge, who met Lukács in Vienna in 1924: 'One day we were discussing the problem of whether or not revolutionaries who had been condemned to death should commit suicide; this arose from the execution in 1919 at Budapest of Otto Korvin, who had been in charge of the Hungarian Cheka, and whose hanging had afforded a choice spectacle for "society" folk. "I thought of suicide", said Lukács, "in the hours when I was expecting to be arrested and hanged with him. I came to the conclusion that I had no right to it: a member of the Central Committee must set the example".'—See *Memoirs of a Revolutionary* (Peter Sedgwick with George Paizis trans.) (New York: New York Review of Books, 2012), p. 220.

2 Thomas Münzer, 'Il giovane Lukács', *Ragionamenti* 9 (1957): 167–72.

3 Cesare Pianciola contests the trajectory that Goldmann attributes to the young Lukács, in his review (see Pianciola, 'L'anima e le forme e Teoria del romanzo', *Rivista di Filosofia* 55(1) (1964): 88–96). Kierkegaard and not Kant would be at the origin of the theme of *Soul and Form*.

4 [In English in the original.] It is curious to note that precisely this variant of the nationalist English motto was explicitly used and justified by Trotsky in his speech at the 13th Congress in May 1924.

VI

The Passage of Joy

1. In a piece about Horkheimer and Adorno's *Dialectic of Enlightenment*,[1] I come across the following sentence, advocating the need to also take into consideration a collection of talks by Horkheimer: 'The reading of this book, in which the popularizing form forces the author to express himself without the refinement of the dazzling prose that often blinds the reader of the *Dialectic of Enlightenment* . . . '

So is 'dazzling prose' something that can be removed without any harm to the substance of the argument? A rhetorical garment? There is an interpretive tradition (deriving from the Enlightenment and then from Romanticism) which contends that this is only true in negative cases, that is, when 'literature' superimposes itself upon authentic thought as a mere ornament. That tradition indicates an increasing split between languages: the language of literature is equivocal or 'expressive', while the languages of philosophy and the human sciences are univocal, translatable and, indeed, 'scientific'. Today we have become sensitive to harmonies and stylistic drifts even in those texts that make the loudest claim to be grounded on a coherent and univocal semantic system (or rather, especially in such texts), but this does not at all mean, of course, that we should happily indulge in a stylistic or structuralist reading (which ultimately means, in a tautological reading) of the texts of the moral and historical sciences or (even worse, and as very often happens) in those digressions halfway between sociology and psychoanalysis which have merely a tranquillizing function.

But in this case—and not just—the 'refinement' and 'dazzling prose' (which then becomes, according to the article's author, the gateway to 'smoke and mirrors') must be recognized as a genuine content, perhaps the most relevant content of the work. What is at stake is the choice of a *genre* and a *style*. That choice is a sign. And, to the degree that it inclines towards aphorism or models itself according to the canons of the essay (it is not by chance that Adorno has written an essay on the essay,[2] drawing upon the history of the genre in German literature and the remote precedent penned by Lukács[3]) this prose wants the logical-dialectical operation to breathe existence. 'The new emotional accent of utopian hope' that Pianciola detects in the book is, very probably, deposited in these very forms.

In light of this observation, I think the criticisms levied against the work of the two German thinkers could and should be even sharper, but it cannot be denied that the work aims at and, to a certain extent, realizes its strongest contestation of Enlightened-bourgeois *ratio* precisely by means of its form. Those who wish to criticize 'essayism' and the literature it implies must also criticize the latter and not treat it as a 'sterile appendix devoid of any function or meaning'. In other words, the work of Horkheimer and Adorno (just like, or even more so, the latter's *Minima Moralia*) does not at all confine itself to postulating utopian hope but wants to realize it *in its own right*, to the extent that its thought aims to escape, if only for an instant, the conditioning of integration. Is it possible? Does the formal anticipation not perhaps imply a double notion of 'time'? It should be clear that this question is posed in order to increase, and not to diminish, the causes for contention. But aggravating the charges against Adorno (or whomever stands in for him) means shifting the whole problem and basically *deciphering Nietzsche*—in other words, the contradiction between the immediate (mystified) consumption of thought and existence and their future realization. This is the problem of the legitimacy of poetry, among others.

2. A not dissimilar doubt occurred to me on a second reading of Sebastiano Timpanaro's[4] beautiful book on classicism and the Enlightenment in nineteenth-century Italy.[5] I am thinking of the essays on Giacomo Leopardi. They deserve commentary by specialists, but I hope that Timpanaro will welcome the opinion of one whose only credentials, when it comes to Leopardi studies, is an article from 1946,[6] which nevertheless already contested the 'white' interpretation given to Leopardi in the previous two decades.[7]

The reconstruction of Leopardi's thought is carried out in a movement which, captivated as we are by the author's lucidity and doctrine, we quickly forget; and it is the right polemical impetus against the traditional devaluation of Leopardi's anti-spiritualism, customarily accompanied by a 'purely aesthetic consideration' of his poetic work or by his reduction to a 'pure poet'. We also quickly forget its author; this too is justifiable, if his aim is that of speaking about Leopardi the thinker and not the poet.

But is it possible to write an essay on Leopardi the thinker without evaluating how much of that 'thought' is conveyed in what popular or professorial speech stubbornly refers to as his 'poetry'? Is it possible to do it with the bare reference to a distinguished work like that of Walter Binni,[8] cited by Timpanaro, and in short without considering that between the Leopardi of the *Zibaldone* and that of the *Canti* and perhaps the *Operette morali*[9] there may be a difference *that cannot be described in quantitative terms (more 'poetry', less 'poetry'; more 'thought', less 'thought'), but only in dialectical ones?* Confident of my agreement with Timpanaro, I refuse to believe that Leopardi's 'poetry' is some ineffable and untranslatable thing, something 'pure' and thus separate from 'thought'. However, I need to affirm just as emphatically that the verbal organs of the *Canti* with their phonetic, lexical, syntactic and metric plexuses, the play of discursive figures and stylistic shifts, their balanced and unbalanced tensions, with that form of theirs (which is, as we all know, content)—those poems, in short, say something (or rather, say multiple things, one after the other and all together) which critical analysis can, at least to a certain degree, translate into discursive terms, that is, into 'thought'. And, finally, this 'thought' of 'poetry' not only does not necessarily coincide with the 'thought' of the 'prose' of the same author but *cannot* and in a sense *must not* coincide with it.

This inquiry, which reassesses Leopardi as an authentic thinker, is no doubt a praiseworthy contribution to the history of Italian and European culture in the age of Restoration; but those who bring not just a historical interest but a properly speculative one to these kinds of reflection will most likely not look for Leopardi's work, but for those of other authors, philosophers (properly so-called), not disturbed by that sphere of shadow or light which is Leopardi's poetry. While anyone who wishes to repeat the experience of a total impetus of life as language will not be able to avoid rereading 'Il tramonto della luna' (The Setting of the Moon) or 'La ginestra' (Broom) or 'Imitazione' (Imitation).[10]

Only an entire volume's worth of examples could at this point elucidate this modest council of prudence. For now it suffices to recall a passage that all Italian high-school students know, that page from De Sanctis' *History* with its famous commonplace: 'the scepticism of a quarter', etc.[11] In other words, what correction to the thought of Leopardi the thinker, to his conception of human life, comes from the images of life positively connoted in his poetry (from the voice of Sappho, if you will, to the figurations of nature, say, the dancing hares, the clear river, the enamoured and evasive gazes and so on), and finally, from the fullness or happiness or completeness associated with making poetry, with expressing a 'thought' in a different way than prose, and thus with expressing a different thought? What is the concrete contribution to 'thought' that follows from the lived contradiction, repeatedly described by Leopardi, between the mythical-irrational lie and its consoling effects? The contribution implicit in the effective overcoming of this lie in poetic writing?

At this juncture, I do not need to anticipate the objections of those who think I am aligned with the aesthetes who saw Leopardi as the high priest of poetry. It was just that myth, matured in the climate of hermeticism but prepared by the followers of Croce, that I tried to contest 20 years ago. But love of a more serious and fuller idea of poetry than that of twentieth-century aestheticism cannot make us act as though in Leopardi poetic activity did not possess a gratifying and eudaimonic function to a high degree; as though it did not, at least partly, make itself into its own object, the poetry of poetry. In short, we cannot omit from Leopardian 'thought' the enormous *joy* of formal adventure, namely, that contradiction which the history of Leopardian criticism has variously voiced. We can and must definitively wrest Leopardi away from yesterday's aestheticism. But we cannot wrest him away from the general condition of the time in which he wrote; a condition that determined him more than his culture and thinking could acknowledge. Now that condition—a phase of the development of bourgeois society, etc.—places him among the first great European interpreters of a tragic dissociation between 'poetry' and 'truth' that continued until our various yesterdays, at least partly justifying with its existence the critical interpretations of which we would have liked to be rid for ever.

What correction, as I was saying, comes to Leopardian 'thought' from the 'poetry' of the *Canti*? First of all, that men are granted the chance to consume in 'form' a vital plenitude or (if you prefer) to enjoy a 'totalizing' experience that in other epochs and societies was configured as religious or mystical, whereas in Leopardi it is aesthetic and poetic. Hence his poetry, in keeping with the necessarily mystified, embryonic, formal character of those 'totalizations', those short-circuits of the absolute, contains two simultaneous and contradictory movements. The first (I am not referring only to the call of 'La ginestra'), is implicitly pedagogical, and it wants to make it so that men—freed from illusions and errors and thus, desperately happy—may also live as actors and spectators but in history, in society, that experience of a formal consummation of existence for which Giacomo, chanting from his gridiron, provides the heroic example. The second renounces the first, refuses to universalize its own example, demand a historical fulfilment of its own prophecy, and devours itself on the spot, in a perfect coincidence between solitude and form, suicide and joy.

It would not be the first time that a 'thought' cunningly introduces within itself the thorn of a contradiction, of the kind about which Kierkegaard says 'were I to remove it, I would die'.[12] We could even say that poetry or, better, lyric poetry (or, better yet, the lyric poetry of the modern age) has been (and *is no longer*) that contradiction and that thorn in the thought of various thinkers. It would be enough to recognize that at least for a given time and society, poetry fulfilled the office of spur towards a real, inter-human, fulfilment of its own formal image and, *simultaneously*, the place of an anticipated (and therefore mystified, like a drug or a communion wafer) consummation of a sudden and imaginary fulfilment. This would help some of us to understand, for example, the motives, limits and authenticity of our own or others' revolutionary vocations, and better to evaluate which is the joy we proclaim to despise, which is the one we seek and would like to attain, and what is their price in contradictions.

1967

Notes

Originally published in *Quaderni piacentini* 6(30) (1967). [Trans.]

1 Cesare Pianciola, '"Dialettica dell'illuminismo" di Horkheimer e Adorno' [Horkheimer and Adorno's *Dialectic of Enlightenment*], *Quaderni piacentini* 6(29) (1967): 68–73.

2 Theodor W. Adorno, 'The Essay as Form' in *Notes to Literature, Volume One* (Shierry Weber Nicholson trans.) (Columbia: Columbia University Press, 1991), pp. 2–23. [Trans.]

3 For a discussion of 'On the Nature and Form of the Essay' in *Soul and Form*, see 'The Young Lukács', pp. 354–59 in this volume. [Trans.]

4 Sebastiano Timpanaro (1923–2000), Marxist philologist, philosopher and literary critic. For an appreciation of his work, see Perry Anderson, 'On Sebastiano Timpanaro', *London Review of Books* 23(9) (10 May 2001): 8–12. [Trans.]

5 Sebastiano Timpanaro, *Classicismo e illuminismo nell'Ottocento italiano* [Classicism and Enlightenment in the Italian Nineteenth Century] (Pisa: Nistri-Lischi, 1965).

6 Franco Fortini, 'La leggenda di Recanati' [The Legend of Recanati], *Il Politecnico* 33–34 (September–December 1946): 34–8. [Trans.]

7 *ventennio*, alludes to the period of Fascist rule. [Trans.]

8 Walter Binni (1913–97), literary critic and historian, anti-fascist politician and Leopardi scholar; author of *La nuova poetica leopardiana* [Leopardi's New Poetics] (Florence: Sansoni, 1947) and *La protesta di Leopardi* [Leopardi's Protest] (Florence: Sansoni, 1973), and co-editor of *Tutte le opere* [Collected Works] (Florence: Sansoni, 1969). [Trans.]

9 The approximate dates of composition for these works are as follows: *Zibaldone* (1817–32, published posthumously in multiple volumes between 1898–1900), *Canti* (1818–36, published in 1835 and posthumously with Leopardi's corrections and the addition of some poems in 1845); *Operette morali* (1824–32, first publication in 1827). For English translations see: *Zibaldone*: *The Notebooks of Giacomo Leopardi* (Michael Caesar and Franco D'Intino eds) (New York: Penguin, 2013); *Canti* (Jonathan Galassi trans.) (New York: Farrar, Strauss and Giroux, 2012); *Operette Morali*: *Essays and Dialogues* (Giovanni Cecchetti ed. and trans.) (Berkeley: University of California Press, 1982). [Trans.]

10 Leopardi, *Canti* (Jonathan Galassi trans.), pp. 280–311. [Trans.]

11

> 'Leopardi's originality is to be found in this tenacious life of the inner world, notwithstanding the collapse of every theological and metaphysical world, which lends his skepticism a religious character. Or rather, it is the skepticism

> of a quarter of an hour in which the sentiment of the moral world vibrates with such energy.'

—Francesco De Sanctis, *Storia della letteratura italiana* [History of Italian Literature], VOL. 2 (Naples: Morano, 1870), p. 490. [Trans.]

12 I have not been able to trace this expression, which Fortini employs elsewhere ('Lettera ad amici di Piacenza. 1961' in 'L'ospite ingrato primo' in *Saggi ed epigrammi*, p. 952), but the reference is likely to Søren Kierkegaard, 'The Thorn in the Flesh', *Eighteen Upbuilding Discourses* (Howard V. Hong and Edna H. Hong eds and trans) (Princeton: Princeton University Press, 1990), pp. 327–46. [Trans.]

PART IV

For Some Books

I

For Herzen

Read Alexander Herzen and you will feel something opening up inside you, a sense of clarity and wholeness. The distance between voice and objects seems optimal. A useful degree of limpidity. The light is that of dialectical reason. It accords with the shadow of the unsaid. As for deeper shadows, you feel how Herzen is aware of their existence but deliberately declines those opacities that seem so important to us. He declines to interrogate them because he knows that they do not actually belong to him as much as to his century or age; and that marvellous man can, without any arrogance, trust the shift of history's magnetic pole so that year after year the sun will reason with those shadows.

This memorialist from a hundred years ago, who comes forward neither with the words of poetry nor with those of the scientific genius, should be very distant from us. And what if the first reason for his closeness were, instead, the contradiction whereby a man of political thought and action, as well as a narrator, leaves the 'best of himself' in a volume of memoirs? A formulation that Herzen himself would not have accepted. Even though the notion of 'life' that he glimpsed in Turgenev and Tolstoy, with its pre-decadent tonalities, was alien to him, he still regarded every manifestation of existence as potentially charged with value; the 'best' is not to be found in an act but like virtue must spread itself through every moment. (This is the difference between 'heart' and 'life'; Belinsky called Herzen 'intelligence . . . armed with a heart, as it were, by its humanist orientation'.) What is astonishing is Herzen's capacity to suddenly escape the twofold tradition of memoir writing that the seventeenth and eighteenth centuries had bequeathed to his own century, the moralistic chronicle (the Cardinal de Retz or Saint-Simon) and the psychological-pedagogical account (Rousseau or Goethe). Belinsky again, in his famous letter from 1846, writes: 'You possess a particular genre'. Herzen indeed creates a genre because he *is* a genre, an exemplary category of the relationship between imagination and intelligence, existence and history, the past and reflection. To speak of integrity and plenitude is insufficient: Herzen is not simply gifted with the voice of the gentleman of genius, of the revolutionary *barin*, the one we hear in Kropotkin and others. It's a whole way of being and expressing himself, which in Italy is matched only by some pages of De Sanctis and Cattaneo.[1] This is a mode of being that we think we have reckoned with only because modern times have vertiginously distanced it from us (Gramsci too has become distant). Would he be merely the peer of men his book allows us to understand, those innumerable Russians from Chaadayev[2] to Bakunin, and those innumerable westerners, from Mazzini to Mickiewicz,[3] Garibaldi to Proudhon? No, because his true comrades are the Baudelaires, Marxs and Tolstoys.

The world of that historical past, the world in which Herzen spent his life, is presupposed or evoked (both inside and beyond his book) within an order of relations which is the same as that of great poetry, the great novel or the great socioeconomic inquiry; it bears the same awareness of structures and the same swarming of details, the same capacity to move from intellectual synthesis (as in the portrait of Chaadayev: 'For ten years he stood with folded arms, by a column, by a tree on the boulevard'[4]) to the sketch of landscape as a 'spiritual state' (as in the pages on the shipwreck of the mother and son). This is a relationship between history and poetry to which Belinsky had already alluded in 1844. It carries the same trust in the continuous unfolding of the tension between objectivity and subjectivity, the same certainty in the univocity of words and images. The 'world'—men, things, peoples, cities, events, affections—is social, meaning you can only possess it along with others, understood as subjects and addressees of communication. Psychologically, it would be easy to attribute this 'realism' to the extroversion of the property-owner; whereby Herzen turns everyone into a knight, including the repellent Tsar Nicholas I and the odious Herwegh[5]. But, in keeping with what Franco Venturi has written in *Roots of Revolution*, its intellectual root must be looked for in that 'rather personal application of Hegelianism' through which Russian socialists before 1848 sought reality 'in considering the ethical relations of the intellectual towards the people; they did not try to apply the philosophy of history to peoples, groups and classes. In short, they preferred a "metaphysic of mind and will" to a "metaphysic of politics", so popular in the Hegelian left wing in Germany and Poland'.[6]

It is precisely this certainty of communicability, that is to say, in the tendency of the lived life and the written life to become identical, that makes it possible for Herzen to compose a life-novel, allowing him to omit the problem of the legitimacy (and therefore the paradoxes) of writing that the German Romantics had illuminated, which Flaubert and Baudelaire were well acquainted with, and which to our very day remains one of the strongest sources of literary inspiration—sometimes the only one. Social or intimate vicissitudes, these are all *res gestae*; one does not write solely to prolong action but because (in a world *'où l'action n'est pas la soeur du rêve'*)[7] one knows that action par excellence, real action, is the one endowed with form or consciousness, coinciding with the greatest possible human plenitude, the greatest possible recovery of totality . . . This is an absolutely Romantic ideal which our Western age consequently rejects to the same degree that it actually rejects the notion of revolution. It is an ideal which, having morphed into a new spectre (we know that dead faiths turn into ghosts and demons), returns to us on the banners of the 'barbarians' from the four points of the horizon. Yet it is the highest and most lucid point of Romanticism when Herzen in his stunning fourth letter (in *From the Other Shore*) to the young man who wants to leave Europe after the failure of the revolution of summer 1848, writes:

> You are irritated because the nations don't fulfil the conception that is dear and close to you, because they are unable to save themselves with the weapons you offer them and to cease suffering. But why do you think that the nation is obliged to fulfil your conception and not its own, and precisely at this time, and not another? . . .[B]ut you, faithful to Romanticism, are angry and want to run away, so as to avoid seeing the truth.

This letter, let us note parenthetically, opens with the description of a military parade at the Tuileries, on an autumn day, which seems as though it had been written on the verso of a page from *Spleen de Paris*.[8]

The secret behind the power of these pages is ultimately not a psychological secret; it is not to be sought in a particular 'genius'. Let us reread what Lenin wrote on the centenary of Herzen's birth. He saw in the '*gentilhomme russe et citoyen du monde*' (as Dostoyevsky disdainfully portrayed him in his *Diary of a Writer*) 'a product and reflection of that epoch in world history when the revolutionary character of the bourgeois democrats was *already* passing away (in Europe), while the revolutionary character of the socialist proletariat had *not yet* matured'.[9] I can thus surmise that the secret is indeed to be sought in the way that Herzen responded to a typical historical situation, refusing to equate the temporary defeat of a cause (that of the revolutions of 1848, which breaks his life in two) with his own existential defeat (age, exile, domestic suffering), refusing to superimpose onto a historical condition—the interval described by Lenin—the so-called human condition, but experiencing and expressing both defeats in keeping with the 'irresistible charm' which, as he declares elsewhere, exists 'in the very oscillation between the two worlds of the universal and the personal'.

'The working man of every country is the petit bourgeois of the future'; 'They look at you with a kind of pity, like a madman . . . '[10] In these two phrases (from his last years and the last pages of *My Past and Thoughts*) we find one of the innumerable proofs of the lucidity that never falls into scepticism, which marks out our distant older brother—phrases that are a hundred years old but whose meaning we can grasp only now. Or this: 'Will the brutalized masses rip from the hands of the monopolists the energies produced by science, that whole complex of technical improvements of human life, turning them into a common good? . . . We won't see the solution. Your hair is grey and I am 44.' I think of the illustrious victims of 1848: Wagner, Flaubert, Belli, Baudelaire, Mazzini . . . Only Marx is more lucid than Herzen.

Today we are all capable of knowing which is the blind spot, the *macula lutea* of that clear sight. After a century-long experience of decadentism, we know what Dostoyevsky meant when he indicted Herzen's lucidity ('the ability to transform the deepest of one's feelings into an object'), namely, that his blind spot is precisely the apparent absence of blind spots, the absence of doubts about the communicability of experience . . . But we take advantage of this easily-gained superiority to refuse the extraordinary usefulness of this teaching. We do not read him. ('They look at you with a kind of pity, like a madman . . . ') We don't even translate him unabridged. We avert our gaze from his time. We think that the keys to our own time are nearer—between 1890 and 1920. We think we have nothing to learn from the age of that 'young man with a thin and delicate neck', son of Prince Andrei, who in the final pages of *War and Peace* listens to the arguments of the future Decembrists, and who has always reminded me of Herzen—who lived between Alexander I and *Capital* and died the year Lenin was born.

1961

Notes

Originally published as 'Dall'altra sponda' [From the Other Shore], *Questo e altro* 1 (July 1962). [Trans.]

1 Carlo Cattaneo (1801–69), philosopher, republican and founder of the nineteenth-century journal *Il Politecnico*. [Trans.]

2 Pyotr Chaadayev (1794–1856), Russian philosopher. [Trans.]

3 Adam Mickiewicz (1798–1855), Polish poet and political activist. [Trans.]

4 Alexander Herzen, *My Past and Thoughts: The Memoirs of Alexander Herzen* (Constance Garnett trans.) (Berkeley: University of California Press, 1982), p. 295.

5 Georg Herwegh (1817–75), German poet and radical. [Trans.]

6 Franco Venturi, *Roots of Revolution: A History of Populist and Socialist Movements in Nineteenth Century Russia* (Francis Haskell trans.) (New York: Alfred A. Knopf, 1960), p. 17.

7 'From this world where the deed and dream do not accord'. A line from Baudelaire's poem 'Le Reniement de Saint Pierre' [St. Peter's Denial] in *The Flowers of Evil*, pp. 265–6. [Trans.]

8 Alexander Herzen, *From the Other Shore, and The Russian People and Socialism, an Open Letter to Jules Michelet* (Moura Budberg and Richard Wollheim trans) (London: Weidenfeld and Nicolson, 1956), pp. 76–8.

9 V. I. Lenin, 'In Memory of Herzen' in *On Literature and Art* (Moscow: Progress Publishers, 1967), p. 64.

10 Herzen, *My Past and Thoughts*, p. 659.

II
Rereading Pasternak

1. This book judges us. That is beyond doubt. One night at the borders of Karelia, my train stopped amid the border forests of the Soviet Union, the fog spread across the fields; in half-sleep, I thought that along that path thousands had dragged the granite blocks to raise Petersburg and the Bronze Horseman over the swamps. In April 1917, it was Lenin's path. In those hours of immobility and silence it was as though a knot had come undone. After many years and many pages, exhausting discussions and contested passions, one could again recognize, across now distant years, the homeland of an undivided truth, the moral place of a greatness forged by humility and terribleness, 'the sixth Continent—by the brief name: Rus''.

> 'Wake up! Wake up!' it called entreatingly; it sounded almost like the summons on the eve of Easter Sunday: 'Awake, O my soul, why dost thou slumber.'[1]

This air of resurrection runs throughout the book. It was not difficult to write in 1956, and after the 20th Congress, that the 'collective historical *pietas* of the Soviet people towards itself, towards its self' prepared it 'to offer new marvels, thoughts and new truths to all men'. Why should I apologize for this self-quotation? Especially since—according to what Mario Alicata[2] said to me then—those pages of mine would have harboured 'anti-Soviet feelings'. But we're the same age and have the same time before us; he perhaps to recognize his error, and me perhaps to excuse it. Why shouldn't I say that I discovered, reading *Doctor Zhivago*, how correct I had been about Pasternak when in 1955 I dedicated to him some verses where I said that, right or wrong, his people without knowing it also spoke in the words of his poetry, and that one day, readers of his poems would have felt remorse, bitterness, love?

This book judges us because it unsettles many of our critical notions. It doesn't fit our calculations; it escapes us. It is easy for us to say what we do not like in it; it is immensely difficult instead to convey what inspires us and why. We can recognize with our eyes closed the reasons to circumscribe and reduce it, while the reasons to appreciate it are almost invariably old weapons of our enemies. The surfeit of polemical light alters the tone, too many among those who write or speak about *Doctor Zhivago* judge it to be either a meteorite or a fossil because they are unable even to glimpse the richness and variety—sometimes visible, sometimes hidden—of Russian literature. They believe (because it humours their laziness) that from the suicide of Yesenin to Fadeyev, for 25 years, the Russian people only wrote or read Stalinist words.

When Piovene[3] writes that 'it is a political event to have heard again the voice of great and unencumbered poetry', he is certainly right (especially in a country where the cream of our criticism puts the entire second half of our century under the sign of Gadda's *That Awful Mess on the Via Merulana*); but I wonder whether he fully realizes the meaning of his own words. We must therefore draw nearer to that strange sphinx that is *Doctor Zhivago* and once again repeat 'blessed is the one who does not condemn himself by what he approves'[4]—or what he disapproves, of course.

2. The principal objection to *Zhivago* came to me from a friend. He argued that the refusal of the revolution and of history more generally, which permeates the book from start to finish, would be legitimate if it were an a posteriori result, the balance sheet of a failed historical commitment. Pasternak's perspective is instead framed in counterposition to sociohistorical experience, not as its result.

If that is true, we can immediately grasp the common cause for the two opposite errors of interpretation that have accompanied the novel ever since its publication. Because the book presented itself as a story set in the revolution, penned by a great poet ill treated in his country by the powers that be, it was natural to expect a novel of education and experience. So it was read either as the experience of a failure, or as the failure of an experience. In both cases, the 'balance sheet of a failed historical commitment' was demanded from the book. However, for one critical camp, the most favourable, that 'balance sheet' is contained in the book, while the other camp is less favourable, precisely because it denies that the book contains such a 'balance sheet'. Yet both ask of the book a historicist reason for its contestation of history.

Does the book justify this dual yet convergent demand? I think so. And this is no doubt the root of its ambiguity. In effect, the first third of the novel seems to be the story of a group of youths between the Revolution of 1905 and the Civil War; the events, public or private, change them and they react to one another. But from a certain point onward, namely, from the journey to the Urals, the book focuses on the love story between Zhivago and Lara Guishar-Antipov. History is adjourned while the characters attain a relative self-identity. We could even say that in the final analysis this also corresponds to the characters' attitude towards the Revolution, which is initially felt as something in which one participated, sympathetically or otherwise, and then turns into naked extraneousness, or destructive animosity. It is true that the vicissitudes that separate or unite the characters, killing their loves or lives, are tragic or lyrical and not epic. We do not find here the ambition of Grimmelhausen's *Simplicius Simplicissimus* or even Hemingway's *A Farewell to Arms*. Consider Zhivago's attitudes towards the revolution: 'Mother Russia is on the move' (p. 136); 'It seems to me that socialism is the sea . . . the sea of each and every one's authenticity'

(p. 136); 'Such a new thing, too, was the revolution, not the one idealized in student fashion in 1905, but this new upheaval, to-day's born of the war, bloody, pitiless, elemental, the soldiers' revolution . . . proceeding full of hope towards the goal' (p. 148). At the same time, during the trip that takes him from the front to Moscow, Spring 1917: 'Just a moment . . . it seems to me that with all that's going on—the chaos, the disintegration, the pressure from the enemy—this is not the moment to start dangerous experiments' (p. 151); 'This was the point of life, this was experience, this was . . . what artists had in mind—this coming home to your family, to yourself, this renewal of life' (p. 152). But, once he is in Moscow: 'I also think that Russia is destined to become the first socialist country since the beginning of the world' (p. 167); 'he could see that his past life and his world were doomed, and that he and such as he were sentenced to destruction' (p. 168). The decrees of October bring to mind 'something of Pushkin's blazing directness and of Tolstoy's bold attachment to the facts' (p. 177). '"So you're working for *them* [the Bolsheviks]?"—"I am," I said, "and may it not displease you, I am proud of our privations and I respect those who honour us by imposing them on us."' (p. 179) Travelling towards the Urals instead, and it is not clear why, this is his reply to a counter-revolutionary argument: 'History hasn't consulted me, I have to put up with whatever happens, so why shouldn't I ignore the facts?' (pp. 202–3). 'The régime is hostile to us', Alexander tells him, 'Not that I would take back the estate on the old terms as a gift . . . That would be as foolish as to start running about naked or trying to forget the alphabet' (pp. 218–19). Halfway through the book, when Zhivago is confronted by Strelnikov, the first and only revolutionary in the book, he replies in the only way that Pasternak can reply to his Soviet censors: 'the point you wish me to discuss with you is one I have been arguing with an imaginary accuser all my life . . . permit me to leave, without having it out with you . . . I have no excuses to make to you' (p. 228).

From here on—without us ever being told what the imaginary argument was—*the refusal of the revolution*, in the guise of the refusal of the mentality of its leaders, seems to be consolidated. What happened? Did Pasternak wish to narrate the story of a sympathizing intellectual, overwhelmed by Bolshevism? But it is precisely *that* story which is absent from the book. Zhivago's intellectual profile, so rich and complex in many respects, is extremely impoverished, even void in this one. Antipov-Strelnikov, in his final speech before committing suicide, is incomparably more coherent with his invocation of nineteenth-century Marxism and Lenin, when he says 'how beautiful she was!' and you don't know whether he's talking about the Revolution or the young Lara.

3. The judgements to which an explicit world-view is entrusted are almost indifferently voiced by various characters or by the author. As with the thesis about the age of the individual inaugurated by Christianity, a thesis from the philosophy of history that we successively encounter in the voice of Vedenyapin (p. 18), Gordon (p. 117) and Sima Tuntseva (p. 370); or the judgement about the revolution which shifts from Zhivago to Lara (p. 365), or about Lenin, from Zhivago to Strelnikov (p. 413). But not just the judgements, the actual tone of some dialogues is often interchangeable. It is often difficult to attribute an exchange to particular characters. Scenes—especially the love scenes between Zhivago and Lara—take on an intense and uniform coloration, becoming veritable duets, such as one might encounter in lyrical opera. We could even speak (to the extent it is possible when dealing with a translation) of a juxtaposition of styles: the 'popular' characters (Ustinya on p. 133; Bacchus, p. 245; Pamphil, p. 314; Kubarikha, p. 326; Vassya, p. 420; Tanya, p. 456) all speak in the same way, in a laborious and rough, immediate and coquetting language like Shakespeare's commoners, while the 'tragic' characters speak in a uniformly elevated language. Entire episodes borrow this dramatic character from Elizabethan theatre; I am thinking of the brief episodes in the village, the scene of the conspiracy of the partisans but, especially, the part that follows Zhivago's return to Yuryatin, where entrances and exits (of Komarovsky, Lara, Strelnikov) follow each other as in Dostoyevskyan 'theatre'.

4. It is tempting to argue that the book never received its final revision—especially in the final pages—or that there were editorial interventions or compromises. Consider, for example, the details of the clash between the partisans and the Whites when Yury Zhivago picks up the rifle and shoots. This part is of significance; decisive for the character and wilfully elusive. Besides the absence of motivation—which makes it difficult to explain why Zhivago, a 'sympathizer' just a few months prior, desires the victory of the Whites, without any declared reason other than the wish to remain aloof from the civil war—Zhivago's incoherence is articulated in two distinct moments, the second of which begins precisely when he, with customary precision, starts to shoot down the branches of the tree that stands in the middle of the battlefield. While taken separately the two moments are acceptable, together they are contradictory. The psychological balance that governs the actions of the characters in the rest of the book means that we cannot find Zhivago's gratuitous act convincing.

Moreover, it is difficult to grasp the meaning of the final part. From the moment of his return to Moscow, Zhivago is presented as a man undergoing progressive mental and moral decadence, as demonstrated by his 'approximate' matrimony; and we can understand why Pasternak chooses to summarize, or to barely hint at the dark twilight story. But later, after Zhivago receives help from his brother, all of a sudden we witness an intense resumption of intellectual activity, unrelated to the environing circumstances, more asserted than motivated . . . And this wilful imprecision comes to a conclusion in the ambiguous 'five or ten years later' which, like an insignificant aside, opens the book's last page.

Or perhaps this is an integral part of Pasternak's narrative technique which, applying a thin and neutral layer of colour, quickly covers over the edges of the book the better to foreground the parts that are treated instead with a richer impasto, in keeping with a taste that was not uncommon in European painting during the years of the writer's formation and youth.

5. A deficient, badly constructed book, which begins in one way, develops in another, only to conclude in a third register; full of unexplained incoherencies; featuring a plot lacking in verisimilitude and replete with diverse materials.

And yet it is a living book, with passages of immense scope, and at least one character who is—to use the common expression—unforgettable: Lara. A book that does not fit, or that fits badly, in traditional categories or in those of yesterday's and today's avant-gardes, and therefore a book which one does not stop rereading in order to hunt down its difficult secret.

Perhaps, I tell myself, this secret is really to be sought in what many have taken to be one of its defects, namely, the lyricism of its descriptions and the tragic-dramatic structure of some scenes.

When I speak of the lyricism of the descriptions, I am thinking especially of the liveliness of the landscapes (and the poetry of Pasternak, the verse poet). No one will argue that this lyricism is superimposed, or juxtaposed, to the properly narrative movement. Reread, for example, paragraphs 18 to 26 of Chapter 7, 'The Journey': 'All at once the weather and the scenery changed' (p. 210)—this is the theme of the thaw and drowsiness. There follows a long descriptive passage (par. 19), on the 'reawakening' of the wood and the hills, which makes way for successive sensations of sleepiness and awakening in Yuri, interlaced with the speeches of the travellers. In the background, the waterfall, the rumble of the waters, 'freshness and freedom' (par. 21, p. 212). The voices, the noise of the water, then that of the armoured train; again sleep overtakes and on awakening a scrum of people, and 'commotion'; but onto these is superimposed the wild cherry tree in blossom (par. 22). Another page of dialogue, of 'chronicle', intercut with the vision of a river that has overflowed its banks, of wild ducks (par. 23). Then another paragraph (par. 24) and we are back with the waterfall but this time it is the flight of Vassya, the boy, that dominates; finally, in the midst of the 'young coppice' (par. 25), the excited happiness of the passengers who descend to cut the wood. In this dense and seemingly disordered score, the thawing nature is a character, a projection of Yury's hopes, the allegory of a secret peace. It is worth noting that nature here is never, or almost never, felt as the place for a pagan identification; it is a 'forest of symbols', not an irrational mother.[5] Neither Yury nor the other characters hanker after it as a sensual life-spring; on the contrary, the very word 'life', often repeated in Pasternak's work, rarely takes on a 'vitalist' meaning. It signifies the stratification rather than the multiplicity of the real. What's more, there is a rather significant passage in which nature, that is, 'everything else' (p. 310) takes on Lara's lineaments. Often that nature bears the mark of human history like the 'stony platform' (p. 319) where the partisan firing squad carries out its execution, or as in that passage where we read: 'Only nature had remained true to human history and had kept the aspect which contemporary artists had portrayed' (p. 341).

We have put our finger on what to my mind is the most particular and deepest meaning of the poetry of this book. It is not to be found in the opposition between the anti-history or sacred history of the 'eternal'[6] man and the history of political events or class struggles (as is the wont of the interpretation advanced by a vulgar spiritualism) but, rather, in the opposition between vulgar historicism, which justifies any present whatsoever, and a broader vision of history. This, after all, is what poetry always does. Like talk of 'nature', recurrent reference to the origins of Christianity as a historical event, to Russian culture—the ancient Slavic of religious hymns, medieval chronicles, and the great literature of the nineteenth century (which elicits from Pasternak some piercing critical remarks)—and finally to the history of socialism tends to suggest a historical dimension opposed to the unbridled attention to current events. If we take the arguments of his characters literally, it is easy to see the errors and limits of Pasternak's philosophy of history, with its Vico-like returns to barbarism. But we would be guilty of gross naivety if we accused Pasternak of excluding from his book the essence of the conflicts of his time.

Pasternak, who certainly is no Marxist, nonetheless expresses a real and current conflict. His is no mere epicedium.

6. The book has a thesis, if that's how one wishes to term the 'whence' that determines the 'whither', to employ an expression from Lukács. It is a familiar thesis which can even seem banal: There is an inalienable value in the existence of men, which must be affirmed and defended; this value does not stem from a biological element but a spiritual one, because it is produced by the history of men, of mankind, which has made them what they are. Lastly, this value is revealed in the highest forms of inter-humanity, one of which is love. This is the meaning of 'be loyal to immortality, which is another word for life' (p. 18) and of 'the love of one's neighbour—the supreme form of living energy' (p. 19), Vedenyapin's words in the first few pages of the novel.

This position or perspective, the product of a particular secular humanism informed by a religious spirit (or, better, by Kantian moralism), is not new to European culture, it must explicitly be referred to the age the book assigns to it, namely, the first 15 years of the century and to that particular form of non-Marxist Russian culture that was readying itself to confront the Revolution to which the likes of Gorky were no strangers.

Positions of this kind are more than familiar to us because they have been repeated in every language and every variation for at least 30 or 40 years over the whole spectrum of the liberal-Christian, social-personalist, anarcho-socialist intelligentsia; to encounter them seemingly unchanged in the pages of a non-Marxist like Boris Pasternak or of a Marxist like Tibor Déry[7] raises a question of method. Is the 'thesis', if that's what we wish to call it, of a Pasternak or Déry the same as those of a Camus, a Vittorini, a Silone, etc.? If a positive answer to this question is more than an empty congressional or convivial motion, it would mean that East and West meet in substance and in front of 'eternal humanity', that socialism and capitalism are equal oppressions, etc. This is in fact the conclusion cherished by a good number of the authors of Western 'humanism'. But if instead our answer is 'no' and we accept, as the undersigned does, that the communist (and in particular the Soviet) 'world' is qualitatively different than the Western 'world', both at the level of institutions and ethos, then we will have to conclude that it has never been as true as in this instance that two people who say the same thing do not say the same thing.[8] The sociohistorical reality that immediately surrounds Pasternak's book determines and modifies it. It is enough to note that the theses of Camus, Vittorini, Silone, etc., are largely shared as a starting-point by the potential public of their books, while for Pasternak and Déry it is legitimate to suppose a considerable degree of rejection or resistance by their readers. As for the official literary and political authorities, we all know how they reacted. In other words, the whole world is not a village. It is one thing to speak of humanism, freedom and socialism from within a society that has not lived or undergone a socialist revolution, and something else to have actively or passively lived through the experience of the revolution. The possibility of misunderstanding should therefore not surprise us, for example (with the secret satisfaction of those who are impatient to agree with the governing authorities of the USSR or Hungary) voices like those of Pasternak or Déry seem to agree with those who among us, denying the possibility of a collective progress of human consciousness, are seized by panic when faced with the advances of technical progress or the frightening possibilities of control that the contemporary world is bringing forth; they clutch onto one of the many by-products of mysticism in order not to see that the struggle for the mastery of the instruments of technical progress and collective control is of a piece with the struggle for socialism. But the decisive difference is this: Pasternak and Déry do not despair of this possibility; instead, they view their own work and vicissitudes as episodes in the struggle for the liberation and realization of man. Is it not highly significant that the themes of alienation and guilt are absent from *Doctor Zhivago*? That Zhivago does not feel responsible for his social condition, or that the voice of unhappy consciousness (typical of the decadent intellectual) is mute? Consciously or otherwise, in practice—that is to say, in poetry—the positivity of socialism is no longer under discussion. It is simply that Pasternak and Déry must fight against mendacity and crime, and they do so at the price of life or liberty with the only political instrument at their disposal: literature. 'The truth is only sought by individuals, and they break with those who do not love it enough' (p. 18), says a character in *Doctor Zhivago*. Let's not make the mistake of thinking that this phrase is the same as the one that can be found in the final pages of Gide's *Journal*: It is not a paean to isolation, but its acknowledgment and indictment, the indictment of political tyranny and of a worse-than-imperfect siting of 'solitude' in the human community.[9] That phrase is written in praise of truth, not of solitude; and the truth it demands from the socialist is by no means that of solitude but of a choice and a historical-political judgement. The judgement is the following: To the degree that Pasternak and Déry are right (at least to that degree), is that part of communism which considers the pages of these writers as enemy pages, a dead branch and obstacle to socialist progress or not? And are the non-Marxist Pasternak and the Marxist Déry, or are they not, also an expression of the forces that hope for that progress, even if the latter do not recognize themselves or only partly in their words—forces in whose existence and capacity it is no longer possible to doubt?

It is impossible to understand anything about this book if one is unaware that the literary artifice thanks to which a drama that consumed the Russian conscience in the 1930s has been retro-dated to the Civil War and the 1920s (which explains a fair few anachronisms and incongruities) is a product of the desire to broaden as far as possible the temporal arc of the novel, to conjoin 1903 and 1943. Zhivago is the progressive petty-bourgeois intellectual of 1905 and 1917, but he is also the foe of the state art of the Stalinist period and of the (ultimately futile) moral compromises of his friends Gordon and Dudorov; Strelnikov is the extremist intelletual of the Civil War, but he is also the man of the 'old guard' destroyed by Stalin only 20 years later.

In Pasternak we can certainly find the idea that the history of socialism should be led back to the history of Christianity, and that Christianity represented the greatest and perhaps the only revolution in human history; but in the reality of his novel, this thesis is almost devoid of significance, what matters is the desperate defence of his own person and affections that a man like Zhivago carries out in the face of an upheaval—war and revolution and civil war—that tends materially to annihilate him, and when he is face to face with the formulaic men of constituted power. If we read the novel as a 'private history of the age of revolution and civil war', that individualism, that 'atrophied social sense' (p. 305) appears to us historically identifiable with bourgeois individualism and egotism. But if we read it—as it was written and as it must be read—from within the already constituted society, the socialist one, we discover that individualism is not defended against a 'collectivist barbarism' as a right to subjectivity and anarchy, but advanced as a warning and a value for the very society for which these texts were written, namely, Soviet society. Art 'is concerned not with man but with the image of man. The image of man, as becomes apparent, is greater than man', Pasternak had written in 1931, in *Safe Conduct*.[10] What does this phrase signify, in connection to *Doctor Zhivago*, if not the announcement of a proposal of integration for communist civilization, one which no poet of the pre-communist West, that is, of our world has yet been able to or would be able to or, most importantly, would be in his rights to make?

7. Piovene and Cassola[11] have underscored the simplicity and bluntness of the novel's characters, one of the book's most prominent and vital contradictions: the introverted intellectual incapable of practical decisions (Zhivago) and the poet nourished by the culture of European decadentism and the whole tradition of the avant-garde (Pasternak) do not even pose themselves the classical dilemma of decadentism—health or sickness?—they call health health, and sickness sickness. Their individuality and that of the other characters enjoys a high degree of homogeneity. Even their contradictions, so to speak, are simple. What is absent is the contemplation of death, horror or abnormality, the dissociation—typical of Western literature—between the in-itself and for-itself. The moral foundations of the main characters—with exception of the 'villain' Komarovsky—are those of self-respect and love of one's neighbour; Zhivago and Lara love each other and they also love their two families, their personal drama is framed and unfolded with the moral clarity that allows Zhivago and Antipov to talk about the woman they both love, as of their youth, Russia and the Revolution. Each of the three main characters has their shadow side, their sins: Zhivago, his intellectual pride, a 'delirium of immobility' that makes him increasingly passive in the face of events until the decadence of his final years; Lara, her obscure absent-mindedness, a kind of hidden (and morbid) wound left behind by the sad experience with Komarovsky, who finally takes her away with him and forces her to abandon her daughter; Strelnikov, the tragic and pitiless abstractness of Nechaev's heir, the absence of that 'unprincipled heart—the kind of heart that knows of no general cases, but only of particular ones, and has the greatness of small actions' (p. 226). And yet you can sense in each of them a dimension, a human scale incomparably superior to that of the

protagonists of our Western literature; what is rightly called a Shakespearean force that signifies freshness or breadth of feelings, integrity. Piovene is very right to recall, with reference to the men of communist countries (and in particular, I would add, the Russians), an 'extraordinary intensity of personal life' which recovers 'a simpler sense of life, which is serious and ancient and therefore more modern than the one which by custom and conformism we still call modern; and a more direct, and I would say more lyrical, consciousness of subjective man, which does not have the least relationship with the individualism of misanthropes and neurasthenics'. This is the intensity revealed to the Europe of 80 and 50 years ago by Russian writers and revolutionary intellectuals and which lies behind the charm felt by every traveller who journeys across those countries, with the obvious proviso (still worth repeating) that the terrible ordeals of socialist construction, and its results, have extended to a whole people—or at least to an ample elite within it—the ethos that had belonged to heroic minorities. It must be said and repeated: Collective political-economic repression and compulsion was matched by an extraordinary empowerment of individualities. Except that we continue, despite everything (that is, despite Christianity) to have an image of the individual inherited from the notion of bourgeois property, continually shifting from the abstract Man of various metaphysics to what Noventa called the John Doe Soul of every John Doe.[12] So that when Pasternak lays claim to the 'Christian' individual against the 'peoples', the 'fathers of the peoples' and the 'chiefs', he fights against the 'Egyptian' conceptions of Stalinism but in the name of a past which is a future: 'the future of man is love'. In that future Christian intersubjectivity and socialist intersubjectivity are united.

Of course, these 'ideas' would remain mere ideas, which is to say, artistically barren, if they were—as they often are—only on the lips of the characters; the greatness of the book lies in having embodied them in its pages, over long sections and rich passages. We must therefore point towards the stylistic instruments of this incarnation, the instruments that orient the book, as I have said, towards drama and lyric; they are the dialogue, as a form of (dramatic) intersubjectivity, and description, as the form of the unity of individuals bound within the lyrical situation.

8. The fragmentation of personalities and the destruction of objective time, to which the contemporary novel has inured us in favour of subjective time, are here replaced by objective fractures that historical movement determines within the lives of the characters,[13] and by the accelerations and decelerations the time of calendars undergoes in order to become, as Lukács terms it, 'historical time'. Here is the reason for the intricate web of coincidences and sometimes mechanical and paradoxical recognitions (no more so, it must be said, than those of classical theatre). Those cases serve as allegories of radical intersubjectivity where one character really extends into another and by moving modifies the motions of the others, as in a celestial mechanism. Then Russia becomes the scene for these situations, which are not so much providential as signs of the responsibility of all towards all: 'You in others are yourself, your soul. This is what you are' (p. 70).

Another mode of this unity is given by metaphor, that is to say, by the relationship with nature. Here too we have neither pantheism nor communion in the great whole. The woods, the hours, the snows are violently invested by the culture of the characters and authors, violently humanized and historicized. Nature is the projection of one of the deepest demands of the two protagonists and the author, the aspiration to a deeper, slower and more organic time for human love than the one that calendars and wars permit. 'Man does not live in a state of nature but in history' (p. 19). Nature is not anti-history but a deceleration of current events. This has been called Romanticism (and there is certainly a ring of Schelling). The chorus of metaphors and images follows the steps and thoughts of the characters, spinning a web of solidarity around them. These are

Baudelaire's *regards familiers*, not a paradise lost but a paradise promised.[14]

9. That is why this book-poem seems to come from afar and to speak of the future. To the end, as you read and reread, you have the impression that you need to let time do its work, as Pasternak-Zhivago says about Pushkin and Chekhov's 'apples picked green from the tress' (p. 259).

I think that *Zhivago*'s rhapsodic nature will become ever more apparent, its lack of unified narrative structure, the element of improvisation and juxtaposition that makes itself particularly felt in the first and last parts. What will remain are great fragments (and a great character): Moscow in 1917, the entire journey to the Urals, the whole section on the 'Forest Brotherhood' (with the extraordinary pages on the firing squad and the spell and that dizzying regression to medieval madness), the nights of Varykino, the pages on Vassya and Zhivago's return to Moscow. In those parts, that is to say, in the substance of the book there is that 'vegetal' nature that Pasternak attributes to history. Something rich and irregular, casual and necessary, oblique, mobile.[15]

Something 'living'—in the dense and contradictory sense, serious to the point of tragic rupture and humble to the extent of the most unassuming everydayness (splendid and modest like Lara, as both the dazzling beauty and the woman burdened by her domestic work) which, from his first book onward, Pasternak granted to the word *life*, the etymological roots of the name of his character,[16] a meaning that is synonymous with truth as in the Gospels. This life and truth of Pasternak can appear as a mystical experience, an invocation of invisible powers. And that is probably why the author for many years, in order to survive, could only reply: 'I have no excuses to make to you'. But for how many have those notions in the meantime become—perhaps once again—nourishment? Inasmuch as we believe that in the Soviet Union, or perhaps here among us, there is a nascent or already mature line of men, ready to know that 'love is the future of man', and to treat this not as matter of mere taste but as a poetics and a politics, will these notions not be, or in part already have been, tested and verified?

1958

Postscriptum

For some of the critics and writers who have dealt with the novel, it seems to have served as a pretext for theses about poetics. Cassola has seen it as the revenge of poetry over ideology; Calvino[17] has taken it as an occasion for one of those declarations of ignorance dear to him (about 'decadentism'), which in proper rhetoric are called preteritions, and yet do not stop him from ideologizing, while others beat their chests. It can be concluded that ideas about narrative literature, about its situation and prospects, are rather confused and that Pasternak's novel is a lousy occasion to debate them, given its enigmatic structure, the indisputable intellectual and poetic excellence of many of its parts, the weakness of others. In short, the judgements can be divided into two groups: those who see a meteor and those who see a fossil. The first—who also tend to accentuate the positive judgement or the positive moment in their judgement—recognize the 'eternal freedom' of poetry shining forth in the book, the spirit that blows where it wants, the expression of something that by nature and definition escapes historico-ideological categories and which comes from above or beneath them; this is the case, for example, of the positions of Piovene and Cassola. The second group of critics underscore their own perplexity and the nineteenth-century traits of the book. When they do not conceal their admiration for some of its parts, they end up like Calvino, either with a tendentious reduction that stresses beyond what the letter of the text permits the complexity of the admittedly central figure of Lara and downplaying the value of the second part of the book in favour of the first, thereby inverting the judgement of the first group; or with a 'historical' liquidation, when they see in the still traditional 'form' of Pasternak's novel something that only the anti-historical and authoritarian Stalinist cultural dictatorship would have kept alive in the USSR while the rest of the world 'moved forward'. The men of the meteor wield Pasternak against the avant-garde; while those of the fossil, obviously, do so to the avant-garde's advantage.

What's curious is that the two groups, in the guise of an apparent irreconcilability, lend each other a hand: the anti-ideologism of the first, with its 'artistic' or 'poetic' prejudice has, or would like to have, a 'historicist' coda in which Pasternak would be the 'truth' of today's Soviet society, the twin of the anarcho-existentialist-vitalist 'truth' of much European and American leftish (but anti-communist) protest literature; while the curious critical canon of the second—opposing the 'old' and the 'new', and wanting to be young at any price—reveals, consistently with its basic neo-empiricism and against its own apparent historicism, a refusal of interrelations. For them literature is literature, a dog is a dog, and just as dogs are divided into bastards and pure-breds, so is literature good or bad, and that is all.

Try to argue instead, as I do, that the poetic quality of *Doctor Zhivago*, its feeling of air and greatness, its complexity and simplicity are not the breath of Spirit in the head of Pasternak but the form assumed by a content—the contradictory and terrible, miserable and august content of the history of the Soviet world and of its society; that moreover there can be no history of literary forms with their relative progress and regression but only a history of contents, that is to say, of culture or at most a phenomenology of genres (so that it makes no sense to speak of the synchrony or asynchrony of Pasternak's book). You will gain a reputation, as I certainly have, of being a late or pseudo-Lukácsian—when as we know even the least experienced high-school student has imbibed with his mother's milk the certainty that the old Hungarian, like his old master Hegel, understood nothing about aesthetics and little about literature.

Or perhaps, even the most authorized Lukácsian in Italy, namely, Cases will chide me, confirming 'in the final analysis' the decadent traits of the novel and aligning himself, albeit by a very different route, with the extremely reductive criticisms of many communists and ex-communists. It is clear then that beyond or before critical argument there is the allergy, or the elective sympathy, for the 'odour of sanctity' rising from the pages of *Doctor Zhivago*.

In the end, we are left with the ghost of Boris Pasternak. But those who are persuaded that the value of great works does not simply consist 'in achieved harmony, in the questionable unity of form and content, inner and outer, individual and society, but in those traits in which the discrepancy emerges, in the necessary failure of the passionate striving for identity',[18] can today shut the pages of that book and continue the dialogue, with themselves or with other men and other books, certain that in the future they will again find within that novel the signs of greatness, of 'passionate striving' and 'necessary failure'.

1958

Notes

Originally published in *Comunità* 12(58) (March 1958). *Comunità* was a journal founded by Adriano Olivetti in 1946 as the organ of his political project, the Movimento di Comunità. It closed when its founder died in 1960. [Trans.]

1 Boris Pasternak, *Doctor Zhivago* (Max Hayward and Manya Harari trans) (London: Collins Harvill, 1988), p. 275. [Page numbers in brackets in the text are from this edition. Some translations have been modified to follow the Italian version more closely.]

2 Mario Alicata (1918–66), literary critic, head of the Italian Communist Party's Cultural Commission, and director of its newspaper *L'Unità*. As emblem and enforcer of communist cultural orthodoxy, he was the frequent object of Fortini's criticism. [Trans.]

3 Guido Piovene (1907–74), writer and journalist. [Trans.]

4 Romans 14:22. [Trans.]

5 An allusion to Baudelaire's poem's 'Correspondences' in *The Flowers of Evil*. [Trans.]

6 See the polemics about Tolstoy by the Hegelian Marxist Mikhail Lifshitz and the Yugoslav critic Josip Vidmar in *Littérature Soviétique* 9 and 10 (1957). It is well known that Lifshitz is very close to Lukács's critical positions.

7 I am referring especially to the central pages against the 'morphinomaniacs of the future' and the 'wolves of mankind' in the short story *Drôle d'enterrement*, published in December 1957, January and February 1958 issues of *Les lettres nouvelles*; and in Italian, in p. 201 of *Il gigante* [The Giant] (Milan 1956), a work that Italian literary scholars—in one of those silent gestures of unanimity that speak volumes about the comedy of their fake conflicts—have decided to leave for another generation. [English translation: Tibor Déry, 'A Gay Funeral' in *The Portuguese Princess and Other Stories* (Kathleen Szasz trans.) (London: Calder and Boyars, 1966), pp. 167–224.]

8 As for those who today (in 1965) would deny that qualitative difference the author can only refer them to the pages of 'Radek's Hands' and 'The Writers' Mandate'.

9 The political indictment and polemic in *Doctor Zhivago*, especially in the last part, is far from negligible. Not to feel the coldness and violence, in Italy some gloss over it in silence (the USSR has a broad back), the others (those with the greatest praise for the book) glide over it, with aestheticizing generosity.

10 Boris Pasternak, *Safe Conduct: An Autobiography and Other Writings* (New York: New Directions, 1958), p. 54. Fortini is quoting from a translation in Italian (from the English version of Pasternak's text) which appeared in *Politecnico* 35 (1947). [Trans.]

11 Guido Piovene, 'Lettera aperta a G.B. Angioletti' [Open Letter to G.B. Angioletti], *La stampa* 14(43) (19 February 1958): 3; Carlo Cassola, 'Dibattito sul *Dottor Zivago*' [Debate on *Doctor Zhivago*], *Il ponte* 14(4) (April 1958): 526–38. [Trans.]

12 *l'Anima Tizia di ogni Tizio* [Trans.]

13 '[C]hildren are children and the terrors are terrible' (p. 463), says a character's daughter. In the whole book, the characters' misadventures find their objective ground in their practical 'cases'—war, prison, etc.

14 Like the earlier reference to the 'forest of symbols', this allusion to 'familiar gazes' also comes from Baudelaire's poem 'Correspondences'. [Trans.]

15 This resonates with the non-superficial artistic taste that in central Europe and the Germanic world was at the source, at the end of the nineteenth century, of the Secession, and then of Expressionism, of Klimt first and Kandinsky or, rather, Kokoschka after. How much of the Scandinavians makes its way to Pasternak, for example, from Jens Peter Jacobsen's *Niels Lyhne* (1880)? But the task of following up the countless cultural components of *Zhivago*'s prose would be endless, especially as the book harbours a far greater expertise about contemporary literary tendencies than a hasty reading might betray.

Revising the proofs for this book I read in *L'Europa Letteraria* 33 the letter that Pasternak addressed to Jacqueline de Proyart on 20 May 1959 about his *oeuvre*, where he speaks of 'universal turbulence', of 'reality as the embodied and rotating spectacle of an inspiration, as an apparition moved by a kind of choice and freedom'. A confirmation of, among other things, the great critical intelligence that lay behind the novel.

16 'Zhivago' is derived from the Russian word *zhiv*, meaning 'alive'. [Trans.]

17 Italo Calvino, 'Pasternak e la rivoluzione' [Pasternak and Revolution], *Passato e presente* 3 (May–June 1958): 360–74 (reprinted in *Saggi*, pp. 1361–82). [Trans.]

18 Max Horkheimer and Theodor W. Adorno, *Dialectic of Enlightenment: Philosophical Fragments*, (Edmund Jephcott trans.) (Stanford: Stanford University Press, 2002), p. 103.

III

Notes on Proust

(a) *Proust as Critic*

We know that Proust did not believe in friendship; similarly, as his life wore on, his belief in intelligence progressively faded. That was obviously the best way to enjoy friendship and be intelligent. But in order not to confuse the argument with an all-too-hasty classification (for what is the decadentism which reappears, like an unwanted ectoplasm, in all our snapshots if not also the theory of the artist and writer as Lazarus, the provisional corpse, the one to whom everything can be restored but only on condition of having lost everything—faith, love, friendship, intelligence, etc.?), we need to ask whether when it came to friendship or intelligence and other such virtues and powers, Proust devalued them absolutely or only at the end of a very private search for happiness.

He does not even believe in books, or at least the more he loves them: 'The taste for books seems to grow as intelligence grows, a bit lower down but on the same stalk'.[1] That was for him the best way to enjoy books, and to write about them. But what did such prideful mistrust aim at? Was there a truth, in the face of which all particular values turned into splendid vices? I think that a reading of Proust's criticism confirms the affirmative reply that the reader of the *Recherche* could already give.

First of all, the force of his critical writings lies precisely in those aspects that provoke the most basic objections: in the attitude that stems from an apparently irresponsible subjectivism of taste. Proust knows that he cannot clear a path towards poetry-truth except through the narrow door of autobiography, pushed to the borders of the ineffable; he knows that he can affirm the plurality of states of consciousness only by continuing to say and to write 'I'. It suffices to read his observations on Nerval: 'the atmosphere of *Sylvie*, a colouring in the air like the bloom of a grape . . . is all among the words, like the morning mist at Chantilly',[2] or on Flaubert: 'Those heavy materials that the sentence . . . lifts and drops with the intermittent noise of a mechanical digger',[3] or on Goethe: 'We often come on a place where there is a wide and varied prospect. Valleys extend before us, with villages and a fine river on which the light of morning dazzles, and we look down on all this from a little mountain'.[4] But what am I saying? It's enough to recall any volume of the *Recherche*. They are examples of reproductive criticism. Proust, gathered in his corner, puts his trust only in his own neurosis and taste, defining himself line after line as an amateur who confused reading with the atmosphere of reading, the taste of poetry with that of a café au lait, pushing his naive coquetry to the point of choosing his mother as his interlocutor in order to argue about Balzac or Baudelaire (but is this not a critically brilliant decision, equivalent to Molière's famous chambermaid,[5] in that imaginary dialogue with that creature 'who does not know' what he, Marcel, knows all too well, and which at the same time, like Françoise, 'knows' everything that for Marcel is irrecuperable . . . ?). And yet he is on his way towards values that transcend or negate that mawkish aestheticism, those subtleties good for *Le Figaro*.

For example, his manner of reading the authors of the past often appears not to differ from his way of living in a room in the country -side, enjoying it not for what it has in common with him, but for the difference he feels within it. However, his words—'I cannot live and think except in a room where everything is the creation and language of existences profoundly different from my own, whose taste is opposed to mine, where my fantasy is exhilarated by feeling itself immersed in the non-I'—offer us the key to a miraculous emergency exit, the *clé des champs*[6] that allows the recluse and asthmatic to understand what his society, his culture, his milieu of snobs and aesthetes would have never allowed him to grasp. For example, to discern in Baudelaire a great classic, a poet 'for the people and for the beyond'[7] (one should reflect today, half a century later, on the formidable critical density of this formula!), to feel, notwithstanding the irony and rebellion of 'taste', the greatness and truth of a Balzac, to contest the mystical aestheticism of a nonetheless admired Ruskin ('I do not venerate the hawthorn, I go to see it and smell it'[8]), to affirm with all his energies the supra-individual character of poetry to the point of making the life of poetry coincide with that of a single poet. How we were deceived by those who spoke to us of Proust's 'fragmentation of personality'! If we do not forget (as Bernard de Fallois remarks in his introduction to the volume under review) that Proust is the author of a single book and almost all of his critical writings, including *Jean Santeuil*, form a single matrix, a single monologue, a single 'monster' fated to morph into the *Recherche*, then we can recognize what a unitary lesson of intersubjectivity and totalizing discourse he has left us. It is a lesson that most of us today—let us admit it—refuse. But we, the administrators of our meagre allotments, are wrong. These critical pages speak *de unitate intellectus.*

An example: It is impossible not to note that for Proust 'the most beautiful thing in *L'Éducation sentimentale* is not a sentence, but a blank',[9] the one that runs between the moment when Frédéric Moreau recognizes Sénécal in the agent who attacks Dussardiers with his sabre, and the following paragraph and chapter, 'He travelled. He came to know the melancholy of steamers'. 'He returned. He frequented the world', etc. Lukács has written in his *The Meaning of Contemporary Realism*:

> The possibility of realism, as we know, is bound to that minimal hope of a change for the better offered by bourgeois society. We have seen that in avant-garde art this

> perspective disappears altogether. The structure of *L'Éducation sentimentale* shows that Flaubert had prophetically anticipated and represented this development . . . during the night of the barricades . . . [t]he realistic novel is done with; Frédéric Moreau begins his *Recherche du temps perdu.*[10]

Proust looks at the 'blank' and sees in the transition carried out by Flaubert—whom he 'does not love much' but about whom he makes some admirable stylistic observations—the capacity to rid oneself of the 'detritus of history' and to render the impression of Time with rare efficacy. That point of view seems immensely distant from Lukács, who in that clause and that return sees an entire historical process 'prophetically anticipated and represented'. For Proust the most beautiful thing about the Flaubertian novel is, basically, his own date of birth. But it means that Proust and Lukács are saying the same thing! However, it is not yet clear to Proust that the Time whose currents he feels coursing through Flaubert's paragraphs is not any time whatsoever but his own social time, the ominous category that he will be obliged to explore and which begins to gnaw at European hearts in the immediate wake of the barricades of 1848, with a fear that will never again be vanquished, an insecurity that will never again be sloughed off. Just as Lukács does not yet see or, better, feigns not to see that if the *recherche du temps perdu* begins at that point for Frédéric Moreau, the discovery of that time is in fact one of the greatest fruits of the struggle between bourgeoisie and proletariat and one of the foundations of the greatness of Proust's poetry.

1958

(b) *Translating* La Fugitive[11]

Mais si la promenade de la petite bande avait pour elle de n'être qu'un extrait de la fuite innombrable de passantes, laquelle m'avait toujours troublé, cette fuite était ici ramenée

> *à un mouvement tellement lent qu'il se rapprochait de l'immobilité.*[12]

1. What if in order to understand Proust we had to seek out the memory of our first imperfect reading? Of my own, 20 years ago, when I was 20 years of age. Not because the vast critical bibliography stands as an obstacle, as it does with so many great writers; ignorance would be a sufficient shield. But precisely because we think we now know something about the structure of the *Recherche* and every rereading is tendentious, already knowing what it's looking for. In reading Proust as one might consult an encyclopedia, not so much hunting down 'selected passages' as individual elements, the immensely useful summaries of the Pléiade edition are harmfully helpful as are the indexes of names and places. We lose something that belonged to our first reading and especially to the first readings of Proust's contemporaries: boredom or impatience, feeling stifled, or wanting to retreat.

To explain some physical phenomena that the theory of phlogiston had rendered mysterious, at the end of the eighteenth century it was ascribed something like a negative weight: when phlogiston left a body, the latter instead of diminishing increased in weight. The hypothesis comes to mind when I reflect on the impact of my first readings of Proust—the march through the pages, notwithstanding its apparent accelerations, tends to slow down to zero and then enter into negative values, and the more you go *forward* (for you do go 'forward' after all) the more you go *backward.* It is as though, in order to become as translucent as air within air, Proust's construction had required that immense abundance of details, which in the end seem (or rather, want to be) almost futile. Even if the conjecture that Proust elaborated the plan of his work like that of a Gothic cathedral turned out to be true, the intention to hide that plan under the creepers of the transitions appears as almost too successful. Avoiding that suffocation reported by his first readers, that negative acceleration in the memory of our own first reading, could only mean avoiding one of the essential components of Proust: the imitation of the multiplicity and dense presence of life, required in order to deceive the reader and allow him the salutary experience of disillusion. But all of this would not set Proust apart from Balzac if the density of objects, events and sensations were not a density of *reasonings*. Unlike Joyce or Musil, in whom encyclopedic ambition stems from the experience of a *descensus* to nothingness and a thoroughgoing scepticism about knowledge, what makes Proust's encyclopedic urge both powerful and harrowing is that it originates in a cultural universe whose structures are for Proust ultimately not in doubt. And that is why he dons the mask of (relative) futility. It was the ensuing decades, as they clarified the aporias of the culture of advanced capitalism, that made Proust's undertaking 'true', revealing as an *itinerarium mentis*[13] what originally had probably wanted to appear as an arduous and incomparably elegant exercise for ascetic aesthetes.

Proustian 'reality', that is to say, reality for Proust, is a complex of structures, a complex structure which he (by writing) and the reader (by reading) must discover beneath its naturalistic appearance. Save that the appearance is given in an implacable ratiocination. For the Joyce of *Ulysses* one can speak of a pursuit, with different instruments, of the positivist project of verism; it is true that Proust too emerges from a naturalistic and psychologistic cultural terrain; but his first datum, his *materia prima* is judgement, in which he mediates characters, dialogues, events, objects. That is why in Proust the dialectic of phenomenon and essence is so complicated and seems to have eluded Lukács, at least in part. For Proust the phenomenal surface is always a finished product, never a datum. What can be termed as Proust's 'essayism' is nothing other than his deep and natural (in the sense of habit or second nature) inclination not to abandon any fragment of thought in its nascent or spontaneous state, but to bring it to conclusion in an exact proposition. It is as though from the inexhaustible compendia of precepts about 'good manners'—undoubtedly one of his biographical obsessions—he had retained, as a well-mannered Frenchman from the last century, the rule which prescribes that when speaking one should conclude every sentence in a syntactically correct fashion. But above all, it is as though by maintaining within a much ampler cubic volume the same definite proportions of the atoms which lyric poetry contracts into a few strophes, his writing made visible the resilient rational ligaments that in lyric poetry are such slender fibres as to deceive sight.

2. The refusal of 'plane geometry' of which Proust speaks is also the refusal of uniform motion.[14] This enemy of clock-time in fact moved like the clocks, by successive units, in discontinuous motion. The continuity effect is achieved through tendentially isochronic starts,[15] each of which is a sentence. A sentence that is never direct and paratactic but wrapped upon itself, helicoidal. Let us listen to Proust's so-called long sentence (in Spitzer's classic analysis as well, of course).[16] No matter how much the initial impulse (which aims exactly at the clause) is deflected from the start by parentheticals or subordinates and broken into multiple directions, it is still strong enough to transmit itself from one device to another, to defeat the final inertial resistances and spring forward, after a dangerous or only apparently reckless hesitation, as in those difficult acrobatic exercises where the pleasure of the onlooker is proportional to the suspense at the outcome. It is as though we were peering into a giant clock. The impetus of the mainspring engages successive serrated gears, each of which is fractionally delayed with regard to the other. And just when you thought it could not go on, all at once the hand moves, and everything has advanced by one unit. This gives way to a moment of silence, before there recommences the obstinate effort to budge once again a device dense with words. The tension or energy of each individual sentence is, as we have said, of a ratiocinating nature; it follows a classical mechanics, abhors imprecision instead of the void, locks any uncertainty into its course and reiterates itself within its clauses. But Proust reveals he has gone beyond any classical mechanics in the fluid, unstable quality of the cohesive force that binds sentence to sentence. The latter do not interlock—they are juxtaposed. The adverbs of connection (*car*, *ainsi*) are mere wedges or pretexts to recommence the internal motion of each individual microcosm. This leads to a structure that is more granular than cellular. Every sentence has its own motion, its own start; but there is no common direction. At most you get a common motion for a group of sentences when the syllogistic, cavilling intent makes what comes before transitive to what comes after. Proust's pages then appear like magnetic fields made visible by iron shavings. The magnet orients; then, having passed, it disorients.

The real Proustian transitions, the novel's sudden shifts of direction, don't happen in the interminable parentheses, or in the ovular niches of the sentence but where a stronger pause (the paragraph) is set down or where, even more abruptly, the argument changes.

The granular structure is so cohesive as to give the impression of continuity, but we are dealing with an optical illusion pure and simple. The effect of a uniform motion is consigned to the great, slow currents of the novel, or to what might be termed structural elements. For the rest, every quantum of intellectual energy must remain distinct from every other, like entries in a great dictionary, each of which can be consumed in turn. Hence the importance of the aphorism, the aside, whether it is introduced without a syntactic nexus and situated betwixt two narrative passages (*Le snobisme est une maladie grave de l'âme, mais localisée et qui ne le gâte pas toute entière*), set in parentheses (*chaque classe sociale a sa pathologie*), or presented as conclusive (*Car la vérité change tellement pour nous que les autres ont peine à s'y reconnaître*).[17] Contrary to aestheticizing interpretations, there is in Proust a desire for these thoughts, maxims, reflections, moral hypotheses, etc., to be easily extractable from the context, useable in their own right and not only as the enduring connotation of the character that says *je*, 'I'. It cannot be said often enough that what Proust wanted from the artwork was less 'poetry' and more a 'guide to the perplexed'. Accordingly, there is a primary surface of the novel which is the implacable reasoning of the character-'I' (who narrates, summarizes and anticipates but, above all, moralizes, demonstrates, interprets, comments). There is then a second stratum, that of events, each of which is enveloped by the dense narrative voice. The third stratum is the demonstrative structure or initiatory itinerary: general pedagogy or integral psychoanalysis *par le langage* (the aspect of Proust's language that vulgar Marxism rejects and that a non-vulgar Marxism should instead both understand and praise) *et par l'imitation*,[18] which comes to a conclusion in the ecstatic consciousness of one's own achieved transformation, in the *persuasion* of the Lazarus or Orpheus who has visited Hades.

(Notwithstanding its position as a 'classic', it is necessary for the *Recherche* to grow even more distant from us, like Goethe's *Wilhelm Meister* or Cao Xuequin's *The Dream of the Red Chamber*. That element which was transmitted immediately, through our fathers, from the beginning of the century, touching us like the memory of a personal experience, must disappear. Only when the fascinating surface of the work will have become either inaccessible to a reader not armed with philology or entirely spent, as once happened to much polychromatic statuary, will the deeper structures appear.)

3. The victory over time is achieved not only through the recovery of time 'lost' or with the casting of the artwork in bronze but, rather, by antiphrasis, by developing permutations which over time destroy each other, celebrating terrible but ultimately pointless victories and conversely conjuring up an identity that is gathered and whole, an instantaneous and eternal present. This is a finite universe, in the sense that all its rectilinear forces curve like light for Einstein and appear in the form of the circle. Does this mean what Proust calls his own three-dimensional geometry is nothing but a physics of the 'psychosphere', of a world beyond the visible one? This would be further proof of his strict fidelity to a French tradition, and of the relationship (even if only metaphorical) between literary creation and the exact sciences, ranging from the mechanism of Pierre Laclos to Balzac's physiologists and the 'diagnoses' of the realists. An immensely vast yet closed universe without transcendence of any kind. When some insist on the meaning of the *Recherche* as a sacred path, an initiatory and mental itinerary, they are, to my mind, saying something very true; on condition, however, of underscoring the work's strict atheism. At the root of the *Recherche* lies the magical experience of the identity of opposites, matter and spirit, death and life, instant and eternity. But it is an experience inseparable from the reading of *every* single element, from the laborious deciphering of every point on the map of existence. For Proust, it is inseparable from the very act of writing, that is to say, of exorcizing or enchanting—while apparently bending to their wishes—the forces of life's surface tensions, but in reality opposing to them an astute resistance. For the reader, it is inseparable from the model-experience that must be repeated in order to 'save' himself. Is Proust's goal the victory over time? In that case the best way of beating the 'infamous retiary'[19] is to go along with it. Whence Proust's equanimity, which apparently rejects nothing of human history and the passions of time, not only because it glimpses in every force-line the application of another line (hence the curvilinear motion of the entirety of the real), but also because the meaning of the 'great vectors' must only surface with difficulty—it must not be available to the impatient.

The strict atheism of the particulars is as though 'guaranteed' by the sacredness of the goal. Only an advocate of finalism like Proust can allow himself to scrutinize the glaring absence of apparent finality in human affairs; his cynicism, like that of true revolutionaries, is not a mask but a precise requisite of his faith.

4. Proust seems to be telling us the story of the decadence of an aristocracy and the progress of the business bourgeoisie, which assumes the trappings of its predecessor. That story was true—but in Balzac's time. That story and that conflict have no basis if referred instead to the time of the events that form the *Recherche*. Those were secondary contradictions. The real conflicts of the French society of that period were those opposing French imperialist capitalism to its German or English counterparts, and those between the propertied bourgeoisie and the anarcho-syndicalist or socialist proletariat. Just like in Germany or Italy. There is little interest in knowing whether Proust was conscious or not of those real conflicts. In other words, those conflicts did not interest him as a writer; their place is taken by the reflections, in civil society, of a type of conflict internal to a fraction of bourgeois society. Just like that seemingly sensational but ultimately superficial conflict that was the Dreyfus Affair. Reflections in the sphere of manners, of behaviour.

In truth, the conflict that Proust represents wants to be the metaphor of an eternal mode of being of society and of the individual himself, of a cycle which (let us note parenthetically) is inhabited in equal measure both by Darwinian notions of a struggle for survival and by those of the sociology of elites which, together with the theme of decadence, was the fashionable argument at the turn of the century. Though we can find some isolated allusions to a working class fated to generate, in a horizon of democratic development, new forms of aristocracy, the class antithesis that Proust presents is the well-known and archaic one between the commoner or farmer (Françoise) and the 'lords', be it the Guermantes, the Verdurins, or the narrator's family. Whether we're dealing with the wisdom of Françoise, so close to that of the major aristocrats or of the 'greatest names in France', or with the soldiers of Robert de Saint-Loup in the trenches, this antithesis resolves itself into a complementarity—in the name of a nation-civilization which if not eternal, at least enjoys an enduring vitality (there is a very strong consciousness of the *grande nation* in Proust). It is not so interesting to know from where he gets this way of thinking about the relationship between classes, even if it is easily referred to the cultural universe of bourgeois positivism and its aesthetic corollaries: '*Aussi la meilleure partie de la jeunesse, la plus intelligente, la plus désintéressée n'aimait plus que les oeuvres ayant une haute portée morale et sociologique, même religieuse*'.[20]

For Proust, the social universe is the exact equivalent of the intrigue in an opera and his ultimate ambition seems to have been that writing a Japanese or Chinese novel set in an undefined historical epoch. As long as we continue to read Proust in terms of the 'triumph of realism', to refer to his 'historiography of private life', we will achieve nothing. Lukács's evasiveness about Proust stems, I believe, from the embarrassment of having to admit that, paradoxically, what is 'recuperable' in Proust's work for a society to come is actually its enormous finalistic pretensions, its desperate ideological ambition and not just the mimesis of a society however exceptional. In sum, if the decisive conflictual figuration is the one that pits '*les passions, les caractères, les moeurs*', that is, '*les vérités que l'intelligence dégage directement de la réalité*'[21] against that other deep and ungraspable 'life' which tends to destroy them, then it is necessary to declare that the apparent primacy of the latter, and of the unconscious that generates and nourishes it is never based on a spiritualist epistemology in Proust. The world of micro-psychology, the demonic universe of the *petites sensations* is continually contested and surpassed not only towards an objectivity which, in positivist terms, Proust regard as 'scientific' but towards a 'truth'—the knowledge of the real through language.

1957–63

Notes

Section 'a' was originally published as '"Giornate di lettura" di Marcel Proust' [Marcel Proust's 'Reading Days'], *Notiziario Einaudi*

7(3) (November 1958). The Italian-language collection reviewed here is Marcel Proust, *Giornate di lettura. Scritti critici e letterari* [Reading Days: Critical and Literary Writings] (Paolo Serini ed.) (Turin: Einaudi, 1958). [Trans.]

1 Marcel Proust, 'On Reading' in Marcel Proust and John Ruskin, *On Reading* (Damion Searls ed. and trans.) (London: Hesperus, 2011), p. 31.

2 Marcel Proust, *On Art and Literature, 1896–1916* (Sylvia Townsend Warner trans.) (New York: Carroll and Graf, 1997), p. 153

3 Marcel Proust, 'À propos du "style" de Flaubert' (1920) in *Chroniques* (Paris: Gallimard, 1927), pp. 193–211.

4 Proust, *On Art and Literature*, p. 363.

5 'Molière, as a naive poet, is said to have left it in every case to the opinion of his chambermaid what should stand or fall in his comedies'—Friedrich Schiller, 'On Naive and Sentimental Poetry' in *German Aesthetic and Literary Criticism: Winckelmann, Lessing, Hamann, Herder, Schiller, Goethe* (H.S. Nisbet ed.) (Cambridge: Cambridge University Press, 1985), p. 292. [Trans.]

6 Literally, 'the key to the fields', a French expression denoting liberty and escape. [Trans.]

7 Marcel Proust, 'Concerning Baudelaire' in *Against Saint-Beuve and Other Essays* (John Sturrock trans.) (London: Penguin, 1994).

8 Marcel Proust, Translator's Preface to *La Bible d'Amiens* in *On Reading Ruskin* (Jean Autret, William Burford and Phillip J. Wolfe eds and trans) (New Haven: Yale University Press, 1989), p. 57.

9 Proust, 'À propos du "style" de Flaubert', pp. 205–6.

10 Georg Lukács, *The Meaning of Contemporary Realism*, p. 68 [translation modified].

11 Sixth volume of Proust's *In Search of Lost Time* (1913–27), also known as 'Albertine disparue' (Proust changed the original title to avoid confusion with Rabindranath Tagore's novel *The Fugitive*). Fortini's translation was published as Marcel Proust, *Alla ricerca del tempo perduto. Albertine scomparsa* (Turin: Einaudi, 1951); and in a new edition as *Alla ricerca del tempo perduto. La fuggitiva* (Paolo Serini ed.) (Turin: Einaudi, 1963). [Trans.]

12 'Though this little sauntering gang of girls was an example of the countless occasions when young passers-by had escaped my grasp, a failure which had always irked me, this time the escapers had slowed their pace almost to the point of immobility'—Marcel Proust, *In the Shadow of Young Girls in Flower: In Search of Lost Time, Volume 2* (James Grieve trans.) (London: Penguin, 2003), p. 377.

13 A journey of the soul or mind, as in the Franciscan theologian Saint Bonaventure's *Itinerarium mentis in Deum* [The Mind's Road to God] (1259). [Trans.]

14 Proust, *Against Saint-Beuve and Other Essays*, p. 234.

15 *scatti* [Trans.]

16 Leo Spitzer, 'Le Style de Marcel Proust' [Marcel Proust's Style] (1928) in *Études de style* (Paris: Gallimard, 1970), pp. 397–473

17 'Snobbery is a grave disease, but it is localized and so does not utterly corrupt the soul' (p. 8); 'every social class has its own pathology' (p. 11); 'For the truth is so variable for each of us, that other people have difficulty in recognizing what it is' (p. 15)—Marcel Proust, *The Captive & The Fugitive: In Search of Lost Time, Volume 5* (C. K. Scott Moncrieff and Terence Kilmartin trans, D. J. Enright rev.) (New York: The Modern Library, 1993). [Trans.]

18 Through language and through imitation. [Trans.]

19 *rétiare infâme*, the phrase is from Baudelaire's poem 'Le Voyage' (Voyaging) in *The Flowers of Evil* (James McGowan trans.), p. 290. A retiary, or retarius, is a Roman gladiator who fights with equipment styled on a fisherman's net (a weighted net, or 'rete'). [Trans.]

20 'the best part of the younger generation, the most intelligent and the most disinterested of them, through a change of fashion admired nothing but works with a lofty moral and sociological, even religious, significance'—Marcel Proust, *Time Regained: In Search of Lost Time, Volume 6* (Andreas Mayor and Terence Kilmartin trans, D. J. Enright rev.) (New York: The Modern Library, 2003), p. 295. [Trans.]

21 'human passions and character and conduct'; 'these truths which the intellect educes directly from reality'—ibid., p. 303. [Trans.]

IV

Tolstoy, the Master and the Man

Leo Tolstoy's profile resembles some natural or artificial phenomena like mountains or monuments, which can be recognized even when they have been reduced to a logo or a stamp, comforting us as secure and immutable things. This is the extraordinary sense of filial security we feel irrespective of our entry point into the immense beech forest that is Tolstoy's *oeuvre*.

Trust stems from the opaque awareness that the author won't leave us on the page where Ivan Ilyich dies or where the *muzhik*, along the train tracks, 'strikes the scrap iron'; the more the page grows dense, thick, imbricated with things and words, the more the other lands, the miles of Russian countryside, deserted with snow or shaken by the wind through the wheat fields, await us all around, anticipating our crossing. Tolstoy speaks to you of envy and sin, but you know he will also speak to you of love. A farmer whiles away half a page putting on his fur coat, but give him a few pages, or many, and the entire artillery of the Great Army will open fire on the redoubts of Borodino. To every thing its time: a cyclical education. There is no rush—this evening we will reach an *izba*, the night will bring us a deeper disquiet, a strange pain in our innards, or a vision that will decide the meaning of our existence. Or perhaps nothing; and, having turned the page, we will set out again in the morning on the sleigh, and we will also say, clapping our gloved hands: What a beautiful day.

Everyone hastens to repudiate the Tolstoyan doctrines of non-resistance and non-violence, or to cite them as readily understandable examples of the damage done to artistic creators great or small by moral or social philosophical doctrines, so that the supreme honesty of a Dante or a Tolstoy, having vanquished as artists the 'stupidities' of Thomism or Humanitarian evangelism, would end up in a supreme idiocy or an affectionate decree of irresponsibility. Yet between those doctrines and the sense of space and time evinced by most of Tolstoy's narrative work, there is nevertheless a direct relationship.

Someone referred to Dostoevsky's narrative-dramatic time as a maelstrom,[1] a progressive acceleration of objects, words and situations until the vortex becomes unbearable anxiety, whirling and senseless rotation and at its crowning moment there falls a lightning strike, a character or a revelation—a Chinese vase or a news story break, and we behold a *coup de théâtre* in the same way that the sacred disease[2] gestates, grows, rises and is finally unleashed. As everyone knows, the movement of Tolstoy's pages is a continuous fugue, the repetition that governs it tends to suggest an ascent but a spiralling one, as though one were discovering an ever-vaster landscape, always promising something more. In supreme abandonment to that movement, one always comes to discover that life and death coincide in one point which is the ultimate wisdom. No resistance to evil means no resistance to death, to grace or to 'simple' life. We know how Tolstoy's characters die, how the conjugal love of *Family Happiness* (1859) dies a death of age, of feelings, of individuals—an inspiring and consuming *largo*. We can read in this the extent of Tolstoy's debt to his own time, how much the horn of the last act of Wagner's *Tristan* sounded in the ears of this Scythian convert.

There is a famous and wonderful short story ('Master and Man') from 1895; foreshadowed, almost 40 years before, by 'The Snowstorm' (1856). A livestock trader and his servant are lost in a storm; the labourer will be found alive lying under his master, who dies protecting him with his own body. The external and internal construction of the story echoes the movement of 'Russian mountains'[3] or the spiral I was referring to. The first part (eight pages) is devoted to the portraits of the protagonists, two men and a horse, and it is brimming with details, pullulating, composed of long sentences, slow. They depart; and in the next six pages the road is lost, until as night falls they come upon a threshing barn. This is the motif of the storm in which the protagonists are dilated and lost. Third part, about seven pages: the journey continues, the road is mislaid again. Our travellers are back at the threshing barn. Fourth part, the pause: six pages in which the initial theme is reprised (the psychology of various characters, defined in their milieu); compact syntax and realist density of the objects.

Fifth part: repetition of the second, a new departure, a new dissolution of individuals in nature and night, another seven pages which conclude with the decision to sleep in the open.

Sixth part: in the heart of the snowy night, the immobility of the two men and the inner monologue of the master—until his decision to save himself by abandoning the labourer—recreates the 'closed' situation (equivalent for Tolstoy to sinful, negative) of the first and fourth parts. At this point there are two brief and symmetrical interludes that form the turning point (little more than two pages for the first part, the seventh chapter, and four in the second part, eighth chapter): Nikita's monologue facing his death by hypothermia. No resistance but acceptance: 'He did not know if he was dying or falling asleep; whichever it was he felt equally prepared'[4]—like Prince Andrei at the battlefield of Austerlitz. Then the monologue by Vasily, the master, his dread of death; the invocation of Saint Nicholas (i.e. Nikita, the servant he has abandoned); his flight takes him back to the point where Nikita lies. There is a repetition in miniature of what had happened at a greater scale in the second and third part, but this time the repetition is decisive. You cannot flee from the snowstorm. The two moments, the open and the closed, individual personalities and incommensurable nature, merge: the two men, lying on top of each other, are joined together and Vasily's dream is very much that conjunction and shipwreck of individuality ('he felt that he was Nikita and Nikita he'[5]). Finally, two pages of conclusion, where all the themes not only are reprised, and like at the beginning we return to daylight and collective life, but also in a final repetition we witness Nikita's death (after 20 years pass in a single line, as in a dream).

A closed strophe:

> No sooner had Nikita driven out of the gate and headed the horse towards the front steps, than Vasily Andreich, wearing a long cloth-covered sheepskin coat tightly belted with a sash low on his waist and with a cigarette in his mouth, stepped from the porch onto the tall steps which were covered with trodden snow and which creaked beneath his leather-cased felt boots. He stopped, took a last draw at his cigarette, threw down the stub and trod on it; then breathing the smoke out through his moustache and giving a sidelong glance at the horse as it came through the gate, he began tucking down the points of his fur-lined collar on either side of his ruddy face—clean-shaven but for the moustache—to prevent the fur catching the moisture from his breath.[6]

And an open strophe:

> Snow whipped up from the fields on either side and there was no telling where earth and sky began and ended. The Telyatino wood which you could always see clearly was just a dark shape vaguely discernible now and then through the clouds of powdery snow. The wind came from the left, driving Dapple's mane persistently to the right of his steep plump neck and blowing sideways his full tail which was tied in a simple knot.[7]

But the opening, dilation and dissolution eventually win out. For every one of Tolstoy's characters there is a personal apocalypse, 'a new name written on the stone',[8] and it is natural that Vasily's

'Coming, coming' full of 'joy and ecstasy' at death's door is but a minor transposition of the last word in the New Testament, the final verse of the Apocalypse.

The myth of the master and the man seems to belong to an ancient religion. The master, 'the one who stands above', covers and presses down with his body on the servant; he oppresses this 'seed beneath the snow'[9] but in dying gives him life. His death is decreed in the moment that he, the master, understands the values of his antagonist and ceases to believe in his own; but that death is also his salvation.

In the embrace of the two men, Nikita is in a certain way the female passivity of the Great Countryside, but also the absolute force to which the master cannot but cede his own heat. The death of Vasily is the symbolic death of the owning class, the price of its salvation—mystical for Tolstoy, historical for us. Not only that: a metamorphosis has taken place in the night; Nikita, owing to the nightly terror and solitude encircling Vasily, and to his own pacific acceptance of hypothermia, dominates—but in the sense of a domination of love—the man who despises him and would have let him die; and Vasily instead serves his servant. What is celebrated in that winter night is really a mystery, with that element of obscurity, tribalism and the orgiastic which lies deep in Tolstoy's nature and ties him, by many threads, to the world of decadentism. A capacity to symbolize which is also his greatest strength, to keep a story within the most straightforward veristic tradition and, at the same time, to shape it into a legend. *Master and Man* has elements of the fable, the *byline*[10] and the great historical realism of *War and Peace* (1869).

Thirty years have passed, and the intervening conversion, since the young count had begun drafting *War and Peace*. Now he writes those folk tales, meant to be his final act of proud literary humility—and the other masterpieces.

But some constants in his technique have not changed, like the downy blond hair on the lip of Elena in *War and Peace*. We find here, for example, the willows that the owner and labourer encounter

('Nikita saw that long dry willow leaves were blowing from the direction of this dark shape ahead',[11] then, after the first halt, 'they came again to the fearful soughing willows',[12] and finally, when they set off on their nocturnal drama, there again are 'the dismally soughing willows that whistled and bent in the wind'[13]). Repetition as cycle; identity in variety—resolution.

1955

Notes

Original publication in 'La verità di Tolstoj nella struttura dei suoi racconti' [Tolstoy's Truth in the Structure of his Stories], *Notizario Einaudi* 6(1) (January 1955). [Trans.]

1 'Dostoyevsky is chaos and fecundity. Humanity, with him, is but a vortex in the bubbling maelstrom'—Henry Miller, 'Letter to Pierre Lesdain' in *The Books in My Life* (New York: New Directions, 1969), p. 223. [Trans.]

2 A euphemism for epilepsy. [Trans.]

3 'Russian mountains' were a predecessor to the modern-day roller coaster; the term continues to be applied in various languages including Italian. [Trans.]

4 Leo Tolstoy, *Master and Man and Other Stories* (Ronald Wilks and Paul Foote trans) (London: Penguin, 2005), p. 271.

5 Ibid., p. 279.

6 Ibid., p. 234.

7 Ibid., p. 237.

8 Revelation 2:17. [Trans.]

9 *Il seme sotto la neve*—the title of a 1941 novel by Ignazio Silone. The reference here too is biblical, it alludes to Isaiah 55:10. [Trans.]

10 In English in the original. [Trans.]

11 Tolstoy, *Master and Man*, p. 242.

12 Ibid., p. 244.

13 Ibid., p. 255.

V

Kafka's Men and the Criticism of Things

This year, in France, there is even talk of the 'popularity' of Kafka's *oeuvre*, and as many explanations are given of his work as 'keys' have been offered by critics to explain it. If the 'all too generous shafts of light' of which Carlo Bo[1] has spoken risk distorting it, rendering it entirely inexplicable and ineffective, I still believe that few authors like Kafka are as deserving of commentary, even if it is enthusiastic. Let me anticipate some of my conclusions: the parable-like (rather than poetic) character of his books demands a perpetual exegesis that may subtly encrust itself into the text, gradually becoming part of it, as happened (especially in Jewish culture) with many ancient texts and the Testament in particular. The attitude of ever-renewed questioning, which belongs to the reader-critic faced with the ambiguity of Kafka's text, is foreseen and demanded by the author—as his Talmudic ancestors also foresaw—because that attitude is part of the ritual. Recall the aphorism in which the leopards overturn the sacred urns and their trespass becomes part of the cultic act.[2] It will be objected that this demand for a commentary, this tendency toward translation, is proper to every work of art. But it is the *non-aesthetic* character of the commentary owed Kafka on which I would like to end these notes, which make no claim other than to add another entry in the rather meagre Italian bibliography on this matter with some annotations on method that in no way claim to advance a new interpretive canon.

Let us see right away what are the paradoxes harboured by Kafka's 'success' and by the 'enemies' of Kafka in order to reckon whether these notes on his current fortunes and misfortunes could ever help us clarify the why and wherefore of the critical commentaries that fluctuate between an aesthetic or aestheticizing interpretation and an ideological one.

Every attempt at a response (with the proviso that the 'popularity' of an author as 'difficult' and 'gruelling' as Kafka should be understood as limited to a tiny portion of the reading bourgeoisie) straightaway runs up against a very well-known formula, which I will term 'sociological'. That formula advance both a critical judgement and a framework that lays claim to history. The argument goes something like this: 'Kafka is the novelist of impotence and annihilation, of decay and guilt, of the human condition equated to that of the animal in fear and slavery, of the impossibility of love and consciousness alternating with an irrefutable verdict; his writing is the most lucid expression of his class and his time (the intellectual middle-bourgeoisie of central Europe in the phase of a self-devouring imperialism, compelled to destroy its own myth of economic power in the ravings and massacres of a "spiritual" myth). That is why, after Hitler, the men of his class recognize themselves in his prophecies, while at the same time they deny them, or pretend to do so, in the only way available to them—by reading and approving them, resolving them into (bad) faith and consciousness, in keeping with an idealist-religious procedure. A secret known by everybody loses its power: Kafka read in the open, exploited in his most mechanical and external aspects, is exorcized, deprived of any salutary or lethal poison. He has been turned into theatre, he will be turned into cinema.'

The description contained in this formula is sufficiently close to the truth. Yet we must object—as one usually must when it comes to this kind of description. If the argument above is centred *only* on Kafka, if besides the widespread hypocrisy that by exorcizing him wants to make him familiar, to dispel the dreadful character of his nature into an idealist-religious consciousness and not into praxis, there is barely room for those (the Marxists, the 'enemies' of Kafka) who at most perceive its value as now obsolete historical sign, a mirror that has become sterile or even dangerous —then what remains of the value, of the importance *for us*, of those writings? Nothing. Just consider the embarrassment, in this regard, of the fine essay by Cantoni prefacing the Italian edition of *The Castle.*[3] There are in fact two ways of getting rid of Kafka (and in general of any complex truth). The first is to render him harmless, reducing him to a very gifted writer of fables or identifying him with this or that mystical, religious or philosophical *experience.* The second method belongs to the current that could be roughly called 'Marxist' (if in so doing we didn't risk offending the name of Marx); declaring that it wants to criticize Kafka with facts, that is to say, with the action aimed at changing the reality that has made the existence of his books possible, it quickly and mechanically shoves them into the past, granting the author at most the 'honourable mention for accomplished complaint' that several major writers of the present bourgeois phase pride themselves on. Either way, Kafka disappears. The first forgets the good arguments of the second, namely, the only definitive criticism and absolutely authentic interpretation of every value—and therefore also of the works of truth of thought and poetry—is the criticism of *things*, *practical* criticism (or better, confirmation). In other words, the quantity, quality and direction of the transformation of the world that such values realize, the 'return to the object' from whence those values emerged. The second mechanically and hastily exaggerates that criticism, considering as done what still demands to be, and betraying Kafka in a paradoxically idealist way—'burning' and 'overcoming' him by affixing a simple negative sign on his values.

Having said that, I have no doubt that it is indeed the 'enemies' of Kafka—namely, those who consider him to be negative, decadent, corrupting or worse—*who are best qualified to interpret him correctly.* The sociological formula which we summarized above contains an incontrovertible truth: Today the honour of man lies in fighting the horror of the world of *The Trial*, *The Burrow*, *The Metamorphosis*, *The Castle* and *Amerika*, to make it so that this horror is no longer *obviously real*. Both a living gloss and a dead one are therefore possible. Earlier in this essay, we spoke of ritual; and I can certainly repeat what I have written elsewhere, that is, Kafka's writing is 'a cultic operation that keeps him alive'. But in order for this work to live again within us, or (to employ the language of the Eucharist) for the transmutation of the species to reproduce itself, those pages do not need sorcerers bound to a mechanical ritual but warm, black blood, the kind drunk by the shades in Homer's Hades; they need violent readers that invade those pages, refusing the world that gazed upon the writing and suffering of Kafka, the world of his Director Generals, of his terrifying Hotel Concierges, of his Civil Servants—in other words, the world that belongs to his many, contemporary and all-too-candid readers.

The recognition of a dispute over the validity and direction of Kafka's contents, of the human and subhuman beings that he presents to us, leads to an inevitable doubt about whether Kafka's fundamental attitude is a 'poetic' one. Not that the 'truths' of poetry should not be objects of dispute—to the contrary. But the quickness and virulence of the for and against is generated partly by the nature of a work, that is, to assume the old Crocean distinction, more 'literary' than 'artistic'. This is the case independently of the poetic character of some wonderful pieces, in particular the brief ones, the 'little poems'.[4]

Future critical study (though we can argue about its scope) will need to devote itself to a patient analysis of each page and only at the end permit itself a conclusion. Allow me however to suggest a first, personal conclusion, resting on old and recent readings of Kafka; his basic attitude is far from the 'conclusion' that we have been trained to recognize (whether rightly or wrongly is not the issue here) as the index of a poetic nature. As in Kierkegaard and

Dostoevsky, the latter is in fierce and irremediable conflict with equally forceful natures, giving rise to an uncommonly acute intensity of vision. But his other natures, the anxious and beleaguered demons, propel him forward, forbid him from reaching conclusions, engage him in those very remote zones where even poetry grows silent. The real meaning of Kafka's symbolism, of his whole work intended as a symbol, testifies for our argument.

In the modern world, his *oeuvre* is in fact the only one to explicitly have as its object the *symbolon*, the small stone marked by a conventional cipher, of which the Apocalypse speaks.[5] To have the symbol as subject, which is to say, to affirm a world in which every thing and every word, every feeling and every reason are signs, symptoms and clues of something else, and where everything is irremediably transformed, really means *writing on water* and therefore accepting (as I was saying before) an infinite gloss, an infinite series of translations; it is deliberately to put oneself outside of poetic language. For poetry *is not* symbolic: Valéry and the doctrine of polysemic and *relative* poetry entail either the obvious variety of interpretations or the inclusion of the poetry-object in a world of floating meanings in which every object (and not just poetry) is or can be the symbol of another; where everything, as in alchemical crucibles, converts into everything else. What Kafka describes is precisely this surprising world, but *in addition* he accepts that this description (in other words, his *oeuvre*) partakes in the perpetual change. When it is said that Kafka's writing is a cultural or magical operation, it means that in a wholly-enigmatic world where the relations of cause and effect are altered by superhuman or demonic powers, Kafka of a region, an event or a character is not, as in Edgar Allan Poe or E.T.A. Hoffmann, a 'travel report' or an 'exciting adventure'. It is a *mediation*, the act of an intermediary, the translation of a symbol into something other *that is also a symbol*. Goethe's statement *Alles Vergängliche—ist nur ein Gleichnis*[6] in reality refuses to be itself *ein Gleichnis*, a symbol: the poet admits of an allegory but cannot help wanting to give an absolute, definitive meaning to his words, and the entire history of a hundred years of poetry and magic confirms our thesis. Even recent studies on kabbalism and magic in the works of Gérard de Nerval, Hugo, Rimbaud and Verlaine confirm that they were 'bad magicians', too wedded to poetry, that is too proud of their expressive capacity to be docile *mediums*. Instead, for Kafka the story has exactly the same import as the famous 'gold button' that serves to distinguish the Court clerks in *The Trial*; and the reader would need to put himself in the state of the 'mystic' or the assistant to the mysteries who, by grasping the dangerous instrument which is capable of operating transmutations and is itself transmutable (like Moses' staff), comes to be suspended between two infinities: that of the mutations from symbol to symbol that preceded the present instant, and that of the mutations or pairings of symbolic equivalences that will follow it. All these infinite and correlated series of equivalences flow of necessity into a God the Father and Absolute Destroyer (the religious prefiguration of the dialectical method whose unity is, in a Hegelian vein, self-consciousness and in a Marxian one, *praxis*), the *vanishing point* of every perspective. This is the meaning (now accepted by everyone) of Kafka's symbol. But the reality of things has cruelly undertaken the task of providing it with its first paradoxical refutation, the first criticism of things levied against the ideas of reason. In fact, if the 'ideas of reason' are unmasterable, if the procedure, the itinerary of the mind towards God the Father and Destroyer appears to the religious (to Kafka, in this case) *never* to cease, in reality the pen falls, the reader grows distracted, the book ends (and it *ends* all the more, the more it is printed and extracted from the testamentary flames . . .). *Herr* Franz Kafka *dies*. Instead of an infinite and infinitely ungraspable series we hold in our hand 'torsos of novels', 'fragments' of transmutations, a world over which *we too* have something to say: The force of things lodges Kafka in history, demands a reckoning with his horrors, recognizes them in present things and men, in contemporary history. Where a testament to the absolute was sought, we find instead a testament to the relative. Just as the smell of a leaf will only last as long as the particles of the volatile substances it contains, dispersing one after the other, so too Kafka's book—not so much in what it wanted to be but in what it is—will effuse its scent, its bitter aroma of absinthe[7] as long as the symbolic series will last among men; as long as a worm will be able to pose as a man and a concierge appear as a powerful tyrant, as long as the construction of a senseless wall will demand incommensurable sacrifices, as long as the crows won't stop (as Kafka himself writes) telling us that 'a single crow could destroy the heavens', while ignoring that 'heaven simply means: the impossibility of crows'.[8]

With these notes I've wanted to warn the very recent friends of the author of *The Castle*, as well as those who reproach men for their overt resemblance to these grim heroes. No doubt for us the positive value of Kafka's *oeuvre* lies in having formulated in an absolutely decisive way the codex of human misery. Only a world in which despair or annihilation into the crowd cannot exist as system, in which there is no longer the fear of secret tribunals and their mysterious legalities, of a police which comes to apprehend suspects in the middle of the night, where man is not a slave of other men and frees himself from the pleasures of slavery—only such a world will be able fully to grasp and therefore thoroughly to criticize the work of Kafka. But it will also be necessary for Titanism and Babelism to have disappeared from this world, those rebellions at the borders of the human condition, the borders of its mortality. It will also be necessary for sin to no longer exist, not only in the sense that the judge be destroyed but also that certain forms of 'evil' shall no longer exist. What sets us apart from the psychological or existentialist (Heideggerian) interpreters is that what they consider in Kafka to be the eternal image of the human condition is historically conditioned. For them, Mr Kafka or Gregor Samsa is man always ready to be devoured by the open mouth of the sacred while for us those 'falls', those 'abjections' are real for the citizen of a Central European city at the beginning of the twentieth century. But what further distinguishes us from the hasty 'sociological' interpreters is the conviction that Kafka's description of man and his fate not only continues to be true for those categories and classes for which it is indeed true but also extends to other strata of humanity and is destined, as a historical inheritance, to remain true for a long time.

Until then, that work will have a right to be respected. In such cases, this means far more than 'aesthetic' admiration—the kind reserved for Sade or Dostoevsky—precisely because, in a coherent and inflexible way, it *despairs* man. In other words, because it has not succumbed to 'reformist' flattery.

There can be no humanly fulfilled life if it does not give a meaning and a place to negation, to evil and death; if it does not give a positive meaning to the 'communion of pasts'. Either the future will have a historical *pietas* towards the past or it will deserve to bear the Babelic fist on its emblems, the symbol of the blows that will have to destroy the human city. Kafka's man, the contemporary of Nazism, lost in the snow-covered village at the feet of the castle, crawling like a worm in a rented apartment, trembling at the bottom of a burrow, slaughtered like a dog in a quarry, will have a right to the vigilant *pietas* of humans present and future. Otherwise, were Kafka's books to be thrown into the mass grave or the crematorium, criticism would be evaded, and we would be consenting—precisely where he is most mistaken, where he sins against spirit and reality, where, *despairing of the very meaning of his own desperation*, he would like his work to be destroyed—to Kafka's own biographical craving for dissolution.

1948

Notes

Originally published in *La Rassegna d'Italia* 4(2) (February 1949). [Trans.]

1 For Carlo Bo's readings of Kafka, see Ursula Vogt, 'Carlo Bo e Franz Kafka', *Studi Urbinati* 82 (2012): 41–57. [Trans.]

2 'Leopards break into the temple and drink to the dregs what is in the sacrificial pitchers; this is repeated over and over again; finally it can be calculated in advance, and it becomes a part of the ceremony'—Franz Kafka, *Parables and Paradoxes* (Willa and Edwin Muir trans) (New York: Schocken Books, 1969), p. 93. [Trans.]

3 Remo Cantoni, 'Uomini contro il destino' [Men Against Destiny] in Franz Kafka, *Il castello* [The Castle] (Anita Rho trans.) (Milan: Mondadori, 1948). [Trans.]

4 *poemetti* [Trans.]

5 ' . . . and will give him a white stone, and in the stone a new name written, which no man knoweth saving he that receiveth it' —Revelation 2:12 (King James Bible). [Trans.]

6 'All that passes away is only a symbol'—the words of the Chorus Mysticus in the final scene of *Faust II*. [Trans.]

7 *assenzio*—a pun on *assenza* (absence). [Trans.]

8 Franz Kafka, *The Blue Octavo Notebooks* (Max Brod ed., Ernst Kaiser and Eithne Wilkins trans) (New York: Exact Change, 1991), p. 89. [Trans.]

VI

Two Returns

I think it is worth reflecting on a coincidence that will probably have been noted by others and which I became aware of in rereading, after many years and with rather different eyes, Thomas Mann's *Tonio Kröger*. What I mean is the repetition, first in literature and then in reality, of a situation typical of the narrative produced by the major strains of decadent literature: the return to the paternal home. Tonio Kröger, after a 13-year absence, takes the train to the 'grey and solemn' city where his father has died. He finds the rooms of his adolescence occupied by a public library and visits them without revealing his identity. 'He felt a sharp pang of grief. He glanced sideways through the window. The garden was neglected and overgrown, but the old walnut tree was still there, heavily creaking and rustling in the wind'.[1] The celebrated short story is from 1903. Forty-two years later, in a memorable letter to his father dated 16 May 1945, at a time when he had already resolved to commit suicide—you can find the letter in his autobiography *Der Wendepunkt* [The Turning Point]—Thomas Mann's son, Klaus describes how in the days of the German collapse he arrived in his American army uniform in Munich, looking for the paternal home and discovering it partially destroyed by the bombing. In what was once his room there now lived a woman all of whose relatives had been killed in the war; conversing with her incognito, she revealed to him that the house has been used as a *Lebensborn*, a site for couplings between SS officers and young Aryan women for the purpose of racial reproduction: 'I was unable to suppress a strange feeling of enchantment faced with that quite unfamiliar garden with its vanished paths and collapsed walls, but where the family hedge remained intact; while that old walnut tree that I have never forgotten . . . '.[2] What is concealed behind these returns of prodigal sons, this insistent myth? I think it is the whole implicit theme of the 'return' and the recovery of lost time, of childhood as golden age; in other words, the innumerable *Nóstoi* of our time.[3] I ask myself if it is possible to lead them all back to the selfsame psychological root, to an eternal moment of the soul. Of course it is possible. But if we see this solely as a normal process of consciousness—the act of remembrance and verification, the assumption of identity in diversity, the dialogue of generations where the son generates his father—it is likely we will miss the specific historical meaning that this process has assumed in *our* time, and the reason for its true significance. For example, we feel that the verdant paradise of childhood love changes its meaning over the course of the Romantic generations, not only from poet to poet, understood as individual personalities, but also in keeping with the mutation of the relationship between poets and society. For the Romantics of the counter-revolution or the Catholic restoration, Novalis or Chateaubriand, the irrecoverable golden age was the multifarious world of feudal fidelities; but who could call Stendhal's Napoleonic myth of heroes nostalgia? For the conclusion of Flaubert's *Sentimental Education* one requires the feeling of horror and fear experienced in the face of social revolution; however, that of the heroes of *War and Peace* in the novel's epilogue is not a 'return to the paternal home', but a restless anticipation of the future. Similarly, for the generations of decadentism the world that they now feel as remote is that of the courageous and constructive bourgeoisie; for Thomas Mann, it is that of the pre-Wilhelmine bourgeoisie, a bourgeoisie that has yet to produce all its grave-diggers. The sons and grandsons have instead discovered that the bourgeois world ends; it really ends not in a revolution, or not yet, but in the gigantism of the imperialist phase and in the ideologies that accompany it. The mother's kiss will never again reach Marcel after his journey through time and *salons*,[4] the blue-eyed people, 'the bright children of life, the happy, the charming and the ordinary',[5] elicit in Kröger-Mann 'longing, and sad envy, and just a touch of contempt, and a whole world of innocent delight'[6] (but please note these last two words in view of what I will say later); for Stephen Daedalus, his maternal Catholicism will be a horrible spectre; Kafka will waver at the threshold of the paternal home or write to his father the words we are now familiar with.[7] But—this, to my mind, is the meaning of the Tonio-Klaus repetition—if the decadence of the sturdy European bourgeoisie, which in its very development loses its grip on the levers of power, has produced a generation of aesthetes and poets, of novelists and psychologists who see themselves precisely as its prodigal sons; the ensuing period, by aggravating the contradictions far more terribly, could only produce a generation of suicides, murderers and murdered. It is one thing to return to the paternal home and find a public library, and another to find it scorched by war, the destroyer of the people who had transformed it—note the lexical irony—into a *Lebensborn*.

But *who are* those men of health who accompany the entirety of Thomas Mann's *oeuvre*, beginning with these stories, and form an antithesis with the men of sickness (the prince of *Royal Highness* [1909] is ankylosed, the little lord Friedemann deformed, the Gabriella of *Tristan* (1903) and the Schiller of *A Weary Hour* (1905) are ill, and the protagonist of the eponymous story [*The Hungry*, 1903] truly is 'hungry', just like Kröger and the Jeronimus of *Gladius Dei* [1902] . . .)? The question is too vast for us to be able even to hint at an answer. Besides, Mann criticism has produced countless variations on this argument. Nevertheless, allow me a suggestion—we may surmise that 'the happy, the charming and the ordinary',[8] those descendants of Hermann and Dorothea[9] are as much the bearers of a positive moral quality, of an authentic attitude towards reality, as the nescient, the innocent, those who do not know and do not see what either sickness or an artistic attitude have disclosed to others. Donkeys bearing sacred things, they seem so lovable because they do not know—not for that reason alone but also because health, trust, hope, 'human understanding' (with which the governess succours Leverkühn in *Doctor Faustus*) are *true* virtues, even if they are a mere memory of virtue, a tradition, a repetition. Only by keeping this doubleness or duplicity in mind, is it possible to understand the author's ambivalent attitude towards them. For Mann—for whom, as for us, no health or happiness can justify giving up on science, on truth and its pain—the health and happiness of the 'bourgeois' are not, as we know, pure negativity but, rather, the caricature or, better, the remainder, the echo of a value. For the Christian too, earthly happiness is the parable or symbol of the eternal kind. But remainder of *what*, echo of *what*?

Of a society where science did not contradict hope, in which there was an identity of nature and language between those who knew and those who did not yet or, at least, the hope and wish of a possible identity, when between the young Goethe and the wine merchant's daughter[10] there was not the desperate, impotent relationship which we find between Tonio Kröger and the blonde Inge. In short, the society that German idealism had prefigured, that the democratic revolution of 1848 had attempted and failed to realize, and whose ideological melody continued to inform, albeit now mendaciously, that German bourgeoisie dead set on confusing it with the trumpets of Prussian anthems and with Tristan's horn. I have always been struck by the coincidence of dates between two passages by Kierkegaard and Marx, both from 1843. The first, in which the 'knight of the infinite' is incarnated in the 'bourgeois' of Copenhagen, is from *Fear and Trembling*:

> He enjoys everything he sees . . . everything that happens . . . engages him with equanimity . . . And yet he is no genius . . . He drains the deep sadness of life in infinite resignation, he knows the blessedness of infinity, he has felt the pain of renouncing everything, the most precious thing in the world, and yet the finite tastes just as good to him as to one who never knew anything higher.[11]

The second is from Marx's letter to Arnold Ruge: 'the world has long possessed the dream of a thing of which it only needs to possess the consciousness in order really to possess it . . . the problem is not some great gap between the thoughts of the past and those of the future but the completion of thoughts of the past'.[12] In the end, for Mann, for this last visitor to Weimar, health is not an unrealizable nostalgia, nor is illness a verdict.

That is not the only aspect which isolates Mann from his contemporaries. When one speaks of the literary quality of these short stories—as of the rest of his work—we must not forget that it contradicts most of the formal experience of our time and presents to us a seemingly friendly visage, yet one that turns out to be impenetrable. We could even say: unlikable. In these stories from the turn of the century—whose quality, I repeat, has been retained and incessantly developed, though at times at the price of its frank and balanced character, all the way up to *Faustus* and *The Holy Sinner* (1951)—the reader feels that almost no concession has been made to naturalist verism, and yet Mann's literary canon remains distant from psychologism and from the would-be avant-garde novel; we have not left the classical schemas of great realism behind. Narration is always placed after, never before, the critical act. That is why the continual presence of Mann the essayist with his cultural irony can be so bothersome, casting suspicion on his craftsmanship. Compared to Chekhov, to Joyce, to Proust, to Kafka, he will look like a philistine. What innocence, true or fake, what unconcealed irony, in *Tristan*, in *The Child Prodigy* (1903), in *Gladius Dei*, in *At the Prophet's* (1904), in *Kröger* itself or in *Royal Highness*. At first, these stories don't tell you anything you don't already know but the impassiveness of the artist, advocated in the poetics of Tonio, is entirely different from the formal and decadent one of the 'haughty artificer'.[13] It is a tenacious, passionate struggle to not lose anything. By way of confirmation, I reread *A Man and His Dog* (1918). This is a theme that could have lent itself to every banality and aestheticism—yet what natural intelligence, and how much of it.

Bashan never ceases being, even in the attentive, patient and deft description of his character, what is he: a dog. The temptation to humanize him always stops at the right moment. Likewise for the natural descriptions, those of the forest and the seasons, the hunting of the hares, the ducks, the seagulls; Mann never indulges in decadent pantheism, lyrical abandon, that rhetoric of the immediacy of the wholesome and virile accord with nature that was rampant among his contemporaries. Natural appearances are intensely alive, particular observations rich and exact, but you feel that the whole is governed by a more complex perspective which, even though momentarily concealed, has not disappeared; a perspective in which hierarchies are well entrenched, the master is a man and the dog is a dog and the life that matters, in the end, is that of men. Let the reader compare these particular observations and the subtleties to which we have been accustomed by so much neo-baroque prose, both Italian and foreign, and they will understand that this art cannot be separated from wisdom, and ultimately from truth. Consider this description of the countryside:

> It is my park and my solitude . . . My thoughts and my dreams are mingled and intergrown with its scenes . . . in autumn when the chemical smell of the fading leaves fills the air, when the white legions of the thistledown have all been blow to the winds . . . And also in winter when the gravel is covered with snow and soft mounds, so that one may walk upon it in one's rubber overshoes, and when the river goes shooting black between the pale frost-bound shores and the cry of hundreds of fresh-water gulls fills the air from morning to evening. But the relationship with nature . . . [14]

This kind of prose is capable of weaving words like 'chemical' and 'overshoes' into an emotive and pathetic descriptive motion, or to begin a sentence after the 'pale frost-bound shores', with 'the relationship with nature', without ever undermining the overall balance or introducing the suspicion of a kind of rash or mottled colouring. Mann will write of the horrid, barking Bashan in the falsetto of passion but in the next line he will continue with: 'And then finally is the hunt after waterfowl to which I must also dedicate a few lines'.[15]

1953

Notes

Originally published in *Comunità* 7(18) (April 1953). [Trans.]

1 Thomas Mann, 'Tonio Kröger' in *Death in Venice, Tonio Kröger, and Other Writings* (Frederick A. Lubich ed., David Luke trans.) (New York: Continuum, 1999), p. 36.

2 A much shorter version of this scene can be found in Klaus Mann, *The Turning Point: The Autobiography of Klaus Mann* (Princeton: Markus Wiener Publishers, 2007), pp. 368–9. That text, written in English, precedes the German autobiography from which Fortini is quoting. I have translated the quote directly from the Italian. [Trans.]

3 The *Nóstoi* (from *nóstos*, 'return home' or homecoming), also known as *The Return* or *The Return of the Greeks*, is an ancient Greek epic poem belonging to the so-called Epic Cycle, which tells the stories of the heroes of the Trojan War as they returned to their kingdoms. Only a few lines of the original poem remain. [Trans.]

4 A reference to Proust's *In Search of Lost Time* (1913). [Trans.]

5 Mann, 'Tonio Kröger', p. 55.

6 Ibid.

7 Franz Kafka, *Letter to His Father* (Ernst Kaiser and Eithne Wilkins trans) (New York: Schocken, 1966). [Trans.]

8 Mann, 'Tonio Kröger', p. 55.

9 A reference to Goethe's epic poem *Hermann and Dorothea* (1796–97). [Trans.]

10 Anna Katharina [Käthchen] Schönkopf (1746–1810), Goethe fell in love with her in 1766. The poem collection *Annette* (1767) and the

pastoral play *The Lover's Caprice* (1768) were inspired by their relationship. [Trans.]

11 Søren Kierkegaard, *Fear and Trembling* (Howard V. Hong and Edna H. Hong eds and trans) (Princeton: Princeton University Press, 1983), pp. 39–40. [Fortini co-translated of this book into Italian, see *Timore e tremore* (Franco Fortini and K.M. Guldbrandsen trans) (Milan: Edizioni di Comunità, 1952).]

12 Karl Marx, 'Letters to Arnold Ruge' in *Karl Marx: Selected Writings* (David McLellan ed.) (Oxford: Oxford University Press, 1977), p. 38.

13 *artefice superbo*—from Gabriele D'Annunzio's poem 'Pamphila' in *Poema Paradisiaco / Odi Navali (1891–1893)*, 4th EDN (Milan: Fratelli Treves, 1899), p. 102. [Trans.]

14 Thomas Mann, *A Man and His Dog* (Herman George Scheffauer trans.) (New York: A.A. Knopf, 1930), pp. 156–7 [translation modified].

15 Ibid., p. 219.

VII

Brecht or the Talking Horse

(a) *Instructions for* The Threepenny Novel

In this book Brecht has again remained faithful to one of his canons of dramatic art, that is to say, of moral life—the principle whereby the conclusion of the work lies beyond the work (not just interpreting the world but also changing it). The work must not contain its own conclusion within itself.

This principle—which can lead us to read at least a part of Brecht's *oeuvre* in an allegorical or symbolic key, showing another point of contact between him and the genius of decadentism—is the same as for Chaplin, who appears as a victim, and only in rare moments, a rebel: *the blindness of the character is the condition for the sight of the spectator.*

The victims of Peachum and Macheath, along with the protagonists and their comperes, are blind indeed: Mary Sawyer, the soldier Fewkoombey, the countless managers of 'B shops', the soldiers shipwrecked with *The Optimist*. No one has refuted the doctrine of the positive hero better than Brecht. He does not show us—at least, not in this work—the virtue of the poor but (as he will have St Joan of the Stockyards say) the 'poverty of the poor', the most repulsive and final form of their degradation, their consent to the morality of property. In *The Threepenny Novel,* antithetical forces are barely alluded to—they remain in the background, the strikers and invisible 'communists' mentioned from time to time. Or they are ironized in the trade union consciousness of Macheath's gang—

with its partial participation in the earnings—or Peachum's beggars whose syndicalist consciousness prevents them from carrying the placards with anti-government slogans. There are many moments, and not only in this text but also across all of Brecht's *oeuvre*, in which the author seems to be telling us that *there is no way out*, that the only way to overcome injustice is not to surrender to it, to illustrate instead the scandal of injustice. But that is natural, to the extent that he is a Marxist, Brecht wagers on a humanity that is not there or which, to be more precise, *is not onstage*; it speaks from the wings, the class or the party, in any case the collective; it is a motor of history but one which as soon as it is embodied, takes on a name and appears, must borrow its positivity from something else. Hence the irony: when the beggars, disguised as war cripples, are sent to demonstrate in favour of war, Brecht's pessimism outstrips Peachum's, who had predicted a fiasco, while hundreds of authentic cripples, spontaneously joining the demonstration, assure its success . . .

It is also singular, and telling, that revolutionary (that is to say, historically possible) reality appears to Brecht's characters (as it does to St Joan) *in their dreams*: the dream of London being invaded by millions of outcasts or the Final Judgement with the trial and sentencing of Jesus Christ, in the epilogue of the *Novel*. For the spectator or reader of the 1930s or 50s, those dreams—in view of the revolutions of our century—are realities. And the 'moral' is indeed the following: Dreams can become real. Yet the poet cannot but remain on this side of or beyond that 'real' in the verbal infrastructure of dreams, which is his only way of acting on reality.

Nor does Brecht simply compel us to this participation, co-responsibility and continuation. For what he shows us is not the struggle between good and evil but between evil and evil; and it is *we* who are entrusted with positivity, which is to say, with justice. Note that the triumph of evil—such a traditional presence in the novel—is so obvious and quotidian, at least for us, as to leave us almost indifferent until we perceive it as the other's triumph over us but, especially, until we have dismissed any prospect of easy or possible restoration of justice. For us, the *contemporary* triumphs of evil always emerge on the background of hope. They always include an appeal, or a hearing, for us who live through them; and the bitterness or rebellion that accompanies them risks being mystified by a concealed or explicit '*there will come a day . . .*'. For evil really to be *an* evil it must be felt to be archived, to be historical, strictly irremediable; and faced with it, we must able to say what one of the Karamazovs says about the boy torn to pieces by the general's wolfhounds.[1] We need to despair of evil's redemption, *to run the greatest risk*, that of cynicism or the religious 'leap', of aestheticism or irrationalism . . . That is why Brecht likes to create distance through the chronological setting of his plays; at the same time he wants the relationship between that 'perfection' and our present not to be arbitrary or symbolic but historical. I have been struck, in a debate between Jean-Paul Sartre, Michel Butor, Roger Vailland, Arthur Adamov and Morvan Lebesque on Adamov's satirical play *Paolo Paoli* (1957), by Lebesque's remark: 'To explain the Algerian war to people, we need to tell them about the Boer War. Reflection can only come from this lag'.[2] Brecht's *Novel* tells indeed of the war against the Boers (on the eve of the civil war in Spain). What matters is that the spectators *do not hear* Mother Courage speak like a contemporary sutler disguised as a sutler from the Thirty Years War, *nor* that they read the name of some modern industrialist or figure from a financial scandal where Brecht has written the name of Macheath, aka 'The Knife'; nor that they *contemplate*, like a romantic vista, those facts and those persons reduced to a 'historical fresco' (here we are simply stating the obvious). The spectators must be put in a position to turn into translators; from the contemplation of apparent and distant orbits they derive the laws of their own motion, they assert them in order to change them.

This, to my mind, was not yet at work in the *Threepenny Opera*: the world of the gutters was synoptically presented as that of the

Edwardian bourgeoisie. But thanks to John Gay's model, to the songs, to the multifarious presence of beggars and prostitutes, the accent falls on the former and not the latter. The culture of the young Brecht and the taste of that period as well as the presence of the post-First World War German *Lumpenproletariat* gave him a profound sensibility for the themes of hunger, sensuality, death—and rags. Brecht was forced to entrust the transposition to the acting technique, to its 'time'; in other words, to scenography instead of text. Today the 'truth' of the *Opera* resurfaces and, as could be seen at the Piccolo theatre in Milan, it is entirely to be found in its decorative, aestheticizing dimension; the dreadful songs have become harmless arias for salons. In the *Novel* instead, the world of the prostitutes and beggars is entirely secondary, as it really is today in our society (perhaps not in Italy but, at least, in today's Federal Germany or in England the word 'hunger' which 50 years ago—or 15, under war conditions—had a precise meaning when it was sung in the second verse of the *Internationale, 'Debout, les forçats de la faim'*[3]—now carries a derived meaning where it is hunger for something other than bread). The substance of the book can be located in Macheath's struggle and his victory over commercial and banking institutions, his wanting to become 'a respectable person' who resorts to murder only under exceptional circumstances; and in his success. If the *Opera* advanced the equation gutters = commercial bourgeoisie, the *Novel* advances a different one, namely, commercial bourgeoisie = international and financial high bourgeoisie (or rather, the political–economic ruling class). Brecht does not at all intend to offer us a picaresque novel or a transcription of Daniel Defoe—even if the precursors, along with Diderot, govern the tone of the book. What he wants, in parallel to the way in which the blindness of the victims is to be matched by the clairvoyance of the reader, is for the 'definite' and 'historical' phase of the development of the bourgeoisie depicted by him—namely, the passage from the entrepreneurial individualism of Peachum's firm and Macheath's primitive gang to the ABC Trust for the systematic and legal exploitation of the poor—to be matched in the reader by the discovery and conscious criticism of the further phase of capitalist development, which leads us from a trust of shops selling at a single price, from the union of two banks and a modest colonial war, to the great international cartels and world wars. The wilful banality and 'vulgarity' of Brecht's exemplification has this exact function: to start from what everyone knows or thinks they know (that the world of business often behaves like that of street muggings, that wives are like hard cash, etc.) in order to lead us to what we know *less*. In fact, notwith-standing everything that we think we know, we would find it very vulgar if one wanted to represent the 1956 Suez exploit as one of the 'coups' arranged by Coax, Hare and Mr Macheath. As one of the characters observes, this capacity for simplification belongs only to great politicians and communists, with their unbearable obsession with presenting everything in black and white.

Brecht seems to carry out this simplification and exemplification by accumulating the data of an incredibly complicated detective intrigue. The figures that emerge from it have the force of those grotesque, wooden ones that adorn the clocks of a German *Rathaus*. There is here an extreme assuredness in defining precise, or as they say, unforgettable situations: the séances of semi-naked businessmen among the steam-clouds of Feather's Baths; Peachum ('I wouldn't give away even the dirt under my fingernails!'), hat cocked back, ruminating in his filthy office; Fanny, intelligent and energetic, with her cigarette and silk stockings; the powerful depiction of Coax's murder; the choral scene in the church, at the end, in the fog . . . Puppets who 'no longer have anything human about them' and because of that seem intensely human. Among them wonders—reminiscent of a Flemish painting—Polly Peachum, aka 'The Peach', repellent and rosy, foul and cheerful, with her rose-apple health, her white arms, her regrets before every adultery and her satisfaction after it.

In translating this book, the undersigned enjoyed himself to the point of laughing, from time to time—alone. Once again, one thinks of Chaplin's Tramp, the one from the comedies set in the same London as Brecht's novel. Paradoxically (but not so much) this is a *popular* book, in the best sense of the word, a book to be *used*. 'The history books and the biographies are not enough! Where are the wage lists?', 'Those who have not been paid fully, please send in your names and addresses!'[4] With these coarse, opaque but irrefutable truths, with this deaf and conventional language proper to the evening tabloid or the protests of bills of exchange, Brecht has woven the argument of a thick, muscular book, full of thrusts and things, that is, of useful poetry.

1958

(b) Tales from the Calendar

In the *Tales from the Calendar*, moral truths are communicated in the form of that 'conscious symbolism' which, according to Hegel, distinguishes the consciousness of meaning from representation. In other words, in the form of parables and apologues. The sources of the 'exempla', 'moralities' or 'instructions' of medieval literature are the same as Brecht's: the Judeo-Christian tradition and the Eastern one. Even the 'modern' interpretation of historical events (the 'facts of Caesar') seems to link to that prolonged Medieval phase. This is the conscious symbolism that we encounter in Kafka, the brother–enemy of Brecht. Kafka, like Brecht, kept in his workroom the image of an ancient Chinese sage. From the East, the homeland of the parable and the apologue.

This is a book of instructions in prose and verse, the almanac of Brecht the 'pietist'. If *The Augsburg Chalk Circle* is of singular importance as the first blueprint for the masterpiece that is *The Caucasian Chalk Circle*, it is because within it we can trace the precursor of judge Adzak in the figure of judge Ignatius Dollinger; if 'Two Sons' does not go beyond the anecdote and 'Caesar and His

Legionary' is the blueprint for the longer *The Business Affairs of Julius Caesar*, but with the comparative advantage of a brevity more suited to the chosen genre, if 'The Soldier of La Ciotat' leaves us rather unmoved, the other pieces in this volume contain some of the most beautiful pages of prose writing in Brecht. They are those in which besides a character that celebrates, with his name, wisdom or science or sacrifice, there appears (like a necessary complement) the figure of a humble person, a face in the shadow, to promote the truth of his enlightened counterpart. The illiterate boy who carries on his own modest experiment after the death of his master Bacon Verulam reveals the essence of the latter's teaching, the proper character of the new science: not to end with biological death. In the splendid tale 'Socrates Wounded', Xantippe is the Socratic 'developer' of the philosopher, the demand for an anti-rhetorical truth, the equivalent of the customs man in 'Legend of the Origin of the Book Tao-Tê-Ching on Lao-Tsû's Road into Exile'; and the Athenian philosopher regards her, 'recognizes' her just like the Chinese sage, as he gazes at the rags of the customs man, understands that he has found the recipient of his own wisdom: 'Xantippe was a being worn down by work, her chest flat as a board and her eyes sad. He knew he could trust her'. Likewise for the tailor and his wife in 'The Heretic's Coat', troubled by an unpaid bill, forcing Giordano Bruno (who is already under the trial because of Mocenigo's accusation) to fight for a small act of justice—a viaticum for the years before his burning at the stake. Even in the minor tale 'The Unseemly Old Lady', the poor scullery maid contributes to the happiness of the Grandmother's last years, the 'short years of freedom'.

Even when they seem to stretch out in the narration, these prose pieces retain an emblematic character in their dry precipitousness. An invisible QED brings them to a close. And, in the final pages, the aphorisms of 'Mr Keuner' are not just 'memorable sayings' but also scenes—exemplary situations, minimal theatre.

The poetic compositions also propose, in another but not too different register, examples and admonitions.

Three of the eight compositions are in the free metre that Brecht amply employed aiming at the same 'estrangement' effect theorized and practiced in his work as a playwright. The verse does not follow the lyrical movement but rather superimposes upon the narrative rhythm simple indications of diction and gesture; solemn cadences derived from Biblical verse or hexameter.

Estrangement is then achieved through the tension between an austere and ample rhythm, as in an ode or hymn, and the unassuming appearance of the narration. Moreover, 'The Carpet Weavers of Kuyan-Bulak Pay Tribute to Lenin' or 'The Buddha's Parable of the Burning House' have a structure analogous to that of the Brechtian 'teaching plays' in which a character or chorus summarizes or interprets the events. 'You have heard how . . .', and then: 'But we . . .'. Similarly in the poem on the weavers, note the precise dialectical motion; in order to honour him with a correct understanding of his teaching, the bust of Lenin has been replaced with barrels of oil used to fight against malaria, but the conclusion is not that of vulgar pragmatism. The unnamed Turkmen comrade, in the second part of the poem, proposes to affix on the station a plaque with an account of what happened:

> Recording these events and containing
> Precise details too of their altered plan, the exchange of
> The bust of Lenin for a barrel of fever-destroying oil.[5]

He represents the moment of historical-ideological understanding which is as necessary as action for real progress. He is, to a certain degree, the poet himself. 'And all this in honour of Lenin'—the principle of the convertibility of theory and praxis is correct. Brecht is never as simple as he seems, even the 'Questions from a Worker Who Reads' are actually questions that Brecht puts to the reading worker. It is not merely a matter of demystifying the history of 'personalities' and replacing it with that of social forces; the point is to bring out, with their clearly delineated faces, those terrible humble executioners, those cooks of Caesar, those masons of the Great Wall, the bearers of 'concrete truth'.

The poem 'Ballad of Marie Sanders, The Jew's Whore' is an example of dramatic concentration in four brief strophes and many voices. In the first and fourth, the impersonal voice of the historian, in the second, that of an 'advisor'; in the third, that of Marie Sanders, to which is added the different voice of the refrain, collective fear expressed in a female tonality, almost like the mental reply of the mother to the girl. But in the final reprise the voice of the author introduces and overlays itself, a high note in the chorus.

The reader can judge for themselves the uncertain 'Children's Crusade 1939' and the epigrammatic 'My Brother was a Pilot' but it is worth pausing on 'The Tailor of Ulm', a brief and perfect 'historical' ballad. Here too it is not a matter of celebrating man's progress and conquests—or not just. Rather, what is at issue is the elucidation of the human moments corresponding to progress and to regression. Here is the humble tailor who, precisely because he neither wants nor knows how to interpret his own attempt as an infraction against natural or divine laws, addresses the bishop with naive childish faith: 'Bishop, I can fly . . . Just watch me try!' Here is the mediation of the people's chorus, hesitating between submission and courage, between deference to authority ('It was nothing but a lie') and compassion for the dead. And here is the bishop, who does not even stop when the tailor speaks to him, who does not have a single word of compassion for the dead man, merely repeating his impoverished wisdom and only capable of thinking of the confirmation of ecclesiastical authority: 'Let the church bells ring'.[6]

But the most difficult and highest point of the book is 'The Legend about the Origin of the Book Tao-Tê-Ching on Lao-Tsû's Road into Exile', perhaps Brecht's most perfect lyric, also made famous by the commentary that Walter Benjamin devoted to it shortly after its initial publication.[7] Yet the richness of moral meanings contained in those 13 strophes does not manifest itself with the same happy immediacy as the represented situations. Benjamin, for example, highlights the values here proposed by Brecht—courtesy, benevolence and serenity. These are Taoist themes but here they are also the transposition of the values of a Marxist ethic that Brecht, on the road of exile and death, wants to bequeath to the German proletariat. They are exactly the values which the harshness of struggle seems to refute, the struggle that 'contorts the features' and 'makes the voice hoarse'.[8] It is not possible to hear the 'courtesy' of the Chinese philosopher and the customs official without the 'wickedness' that rages behind their backs.

We need to devote a lot of attention to the limpid structure of the short poem, to the *mise en scène* of the dialogue, to the denouement (at once cautious and precipitous) and the vivid insertion of the concluding comment. It is not just an astounding page of poetry, in the precise and delicate mark carried by every object, borne by a strong yet flexible rhythm, entrusted to such a subtle movement of lexical subsidence between *Umgangsprache*[9] and a language veiled by archaisms and solemnities that no attempt at translation can match, reflecting and redoubling the very essence of the poem, namely, the connection between aristocratic wisdom and humble wisdom. Evidently, it is also a poetics and an ethics: the poetics of the 'social mandate' for which the non-poet is the poet's indispensable collaborator; and the ethics of man who is an aid to man. Here we touch upon one of the two poles of a tension typical of Brecht: the pole of 'benevolence' and 'non-resistance' which is the invincible weapon of sages and the poor; and their necessary 'meanness' and inflexible 'resistance'. These are the two dialectical themes that accompany Brecht's poetry from beginning to end. This 'master of impatience' is also a master of patience.

1958

(c) *Readings of Some Poems*

1. '*A Bed for the Night*'

It tells of unemployed Americans during the great crisis of 1929, finding shelter for a night thanks to private charity. The structure of the composition results from overcoming the apparently positive character of the philanthropic intervention. But what allows the poem to be a poem and not a mere caption is the way it centres on the human activity which is responsible for this state of affairs, that of mere 'reformism':

> For a night the wind is kept from them
> The snow meant for them falls on the roadway.[10]

'Kept from them' suggests something that counters the wind's intent to assail the homeless; the snow 'meant for them' speaks of an averted predestination and of the fall on the asphalt of the snowflakes that no longer meet their original target. Wind and snow depict an intentionality, even metaphorically alluding to an ill will. With extreme plastic simplicity, one *sees* the wind ceasing because something has been interposed and the snow incessant because the men have been removed from the place where they were present. The whole poem draws its power from this concrete but insufficient victory over nature.

2. '*Epitaph for Karl Liebknecht*'

'Here lies / Karl Liebknecht / Against war he carried on a fight / When he was killed / Our city was still standing on the site.' This epitaph draws its force from the suppression of the intermediate steps of an argument. Yet consider the difference between this and the short-circuits of surrealist analogy. The difference is that in surrealist analogy the shock of the short-circuit is possible for anyone who partakes of common sense (like saying that black is white, or two plus two equals three), while the shock of Brechtian abbreviation can only be perceived by those who, at least for a moment, partake of a specific ideology, namely, the one that explains why those who fight against war are murdered and why the ultimate consequences of these murders is the destruction of our cities.

3. '*Difficult Times*'[11]

The model is that of the example, an example of situation and morality. The expressive formula is that of the translation from the Chinese. The time is the present. A poem of this kind exists through its omissions. It must, therefore, be all the more rigorous the more it is concise and apparently devoid of form. In this poem, composed during his final years, Brecht plays the role of Eastern sage. The poetry is without rhyme but not because of diction and *gestus*. Rather, everything must rest on the objective thrust of the poetic machine, the fast and precise dagger strike of disappointment and truth. The pivot is 'I debate / Quite seriously'. The reader must not share in the feeling, in the memory of childhood, he is only granted the possibility of feeling. Following this, the author and reader are put in a condition of ironic doubt that places a question mark over the very value of the childhood memories. There is no conclusion but we are made to understand that he will not go and pick up the spectacles. The return is refused, not the remembrance. The berries exist, no doubt, but there is no need to see them again. Till here, all we have is the affirmation of a hierarchy between the different moments of a human life. And a half-serious, half-joking profile: 'I debate / Quite seriously'. But then there is the title, apparently incongruous (Brecht will use it for another poem; many years before, he had already entitled one of his poems 'Bad Time for Poetry'). Bad times are those, he had said 18 years before, when 'talking of trees is almost a crime / Because it means keeping silent about too many massacres'. And in 'Bad Time for Poetry': 'Inside me contend / Delight at the apple tree blossom / And horror at the house-painter's speeches. / But only the second / Drives me to my desk'.[12] But they are not 'bad' or 'ugly' times; here they are 'hard', *Schwierige Zeiten* (or rather, 'difficult'). There is a coincidence and overlap between a judgement on the historical epoch (cold years, the social tension surrounding him, the imminence of the anti-Stalinist crisis) and of a judgement about his own biography which, having reached the age of weak eyesight, is still capable of perplexity to the point of not knowing for *mehrere Minuten* (several minutes) if it's worth stepping away from the writing desk, where Brecht worked standing up, to fetch from the table the glasses for the longsighted.

4. '*Changing the Wheel*'[13]

In 'conscious symbolism [. . .] the meaning is not only explicitly known but also *expressly* posited as different from the external way in which it is represented'.[14] So says Hegel. Each word in this briefest of poems expressly posits a distinction between meaning and representation. The margins of the road tell of one who is 'at the margins' of a situation. The driver is also the 'guide', the authority, the Party. The wheel has to be changed because it is deflated, blown, dead. Is this the change that followed Stalin's death or, more likely, the one after the events of Berlin?[15] The travelling verbs (*herkommen*, *hinfahren*) carry the obvious doubleness of 'life's journey'. The 'disliking' too is historical and existential. And the contradiction between 'disliking' and 'impatience' no longer carries the triumphant accent of the verses from the 'The Buddha's Parable of the Burning House' ('we too, no longer concerned with the art of patience / Rather with that of impatience'[16]) nor that of he who, after 'the travails of the mountains', sees before him 'the travails of the plains'.[17] Instead, there is pride in hope and rage for its corruption. Hope is violent and life is slow, a poet had written 40 years before, adding: *Allons plus vite, nom de Dieu, allons plus vite.*[18] But since then something terrible has happened, the acceleration of history has shown itself to be possible and impatience has become an essential ingredient of politics . . . I know of no more precise and succinct portrait than this of a historical turning point, of a lull in the wind, of a man at the margins—uselessly impatient, nearly dead already—who tells us that we need to change that wheel, soon.

(d) *The Talking Horse*

Brecht's sole collaboration with the journal *Die Weltbühne*, with the exception of a short polemical letter that appeared on 20 November 1928, is—according to W. Nubel's bibliography—from 17 January 1933 (Issue 3, pp. 100–1). It is a poem, which at least in that version, has never been republished. It is entitled 'Oh Falladah, die du hangest!'.

Thirteen days after its publication, Hitler was named Reich Chancellor. Nazism seized power. Brecht left Germany. That poem was his last text to be published in his homeland. In December of the same year he published a piece in a émigré magazine.

Brecht died on 14 August 1956. Two days before, in the Sunday literary supplement of the daily *Neues Deutschland* 191–192 (11–12 August) the same poem 'Oh Falladah, die du hangest!' appeared beneath the reproduction of a lithograph by Fritz Cramer. The poem carries in parentheses the date 1918. It is the last text to be published while Brecht was alive.

The fact that, with an intervening gap of 23 years, the publication of the same poem precedes both the exile and the death of its author is probably a mere coincidence. But it deserves a closer look, for reasons we will presently consider.

The poem published in *Die Weltbühne* (which is preceded by the statement *Alle Rechte vorbehalten*, 'All Rights Reserved', a rather singular occurrence, but one that points to the intensity of Brecht's practical preoccupations) is presented as a dialogue between a reporter and a dead horse. The reporter broadcasts or describes an episode reminiscent of a horror tale (*Schauermärchen*) said to have happened on the Frankfurter Allee. A draught horse was assailed while still alive by the famished population for 10 minutes, leaving only his bones behind. The horse recounts his end. The reporter speaks for four strophes and so does the horse. The latter ends on a note that is not grotesque but tragic:

So helfet ihnen doch! Und tut es in Bälde!
Sonst passiert euch etwas, was ihr nicht für möglich haltet![19]

As for the title of the poem, it comes from a tale by the Brothers Grimm, 'The Goose Girl'. But we will have to come back to it.

Brecht left Germany. His last poetic utterance was consigned to a poem published in the small review run by K. von Ossietzki, who will be murdered by Hitlerites. It was chiefly a political publication whose positions did not at all coincide with the official ones of the KPD.

Eighteen years later, in the edition of *Hundert Gedichte* (Berlin 1951)—which was not edited by Brecht—the poem appears in a different form. The parts attributed to the reporter are eliminated, and it becomes a monologue by the horse. And in the index of the collection the poem is dated 1932, the year when Eisler had set it to music.

Why did Brecht need to republish the poem in 1956? We can rule out that the initiative came from the editors of *Neues Deutschland* who would not have reproduced the text on the occasion of Cramer's (utterly mediocre) lithograph without the poet's authorization. Not only because the penultimate verse of the first strophe ends in *Neues Deutschland* with an ellipsis (*zusammenbreche . . .*) but also because of the date 1918, *which has absolutely no precedents and is an obvious sign of the author's intervention.* Let me note in this regard that the edition of the *Gedichte* by Suhrkamp Verlag (Volume 3, p. 172) does not reprint the version from the *Weltbühne* but only that from the *Hundert Gedichte*, even if it puts it under the rubric of 'unpublished and uncollected' poems. Neglecting the dating by *Neues Deutschland*, it is included in the volume covering the period 1930–33, while in the index it is placed without a date between two poems dated 1931. An eminent German scholar, an authority on and acquaintance of Brecht as well as the author of critical studies on him, has suggested to me in conversation that we are really dealing with a piece from Brecht's youth, which relates to a real episode that took place during the last year of the war or in its immediate aftermath. I myself seem to recall a fragment of a documentary about Germany in that period, where one could see citizens wielding knives and cutting pieces of meat out of the carcass of a horse that had died in the middle of the road.

With these elements in hand, it seems legitimate to suppose the initial publication had a clear political intent. On the eve of the Nazis' rise to power, in the tense climate of those terrible months, Brecht publishes the angst-ridden appeal of the mauled horse which he had written almost 15 years before. Help men, it implores, 'Or a thing you thought never could might happen to you!' Well, Brecht's state of mind in the last three years of his life, and particularly in his last months, is just as angst-ridden, albeit in a very different direction: if 1953 saw the bloody events of Berlin (which had been followed by the episode of Brecht's letter to Ulbricht, only partially made available to the press of the GDR), 1956 began with the thunderclap of the 20th Congress and the Khrushchev Report. On 28 June, 50,000 workers in Poznań went on strike and marched, demanding the departure of the Soviet troops. The following day one could count 53 dead and 200 wounded. On 22 July, Gerö replaced Rákosi in the secretariat of the Hungarian party, declaring that *a Hungarian Poznań must be avoided* . . . In short, the storm was gathering that would eventually explode in the Polish and Hungarian October; but, more generally and deeply, we are at the beginning of a crucial crisis not only for peace but also for the prospects of international communism, as we can indeed register today. I offer this as a simple hypothesis: Brecht, conscious of that crisis, if not also of his impending death, republishes the prophecy of the horse and at the same time—also as to avoid every interpretation that would attribute to him a parallelism between Nazism and the Communist regime—restores the real date, 1918.

We still need to elucidate, along with the title, the symbolic meaning of the mauled horse. In the tale by the Brothers Grimm ('The Goose Girl'), the little princess starts on a voyage with the evil maidservant on a horse that 'was called Falada and knew how to speak'. When the maidservant tries to pose as the princess and the real princess becomes the keeper of the geese, Falada is killed. But every time the young woman comes out and addresses it with the call *O Falladah, die du hangest*! ('O Falada, thou who hang there!') his head, nailed over the arch of the city gate, responds with a little strophe that calls her 'the little queen' ('Little queen passing down there, / if your mother knew, / her heart would burst'). News of that wonder leads the king to uncover the deception and to the brutal punishment of the usurping maid. It seems clear then that the relationship between the horse of the fable and that of the Frankfurter Allee lies in the fact that both 'tell the truth' and prophesy.

We are dealing with an animal that has the features of the 'giver from the afterlife' and the 'bewitched helper',[20] to use the designations proposed by Vladimir Propp. In other words, with an animal which symbolizes an ancestor and helps the hero in a prodigious manner, not only speaking while alive but also surviving his own death. But this mauled and devoured animal is . . . Orpheus. (Not too many years later, in Jean Cocteau's piece, Orpheus will devote much of his time to the construction of a talking horse.) Orpheus embodied in the miserable draught horse—or, ironically, Brecht himself. Or better, the poet as prophet or helpful genius is disguised, buried in an animal. The myth dear to all decadents could be reprised by Brecht in the tone of sarcasm, but sarcasm is only a more intense way of pointing, a mask affixed on the door which sees us leave every day is only another necessary difficulty for those who want to write the truth.

'Falada, Falada, There Thou Art Hanging!'

I hauled my cart though I felt weak
I got as far as Frankfurt Street
There I start thinking: Oh, Oh
How weak I feel. Perhaps
If I let go
I'll collapse.
Ten minutes later just my bones were on the street.

For I'd hardly fallen flat
(The driver rushed to the telephone)
When up the street
Ran hungry people, pitterpat, pitterpat
To get their pound of meat.
They hacked my flesh from the bone
And me still alive! Hadn't yet done with dying.

These people, I'd known them before!
Draped me with sacks, they did, to keep the flies away
Gave me bits of old bread
And more—
To the driver, *You be nice and kind*, they'd said.
Such friends once; such enemies today.
They were suddenly different; what on earth happened?

The I asked myself: this coldness, why? Now what
In all the world can have come over them?
Who's bugging this lot
To make them act
As if they're cold right through?
Help them. Be quick, too.
Or a thing you thought never could might happen to you.[21]

Notes

Section 'a' was originally published as 'Alcune "istruzioni per l'uso" del "Romanzo da tre soldi" di Brecht' [Some 'User's Instructions' for Brecht's *Threepenny Novel*], *Notiziario Einaudi* 7(1) (March 1958). Section 'b' was originally published as the preface to Fortini's translation of Bertolt Brecht, *Storie da calendario* [Tales from the Calendar] (Turin: Einaudi, 1959). Sections 'c' and 'd' appear here for the first time. [Trans.]

1 A reference to a tale told by Ivan Karamazov to his younger brother Alyosha in Part II, Book V, Chapter 4 of Fyodor Dostoevsky, *The Brothers Karamazov* (Richard Pevear and Larissa Volokhonsky trans) (London: Vintage, 2004), pp. 242–3. [Trans.]

2 Morvan Lebesque in 'Le théâtre peut-il aborder l'actualité politique? Une "table ronde" avec Sartre, Butor, Vailland, Adamov' [Can Theatre Deal with Contemporary Political Reality? A 'Round Table' with Sartre, Butor, Vailland, Adamov], *France Observateur* (13 February 1958). [Trans.]

3 'Arise, ye prisoners of want', in the English version. [Trans.]

4 Bertolt Brecht, *The Threepenny Novel* (Desmond I. Vesey and Christopher Isherwood trans) (New York: Grove, 1956), p. 396. [Trans.]

5 Brecht, *Poems 1913–1956*, (John Willett and Ralph Manheim eds) (London: Methuen, 1987) p. 175. [Trans.]

6 Ibid., p. 244. [Trans.]

7 Walter Benjamin, 'Commentaries on Poems by Brecht' in *Understanding Brecht* (Anna Bostock trans.) (London: Verso, 1998), pp. 70–4. [Trans.]

8 Brecht, 'To Those Born Later' in *Poems 1913–1956*, p. 320. [Trans.]

9 Vernacular. [Trans.]

10 Brecht, *Poems 1913–1956*, p. 181. [Trans.]

11 'Standing at my desk / Through the window I see the elder tree in the garden / And recognize something red in it, something black / And all at once recall the elder / Of my childhood in Augsburg. / For several minutes I debate / Quite seriously whether to go to the

table / And pick up my spectacles, in order to see / Those black berries again on their tiny red stalks'—ibid., p. 449. [Trans.]

12 Ibid., p. 331. [Trans.]

13 'I sit by the roadside / The driver changes the wheel. / I do not like the place that I have come from. / I do not like the place I am going to. / Why with impatience do I / Watch him changing the wheel?' [Trans.]

14 G. W. F. Hegel, *Aesthetics: Lectures on Fine Art, Volume 1* (T.M. Knox trans.) (Oxford: Oxford University Press, 1975), p. 378. [Trans.]

15 A reference to the 1953 uprising set off by a strike of construction workers on the Stalinallee in Berlin on 16 June. Brecht's own response to those events is to be found in the poem 'Die Lösung' [The Solution] in *Poems 1913–1956*, p. 440. [Trans.]

16 Ibid., p. 291 (translation modified). [Trans.]

17 Brecht, 'Observation' in *Poems 1913–1956*, p. 416. [Trans.]

18 'We must go faster, in God's name, we must go faster'—Guillaume Apollinaire, 'Allons plus vite' in *Oeuvres poétiques* (Marcel Adéma and Michel Décaudin eds) (Paris: Gallimard, 1956), p. 364. [Trans.]

19 'Help them. Be quick, too. / Or a thing you thought never could might happen to you'—Brecht, *Poems 1913–1956*, p. 32. [Trans.]

20 *donatore d'oltretomba* and *aiutante fatato* are categories and section-headings in Vladimir Propp, *Le radici storiche dei racconti di fate* [Historical Roots of the Fairy Tale; orig. Russian title, *Istoriceskie Korni Volsebnoi Skazki*] (Clara Coïsson trans.) (Turin: Einaudi, 1949). [Trans.]

21 Brecht, *Poems 1913–1956*, pp. 32–3. [Trans.]

VIII

The Chinese Spectre

The essays of Lu Xun are both useful and timely. They prove to us that between the two world wars the basic themes of intellectual consciousness were, despite appearances, the same in the West and in China. They also bear witness against many today, among the youngest and most generous, who have been led to think that an attempt at a synthesis between 'transformation of the world' (revolution) and 'life change' (personal salvation) is possible without a preliminary defeat of the individual. I don't want to say anything here about the formal beauty of the essays—too bad for those who don't detect it. Anyone can note the taste for rich irony, wise futility, stylistic fencing; no one among us is so ill equipped not to understand certain things, and perhaps just those. In any case, Edoarda Masi's introduction,[1] along with the 16 dense pages of text comprising brief biographies of the Chinese names, for the first time places Lu Xun—one of those authors who like Boris Pilniak and César Vallejo has had to wait for a whole cultural about-turn to come, or come back, face to face with us—in such clear historical and cultural terms as to condemn any further laziness in his regard. Lu Xun the rationalist, the man of 'light', pedagogue, fighter, politician, narrator, translator. But also the man of 'darkness' who knows very well that his own work, though assumed as vocation and service, 'intrinsically consists in the ongoing search for a formal solution' and therefore does not 'serve' the revolution; and, though it fights against tradition testifies how in the lowliest levels of archaic and peasant life—in the 'living death' of the villages and of its own memory—a precious truth is contained, a truth that can and must be restored in line with the liberation from oppression, a filial piety that must simultaneously express itself in the destruction of the parental home. Those who find it difficult to grasp this argument should recall that in Western poetry the most tragic figuration of this truth is found in the dialogue of the wayfarer with Philemona and Bauci, in the fifth act of Goethe's *Faust II*.

I remember Lu Xun's house in Shanghai, how the leaves of a plant in the courtyard moved their shadows across the small worktable. 'Over the past 30 years, under my eyes the blood of so many youths has massed layer by layer to the point of burying me, forbidding me from breathing; I can only write something with this pen and ink as if I were digging a small opening in the mud, putting my mouth to it for one last breath—what a world is this.'

Evil and negativity is rejected with vigour; but what has happened and is happening is irrecuperable and irremediable. Lu Xun detested Dostoevsky but he was pushed towards his writing table by a horror that the Russian knew well; except that in the Chinese writer this was overtaken by the certainty of the irrelevance of the individual. Irony dispersed any remnant of rhetoric. Yet read with caution: You risk missing out the best parts if you let yourself be tricked by the apparent lightness.

Following the line of Mao's thought ('Put destruction in first place and in the course of the process you shall have edification'), Masi writes in the introduction of 'the recovery of tradition, possible only to the degree that its domination is destroyed'. For this tradition (understood as authority or past) to be efficiently fought, it must be the *dominant* one. The particular form of power represented by ideological power becomes all the more powerful the more it is petrified, reified, close to becoming, or being, a structure. Whence the revolutionary command to strike at the 'root', but that root as we know is 'man himself'. Where you thought you would find a mode, a form, a structure, you find men, namely, something that must always and again be resolved into modes, forms and structures. Scientific minds grow impatient here; they say that the idea of man as a 'microcosm' is the province of literati. Yet it's enough to turn your gaze and what you had abstracted has once again congealed, merged. In that search for tradition, which is a search for your *dominant determination*, you are no longer able to distinguish the 'material' compulsion of your biological structure and the modes of production in which you are immersed from the weight of ideological criteria (for example, the ethical or aesthetic ones). The 'last instance' of Engels' famous phrase continues to be postponed.[2] Hence the inevitable tendency towards false ends, interlocutory objects; towards battles waged against partial traditions.

More than 30 years ago, speaking of Italian culture, had Gramsci not opposed one tradition to another? In the same period, had Lukács not done the same with regard to classical German philosophy and Marxism, at the 'Western' level? Now the revolutionary West, where it exists, knows that if it really wants to bring to light the class characters of its own cultural tradition—the one it usually terms feudal-Christian, bourgeois-Enlightenmental, social-democratic—and overcome it. It can only do so by measuring against the major undertaking of its fellow citizens, the colonial or semi-colonial subjection of the rest of the world (and of its own oppressed classes). Needless to say, such a description has already been carried out, by historiography and anthropology; though standing on opposite sides, Claude Lévi-Strauss and Frantz Fanon —to mention only the first names that come to mind—are certainly offsprings of the West. But Tacitus too wrote on the Germanic tribes long before the bishops started to consider the invasions as nemeses of overweening imperial power. The 'destruction of domination', that is, of the 'tradition' of the West continues to be a fact of cultural consciousness—which is really to say, a case of false consciousness—until political revolution takes place in the West.

Let us ask ourselves if this theme has ever been posed in these terms, and before today, to the West. Not even the October Revolution could do it. But now it is possible. Because the 'negation of the negation' is that new form of 'proletarian' which is properly called the old and new colonized, the 'national colonized' of industry (cultural and otherwise) and the 'international' one, near or far, American, Brazilian or Indian, as you will.

Within this process, as Masi observes, the condition of the Chinese continent is paradoxical. It is the condition of a culture with an exalted tradition that wants to negate and overcome itself in the presence of two contradictory elements which face off against each other in modern China: Western culture–science —already used as a destructive tool by the 4 May generation—which, partly adopted and partly combated, presides over socialist construction; and the form which, as a 'language of slaves', culture–science has assumed in the colonial universe. Hence, the ambiguity of the Chinese experience of the West, and the violent reactions it elicits in the Soviet Union. For the West it is easier to confront—and if needs be to integrate—the Cuban or Congolese 'man with the machete' of which Fanon spoke, than the ungraspable (more 'advanced'? more 'backward'?) Chinese revolution.

The problem of revolutionary destruction posed itself to Lu Xun's consciousness, in the China of 1915–35, with an evidence it had not possessed in the Soviet revolution. In Tsarist Russia, 50 years of ideological and political struggle had seen a thorough debate about the relationship both with the national historical past and with western Europe. And the result was nothing short of Lenin. In China, everything had taken place instead amid the colonial putrefaction of a unified universe. That is why I think in a figure like Lu Xun, the violence of lacerations (which could find expression only by way of irony), the extreme fragmentation of the written work (it is almost as if one were dealing with the fragments of an explosion, the fragments of an incredibly complicated tradition . . .)—what many years ago, speaking about Lu Xun in a language that was still rough and metaphorical, I called 'the relationship between decadentism and revolution'—is nothing other than the voice of the truth of which I have spoken above. That truth is the union between biological–economic necessity and ideological necessity. It reveals itself, blindingly, in the moments of revolution-conversion when a formal choice (of language, writing, ethical criteria) becomes—for one who wishes to undertake it—indistinguishable from the historical massifs, the vast alluvial plains of the property regime of post-imperial China, from the river of conflicts that overwhelm that regime and from the Kuomintang's volleys of lead.

Literally dying of the contradiction, Lu Xun—who in 1927 had said to the officers of the military academy of Huangpu, 'I think you had better not admire literature just yet . . . at most you may write a battle song which, if well written, may make pleasant reading when you rest after fighting'[3]—knew this 9 years later, shortly before his death, when he wrote: 'the everyday life of a combatant is not all songs and laments; but when everything is tied to songs and laments, then you have a real fighter'. The self-destruction of the intellectual is no longer, perhaps, the one of the poet-suicides of the October Revolution of which Lu Xun also speaks, neither is it to be found in the historical prospect of a disappearance of the division of labour; and never ever, of course, in the 'commitment' of a revolutionary mandarin clerk. It is perhaps to be found in a 'contemplation of death' that is not complacent or voluptuous but ironic, in the consciousness of truly being *the union of a dead man and a living one*. But what is this union? It is a spectre. This is what literature can be in an age of revolution.

As a young man in his village, Lu Xun would spend evenings playing the part of the ghost in open-air traditional theatre before an audience of peasants. The theme of the spectre recurs in many of his pages. And the man who at death's door dictates his magnificent and implacable testamentary arrangements, which look towards life, is the same who always also looked towards the creatures from the past, from tradition, who feast on our blood. 'If in the dim light after midnight a woman with a powdered face and red lips like this appeared faintly in the distance, old as I am I might still run over to look at her . . . '[4]

This is why Lu Xun's *oeuvre* is an episode in the world revolution. It destroys the tumuli of the ancestors and scatters their remains, planting on them the cereals that will feed the survivors. Terrified, it carries out the necessary filial impiety.

1968

Notes

Originally published in *Libri nuovi* 1 (June 1968). The essay is a review of Lu Xun, *La falsa libertà* [False Freedom] (Edoarda Masi ed.) (Turin: Einaudi, 1968). [Trans.]

1 Edoarda Masi (1927–2011), essayist and translator, specialist in Chinese literature and culture. A friend of Fortini, she participated alongside him in the journals *Quaderni rossi* and *Quaderni piacentini*. She translated Cao Xueqin's *Dream of the Red Chamber* into Italian. Masi played a critical role in introducing Maoism and Chinese politics to a New Left public in the late 1960s and 70s; see Edoarda Masi, *China Winter: Workers, Mandarins, and the Purge of the Gang of Four* (Adrienne Foulke trans.)(New York: Dutton, 1982). She was actively involved with the Centro studi Franco Fortini since its foundation in 1995.[Trans.]

2 A reference to Friedrich Engels, 'Letter to Joseph Bloch (21/22 September 1890)' in Karl Marx and Friedrich Engels, *Collected Works*, VOL. 49 (London: Lawrence & Wishart, 2001), pp. 33–6. [Trans.]

3 Lu Xun, 'Literature of a Revolutionary Period', *Chinese Literature* 9 (1977): 9. [Trans.]

4 Lu Xun, *Selected Works of Lu Hsun*, VOL. 1 (Peking: Foreign Languages, 1956), p. 438. See also Wang Hui, 'Dead Fire Rekindled: Lu Xun as Revolutionary Intellectual' in *The End of Revolution: China and the Limits of Modernity* (London: Verso, 2009), pp. 191–210. [Trans.]